Sibelius

**A Comprehensive Guide to
Sibelius Music Notation Software**

Sibelius

A Comprehensive Guide to Sibelius Music Notation Software

Thomas Rudolph and Vincent Leonard

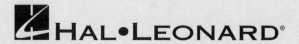

Jacket design by Kristi Montague.
Book interior by Snow Creative Services.

Published by Hal Leonard Corporation
7777 Bluemound Road
P.O. Box 13819
Milwaukee, WI 53213

Trade Book Division Editorial Offices
19 West 21st Street
Suite 201
New York, New York 10010

Library of Congress Cataloging-in-Publication Data

Rudolph, Thomas E.
    Sibelius : a comprehensive guide to Sibelius music notation software / Thomas Rudolph and Vincent Leonard. — 1st ed.
        p. cm.
    Includes index.
    ISBN-13: 978-1-4234-1200-7
    ISBN-10: 1-4234-1200-1
    1. Sibelius (Computer file) I. Leonard, Vincent A. II. Title.
    MT39.R84 2007
    780.1'48—dc22

                                                                          2006036541

Printed in the United States of America

First Edition

Contents

Introduction

This text is meant to be a resource and a method book for how to learn and how to use Sibelius. It is not an attempt to replace the Sibelius reference manual. We have addressed most of the common and not-so-common musical needs of most composers, arrangers, and educators. The screen shots were done using Sibelius 4.

This text is designed for both novice and experienced Sibelius users. Section 1 addresses single-staff parts. Sections 2 and 3 address grand-staff scores and part extraction. Section 4 features importing and exporting files, education applications, and Sibelius support.

If you are a beginner at using Sibelius, we suggest you start with Chapter 1 and proceed sequentially through the text. If you are already using Sibelius, peruse the chapters and look for musical examples that contain information you would like to review. You can skip around to specific topics as needed.

This book assumes that you have a basic knowledge of music theory and are familiar with using the computer's mouse.

Compatibility with Mac OS and Windows

This book covers Sibelius versions for both Mac OS and Windows. Throughout, there are references to both Mac and Windows versions of Sibelius. Both Mac and Windows screen shots are included. When both Mac and Windows screens are used simultaneously, the Mac version is on the left and the Windows version on the right.

Sibelius Support Files and Using the Book with Courses

This book has a companion Web site at *www.sibeliusbook.com*. The site includes files and templates that can be used with this book. The files can be downloaded and used with Macintosh or Windows versions of Sibelius.

The files on the Web site correlate to each chapter. For most chapters, there are several versions of each file. Instructors using this book with a course and experienced Sibelius users may want to use these files from time to time. For example, the chapters that include lyrics have versions of each file, with and without the lyrics. Whenever there is a relevant file on the Web site, you'll see an icon in the book text:

www.sibeliusbook.com

The Goal of Notation Software

Before you read on, be sure you are attempting to learn Sibelius for the right reasons. Sometimes people spend significant time learning a music software application, only to realize that they really needed another type of software. Sibelius is primarily a notation/composition program. There are other programs designed to help you record audio, create accompaniment parts, or learn about music. Sibelius was designed to produce printed notation.

A music notation program such as Sibelius is to music what a word processor is to writing text. Be sure that your goals match the design of the program: to notate and print out scores and parts.

The Latest Version

To get the most out of this book, we recommend using Sibelius 4 or the most current version of Sibelius that is available. As of this writing, Sibelius 4 is the most recent. However, approximately 90 percent of Sibelius version 4 features are accessible to Sibelius version 3 users. Since some features have clearly changed, we recommend that you upgrade. Upgrades for existing Sibelius users are cheaper than the complete program. Check the Sibelius Web site (*www.sibelius.com*) for information on the most current versions of the program.

Purchasing and Registering Your Software

You can purchase Sibelius directly from *www.sibelius.com* or from just about any music dealer or software vendor. If you are an educator or work for a nonprofit organization such as a religious institution, Sibelius offers a special discount. Contact them for details.

We welcome your feedback. Please feel free to contact John Cerullo at Hal Leonard or us with your comments: Tom Rudolph (www.tomrudolph.com) and Vince Leonard (VincentL10@comcast.net).

Acknowledgments

The authors, Tom Rudolph and Vince Leonard, would like to thank the following individuals for their help and assistance with the book:

The beta testers Michael Fein, Dan Newson, and the teachers who attended summer Sibelius workshops with Tom over the past two summers at Villanova University and Berklee College of Music. In addition, Tom and Vince wish to offer their sincere thanks to Robin Hodson, Sibelius trainer, who offered countless edits and advice on every single chapter. Robin's input was invaluable.

The authors would also like to thank project editor Belinda Yong, copy editor Leslie Kriesel, graphic designer Michael Snow, John Cerullo, Brad Smith, Daniel Spreadbury, Sammy Nestico, Stefani Langol, Ron Kerber, Mike Moniz, Steven Estrella, Ken Peters, Lorry Lutter, Laurie Wilde, Tiiu Lutter, and Getrude Leonard.

About the Authors

Thomas Rudolph, Ed. D. is an educator, author, and performer. He has taught workshops in music technology at seventeen institutions of higher learning and has trained over 4,500 music educators. Among his seven books include *Teaching Music with Technology, Finale: An Easy Guide to Music Notation*, and *Recording in the Digital World*.

Producer and composer **Vincent Leonard Jr.** has had works premiered nationally and internationallty. Widely known as a copyist and arranger, he has worked on projects with Peter Nero, Doc Severinsen, the London Symphony Orchestra, Chuck Mangione, and many others.

SECTION I

Single-Staff Parts

1

Getting Started: Overview
(Musical Example: None—Mouse Input)

A notation program such as Sibelius can be an extremely powerful tool, if you learn to use it properly. This chapter will familiarize you with the Sibelius interface and how to move around the score. There are no exercises or example that will be produced; we'll just spend some time getting acquainted with the look and feel of the program.

Throughout Section 1, we will give you specific recommendations for entering notes and other markings in your scores, based on our experience using the program. This is not to say that our way is the only way. Just like any method book for learning a musical instrument, this book contains our best recommendations for learning and using Sibelius. We hope that by completing the examples that follow, you will be able to use the program to suit your own needs.

If you are new to Sibelius, then go through each chapter sequentially. If you have some experience using the program, peruse the chapter examples and select the chapters that seem appropriate for your needs.

Topics and skills to be covered in this chapter include:

- using a two-button mouse
- keyboard terminology (Mac and Windows)
- installing and launching Sibelius
- registering Sibelius
- starting Sibelius
- the Quick Start menu
- selecting menus and submenus
- Navigator, Keypad, and Playback windows
- scaling the size of the score
- entering notation with point and click
- editing notation
- fixing mistakes
- Undo and Redo
- the Create menu
- contextual menus
- menus: View, Notes, Play, Layout, and House Style
- the Help menu

Using a Two-Button Mouse

Sibelius takes full advantage of a two-button mouse, the kind shipped with most computers made today (Windows and Mac). If you have an older Macintosh computer with a one-button mouse, we highly recommend you purchase a two-button mouse. This will save you a lot of time using Sibelius (and other programs). If you are a Mac user and you only have a one-button mouse, it is possible to access the right-click button by holding down the CTRL key and clicking the mouse.

Keyboard Terminology

Before you begin using this book, become familiar with the key commands that are used in Sibelius.

Mac OS

1. The Command key is next to the space bar and looks like ⌘.
2. ⌘-A (or any letter): Hold down the ⌘ key and press the letter A.
3. ⌘-click: Press the ⌘ key and click the left mouse button.
4. Option-click: Press the Option key and click the left mouse button.
5. Shift-click: Hold the Shift key down and click the left mouse button.
6. Option-⌘-[letter]: Hold down the Option and ⌘ keys and press the desired letter.
7. Double-click: Click the left mouse button twice.
8. CTRL-click: Hold down the CTRL key and click the mouse. This can also be accomplished with a two-button mouse by pressing the right button by itself.
9. Right-click: Click the right mouse button.
10. Click: Click the left mouse button.
11. Double-click: Click the left mouse button two times in quick succession.
12. Triple-click: Click the left mouse button three times in quick succession.

Windows

1. CTRL-A (or any letter): Hold the Control (CTRL) key down and press the letter A.
2. CTRL-click: Press the CTRL key and click the left mouse button.
3. Shift-click: Hold down the Shift key and click the left mouse button.
4. Alt-CTRL-click: Hold down the Alt and CTRL keys and click the left mouse button.
5. Right-click: Click the right mouse button.
6. Click: Click the left mouse button.
7. Double-click: Click the left mouse button two times in quick succession
8. Triple-click: Click the left mouse button three times in quick succession.

Installing Sibelius

The first step is to read the manual (yes, this is a chore for most of us, but necessary at this juncture). Read the "Before You Install" and "Installing" sections for Mac or Windows. Be sure to connect your MIDI keyboard before installation, as Sibelius will "see" what equipment is available and help to get the proper connections made.

Take time to install Kontakt Player, Photoscore Lite, and Scorch (see the user guide). These will all be addressed in the chapters that follow. Take your time now, and it will save some headaches later.

Registering Sibelius

Sibelius needs to be registered. If you have an Internet connection on the computer where the program is installed, launch Sibelius, and from the Help menu, select "Register Sibelius." You can also consult your *Sibelius User Guide* under "Registering Sibelius." If you do not register your copy of the program, it will stop saving after thirty days, so you should deal with this soon, preferably the first time you use the program.

Starting Sibelius (After Installation)

Mac OSX: Sibelius installs an icon on the Dock when it is installed. Simply click on the Dock's Sibelius icon. The other option is to open the Sibelius folder on your hard drive and double-click on the Sibelius icon.

Windows: Sibelius installs a shortcut on the desktop when it is installed. Simply click on the shortcut to launch Sibelius. The other option is to go to the Start menu, select the Sibelius folder, then Sibelius.

Sibelius will always look at your MIDI settings when the program launches. Be sure to review the MIDI setup procedures in the Sibelius manual.

The Quick Start Menu

When Sibelius first launches, the Quick Start window appears. In this chapter, you will explore Sibelius without creating a specific piece of music. This will give you an introduction to the look and feel of the program. If you are ready to write some real music, jump to Chapter 2. But do look through this chapter first so you have an idea of what is in store.

If Sibelius is already open, you can access the Quick Start screen:

1. From the File menu, select "Quick Start."
2. Choose the "Start a new score" option.
3. Click OK.

5

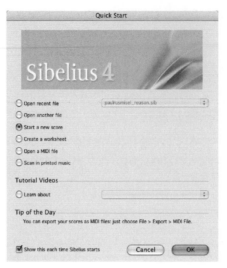

Sibelius next shows the New Score window. From here you have the option of selecting a premade score or Manuscript Paper, as it is called in Sibelius. The manuscript option includes premade blank scores or templates. It is also possible to build an entire score from scratch. You will be building scores in the chapters that follow. For this example, you will use one of the built-in Manuscript Paper options.

4. Scroll down under Manuscript Paper and select "Treble staff." If you type a letter, Sibelius will automatically jump to the first option beginning with that letter. Type a T and Sibelius will automatically select "Treble staff."

5. Click the Finish button. Sibelius will create a score based on the settings that you entered in the New Score window.

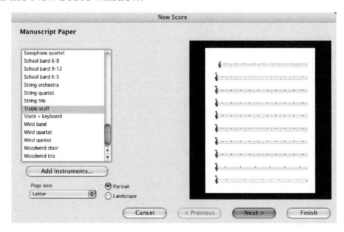

Selecting Menus and Submenus

Menus, along the top of the Sibelius windows, are indicated in this book, beginning in Chapter 3, with the menu name first and each submenu indicated with a >. From Chapter 3 through the end of the book, you will see references such as:

Edit > Select > Select All. This means go to the Edit menu, select the Select submenu, and release the button on the menu choice "Select All." In chapters 1 and 2, all of the steps will be written out such as, "In the Edit menu, choose 'Select' and from the sub-menu choose 'Select All.'"

Navigator, Keypad, and Playback Windows

In order to use Sibelius effectively, you must be familiar with how to display the various windows. The first way is by using Navigator. This allows you to quickly skip around a piece of music.

Check to be sure Navigator is displayed.

1. From the Window menu, look to see if Navigator is checked. If it is not, select it. Navigator can also be selected by using the buttons at the top right of the Sibelius window.

2. Once Navigator is displayed, press and hold the mouse down inside the Navigator window to quickly jump around the score.

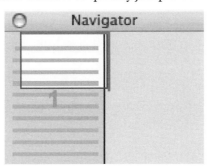

 Shortcuts can save you a lot of time using Sibelius. The shortcut to show or hide Navigator is displayed in the Window menu: hold down ⌘-Option at the same time and press the letter N (Mac) or hold down CTRL-Alt at the same time and press the letter N (Win).

You can also move around the page by clicking the mouse and dragging on the white portion of the music. Do not click on a staff! If you do, you will move the staff location.

• Click on the white portion of the manuscript and drag it up or down with your mouse. The cursor will turn into a hand.

 Being able to drag the manuscript paper with the mouse is a default preference. In other words, if you don't make changes to the Sibelius preferences, this is the way it will work.

Scaling the Size of the Page

8

It is often helpful to make the music larger or smaller for viewing or entering purposes. This process is called zooming *in* to make things bigger and zooming *out* to make them smaller. The view percentage will not change the look of the printout. Changing the size of the printout will be reviewed in later chapters.

1. To resize the view percentage, in the menu bar at the top of the Sibelius screen, click and hold on the drop-down menu (arrow) to the right and select a percentage size.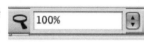
2. The percentage can also be changed using keyboard shortcuts. Hold down ⌘ (Mac) or CTRL (Win) with your left hand. Press the + or – keys (above the P key on your computer's keyboard) with your right hand to make the percentage change. The percentage will be displayed in the menu bar.
3. Return to 100% before moving on to the next step.

Entering Notation with Point and Click

There are several ways to enter notation in Sibelius. They include point and click, typing letter keys, using a MIDI keyboard, and scanning. All of these options will be included in the chapters that follow.

> I find the point-and-click note entry option to be the slowest. For this reason, I rarely use it. It is shown in this initial chapter, as it can be used in some instances. However, the majority of note entry will be using other methods described in the chapters that follow.

Entering notes and rests via the point-and-click method:

1. Press the Esc (Escape) key.
2. Go to the Keypad and click on the quarter-note value.
3. The cursor will turn blue. This means the cursor is loaded.
4. Roll the mouse to a measure. Sibelius will display a shadow note of the pitch in gray. When you get to the desired pitch, click the mouse to enter a quarter note.
5. Enter more quarter notes into the score. No particular musical goal here—you are just getting used to this input method.

You will notice that once a note is entered, Sibelius fills in the rests. If you want to replace a rest with a note, just click on it. You do not need to erase rests first. Also, you can click anywhere in the measure to enter a note on any beat of the bar.

Editing Notation

When you want to do something other than enter notation, such as moving the notation with Navigator, you must first clear the cursor of the current selection.

1. To clear the cursor, press the Esc key (Escape) in the upper left-hand corner of the computer keyboard.
2. When entering notes, you may have to press Esc twice. The first time removes the cursor line, and the second time removes the highlighting.

1. Enter notes.	2. Press Esc. (entry cursor disappears, note turns blue)	3. Press Esc again. (note turns black— nothing is selected)

Repeat the above steps. Remember, when you select a note value in Sibelius, the cursor turns blue to indicate it is loaded. To clear the cursor, press the Esc key. Sometimes you have to press the Esc key twice. The cursor is clear when it is black.

Fixing Mistakes

You will inevitably enter some incorrect notes. There are several ways to correct mistakes.

Correcting the Pitch

If you entered the wrong pitch and the note is blue or highlighted:

*   Use the up and down arrows on the computer keyboard to change the pitch.

If the note is not highlighted and you want to change the pitch:

1. Press Esc (two times, just to be sure nothing is selected).
2. Click on the note to select it (it will turn blue).
3. Use the up and down arrows on the computer keyboard to change the pitch (you can also drag the note with the mouse, but the arrow keys are faster and more accurate).

Correcting the Rhythmic Value

If you entered the wrong note value (rhythm):

1. Select the note value you want to change (it will be blue).

2. On the Keypad, select the desired duration, for example a half note.

 Do not delete rests in measures. In Sibelius, when you select a note and press Delete, the selected note turns into a rest of the same value. If you select a rest and press delete, Sibelius hides the rest. Follow the above steps to edit pitch and rhythmic values.

Undo and Redo

One of the best ways to erase mistakes is using the Undo command.

- From the Edit Menu, select Undo.
- It also can be selected from the toolbar at the top of the Sibelius window.

Undo can also be accessed using the short-cut command ⌘–Z (Mac) or CTRL-Z (Win).

If you keep pressing the Undo command, it will continue to erase your previous steps.

The Create Menu

The same process that is used with notation applies to other aspects of the score. Anything that you want to create comes from the Create Menu. For example, if you want to insert a clef change, time signature, or key signature change, the following steps are recommended:

1. Press the Esc key to clear any selection (you will be pressing Esc a lot when using Sibelius).
2. From the Create menu, select "Key Signature..." (shortcut: the letter K).
3. Select the desired key signature and click OK.
4. The cursor will be loaded and turn blue.
5. Click in the desired measure.
6. Press Esc after the key signature is entered.

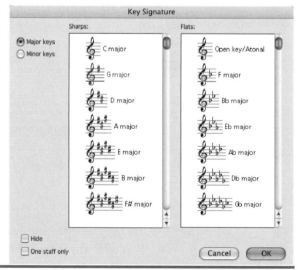

Contextual Menus

A contextual menu appears in the piece when you right-click with a two-button mouse or CTRL-click on a Mac with a one-button mouse. Contextual menus are menus that appear within the context of a piece of music (they are available in many other music and nonmusic programs).

To access the contextual menus:

1. Press Esc to clear the cursor selection.
2. Right-click the mouse. You will notice that the exact options in the Create menu are displayed. This gives you a shortcut to the menu.
3. Select a note, rest, or measure. Click on it so it turns blue.
4. Right-click to show the contextual menu. This is an abbreviated list of items from the Edit menu.

Sibelius has two main contextual menus to remember. When something is selected (it is blue), a portion of the Edit menu appears. This is handy if you want to delete or hide something. Copy and Paste can also be accomplished from this menu, but wait until Chapter 2 to learn the fastest way to copy and paste.

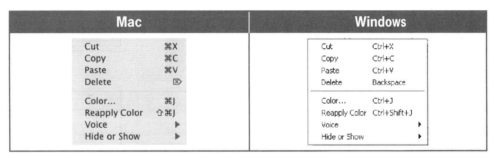

When nothing is selected, the Create menu appears when you right-click. This is a handy way to access the Create menu without going to the menu bar.

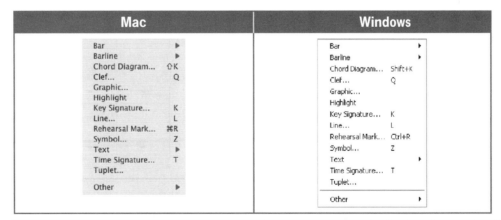

 Sibelius makes frequent use of contextual menus. If you are a Mac user with a one-button mouse, replace it with a two-button mouse. You will be much more productive using Sibelius with a two-button mouse.

The View Menu

The items in the View menu have no impact on the printed score. They are designed to adjust the computer screen view for a variety of note-entry options. These include rulers and the display of various items. A check next to an item means it is active. You can use the mouse to turn these options on and off. These will be covered in the chapters that follow.

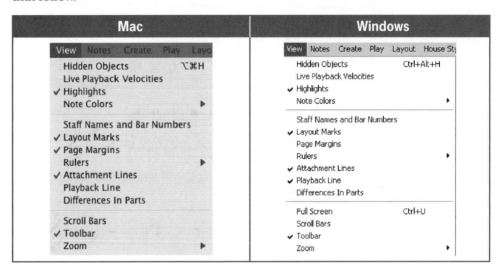

The Notes Menu

This menu is typically used to modify notes that have already been entered. Again, these options will be addressed in the chapters that follow.

The Play, Layout, and House Style Menus

The Play menu is used to change your input and playback options and to select Play or Stop as well as other functions. It is also the menu that has a link to the Sibelius built-in Dictionary.

The Layout and House Style menus (on the next page) are used to adjust the look of the printout, usually after you have entered the notation, lyrics, and other text. The House Style menu is where you go to customize the look of your score.

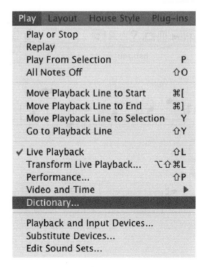

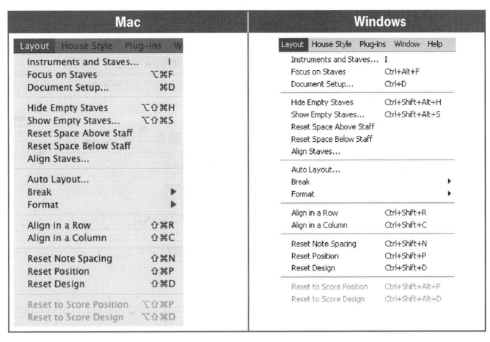

The Window menu controls the various Sibelius tool windows. The windows used so far include Navigator, Keypad, and Playback. Other options will be introduced in later chapters. The windows that are displayed have a check next to them.

There are two helpful shortcuts to access these windows.

1. Click on the appropriate icon on the toolbar at the top of the Sibelius screen.

2. Use the keyboard shortcut commands that are listed next to each menu item:

    a. Navigator: CTRL-Alt-N (Win); ⌘-Option-N (Mac)

b. Keypad: CTRL-Alt-K (Win); ⌘-Option-K (Mac)
c. Playback: CTRL-Alt-Y (Win); ⌘-Option-Y (Mac)

Using the above shortcuts, turn the above options on and off, just for practice. Of course, you can move the various tool windows around the screen by dragging the bar at the top of the window.

The Help Menu

There will be times when you won't remember how to do something in Sibelius. Fortunately, there is an excellent manual that can be accessed from the Sibelius Help menu.

• From the Help menu, select "Sibelius Reference."

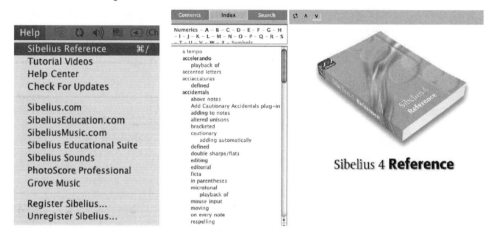

Sibelius 4 **Reference**

This allows you to select concepts via the table of contents, the index, or a specific word search. You can also purchase the printed version of this manual to look things up the old-fashioned way. The printed reference manual can be ordered from the Sibelius Web site.

Tutorial Videos

Another excellent resource provided to Sibelius users is in the Tutorial Videos, introduced in Sibelius 4. These videos provide a short, informative overview of literally every aspect of the program. To access the videos:

1. From the Help menu, select "Tutorial Videos."
2. From the Sibelius menu, select "Quick Start" and then click on the Learn About button and select one of the nineteen videos.

Summary

The main objective of this chapter is to help you become familiar with the basic operation of Sibelius. The following chapters will involve real musical applications of these Sibelius skills:

1. Using a two-button mouse.
2. Keyboard and menu terminology used in this book.
3. Installing and registering your copy of Sibelius.
4. Accessing the Quick Start menu.
5. Accessing the Navigator, Keypad, and Playback windows.
6. Scaling the view size of the page.
7. Entering notation using the mouse (point and click).
8. Editing notation using Undo and changing note values and rhythmic values.
9. Using the two Sibelius contextual menus.
10. Accessing the various menus at the top of the Sibelius window.
11. Getting help via the Sibelius Help menu and Tutorial Videos.

Review

1. Go back through this chapter and review the areas that seem a little strange to you. Remember, you will have to do skills multiple times before you will have them memorized.
2. Keyboard shortcuts: test yourself to see if you remember any of the keyboard shortcuts introduced in this chapter. Go to the Window menu and review the keystrokes to show the Navigator and Keypad controls.

2

Alphabetic Input and Ties
(Musical Example: "Finlandia" by Sibelius)

Each chapter in this section will introduce a specific set of notation skills. The first piece of music to enter into Sibelius is a single-line example, "Finlandia." I thought it would be fun to learn how to use Sibelius by writing a piece by Jean Sibelius. First, look at the final printout of the piece below. The goal is to reproduce this using Sibelius.

The skills to be covered in this example include:

• automatically setting the title, composer, time, and key signature
• entering the notation by typing the letters on the computer keyboard

- entering ties
- entering accents, slurs, and dynamics
- adding and deleting blank measures (called "bars" in Sibelius)
- playing back to check for mistakes
- changing the number of measures on a line (page layout)
- saving to disk
- printing the example

Setting Up the Score

If Sibelius is not already launched, launch it now by double-clicking on the Sibelius icon.

1. If the Quick Start screen is not visible, go to the File menu and choose "Quick Start."

2. Choose the "Start a new score" option and click OK. You can also start a new score by clicking the icon in the upper left-hand corner of the Sibelius screen.

3. In the New Score window, under Manuscript Paper, choose "Blank."

4. Click the Add Instruments button.

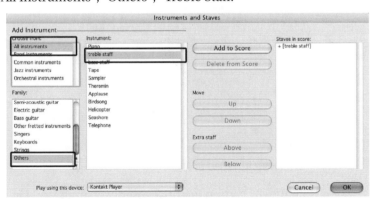

5. Select "All Instruments"; "Others"; "Treble Staff."

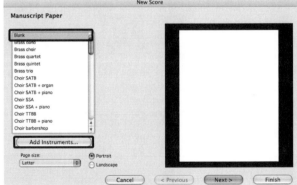

6. Click the Add to Score button. Be sure there is an instrument listed in the column to its right, or you will get a blank piece of paper with no lines or spaces.
7. Click OK.

This is another way of selecting a treble staff. As shown in Chapter 1, you could also select "Treble staff" from the Manuscript Paper options.

8. This returns you to the New Score window. Click Next.

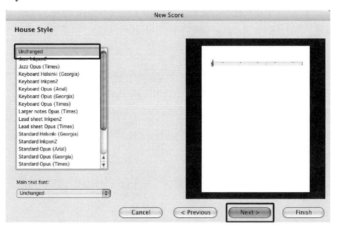

9. Select the notation style: "Unchanged."
10. Click Next.
11. Select "4/4" for the Time Signature.

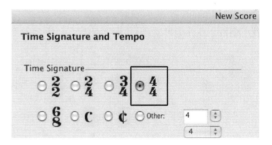

12. Click Next.
13. Select the Key Signature "F major" (one flat).

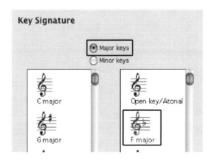

14. Click Next.
15. Enter the Title: "Finlandia"; the Composer/Songwriter: "Jean Sibelius"; and the Lyricist: "Notation entered by [your name]".
16. Before you click Finish, press the Previous button to be sure you selected the right choices. Taking your time at this stage will save you many headaches.
17. Click Finish.

Sibelius creates a file with all the information you entered. It initially creates one line of blank measures.

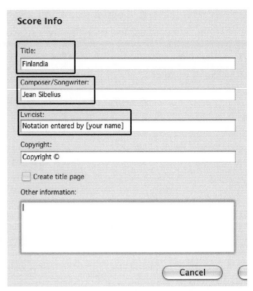

Adding Additional Measures (Bars)

Sibelius will automatically create new measures as notation is entered. You can also manually add measures to a score. When entering an example from printed notation, you may prefer to add the measures at the beginning of the score entry process. Since "Finlandia" has twenty-four measures, add the additional measures to the blank score.

1. From the Create menu, select "Bar" and then "At End" from the submenu. This will add 6 bars or measures to the score.
2. Since "Finlandia" requires an additional eighteen measures, use the shortcut command to add bars (measures): ⌘-B (Mac); CTRL-B (Win).
3. Hint: when you hold down keys on a computer keyboard, they will automatically repeat. Hold them down and add a bunch of measures. Add more than twenty-four so you can practice deleting extra measures.

Notice that Sibelius automatically reformats the score as additional bars (measures) are entered. Your score will look something like the following, depending upon how long you held down the shortcut keys.

Displaying Measure Numbers on Every Measure

Before learning how to delete the extra measures, stop and make a change to the way the music is displayed. Even with a large computer monitor, you can get lost in a score. Sibelius has an option to show the staff names and measure numbers. These will not print, but the reference numbers are really helpful during note entry.

• From the View menu, select "Staff Names and Bar Numbers."

Deleting Additional Bars (Measures)

If you don't have more than twenty-four bars in your score, add them now. Next, we'll practice deleting bars from the score.

To select a bar, click on it. To delete a bar you must:

1. Hold down ⌘ (Mac) or CTRL (Win) and click inside measure 26. This will place a double box around the measure.
2. Press the Delete key on the computer keyboard.

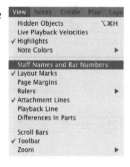

To delete a range of bars:

1. Hold down ⌘ (Mac) or CTRL (Win) and click inside measure 25, the leftmost measure of the block.
2. Release the ⌘ (Mac) or CTRL (Win) key.

3. Press and hold the Shift key and click inside the last measure in the score. This will highlight a group of measures with the double box.

4. Press the Delete key to remove the block of measures.

 Be careful not to delete the first bar (measure) of a score. All of the titles that are entered using the New Score setup are connected to measure 1. If you delete it, all of the titles at the top of the page will go away with it.

Entering Notation by Typing the Letter Names

The fastest way to enter notation in Sibelius is using a MIDI keyboard. This option will be discussed in Chapter 4. If you do not have a MIDI keyboard, the fastest way to enter notes is by alphabetic input (typing the letters A through G directly on the computer keyboard). Using the mouse to click on notes, as introduced in Chapter 1, is the slowest option.

The fastest way to enter music using the computer keyboard is to use your left hand over the letters A through G and your right hand over the numeric keypad. Don't use the mouse at all. With practice, your entry speed will increase dramatically.

 Laptops do not have a numeric keypad. Users have a couple of options. The best option is to purchase a USB keypad from any computer store and plug it into an empty USB port on your laptop. The next best option is to use your left hand to enter the letter names and your right hand to click the mouse on the desired duration on the Keypad on screen. There is yet another option, but it's no faster than either of the above: hold down the fn key and press the appropriate letter that corresponds with the keypad: J = 1; K = 2; L = 3, and so forth.

 Consider purchasing the Sibelius customized computer keyboard. It can be used with desktops and laptops and plugs into a USB port. There are a lot of great features, including color-coded shortcut keys and a numeric keypad. Check out additional information at http://www.sibelius.com/products/keyboard/index.html.

To enter notation:

1. Be sure that the first measure of the piece is visible. If not, use the navigation bar or drag the score with the mouse so it is visible.

2. Ensure that nothing is already selected by pressing Esc (the Escape key), the upper-left key on the computer keyboard. The cursor should be black, not blue.

3. Click inside measure 1 to select it. A blue rectangle will appear around the measure.

4. Press the letter N on the keyboard to input notes. The input notes option can also be selected from the Notes menu.

5. Next, select the quarter note value from the Keypad. If the Keypad is not visible, go to the Window menu and select Keypad.

6. Place your right hand over the numeric keypad. Press the quarter note value on the keypad, or the 4 key if your computer has a numeric keypad. You can also click on the quarter note value with your mouse. Whichever method you use, be sure to select the note duration *before* entering the pitch.

> Place your right hand over the numeric keypad with your middle finger over the 5 key. With practice you will begin to "feel" the different note durations: 5 = half, 4 = quarter, 3 = eighth, and so forth.

7. To enter a quarter rest, with the quarter note value selected, press the 0 (zero) key on the keypad.

8. Since the next three notes are all quarter notes, type the letters A, G, A.

9. To enter the B♭ dotted half note, first select the half note value by pressing the 5 key on the numeric keypad. Add the dot by pressing the period on the keypad. Type the letter B on the keyboard. Sibelius assumes you mean B♭ since it is in the key signature. You can override this by selecting the appropriate accidental on the keypad.

10. To enter the A quarter note in measure 2, press the 4 key on the keypad with your right hand and type the letter A with your left. Getting the hang of it?

Correcting Mistakes (Edit > Undo)

The quickest way to correct a mistake is to use the Undo command, which you can access from the Edit menu. You can also click on the Undo icon on the toolbar at the top of the screen or use the shortcut key: ⌘-Z (Mac); CTRL-Z (Win). Unfortunately, the Undo command does not work after you've printed out an arrangement and your ensemble plays a wrong note.

Entering the Notation in Measures 3 Through 8

1. Enter the G and A quarter notes on beats 1 and 2 of measure 3.
2. To enter the F dotted quarter note, select the quarter note value and press the period on the numeric keypad *before* entering the note. Enter the G eighth note to complete measure 3.
3. In measure 4, enter the G quarter note. To enter the A dotted half note tied to measure 4, select the half note value and press the period to add a dot. Type the letter A.
4. After entering the A, press Enter on the keypad to add the tie. Ties are always added after the note is entered.

 Another way to enter an automatic tie is to enter a note value that is too large for the bar. For example, if you enter a whole note on beat 2 of bar 12, Sibelius will automatically create a dotted half note and a tie over the bar to a quarter note. Very cool, indeed!

5. Enter the rest of the notation in measures 5 through 16. Remember, to enter a rest, select the appropriate duration and press zero (0) key on the keypad.

 Be sure to enter all ties when you are entering the notation, using the tie value on the keypad. Slurs are handled differently and will be covered in a later chapter.

Copying and Pasting with Shift-Click

You can save a huge amount of time entering notation by using Copy and Paste. Note that measures 17 through 24 are identical to measures 9 through 16 except for the last two notes. For this example, you will copy the measures and then use Re-insert Pitch to change the last two notes.

1. Press Esc to clear the cursor so it is black, not blue.

2. Click inside measure 9 on the lines and spaces to high-light it.

3. Hold down the Shift key and click the mouse in measure 16. Click inside the lines and spaces, not on a note.

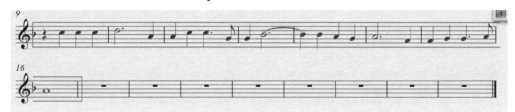

4. Sibelius has a special way of pasting notation that replaces copying and pasting in the traditional manner. Simply hold down the Option (Mac) or Alt (Win) key and click in measure 17. Whatever is currently selected will be pasted into the new location.

Correcting Pitches

There are several ways to change pitches once they are entered. For example, the last two notes in "Finlandia" need to be changed from A to F. Let's make the changes in two different ways.

1. Press Esc.
2. Click on the A eighth note at the end of bar 23.
3. Press the down arrow key on the keyboard two times to move the pitch to an F.
4. Press the right arrow key to move the cursor to the whole note and press the down arrow key two times.

Sibelius offers another helpful way to change pitches without altering the duration of notes. This technique is especially helpful if you copy a first part to a second and then want to change only the pitches. Before trying this option, undo the steps you just took.

To Undo Multiple Steps

You can undo multiple steps by using the Undo command several times. You can click on the icon at the top of the page or use the short-cut key: ⌘-Z (Mac); CTRL-Z (Win).

It is also possible to view the list of steps that have been done and delete them in one simple click of the mouse.

1. From the Edit menu, select Undo History.
2. Click the mouse at the desired location in the list—in this case, the last few steps that you took to move the A pitches to F.
3. Click OK.

Re-Input Pitch

The Re-input Pitch option is another excellent way to change pitches without affecting the note value.

1. Press Esc.
2. Select the first note in the passage that you want to re-pitch. In this case, it's the A eighth note in measure 23.
3. From the Notes menu, choose Re-input Pitches. A dashed cursor line will appear to distinguish Re-input Pitch from normal note entry.
4. Press the letter F two times. You can also enter the notes from a MIDI keyboard. This will be introduced in Chapter 4.

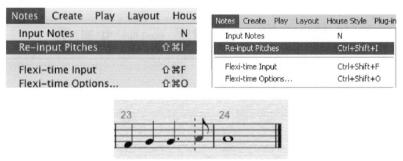

Entering Expressions (Dynamics)

Sibelius handles text in a variety of ways. Dynamics and similar instructions to players such as legato, marcato, and so forth are indicated in italics and are entered below the staff. You can easily move anything on the screen by clicking and dragging it. In this example, there are several dynamics that are entered via expressions.

To enter the dynamics:

1. Press Esc (just in case something is already selected).
2. Click on the quarter rest in bar 1. It will turn blue.
3. From the Create menu, select Text and then Expression from the submenu.
4. A blinking cursor will appear below the staff. Right-click (CTRL-click if you are using a Mac with a one-button mouse) on the cursor to display the list of dynamics and other markings. Drag to the *mp* dynamic marking. Release the mouse button.
5. Press Esc.

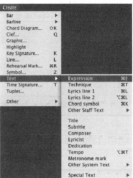

6. Since the expression is blue, you can drag it to any location on the screen. Press Esc to clear the selection.

Entering Expressions via Shortcut Keys

The fastest way to enter expressions is to use the shortcut keys. Remember, the letter E stands for expression.

1. Press Esc (to clear anything that could currently be selected).
2. Click on the quarter rest in measure 9 to highlight it.
3. Use the shortcut command for entering expressions: ⌘-E (Mac); CTRL-E (Win).
4. Right-click on the blinking cursor and select the dynamic marking *mf* (Mac users with a one-button mouse, press the CTRL key and click the mouse. Get rid of that one-button mouse before you start Chapter 3!).
5. Press Esc to enter the dynamic. Press Esc again to clear the *mf* selection.

> You can also type letters by following the above steps (1, 2, and 3) and then holding down ⌘ (Mac); CTRL (Win) and typing the dynamics: *ff*, *mp*, and so forth. They will appear in the correct font.

6. Repeat the above steps to put the *f* (forte) expression in measure 17.

Playback for Proof Listening

Music entered in Sibelius can be played using either a MIDI keyboard or the computer's internal sound source or software synthesis. Be sure you have configured your MIDI setup as described in the Sibelius manual.

To play back the piece:

1. Press Esc.
2. Check to see if the Playback controls appear on the screen. If not, press the right arrow on the toolbar at the top of the screen or select Playback controls from the Window menu.

3. Press the green play arrow or simply press the space bar to start the playback. Listen for mistakes. It is much easier to find any incorrect notes via listening.
4. Press the square button or the space bar to stop playback.
5. Press the play (right arrow) button located in the menu bar at the top of the screen. You can also press the letter P to start and stop playback.

Zooming in and Zooming Out

Review the file before printing. First view the entire document on the screen. You can zoom in and out of the score at any time by selecting a percentage from the menu at the top of the screen.

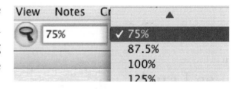

A faster way is to use the shortcut keys: the plus (+) and minus (–) keys above the P key on the computer keyboard (not the ones on the numeric keypad).

Mac: hold down ⌘ and press the plus key multiple times to zoom in (bigger) and the minus key to zoom out (smaller).

Windows: hold down CTRL and press the plus key multiple times to zoom in (bigger) and the minus key to zoom out (smaller).

This will not affect the size of the printed music, just the onscreen display size.

Centering the Music in Page View

There are two ways to center music in the window.

1. Press Esc so there is nothing selected.
2. Click on the white area of the page and drag it up or down. Don't click on the staff, as that will move the staff position.

You can also use the Navigator window, usually displayed at the bottom left of the window. If the Navigator window is not visible, go to the Window menu and select Navigator.

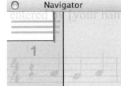

3. Click inside the Navigator window to scroll the score.
4. Use the shortcut keys to turn Navigator on and off: Option-⌘-N (Mac); Alt-CTRL-N (Win).

Measures per Line

Unless you tell it otherwise, Sibelius will automatically format the number of measures per line according to the density of the notation, lyrics, and other score markings. In this case, Sibelius grouped the measures to eight per line. Often, you will want to customize this; for example, to create four measures per line.

To change to 4 bars per line:

1. Press Esc.
2. Click on the barline at the end of measure 4 to select it. It will turn purple.
3. Press Return (Mac) or Enter (Win) to move measure 5 to the next line. You can also access this option from the Layout menu: select Break and then System Break from the submenu.

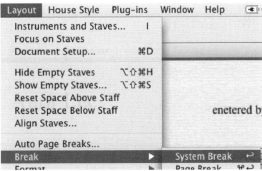

4. Click on the line at the end of measure 8. Press Return/Enter to move measure 9 to the next line.
5. Repeat the above steps and break the system after measures 12, 16, and 20.

Your file should now look like the printout on the next page. The blue return arrows at the end of systems 1 and 2 will not print. They are to remind you that you manually moved the measures in this systems. These are called Layout Marks and can be turned on or off from the View menu.

Saving and Printing ☺

It is important to save your work frequently. If a file has not been saved to disk, it can be lost due to a power failure or a computer crash. I like to use the saying: *When you smile,* ☺ *save.* In other words, if you accomplish something you like, save it! I try to save every sixteen measures, or every page of music. Saving frequently is a habit that you will be glad you adopted. To save a file:

1. From the File menu, choose Save.
2. Name the example "Finlandia" and save it to your hard drive.
3. To print the file, go to the File menu and choose Print.

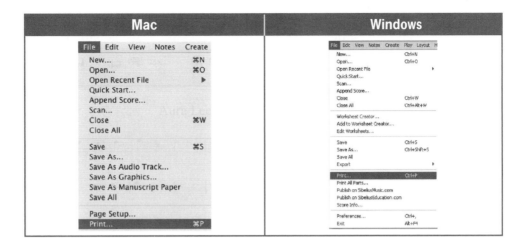

Sibelius Preferences

Sibelius offers a wide range of options with regard to saving files. It can be told to automatically back up at any time interval. It can also automatically create a second copy, or backup, of the piece you are working on.

To select the Sibelius Preferences:

Mac: from the Sibelius menu, select Preferences and then General from the submenu. Windows: from the File menu, select Preferences and then General from the submenu.

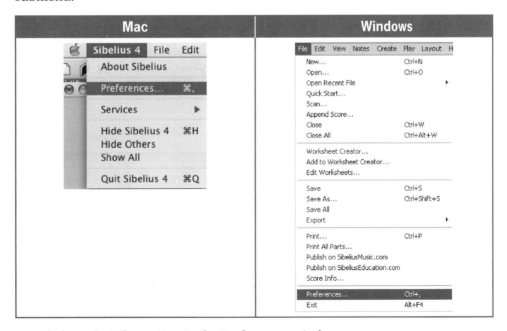

- Click on the Files option in the Preferences window.

These are the Sibelius 4 default settings. The program is set up to save automatically every ten minutes. It places a copy in the AutoSave folder on your hard drive and does not affect the file you are working on.

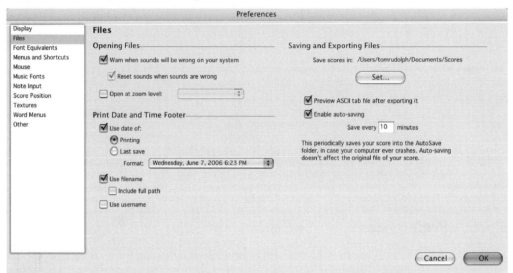

 It is not a bad idea to automatically save, especially if you are not in the habit of saving your work frequently. Making backups is also a good idea. Sometimes the file you are working on will become corrupted and the backup can be a real asset. All of these options can be selected and then are retained even after you quit the program.

Congratulations! You have successfully entered and printed your first Sibelius example.

 Use a copying machine if you need more than two or three copies of a piece of music. It is usually cheaper to print one and take it to a copying machine to make more than to print a large number of copies from the computer.

Plug-Ins

Sibelius comes with a host of plug-ins designed to save you time with specific tasks. The effects of plug-ins cannot be undone, so it is a good idea to save a copy of your file before applying any plug-ins. In this example the solfeggio plug-in will be used.

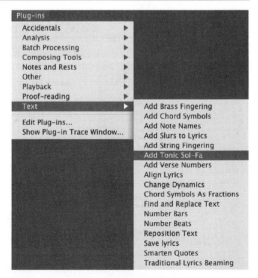

1. From the File menu, choose Save As to rename and save a copy of "Finlandia." Name it "FinlandiaSolFa."

2. Plug-ins can be applied to parts or all of a score. To select the entire score, from the Edit Menu, choose Select All. You can also use the Sibelius shortcut: triple-click inside the lines and spaces in measure 1. Yes, that is triple-click the mouse (three times quickly in a row).

3. From the Plug-ins menu, choose Text, and then "Add Tonic Sol-Fa" from the submenu.

4. You will get a warning about the actions of plug-ins not being able to be undone. Click Yes.

5. In the "Add Tonic Sol-Fa" window, uncheck the button next to "Add rhythmic markings" and click OK.

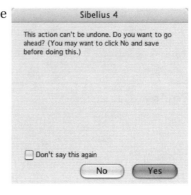

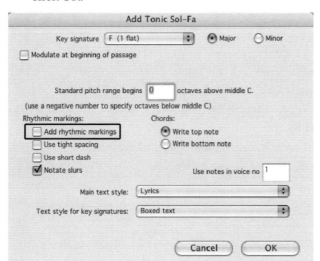

Summary

For this example, only the necessary tools were used. These basic steps can be used to enter similar music examples:

- launch Sibelius
- set up the score
- add additional measures
- display measure numbers on every bar
- enter the notation via alphabetic entry
- correct mistakes

- copy and paste with Shift-click
- correct pitches with Re-input Pitch
- enter expressions
- use Playback to check for errors
- zoom in and out
- center music on the screen
- adjust the page layout to fit the measures four per line
- save a copy to disk to protect against Murphy's Law
- print a copy of the score
- view Sibelius preferences
- apply the Sol-Fa plug-in

Review

1. Review the list of Sibelius skills above. To review any or all, go to the Sibelius Help menu and search for the specific item.
2. Reenter the piece, starting from scratch. Refer only to the list of steps above to relearn the skills.
3. Enter a similar piece of music using alphabetic entry.

3

Chords, Lyrics, and Slurs (Musical Example: "Greensleeves")

This chapter will focus on practicing and extending the Sibelius skills introduced in earlier chapters.

The new areas for this example include:

- deleting extra bars
- entering notation via the keypad and editing mistakes
- changing the tempo of playback
- entering chord symbols
- adding a double barline
- lyrics: entering, editing, and changing the font size
- changing the text style of the title
- entering slurs
- adjusting the space between staves
- transposing the key
- changing page size and format

- realizing chord symbols
- displaying selected staves
- deleting unwanted staves
- developing a Sibelius checklist of steps for creating notation

Selecting Menus and Submenus

Throughout this and subsequent chapters, menus, along the top of the Sibelius window, are indicated with the menu name in bold, and each submenu or choice indicated with a >. You will see references such as: "**Edit** > Select > Select All." This means to go to the Edit menu, choose the Select submenu and release the mouse button on the menu choice Select All.

Setting up the Score

The first step is to prepare the score. See Chapter 2 for details or refer to the *Sibelius User Manual* or Help menu. Carefully follow each step below.

1. To create a new file, use the shortcut keys: ⌘-N (Mac); CTRL-N (Win).
2. Under "Manuscript Paper," click Blank.
3. Click the Add Instruments button.
4. Under "Choose from," select All Instruments; Family: Others; Instrument: treble staff; click the Add to Score button. Click OK. Click Next.
5. Under House Style, click on "Unchanged." Click Next.
6. Set the Time Signature to 6/8.
7. Check the Pickup (Upbeat) bar and change the duration of the pickup to an eighth note. Click Next.
8. From the Key Signature window, select "Minor keys" and click on F♯ minor (three sharps). Click Next.

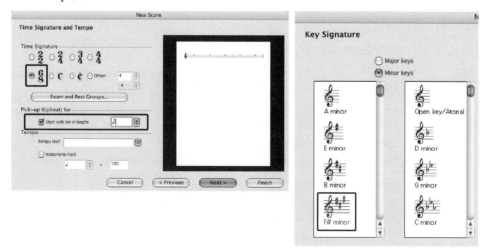

9. Enter the Title: "Greensleeves," the Composer/Songwriter: "TRADITIONAL," and the Lyricist: "Entered by [your name]."

10. Before you click the Finish button, go back and double-check your entries by clicking the Previous and Next buttons. Return to the last screen and click Finish.

 Take your time while going through the New Score setup screens. While you are making your selections, go back and forth between screens and make changes by clicking the Previous and Next buttons. Once you press the Finish button on the last screen, you will have to make changes directly in the score or delete it and start over. So double-check your entries before clicking Finish. You will save time for sure.

Your score should look like the following. If you missed something, the best option is to close the file (**File** > Close) and start a new score (**File** > New) and repeat the above steps.

Adding Bars (Measures)

You should add more bars than you need to again practice deleting unwanted bars.

1. To add one bar and the end of the score: **Create** > Bar > At End.

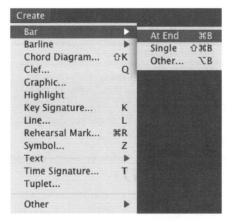

2. Use the shortcut keys to add another bar: ⌘-B (Mac); CTRL-B (Win).

3. To add a lot of bars, hold down the above shortcut keys and the computer will repeat adding them. Add a bunch, more than sixteen. You'll delete what you don't need later.

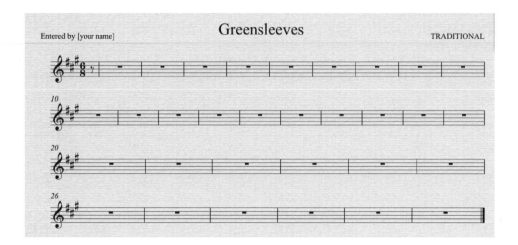

Deleting Bars (Measures)

1. To show the staff names and bar numbers onscreen, go to **View** > Staff Names and Bar Numbers.

There are sixteen measures in "Greensleeves." The pickup bar is measure 0. To delete unwanted measures:

2. Hold down ⌘ (Mac) or CTRL (Win) and click inside the lines and spaces in measure 17. A double box will appear around it.

3. Hold down the Shift key and click in the last measure of the section that you want to delete (or press the End key on the computer keyboard).

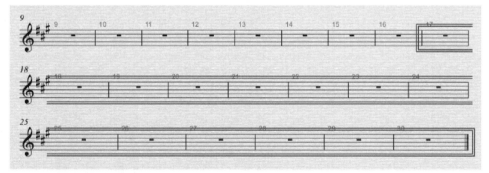

4. Press the Delete key to remove the unwanted bars.
5. If you made a mistake, undo it: ⌘-Z (Mac); CTRL- Z (Win).

Entering Notation with Alphabetic Input

Before starting to enter the notation, be sure the Keypad is on the screen: **Window** > Keypad or use the shortcut keys: Option-⌘-K (Mac); Alt-CTRL-K (Win).

1. Press Esc (just in case something is already selected).
2. Click inside the pickup measure (measure 0).
3. Press the letter N (shortcut for **Notes** > Input Notes).
4. Place your right hand over the keypad. Press the 3 key to select the eighth note value.
5. With your left hand, press the letter F to enter an F♯ eighth note (sharps and flats in the key signature are added automatically).
6. Change the value to a quarter note by pressing 4 on the keypad.
7. Type the letter A.
8. Change the value to an eighth note by pressing 3 on the keypad.
9. Type the letter B.
10. Change the value to a dotted eighth note by pressing the period on the keypad.
11. Type the letter C to enter a C♯.
12. Press the 2 key on the keypad for a sixteenth note value; press the 8 key to add the ♯. Whenever possible, accidentals should be added *before* entering the note.
13. Type the letter D.
14. Type the number 3 on the keypad to select an eighth note value.
15. Type the letter C to enter a C♯.
16. Enter the rest of the notation in bars 2, 3, and 4.

Editing Mistakes

If you enter an incorrect pitch or duration, use Undo to delete it. You can also move the cursor from note to note using the arrow keys on the computer keyboard.

Copy and paste can save note-entry time. To copy measures 1 and 2 into measures 5 and 6:

1. Press Esc (to clear anything that might already be selected).
2. Click inside the lines and spaces in measure 1 (not the pickup bar).
3. Hold down the Shift key and click inside the lines and spaces in measure 2.

4. Hold down Option (Mac) or Alt (Win) and click inside measure 5.
5. Press Esc to clear the selection.

Enter the notation for measures 7 through 12:

6. Click inside measure 7.
7. Press the letter N to enter notation.
8. Enter the rest of the notation for measures 7 through 12.

Entering Harmony

The easiest and fastest way to enter harmony in Sibelius is to play two or more notes at the same time using a MIDI keyboard. This will be covered in Chapter 4.

When using alphabetic or mouse input, harmony can be entered above or below a note using the numbers at the top of the computer keyboard (not the numbers on the keypad). Each number represents the interval above or below the note entered: 2 = second; 3 = third; 4 = fourth, and so forth. If you press the number alone, the harmony will be entered above the entered note. If you hold down the Shift key and then press the number, the harmony will be entered below the entered pitch.

1. In measure 13, enter a C♯ dotted quarter note (the bottom note).
2. Press the number 3 along the top of the computer keyboard to enter the harmony (do not use the numeric keypad).
3. Change the duration to a dotted eighth note (press 3 on the numeric keypad, then press the period). Type C to enter the C♯.
4. Press the number 3 along the top of the keyboard to add a third above.
5. Continue to enter the notation by first entering the bottom note and then pressing the appropriate number to add harmony above (3 = third; 4 = fourth, and so forth). If you make a mistake, Undo and reenter the note.

 Sometimes when you type a letter name on the computer keyboard, it will enter in the wrong octave. You can change the octave by pressing the up arrow on the keypad. There is also a shortcut to move a note up or down an octave. With the note selected, press ⌘-up arrow (Mac) or CTRL-up arrow (Win). The down arrow will move the note down an octave.

Playback

After the notes and rhythms are entered, proof-listen to check for mistakes.

1. Be sure the Playback window is visible on the screen. You can turn it on and off by pressing the right arrow on the toolbar at the top of the screen or using the shortcut: Option-⌘-Y (Mac); Alt-CTRL-Y (Win).

When you proof-listen to a piece, you can speed up the tempo using a control on the Playback toolbar.

2. Drag the Tempo control to the right to speed up the tempo.
3. Press the space bar to begin playback. Press it again to stop playback.
4. It is also possible to go to specific measures. Drag the measure locator to a specific measure, and press the space bar to start playback at that location.

Another way to play back from a specific location is to click on a notehead or rest.

5. Press Esc.
6. Click on the note or rest where you would like to start playback, for example, measure 5.
7. Press the letter P on the keyboard to playback from the selected note or rest.

Entering Chord Symbols

After the notation is entered, go back and add the chord symbols. As with most tasks, Sibelius has several ways to do this. Chords can be entered by analyzing existing music and by manually typing into the score. This example uses the type-into-score method.

1. Press Esc.
2. Click on the A in the first measure.
3. From the Create menu, select "Text" and then "Chord Symbol," or use the shortcut: ⌘-K (Mac); CTRL-K (Win).
4. Type "F♯m" (for F♯ minor).
5. Press the space bar five times to advance the cursor to the first note in the second bar.
6. Type E.
7. Continue to use the space bar to advance and enter the rest of the notation.

You can also select chord symbols and chord suffixes from a pull-down menu. After pressing ⌘-K (Mac) or CTRL-K (Win), enter the chord root, then right-click (two-button mouse) or CTRL-click (Mac, one-button mouse) and select the chord suffix from the list in the menu. This is not necessary for the simple chords in "Greensleeves," but when entering more complex chords, it is a fast way to enter suffixes.

To edit a Chord Symbol that has been entered:

1. Press Esc.
2. Double-click on the chord you want to edit. The cursor will appear at the end of the chord.
3. Press Delete to remove the incorrect chord and then type in the correct chord.
4. Press the space bar to advance the cursor to continue editing, or press Esc to start over and repeat the above steps.

Adding a Double Barline

To create the double bar at the end of measure 8:

1. Press Esc.
2. Click on the barline at the end of measure 8 to highlight it.
3. Select **Create** > Barline > Double.
4. Press Esc to clear the selection.

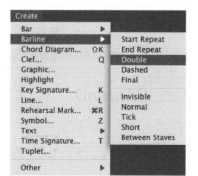

Lyrics

There are two ways to enter lyrics in Sibelius. You can type them directly into the score, similar to chords, or type the lyrics into a word processor and then copy and paste them into the score. This chapter will focus on entering the lyrics by typing them into the score. Chapter 8 will address the copy-and-paste option.

Lyrics basics:

- When there is a syllable break, just type the first syllable and enter a hyphen (-) after it. Do not enter a space before the hyphen! Sibelius will automatically jump to the next note. Take your time and be sure to enter the lyrics under the proper notes.
- If there is a melisma (more than one note per syllable), enter the lyric and press the space bar. Sibelius will create a word extension.
- If you make a mistake, press the left arrow key and edit the lyrics as needed.

Entering lyrics:

1. Press Esc.
2. Click on the F♯ in the pickup measure to select it. It will turn blue.
3. Select **Create** > Text > Lyrics or use the shortcut: ⌘-L (Mac); CTRL-L (Win).
4. A blinking cursor will appear beneath the note. Type in the first syllable: "A" and press the dash key (–) to make a syllable break. The cursor will jump to the next note.

5. Under the note A, enter the lyric: "las,".
6. Press the space bar to move to the next note.
7. Enter the next word: "my."
8. Press the space bar and enter the word "love."
9. Press the space bar and enter the word "you."
10. Press the space bar twice to skip the note C♯, as this is a melisma. Sibelius will automatically enter a word extension (or a lyric line) for all melismas.
11. Continue to enter the rest of the text on the next page.

Fixing a Lyric

There will be times when you have to correct a lyric that was entered. Here are the steps:

1. Press Esc.
2. Double-click on the syllable you want to edit. The cursor will be placed at the end of the entry.
3. To delete it, press the Delete key and reenter the lyric.

44

Changing the (Font) Size of the Lyrics

The font size of the lyrics can be changed at any time. To change the size of the lyrics for the entire piece:

1. Select **House Style** > Edit Text Styles.
2. Select "Lyrics line 1."
3. Click Edit.
4. Adjust the font size, font, or any other font characteristic.

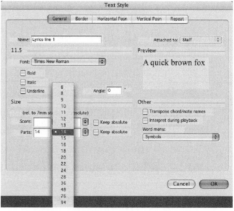

The normal size for most lyrics is 10 to 11.5 point. If there are a lot of lyrics in most measures, a smaller font size will permit more to be printed per line. For a larger font size, use 12 or 14.

 At point sizes of 10 or smaller, it is best to use a serif font like Times because it is easier to read than sans-serif fonts such as Helvetica. A serif is a small decorative line added as embellishment to the basic form of a letter. Typefaces are often described as being "serif" or "sans serif" (without serifs).

Saving the Style for Future Reference

It is possible to save the above lyric settings for future use.

1. Select **House Style** > Export House Style.
2. Name the custom House Style you've created with a descriptive name, such as "Lyrics at 10 point size."
3. Click OK.

You can now import this font size from the House Style menu for future documents.

Changing the Text Style of Individual Items

In Sibelius, use House Styles when you want to affect everything in the score. If you only want to change some items, use the Properties window. For example, perhaps you want to change only the size of the title:

1. Press Esc.
2. Click on the title (Greensleeves) at the top of the score to select it.
3. Select **Window** > Properties, or use the shortcut command: Option-⌘-P (Mac); Alt-CTRL-P (Win), or click the Properties button at the top of the screen.

Properties

4. Click on the Text tab in the Properties window to open it.
5. Change the text size by clicking the arrows next to Size.
6. Change the style by checking B for bold, I for italics, etc.
7. Close the Properties window when you've finished, to keep the screen clutter-free.

Slurs

Recall that in Chapter 2, ties were used. Be sure not to confuse a slur with a tie. A tie connects two notes of the same pitch. A slur is a phrasing mark that connects two or more notes. Enter ties from the keypad (see Chapter 2). Enter slurs as follows:

1. Press Esc.
2. Select the D♯ in measure 1.
3. Press the letter S by itself to enter a slur (or **Create** > Line and select Slur from the window).
4. Repeat the above in measures 2 and 3.

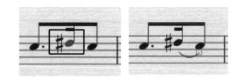

To enter a three-note slur in measure 5:

1. Click on the C♯ in measure 5.
2. Press the S key to enter a two-note slur.
3. Press the space bar to extend the slur to the next note.
4. Enter the rest of the slurs using the above steps.

> You can also enter two-note slurs during the notation-entering process. For example, after entering a note, press the letter S and then enter the next pitch. You may prefer to enter the notation and then go back and do the slurs, but either way works.

Changing the Measure Layout with a Plug-in

In Chapter 2, the measure format was changed one line at a time. Sibelius offers another option via a plug-in.

1. Press Esc.
2. Select the entire piece by triple-clicking inside any measure. Yes, that is a triple-click—click the mouse button three times. Another option is **Edit** > Select > Select All or the shortcut: ⌘-A (Mac); CTRL-A (Win).
3. Since plug-ins cannot be undone, save the file before applying the plug-in.
4. Select **Plug-ins** > Other > Make Layout Uniform.
5. You will get a warning that plug-ins can't be undone. Click Yes.
6. In the Make Layout Uniform window, be sure that "Ignore pickup bar" is checked. Click OK.

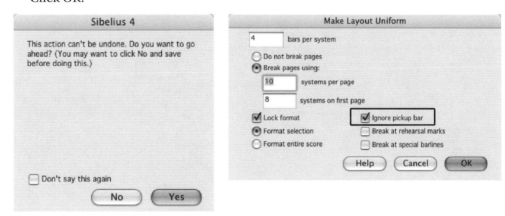

If you want to return to the default layout:

1. Select some or all of the score (shortcut: shift-⌘-A [Mac]; Shift-CTRL-A [Win]).
2. Select **Layout** > Format > Unlock Format (shortcut: Shift-⌘-U [Mac]; Shift-CTRL-U [Win]). This will return the selection to the default format.

Print

Congratulations! You are now ready to print the "Greensleeves" example. Be sure to save before going to **File** > Print.

Adjusting the Space Between Staves

When entering lyrics and chords, you may want to have more room between the staves or systems. The Sibelius default is usually acceptable, but it does come out looking pretty tightly spaced.

There are several ways to control the spacing between the staves. First, set the space between all staves using the Engraving Rules.

1. Select **House Styles** > Engraving Rules.
2. In the Engraving Rules dialog box, select Staves.
3. The Engraving Rules screen has the setting "Justify staves when page is at least 50% full." Changing the percentage figure to 90%, for example, may change the layout

of your score and force white space to the bottom of the screen. In Sibelius, think of the word "justify" as synonymous with "spread out."

4. Next, change "Spaces between staves" to a larger number to add space between all staves. A space in Sibelius is the distance between two staff lines. The larger the number of spaces, the more space there will be between all staves. Try 14.5 spaces and see if you like it.

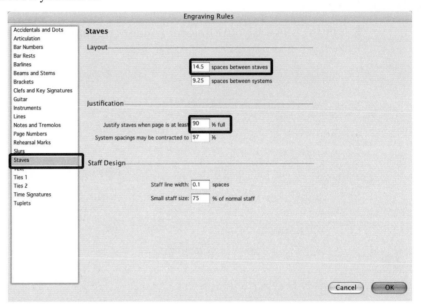

 It is important to understand the difference between a staff (stave) and a system. In this example, there is one stave, but several systems, usually eight to ten on a page. Think of systems as the number of lines in a score. In multiple-stave scores, a system is usually joined internally via barlines.

Saving Copies of the File in Different Keys

Now that you have saved the file (with the name "Greensleeves") in the key of F♯ minor, you may want to save another version in another key, perhaps for a transposing instrument such as a saxophone or to raise or lower the key for a specific vocal range. One way to accomplish this is to use the Save As command to rename and save a second file without erasing the first. For practice, lower the key to E minor. First save a new file, then change the key as needed:

1. Select **File** > Save As to save the file with a new name: "GreensleevesEmin."

2. Select the entire piece by pressing the shortcut keys: ⌘-A (Mac); CTRL-A (Win), or by choosing **Edit** > Select > Select All.

3. Select **Notes** > Transpose (or use the shortcut, Shift-T).
4. Set the direction to down and the interval to Major/Perfect 2nd. Click OK. Sibelius will transpose notes and chords to the selected interval.
5. Save and print the file in the new key.

Change to Hymnal Format

It is easy to change the page size and format of any score. For example, if you would like to print this example out in hymnal format:

1. Select **Layout** > Document Setup (shortcut ⌘-D [Mac]; CTRL-D [Win]).
2. Be sure that Inches is checked at the top of the window.
3. Select Hymn from the "Page size" pull-down list.
4. Reduce the staff size so the same number of measures will be printed on each line. A staff size of 0.17 did the trick this time around.

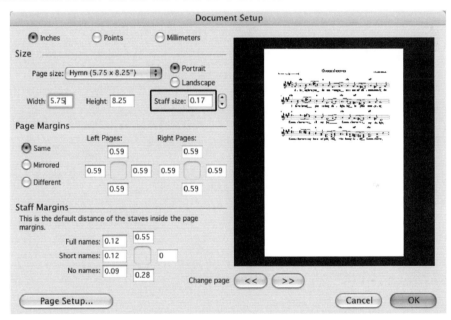

 Do not use the Page Reduction Options in the Page Setup window for your printer. It is much more precise to control the print size in Sibelius.

Realize Chord Symbols Plug-in and Focus on Staves

When you press the Play button, Sibelius does not play back the chords as shown in your file. However, there is a plug-in that can do this.

1. Select **File** > Save As and name the new file "GreensleevesChords."
2. Press Esc.

3. Select the entire piece by triple-clicking inside any measure or choosing **Edit** > Select > Select All.
4. Select **Plug-ins** > Composing Tools > Realize Chord Symbols & Diagrams.
5. Set the Chord style to "Chord every chord symbol" and the New instrument to "Piano." Click OK.

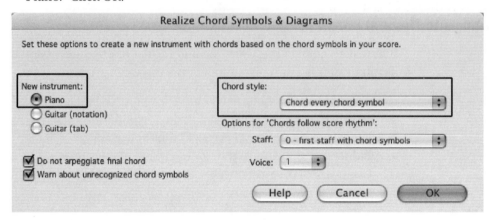

Sibelius will realize each chord symbol. When you press the Play button or press the space bar, you will hear the melody with chords.

Focus on Staves

You can also show specific staves, for example the melody, while the chords are playing back by using the "Focus on Staves" feature.

1. Select the staff you do want to see, in this case the melody. Click in any measure to select it.
2. Click the Focus on Staves button or use the shortcut: ⌘-Option-F (Mac); CTRL-Alt-F (Win).
3. Press Esc to deselect the melody staff. If one or more staves are selected, Sibelius will only play back the selections.

4. Press the space bar to play back the file. You should hear the chords created by the plug-in and see only the melody.
5. To turn off this feature, click the Focus on Staves button or use the shortcut again.

Eliminating Extra Staves

Plug-in effects can't be undone, but it is easy to remove unwanted staves from the score. For example, if you want to delete the Piano part added by the Realize Chord Symbols plug-in:

1. Deselect the Focus on Staves button.
2. Select **Layout** > Instruments and Staves (the shortcut is the letter I).
3. Under "Staves in score," click Piano (a), hold down the Shift key, and click on Piano (b).
4. Click the Delete from Score button.
5. Click Yes to remove the staves from the score.

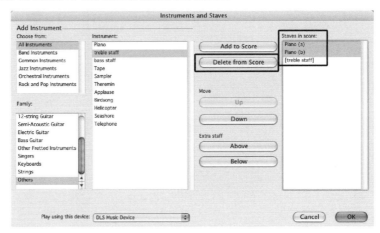

Summary

The steps to enter "Greensleeves" are summarized below. These general steps can be used for future notation projects.

- launch Sibelius
- use the New Score setup to format the piece
- display measure numbers on every bar
- enter the notation
- enter the chords
- enter the lyrics
- enter slurs and other text and graphics above and below the staff
- enter and adjust the titles and credits at the top of the page

- lay out the music to specific measures per line; adjust the spaces between staves and score size
- save a copy to disk
- print the score

Review

1. Try to reenter "Greensleeves" referring only to the general areas listed in the summary above.
2. Consult the Sibelius Reference (**Help**> Sibelius Reference) to review the skills presented in this chapter.

4

Articulations, Expressions, and D.S. al Coda (Musical Example: "Rondeau and Fanfares" by Mouret)

Review the "Rondeau and Fanfares" printout below. You will notice that the notation is more complex than in the earlier chapter examples. This chapter introduces the use of articulations, dynamics, a D.S. al Coda, and other markings.

The new areas addressed in this chapter include:

- new items in score setup: selecting Orchestra > C Trumpet; entering "Tempo text" (Allegro); entering 2/2 time signature; adding copyright at the bottom
- creating an instrument name and arranger at the top of the score
- changing the font of the title and other text
- removing staff names via Engraving Rules
- exporting (saving) a House Style for later use and importing it into an existing document
- displaying bar numbers under every measure
- entering notation with a MIDI keyboard: step time
- entering articulations
- creating lines: slurs and crescendos/decrescendos (hairpins)
- creating rehearsal letters
- entering tuplets and grace notes
- controlling the display of out-of-range notes
- entering cue-size notation
- entering Technique Text above the staff
- entering a D.S. al Coda and splitting a system for the Coda
- entering a fermata
- entering 8va lines above selected notes
- displaying multirests
- laying out the page with four measures per line
- breaking the Coda system and indenting the system to the right
- creating an Ossia
- adding brass fingerings via plug-in and moving items using Select More

Preparing the Score

1. Open a new file in Sibelius: **File** > New.
2. Choose Blank Manuscript Paper and click on the Add Instruments button.
3. Select Orchestral Instruments > Brass > Trumpet in C. Click "Add to Score" and click OK. Then click Next.

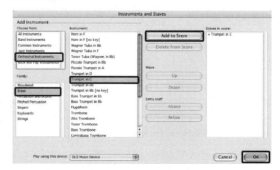

4. Select the House Style "Unchanged," and click Next.

5. In the Time Signature and Tempo window:
   a. Under Time Signature, select 2/2.
   b. Click "Pick-up Bar" and enter a duration of a quarter note.
   c. Click on the pull-down menu next to "Tempo text" and choose "Allegro."
   d. Click Next.
6. Choose the key of D major (two sharps) and click Next.
7. In the Score Info window, enter the titles and copyright notice:
   a. Title: Rondeau and Fanfares
   b. Composer/Songwriter: Jean Joseph Mouret
   c. Lyricist: Entered by [your name]
   d. Copyright: This arrangement copyright © 2006 by Tom Rudolph
8. Click the Previous button and review your selections to be sure they are accurate. When you are satisfied, return to the last score setup window and click Finish. Your score should now look like the following:

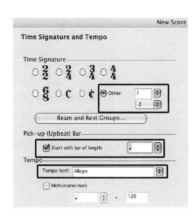

Customizing the Text at the Top of the Score (System Text)

This example requires the insertion of two text items at the top of the score: one for the instrument name, C Trumpet, and one for the arranger. Sibelius has a huge list of text options, which are presented in the menu **Create** > Text. There are then several submenus of options. System Text contains items typically displayed at the top or bottom of the score and D.C./D.S./To Coda signs. Staff text includes those items that typically appear above or below the staff. The advantage of using these specific menu options is that you can select the recommended text style, location, and size. Also, in scores, system text applies to all staves; staff text applies to specific staves. This will be covered in later chapters.

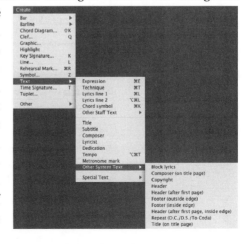

All of the titles at the top of the page are linked to the first measure (bar) of the score. If you delete the first measure, all of your titles will also be deleted. Keep this in mind when editing the notation in the first bar of any score.

Entering an instrument name and arranger at the top of the score

1. Press Esc.
2. Click inside the pickup bar.
3. Select **Create** > Text > Special Text > Instrument Name.
4. Type the text: "C Trumpet."
5. Press Esc. The text you just typed should be selected (highlighted in blue).
6. Use the up arrow key on the computer keyboard to move it up. Using the up and down arrow keys is more accurate than dragging text with the mouse.
7. Click the mouse inside the pickup measure.
8. Select **Create** > Text > Composer.
9. Enter the text: "Arranged by Tom Rudolph."
10. Press Esc.
11. Use the down arrow to move the text beneath the composer's name (Jean Joseph Mouret).
12. Press Esc and compare your score with the graphic below.

To remove the staff or instrument name

Sibelius automatically names staves in a score. In this example, we want to remove the staff titles that appear to the left of every staff. One option is to just select them and press Delete. Another option is to turn them off via Engraving Rules.

1. Select **House Style** > Engraving Rules.
2. Select Instruments.
3. Under Instrument Names, check None under "At start," "Subsequently," and "At new sections." Then click OK. This will remove the staff name from the left of the system.

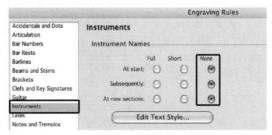

Editing the Font, Size, and Style of Text

All of the text entered in Sibelius can be altered via the Properties menu. For example, you might want to use your favorite font for the title.

To change the font of the title:

1. Press Esc.
2. Click on the title "Rondeau and Fanfares" to select it.
3. Select **Window** > Properties.
4. Click the arrow next to the Text tab.
5. Change the font as desired. You can also change the size and the style: B = bold; I = Italics; U = Underline. You may not have the font I selected on your computer. Use the font you think fits best.

Displaying Measure (Bar) Numbers Beneath Every Measure

In the previous chapters, the measure numbers were displayed to the left of every staff system. For instrumental parts, I usually display the measure numbers on every measure to help the performers when reading the part (they still get lost sometimes, but it does save rehearsal time when you can say something like, "Let's start at bar 57").

1. Select **House Style** > Engraving Rules.
2. Choose "Bar Numbers" in the left column.
3. In the "Bar number frequency" list, choose "Every bar." "Center range on multirest" will become active and checked at the same time. Click OK.
4. Check "Show at start of sections."
5. Click the "After clef" button.
6. Select **House Style** > Default Positions.
7. Select "Bar numbers."

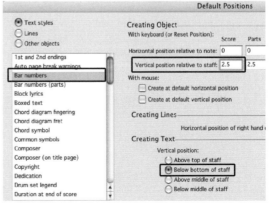

8.   Change the "Vertical position relative to staff" to 2.5 spaces for the score.
9.   Under Creating Text, choose "Below bottom of staff" and click OK.

That was a lot of work. Save the file: **File** > Save, in the Documents folder or another location you will remember. Give it the file name "Rondeau."

Saving the House Style Settings for Use in Other Scores

One of the best time-saving options in Sibelius is being able to save the settings for specific House Styles for future use. It is possible to export and import custom settings so you don't have to go through all of the steps on every score.

1.   Select **House Style** > Export House Styles.
2.   Give your house style a descriptive name, such as "Number bars below staff." Click OK.

Opening a Saved House Style

1.   Select **File** > Open Recent file > Finlandia (if you did not save the Chapter 1 example, open a blank new score).
2.   Select **House Style** > Import House Style.
3.   Choose the style you just saved: "Number bars below staff."

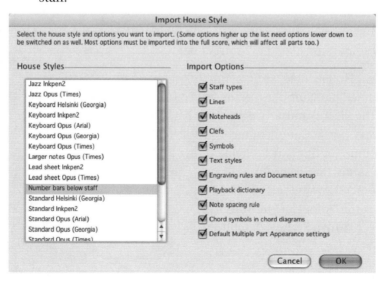

These custom House Styles will also show when you start your next score from scratch.

1. Select **File** > New.
2. Choose a Manuscript Paper option other than Blank; for example, Brass Quartet. Click Next.
3. Under the House Styles list, the custom setting "Number bars below staff" should be in the list.
4. Click Cancel.

Now, back to "Rondeau and Fanfares." If it is not on the screen, go to the Window menu in Sibelius and choose it from the list of all open files at the bottom of the menu.

Adding Bars (Measures)

There are a total of fifty-eight measures in Rondeau. Use one of the methods to add 53 measures from **Create** > Bar. When you know how many measures there are, you can use the Option-B (Mac); Alt-B (Win) method to enter the exact number of measures or select **Create** > Bar > Other.

Entering the Notation with MIDI (Step Entry)

There are several ways to enter notation in Sibelius. Each type of input has its strengths and weaknesses. The previous chapters dealt with the mouse and alphabetic entry modes, which do not require a MIDI keyboard. Without a doubt, the fastest way to enter notation into Sibelius is using a MIDI keyboard, assuming, of course, that you have some familiarity with playing the piano keyboard. You do not have to be a piano performer. Both of us (Vincent and Thomas) have extremely limited piano skills, but we find MIDI entry to be the fastest way to get notation into Sibelius.

This chapter will focus on using a MIDI keyboard to enter notation one step at a time, hence the name step entry. If you don't have a MIDI keyboard, skip this section and continue entering notation using alphabetic entry.

In order to use a MIDI keyboard, you must have it connected to your computer via MIDI. Refer to the Sibelius user manual for instructions on connecting the instrument. Check the Playback and Input Devices settings: **Play** > Playback and Input Devices...

Step entry with a MIDI keyboard is faster than either mouse or alphabetic input for several reasons. Accidentals do not have to be selected, since they are simply played on the keyboard. Chords are much easier to enter, since you just play the chord.

Be sure to set up your keyboard so you can play comfortably and efficiently. For example, placing the keyboard to your right allows you to play the pitch with your right hand on the MIDI keyboard and use your left hand to identify the duration using the numeric keypad.

The fastest way to enter notation may be to place one hand on the MIDI keyboard and the other hand over the keypad. Take some time to experiment and decide which hand works best in which position. The goal is to develop a feel for touch-typing the notes to speed the notation-entry process.

Getting to Know the Keypad Shortcuts

Get familiar with the Keypad and the shortcuts using the numeric keypad rather than the mouse. With practice, pressing the numeric keypad keys will be faster. If you have a laptop, you have to use the mouse or purchase a USB keypad.

The computer numeric keypad layout is slightly different on Mac and Windows computers. Try the following:

- Click the note values. 4 = quarter note. Values larger than a quarter note are selected with larger numbers: 5 = half note, 6 = whole note. Lower values are selected by smaller numbers: 3 = eighth note, 2 = sixteenth note.
- You can also enter three articulations from the Keypad. These should be selected before the note is entered to save time.
    a. Accent: = (Mac); / (Win)
    b. Staccato: / (Mac); * (Win)
    c. Legato: * (Mac); - (Win)
- Be sure not to confuse the two periods on the keyboard. The period at the bottom of the Keypad must be used to add a dot. Click this before entering the note.
- 0 (zero) enters a rest.
- The Enter key (on the numeric keypad) adds a tie (not to be confused with a slur). Add ties after the pitch/duration has been entered. Or, if you're clever, you won't need to enter ties at all: add up the total duration of the note (both notes together) and choose that duration on the keypad.

Enter the notation and articulations in measures 1 through 6, including the pickup measure:

1. Press Esc.
2. Click inside the pickup measure.
3. Press N to display the note entry carat (or use the menu option: **Notes** > Input Notes).
4. Select the note value for the first note, an eighth note, by pressing 3 on the keypad.

5. Since there is also an accent, select it *before* you enter the note by pressing on the Keypad: = (Mac); / (Win).
6. Play the A above middle C on the MIDI keyboard twice to enter the two eighth notes in the first measure.
7. Enter the notation in measures 1 and 2. Since they all have accents, leave it selected.

Entering Notation, Slurs, and Rehearsal Marks

If you memorize a few simple keystrokes, you can enter slurs and rehearsal letters as you are entering the notation for "Rondeau and Fanfares."

1. Enter the D dotted half note with an accent in measure 3.
2. Select the eighth note value and play F♯ on the MIDI keyboard.
3. Press the letter S to enter a two-note slur (**Create** > Lines > Slur).
4. Play the note E on the MIDI keyboard.
5. To insert a rehearsal letter, press the shortcut ⌘-R (Mac); CTRL-R (Win) or select it from the menu: **Create** > Rehearsal Mark.
6. To enter the double bar, press Esc.
7. Select the barline at the end of measure 3 by clicking on it.
8. Select **Create** > Barline > Double.
9. Press Esc.
10. Click inside measure 4.
11. Press the letter N for notation.
12. Choose the quarter note value from the keypad and add the staccato marking (dot).
13. Enter the rest of the notation in measures 5 and 6. Be sure to include the slurs and articulations.

 Sibelius note entry is very intuitive. Things that appear before, over, or under a note such as an accidental, accent, and staccato are selected *before* entering the note. Things that attach the note to another, such as ties and slurs, are selected *after* the note is entered.

Editing Articulations

You will undoubtedly enter some notes with the wrong articulation or want to add an articulation after a note is entered. The process of editing is the same for all articulations or markings that are attached to notes:

1. Press Esc.
2. Click on the note or notes that you want to change. If there are multiple notes consecutively, select entire measures by clicking inside the lines and spaces or hold down Shift and clicking on a specific note. If there are noncontiguous notes you want to change, hold down ⌘ (Mac) or CTRL (Win) and click on the notes to highlight them.
3. Select the desired articulation, such as an accent, on the Keypad. If you want to remove an articulation, uncheck the selection.

Entering Grace Notes

To enter the B grace note in measure 7, there are two steps. First, select the note value of an eighth note. Then switch to the second Keypad layout and select the grace note. There are two grace notes, one with a slash through the flag and one without. Use the slash when you enter a single grace note and the non-slash when you enter two or more grace notes. This example includes only single grace notes, so use the slash version.

1. In measure 7, select the eighth note value by pressing the number 3.
2. Move to the second Keypad layout by pressing the + key on the Keypad. Click the grace note icon or press / (Mac) or * (Win).
3. Play the note B on the MIDI keyboard.
4. Go back to the second Keypad and uncheck the grace note—otherwise every note from here on will be entered as a grace note.

Entering Tuplets

A tuplet is a group of notes evenly condensed or expanded over a specific duration of time. For example, a group of three eighth notes may be played within the space of one quarter note. This is called a triplet. Other tuplets include quintuplets (5 notes), sextuplets (6 notes), and septuplets (7 notes). Sibelius automatically places the tuplet sign above or below the group of notes. "Rondeau and Fanfares" has several sextuplets to be entered.

1. After entering the B grace note, be sure to uncheck the grace note on the second Keypad.
2. Next, enter a sixteenth note A above the staff.
3. To enter the sextuplet, press ⌘-6 (Mac); CTRL-6 (Win) after entering the first note of the tuplet. This is the 6 key that is above the T key on your computer keyboard, *not* the one on the keypad. You can also enter a nonstandard tuplet by entering the first note, selecting **Create** > Tuplet, and entering the tuplet number in the dialog box.
4. Play in the rest of the 5 notes in the sextuplet.

This is the fastest way to enter tuplets such as triplets, septuplets, and sextuplets. To set up a custom tuplet or to make changes in the way the tuplet is displayed, use the menu: **Create** > Tuplet and change the options as needed.

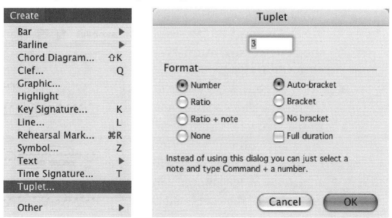

5. Complete the rest of the notation in measure 7, then enter the multinote slur.

6. To add the slur, press Esc.
7. Click on the first note of the tuplet in measure 7.
8. Press the letter S to create a two-note slur (**Create** > Line > Slur).
9. Press the space bar five times to extend the slur to the A on beat 2.

 There are times when you may want to flip a slur. Press the X key to flip it (**Edit** > Flip). This can also be used to flip stems of notes, articulations, or any other marking that is attached to a note.

Out-of-Range Notes

Sibelius is programmed with instrument ranges and will turn notes red when they are out of the specified range. The coloring of the notes will not print; it is designed to be a warning to the composer/arranger regarding instrument range issues. This feature can be turned on or off in the View menu: **View** > Note Colors > None.

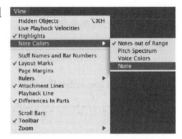

☺ **Have you saved, lately?** ☺

Altering the Range of an Instrument

You can also adjust the ranges of instruments via the Properties window.

1. Turn out-of-range notes back on: select **View** > Note Colors > Notes out of Range.
2. Select a measure in the staff you want to affect. Any measure will do, as this is a single-staff example.
3. Select **Window** > Properties or use the shortcut keys: Option-⌘-P (Mac); Alt-CTRL-P (Win).
4. Open the Staves tab of the Properties window by clicking the arrow.
5. Under Range: Comfortable, change the right column selection to D6. For this piece, the range will now be adjusted. The left column controls the lower note of the suggested range.

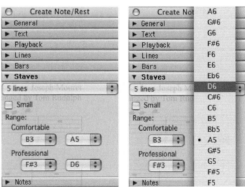

Enter the notation and articulations in measures 8, 9, and 10:

1. Press Esc.
2. Click inside measure 8.
3. Press N for notation (**Notes** > Input Notes).

4. Select the quarter note value and enter the notation. Be sure to add the articulations before entering and the two-note slurs after entering the first note of the slur.
5. Measure 11 has thirty-second notes. Press the number 1 on the keypad.
6. The multinote slur in measure 11 will have to be entered after the notation. To select the first note of the slur, press the letter S and then press the space bar to extend the slur.

*Entering a crescendo (hairpin) and **ff** (expression) in measure 11:*

1. After entering the notation, press Esc.
2. Click on the first note in measure 11.
3. Press the letter H (hairpin). This can also be accessed via **Create** > Line.
4. Press the space bar to extend the crescendo.
5. Press Esc. The hairpin should be selected.
6. Press the down arrow key to move the crescendo a bit lower.
7. Enter the **ff** mark under the F♯ eighth note on beat 4. Select the F♯ and press the shortcut keys: ⌘-E (Mac); CTRL-E (Win). Right-click (CTRL-click on a Mac with a one-button mouse) and select the **ff** marking.

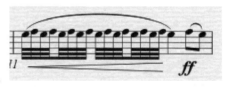

To save time, copy and paste measures 4 through 9 into measures 12 through 17, as they are identical:

1. Press Esc.
2. Click inside the lines and spaces in measure 4 to select the entire measure (not a single note).
3. Hold down the Shift key and click inside the lines and spaces in measure 9. Be sure the entire measure is selected, not just one note.
4. To copy the selection, press Option-click (Mac); Alt-click (Win) inside measure 12.
5. Select the barline at the end of measure 11 and press the shortcut keys: ⌘-R (Mac); CTRL-R (Win) to enter the letter B rehearsal letter. Sibelius keeps track of the rehearsal letters as they are entered.

Enter the notation, rehearsal letters, slurs, and crescendos/decrescendos for measures 11 through 52 (see the next page). *Do not* enter the whole rests, as we will ask Sibelius to display multirests. If you enter whole rests, multirests will not appear.

Some suggestions:

- Copy and paste measures 12 through 19 into measures 28 through 35, as they are identical.
- Entering the decrescendo in measure 19: After inputting the D dotted half note, hold down the Shift key and press the letter H for hairpin (**Create** > Line).
- Entering expressions in bars 27 and 43: enter the Expressions (dynamics) in bars 27 (*f*) and 43 (*mp*). Select the note in the measure and press ⌘-E (Mac); CTRL-E (Win). Right-click and select the appropriate dynamic marking.
- Respelling the accidental in measure 44: If you play a B♭ on a MIDI keyboard in measure 44, an A♯ will appear. As soon as the note is entered, you can respell the accidental by pressing Return (Mac); Enter (Win) when the note is selected. You can also go the slow way and use the menu: **Notes** > Respell Accidental.

☺ **Save often** ☺

 A question frequently comes up: which is faster, entering the notes, dynamics, expressions, text, etc. as the notes are being entered; or entering all the notes, and then going back and adding the articulations, expressions, and so forth. When entering a complete score from a printout, the answer may be to enter everything as you go. When composing or creating a new part from scratch, it may be more efficient to enter the notes and then go back and enter the rest of the markings—articulations, expressions, etc. There are some things that must be entered after the notation, including slurs of three or more notes and crescendo and decrescendo (hairpin) marks that span more than one note.

Cue Notes

There is an organ cue in measures 53, 54, and 55. To enter cue notes:

1. Press Esc.
2. Click inside measure 53.
3. Press the letter N for notation (**Notes** > Input Notes).
4. Select the quarter note value on the Keypad and press the number 0 on the Keypad to enter the quarter rest.
5. Select the eighth note on the Keypad.
6. To choose cue-sized notes, open the second Keypad by clicking on the whole rest icon or click the arrow key on the Keypad.
7. Select the cue notes option by clicking the button or pressing the Enter key on the Keypad.
8. Return to the first Keypad by clicking on the whole note or click the double left arrow key on the Keypad.
9. Enter the G eighth note.
10. Change to the quarter note value and enter the B quarter notes.
11. Continue to enter the notation in measure 54 and the first 3 beats of measure 55.
12. Before entering the normal notation in measure 55 on beat 4, be sure to turn off the cue note selection on the second Keypad. You can always tell when multiple items are selected, as the Keypad icons are highlighted.

13. Enter the F♯ as normal notation.
14. Press the letter S to enter the two-note slur.
15. To enter the *f* marking, press the Expression shortcut keys: ⌘-E (Mac); CTRL-E (Win), then right-click and select *f*. Press Esc and enter the E eighth note.

> The function keys on a Windows computer can be used to select the various keypads: F8, F9, F10, F11. On a Mac, these keys are assigned by default to the Expose function. Mac users should go into the System Preferences and use the Expose option to reassign these shortcuts to other keys; for example, F2, F3, F4, and F5.

Entering Text (Organ) Above the Staff

You can enter text as you are entering notes or go back and enter it afterward. To enter "Organ" over the cue notes in measure 53 after the notation has been entered:

1. Press Esc.

2. Click on the G eighth note in measure 53.
3. Press the shortcut keys: ⌘-T (Mac); CTRL-T (Win). The letter T stands for Technique, meaning instructions that are typically placed above the staff.
4. Type "Organ" and press Esc. (A list of options in **Text** > Technique is accessible by right-clicking on the cursor. "Organ" is not one of them.)

Remember, you can always enter technique or expressions immediately after the note is entered.

☺ **Have you saved, lately?** ☺

D.S. al Coda, Splitting Staves, 8va

There are several steps to enter in the last few measures.

To enter the D.S. al Coda sign:

1. After entering the E eighth note on the last half of beat 4 in measure 55, select **Create** > Text > Other System Text > Repeat (D.C./ D.S./To Coda).
2. Right-click on the cursor above the staff and select D.S. al Coda.
3. Be sure the D.S. al Coda is connected to measure 55. Check the dotted line that connects it.

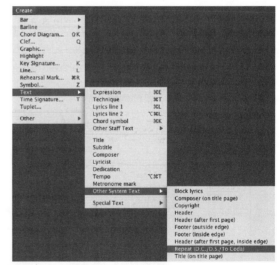

4. Select the barline at the end of measure 55 and create a double bar: **Create** > Barline > Double.

5. To split the system for the Coda: **Layout** > Break > Split System.
6. Enter the D dotted half note in measure 56.
7. Select **Create** > Text > Other System Text > Repeat (D.C./D.S./To Coda)
8. Type the word "Coda."
9. Enter a space by pressing the space bar.
10. Right-click (CTRL-click on a Mac with a one-button mouse) and select the (Coda) sign.
11. Press Esc. The sign should be selected. Open the Properties window and select the Text option. Change the size of the to 17.9.
12. Drag the sign to the right.

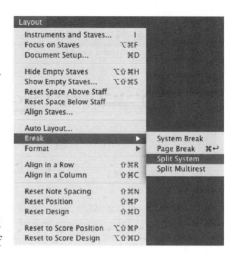

Entering the D.S. and to Coda signs in bars 4 and 18:

1. Press Esc.
2. Drag the score so bar 4 is visible.
3. Click the D on the first beat in measure 4 to select it.
4. Select **Create** > Text > Other System Text > Repeat (D.C./D.S./To Coda).
5. Right-click (CTRL-click on a Mac with a one-button mouse) and select the 𝄋 sign.
6. Press Esc and change the font size in the Properties > Text menu to 17.9.

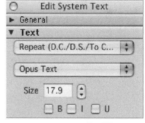

7. To enter the To Coda sign, select the D eighth note at the end of bar 18.
8. Select **Create** > Text > Other System Text > Repeat (D.C./D.S./To Coda).
9. Right-click (CTRL-click on a Mac with one-button mouse) and select "To Coda." If this is not entered in the measure, the D.S. will not play back properly.
10. Press Esc. Again click on the D eighth note in measure 18.
11. Select **Create** > Text > Other System Text > Repeat (D.C./D.S./To Coda)
12. Right-click (CTRL-click on a Mac with a one-button mouse) and select the Coda sign .
13. Press Esc, and the To Coda sign will be selected. Change the font size in the Properties/Text menu to 17.9. Drag the sign slightly to the right.

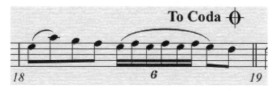

Enter the rest of the notation in measures 56 and 57.

Entering the fermata in measure 58:

1. Select a dotted half note on the Keypad.
2. Advance to the fourth Keypad or click on the fermata icon at the top of the Keypad.
3. Click on the fermata button to select it.
4. Play a D on the MIDI keyboard.
5. Be sure to deselect the fermata, or every note that you enter from here on will have a fermata attached to it!

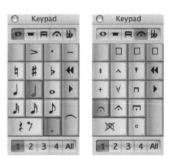

Entering the 8va mark over the last three measures:

1. Select the A eighth note on the fourth beat of measure 56.
2. Press the letter L for line, or choose it from the menu: **Create** > Line.
3. Select the 8va mark and click OK.
4. Press the space bar (or right arrow key) to extend the mark, just like the slur and crescendo/decrescendo markings entered earlier.
5. Enter the crescendo (hairpin) in measure 57 and the expression (*ff*) in measure 58. If you forgot the steps, review them above.

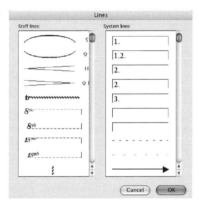

 Another way to select the correct size for a line, such as an 8va mark or a hairpin, is to select the notes or bars first and then choose the Lines menu (by pressing the letter L). Sibelius will make the marking conform to the notes/measures selected.

Deleting Extra Measures

If you followed the steps at the beginning of the chapter, you should not have any extra measures. However, there may have been one or more extra measures entered along the way. To delete them, ⌘-click (Mac); CTRL-click (Win) inside the empty measures. Press Delete to remove them from the score or use the menu: **Edit** > Delete.

☺ **Have you saved, lately?** ☺

Playback to Check for Mistakes

Now that all the notation is entered, play it back to proof-listen. Note that the articulations and dynamic markings and crescendos and decrescendos play back.

1. Select **Window** > Playback Controls.
2. Press the Space bar to start playback.
3. When you get to the measure rests, press the fast-forward button to save time.

Adjusting the Playback

Sibelius also has a built-in performance feature that can be helpful. For example, if you want to play back the score in a swing or dotted eighth note style, this can be accomplished without changing the note values.

1. Select **Play** > Performance.
2. Next to Rhythmic Feel, click on the pull-down menu and select Dotted Eighths.
3. Press the space bar to play back the score. Notice the altered performance style of the eighth notes.
4. Repeat the above steps and return the Rhythmic Feel back to Straight.

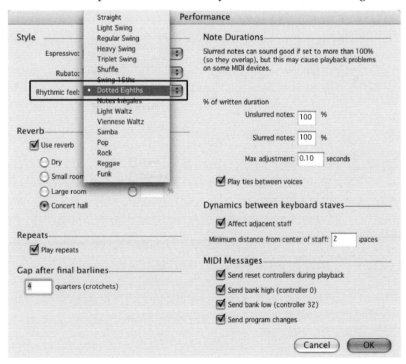

Displaying Multirests

To display multirests in a score:

1. Select **Layout** > Auto Layout.
2. In the Auto Layout window, check "Use multirests." Sibelius will automatically create multirests throughout the entire score. There is a special shortcut for this: Shift-⌘-M (Mac); Shift-CTRL-M (Win). Nothing needs to be selected for this to turn on and off.

Page Layout

You may find it easiest to tackle the page layout and overall appearance of the page after all the notes and other markings have been entered.

1. Zoom in so you can see the entire score on the screen: hold down ⌘ (Mac) or CTRL (Win) with your left hand and press the minus (–) key with your right hand to zoom in. You can also use the menu bar to change the viewing size of the notation.
2. Save the file before applying the layout plug-in, as it cannot be undone: **File** > Save.
3. Use the plug-in to lay out the entire document: select **Plug-ins** > Other > Make Layout Uniform.
4. Change the number of systems on the first page to 11 and click OK.

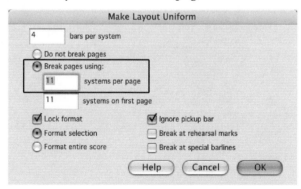

System break in measure 55

Force the Coda bars to the last line. This will make it easier for the performers (and give them one less excuse when they miss the Coda the first time through).

1. Select the barline at the end of measure 55.
2. Press the Return or Enter key to force the system to the next line, or do this via the menu: **Layout** > Break > System Break.

Indenting a system

Indent the Coda a bit to the right. This can also be done to indent a system to the left.

1. Press Esc.
2. Click the mouse just to the left of the system on the third line of the staff. A box will appear when you have selected it. This might take a few tries, as the handles to move systems are one of the few things in Sibelius that are difficult to find. The left is easier to locate than the right. Just click on the invisible barline before the clef.
3. Click and drag the handle to the right to indent the system. Or use the right arrow key for greater accuracy.

Printing the Score

Congratulations! This was a lot of work, for sure. Save your work and then print it via **File** > Print. Put it up on the refrigerator!

Creating an Ossia

An ossia (pronounced *oh-see-ah*) is a bar of music above the normal music that designates an alternate section or passage. Typically, this is an easier version of the original. In Sibelius, creating an ossia is a snap. To practice, you will create an ossia in measure 7 as an alternative to playing the sextuplet on beat 1.

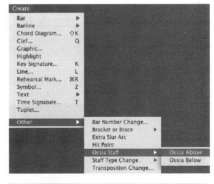

1. Select **File** > Save As and save a copy of your project as "RondeauOssia."
2. Click inside the lines and spaces in measure 7 to select it.
3. Select **Create** > Other > Ossia Staff > Ossia Above.

4. Enter the notation in the Ossia measure. To create a triplet, enter the first note and then press the shortcut keys: ⌘-3 (Mac); CTRL-3 (Win) after entering the first note.

Sibelius creates another staff and automatically hides everything except the selected ossia measure. Sibelius also moves the bar number (7) up to the ossia staff.

Add Brass Fingering Plug-in

Another helpful plug-in shows selected instrument fingerings, in this case the fingerings for C Trumpet. This can be helpful when working with students or learning a new instrument. I do not advise making a habit of displaying fingerings on entire pieces of music, or you and your students will become excellent fingering readers but not very good music readers. Here are the steps:

1. Save a copy of the file via **File** > Save As; name it "RondeauFingerings" (since plug-ins cannot be undone).
2. Click inside measure 10 to select it.
3. Select **Plug-ins** > Text > Add Brass Fingerings.
4. Select C Trumpet and click OK.

To move the fingerings up:

There is a helpful option in Sibelius called Select More. It selects items for the rest of the system.

1. Press Esc.
2. Click on the first fingering over beat 1 to select it.
3. Go to **Edit** > Select > Select More.
4. Press the up arrow key to move all the fingerings up so they are not colliding with the notation.

Summary

- use New Score setup to create C Trumpet, enter "Tempo text" (Allegro), and add a copyright at the bottom of the score
- create an instrument name and arranger at the top of the score
- change the font of the title and other text
- remove staff names via Engraving Rules
- export (save) a House Style for later use
- import a House Style into an existing document
- display bar numbers under every measure via House Styles
- enter notation with a MIDI keyboard (step entry)
- enter articulations via the Keypad while entering notation
- create slurs and crescendos/decrescendos (hairpins)

- create rehearsal letters
- enter grace notes and tuplets
- change the range of the instrument
- enter cue-size notation
- enter Technique Text above the staff
- enter a D.S. al Coda; split the system for the Coda and change the size of the D.S. al Coda
- enter a fermata
- enter 8va lines above selected notes
- display multirests
- lay out the page with four measures per line
- create an ossia
- add brass fingerings via plug-in
- move items using Select More

Review

1. See how well you do with the following questions. Correct answers are printed at the bottom of this page. No fair looking!

   a. Articulations such as accents and staccato markings are entered using:
      1. Text > Expressions   2. Keypad   3. Text > Technique   4. Lines

   b. Dynamics (*mf*, *mp*) and text below the staff are typically entered using:
      1. Text > Expressions   2. Keypad   3. Text > Technique   4. Lines

   c. Crescendos and Decrescendos (hairpins), slurs, and 8va marks are entered using:
      1. Text > Expressions   2. Keypad   3. Text > Technique   4. Lines

   d. Directions above the staff are typically entered using:
      1. Text > Expressions   2. Keypad   3. Text > Technique   4. Lines

2. Reenter this composition, or one like it, using the steps listed in the summary above.

3. Review how to enter tuplets. Practice entering triplets using the steps explained in this chapter.

4. Try transposing the score to another key for a B♭ trumpet. Change the text to read B♭ trumpet.

5. Review the **Plug-ins** > Text options. Are there others that you would like to try?

Answers to question 1 above: a-2; b-1; c-4; d-3.

5

Real-Time Note Entry and Page Layout (Musical Example: "Carnival of Venice")

All of the previous chapters dealt with some form of step entry of music notation: select the value and enter the pitch for each individual note. Sibelius provides other ways of entering notation that can be useful. This chapter focuses on entering music using Sibelius's real-time tool: Flexi-time. In addition, page layout, hiding metronome markings, and manually adjusting note beaming will be addressed.

The new areas explored in this chapter include:

- manually entering the time signature
- moving staves in Page Layout
- creating two sets of measure numbers in the same piece
- setting the notation (quantization) level
- entering music in real time using Flexi-time
- changing tempos for playback
- transposing pitches diatonically
- using the Selection feature to isolate specific parts of a score

You should be familiar with the score setup steps by now. If not, review the previous chapters. Here is a summary of the steps:

1. Select **File** > New.
2. Under Manuscript Paper, choose Blank.
3. Click the Add Instruments button.
4. Choose "Band Instruments"; "Woodwind"; "Clarinet in B♭" and click the Add to Score button. You can also double-click on "Clarinet in B♭" to add it to the Staves in Score column.
5. Click OK.
6. Click Next.
7. Under House Styles, select the custom style "Bar numbers below the staff." If this is not visible, review the steps for creating a custom House Style in Chapter 4 (p. 58).
8. Click Next.
9. In the Time Signature and Tempo window:

   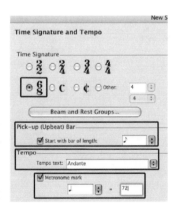

   a. Select 6/8.
   b. Set the Pick-up Bar to the length of an eighth note.
   c. Select the Tempo text: Andante.
   d. Enter the "Metronome mark" ♩.= 72 . First select the quarter note value; then go back and select the dot at the bottom of the list.
   e. Click Next.
10. Select the concert key for the piece. Since the clarinet is a B♭ instrument, choose the key of Eb. The clarinet will be automatically transposed to the key of F.

11. Click Next.
12. Enter the following Score Info:
    a. Title: "The Carnival of Venice"
    b. Composer/Songwriter: "Traditional"
    c. Lyricist: "entered by [your name]"
13. Click the Previous button and double-check that everything has been entered correctly.
14. Return to the Score Info page and click Finish.

Your score should look like the following:

Adding the Instrument Name

The instrument name, "Clarinet in B♭" has been turned off via the custom House Style that was created in Chapter 4. These settings were imported into this score. There are a couple of ways to get the instrument name printed in the upper left-hand corner of the score. One option is to reenter it as follows:

1. Select the pickup measure.
2. Select **Create** > Text > Special Text > Instrument Name at Top Left.
3. Type: "Clarinet in B♭."
4. Press Esc.
5. Use the up arrow to move the name up above "entered by [your name]."

Concert and Transposed Scores

When Sibelius opens a new score, it initially shows it in concert pitch. However, since this clarinet part is transposed, set Sibelius to view the part in transposed format.

To change to a transposed score (for transposing instruments like clarinet):

- Click the Transposing Score icon on the toolbar. It looks like the key of B♭: Or select **Notes** > Transposing Score. You may also use the shortcut command: Shift-⌘-T (Mac); Shift-CTRL-T (Win).

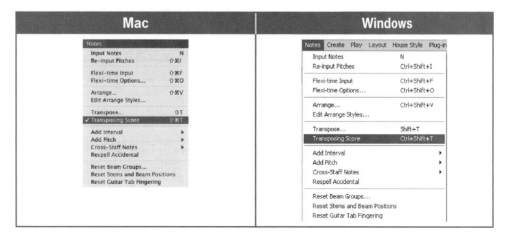

The score should be transposed in order to enter the Clarinet in B♭ "Carnival of Venice" part:

Recording/Entering Transposed Pitch

With transposed parts, such as the clarinet in B♭, Sibelius needs to know if you are inputting the written pitches (the way they look on the transposed part) or the sounding pitches, or the untransposed pitches. For a transposed part (or score) such as this, make sure the following settings are in place:

1. Mac: select **Sibelius** > Preferences > Note Input; Win: select **File** > Preferences > Note Input.
2. Under Transposing Staves, check "Input written pitches." Note that this setting, like all Preferences settings, will remain even after you shut down Sibelius.

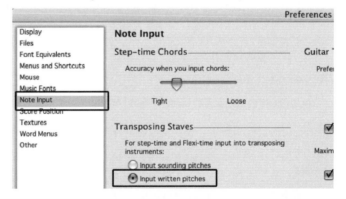

> If you are using a MIDI keyboard (as opposed to a MIDI controller), be sure to turn off "local" on your keyboard. Every MIDI keyboard does this differently, so consult the owner's manual for your synth. If you do not, you will hear two pitches while entering, a major second apart.

Adding Bars

"Carnival of Venice" and the variation is 32 bars plus two pickup bars, for a total of 34 bars. You can use the method described in previous chapters to add bars, using the shortcut command: ⌘-B (Mac); CTRL-B (Win). Another way to enter a specific number of bars is:

1. Select **Create** > Bar > Others (shortcut: Option-B [Mac]; Alt-B [Win]).

2. Enter 27 in "Number of bars" in the Create Bars window. Click OK.

3. Click on any measure in the score *except* measure 1 (which is the pickup bar). If you click inside measure 1, it will be replaced, and since all the titles are connected to this measure, they will have to be reentered.

 Page layout is something that Sibelius does a pretty good job of all by itself. This example, however, requires quite a bit of tweaking of the layout. There are two ways to address this: enter the notation, then go back and lay out the page. This is the way I address page layout most of the time. However, for examples when the page layout is complex, complete the page layout before entering the notation. Either way works.

Measure Layout and Inserting a Time Signature

Here are the steps to make the first 16 measures format correctly:

1. Select the barline at the end of bar 4. This is actually the right barline of measure 4.
2. Press Return (Mac); Enter (Win) to break the system or use the menu: **Layout** > Break > System Break.
3. Repeat the above steps at the ends of measures 8, 12, and 16.

Next, add a final barline at the end of measure 16:

4. Since the barline at the end of bar 16 is still selected, select **Create** > Barline > Final. If it is not selected, click the mouse on it to select.

Add the pickup bar in original measure 17:

5. Press the letter T (all by itself) to select the Time Signature window, or use the menu: **Create** > Time Signature.
6. In the Time Signature dialog box:
   a. Select 6/8.
   b. Check "Start with bar of length" and choose an eighth note.
   c. Uncheck "Allow cautionary."
   d. Click OK. Since the barline at the end of measure 16 was selected, Sibelius enters the time change in the next bar. If nothing was selected, you would have to click the mouse in the appropriate measure.

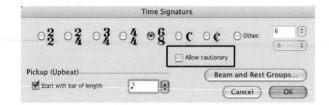

You have to uncheck "Allow cautionary" because in this example, a cautionary time signature in the line previous to the time signature change is not wanted. Typically, when a time signature does change in a score, a cautionary symbol is printed on the line before.

7. Make the layout of the rest of the example 4 measures per line (not counting the pickup bar) by breaking the systems after measures 20, 24, and 28.

Making a Bar Number Change

Since the goal is to have this document appear to be two separate examples, you need to renumber the measures starting in the pickup bar of the variation.

1. Press Esc.
2. Right-click (or CTRL-click on a Mac with a one-button mouse) to access the Create menu via contextual menus.
3. Select **Create** > Other > Bar Number Change.
4. Enter the number 1 in the dialog box. Click OK.
5. Click on actual measure 17 to enter the bar number change. Notice that Sibelius displays the new number 1 in a lighter color. This is just to remind you that a bar number change has been entered.

Page Layout Settings

There are a couple of settings that need to be adjusted when you are attempting to override the default page layout settings in Sibelius.

1. Select **House Styles** > Engraving Rules.
2. Click on Staves.
3. Under Justification, change the top setting to read: "Justify staves when page is at least" 95% full. When this setting is at the default of 65%, staves will automatically spread out to fill the entire page. In this example, that is not wanted.

Justification

Justify staves when page is at least `95` % full
System spacings may be contracted to `97` %

Next, space needs to be made between the first and second examples. One option is to just drag the staff with the mouse.

1. Select the second pickup measure.
2. Click and drag the staff down slightly to make room for the second title ("Variation"). Another way to move the staff with finer control is to hold down ⌘-Option (Mac); CTRL-Alt (Win) and press the down arrow on the keyboard.

 In some cases, you may want to move one specific staff system by itself, perhaps to bring it down slightly or to create a custom page layout. To move just the selected staff system up or down, hold down the Shift key and drag the staff with the mouse. For more fine-tuned movements, select the staff and then hold down ⌘-Option (Mac); CRTL-Alt (Win) and use the up or down arrows to move the staff as desired.

In Chapter 4 we exported the measure number settings for future use. You may want to export these staff settings when working on music that requires fine-tuning of the staff positions.

1. Select **House Style** > Export House Style.
2. Give the custom House Style a descriptive name, such as: "Bar numbers below & 95% staff justification."
3. Click OK.

This custom House Style will now appear in the New Score > House Styles window and you can import it into an existing document or by selecting **House Style** > Import House Style. Building a list of your custom settings in House Styles will save you time when creating similar scores in the future.

Adding a Second Title

So far, all of the titles have been entered using the New Score setup. It is also used to place a title above any staff system.

1. Click inside the lines and spaces of the second pickup measure, after measure 16. A blue box will appear to show it has been selected.
2. Select **Create** > Text > Title.
3. Type the title: "Variation."

The page layout should now be complete. Compare your example with the following printout:

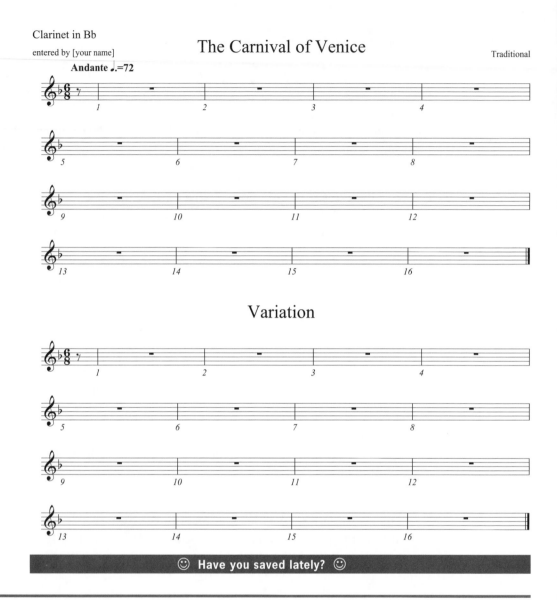

Adding Double Barlines

There should be a double barline after each of the pickup measures.

1. Press Esc.
2. Right-click (CTRL-click on a Mac with a one-button mouse) to display the Create menu.
3. Select **Barline** > Double.
4. Click in the selection after each of the pickup bars in both examples. Be sure to press Esc after you create each double barline, or the contextual menu will not give you the correct options.

Another method is to select the barline you wish to change *first,* then follow steps 1, 2, and 3 above. Sibelius will place the double barline in the selected measure.

Real-Time Entry with Flexi-Time

Imagine if Mozart had had a tool with which he could sit at the keyboard and play in all of the music already composed in his head, rather than drawing noteheads on paper with ink and a quill pen. Using Sibelius's Flexi-time, it is possible to play music on the MIDI keyboard as Sibelius attempts to transcribe what is played. In some cases, Flexi-time can be a fast way to enter notation into your score. Entering music in this way is called *real-time entry*. All other entry methods introduced in previous chapters are considered *step-time entry*.

To demonstrate the advantages and disadvantages of using Flexi-time, you will enter the melody "Carnival of Venice" and a rather intricate variation.

Entering in Real Time with a Metronome

In order to use Flexi-time, you must have a MIDI keyboard or other MIDI controller connected to your computer.

MIDI Tips

Take time to be sure your MIDI keyboard is properly connected and working. The best place to start is to review the installation manual that came with the software. You can also use Sibelius **Help** > Reference. Search for topic 4.10, "Playback and input devices."

If you don't like to read manuals, here are the essential steps for getting the MIDI connection to work properly. If you are recording and the keyboard is not working, you will have to resort to that dreaded manual!

1. Be sure that the keyboard is connected to your computer, and switched on if it has an on/off button, before you launch Sibelius. If Sibelius is already launched, quit, check to be sure that your MIDI instrument is on and properly connected, then relaunch the program.
2. Check that your USB or MIDI cable is connected correctly. If you are using a MIDI interface, there are MIDI IN and OUT cables to connect.
3. After Sibelius launches, check your keyboard connection by selecting **Play** > Playback and Input Devices. This screen has two tabs at the top.

4. Click on the Input Device tab and be sure your MIDI device is working properly.
5. Click on Playback Devices. Don't use Kontakt if that is an available option. Use this when the score is completed, since it takes time to load the sounds each time you press play. (Kontakt will be addressed in detail in Chapter 7.) If you are using an electronic keyboard with good-quality sounds, use it for playback. If you are using a MIDI controller with no sound output, you should use the computer's built-in sounds for playback.

If the above steps do not work, then go to the manual for reference or contact the maker of your MIDI device for assistance. There is also a helpful tutorial video on the topic. Select **Help** > Tutorial Videos and then click on #12, "MIDI input."

Setting up the Click and Countoff (Flexi-time Options)

There are two ways to enter with Flexi-time: having the computer play the pulse like a metronome or asking Flexi-time to follow your tempo as you play. Following you as you change tempo is an option that is unique to Sibelius. In this chapter we'll use the traditional way to enter notation in real time, with the computer supplying a steady pulse.

1. Select **Notes** > Flexi-time Options. This screen has two tabs at the top, one for Flexi-time and one for Notation.
2. On the Flexi-time tab, set the "Flexibility of tempo" to "None (non rubato)." You must play in tempo with the click.
3. The number in the "Introduction" box is the number of count-off measures. The default is set to 1. In this example, the count-off will include one full measure before the pickup measure. So you will hear six beats and then five before you should play the pickup eighth note.
4. Change the "Record up to…" value to 0. If you don't, Sibelius will add the number of measures in this box to the end of the score.
5. Be sure that the "Record into multiple voices" option is unchecked and that "Replace" is checked under Existing Music. Voices will be covered in Chapter 8. The "Replace" option means that all existing music in any stave being recorded will be erased.
6. Click on the Click button to review the Click options. I usually leave these as they are.

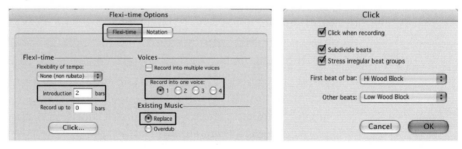

The next setting is to determine is the notation or quantization level. *Quantization* refers to Sibelius's capability of rounding to the nearest note value. Perhaps you actually played a note ahead of the beat. If you set the note value to an eighth note, Sibelius will round your note to the nearest eighth note.

To choose the best notation (quantization) level, let the music be your guide. Examine the first 16 measures of the "Carnival of Venice" melody. The smallest value in the piece is an eighth note; therefore, you should ask Sibelius to notate, or round to, the nearest eighth note. This will help forgive some of the timing problems when you enter in Flexi-time.

Setting the Notation (Quantization) Level

1. In the Flexi-time window, click the Notation tab at the top.
2. Under Note Values, set "Adjust rhythms" "Minimum duration" to an eighth note since this is the smallest note value in the melody.
3. Under "Allow these tuplets," change all options to None, since there are no triplets or tuplets in the melody.
4. When you're satisfied you've made all the changes you need, click OK. Sibelius will remember these settings for all your future scores unless you return to this screen and make changes.

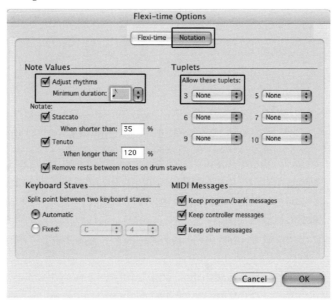

Start Recording

Before recording a "take," as it is referred to in the recording world, you might want to practice the piece a few times. When you are ready to give the recording process a try:

1. Press Esc.
2. Click inside the first measure of the first pickup bar.
3. Set the recording tempo on the Playback controls. I usually slow it down significantly. For 6/8 time, it's most accurate around 40 beats per minute.

4. After setting the desired tempo, press the red Record button on the toolbar.
5. Wait for one bar and then the first five beats of the pickup bar and then start playing the melody to "Carnival of Venice."

If you don't like your first take, no problem! Just choose **Edit** > Undo. This will erase your last recording. By now, you should have the Undo shortcut memorized: ⌘-Z (Mac); CTRL-Z (Win).

Click in the first measure and try it again, or go back through the above steps and make any necessary changes, such as slowing down the tempo.

Usually, there will be a few places where editing is necessary. Use mouse or alphabetic entry to fix minor mistakes. Remember, don't delete notes or rests! Rather, select the note or rest and then choose the correct rhythm from the Keypad and/or drag the note to the correct pitch.

☺ **The next time you enter something that makes you smile, save it!** ☺

With the above settings, your ability to play the keyboard in tempo with the metronome will determine the accuracy of your results. Don't give up after one or two tries. Usually, with practice, melodies such as "Carnival of Venice" can be entered quite accurately in Flexi-time. Also, don't try to play everything in one take. Play the first few measures, then come back later and record more bars.

 Another option is to use Flexi-time to follow you as you change tempos when you are recording. This can be helpful, especially if you have trouble playing in time with a metronome or if the music has several *ritards*. I have found that I get the best results when using the setting "None" for Flexi- 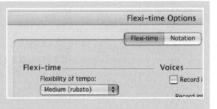 time and playing in strict tempo. Go to **Notes** > Flexi-time Options. Then change the setting for "Flexibility of tempo" to something other than None.

Erasing Music Without Deleting the Measures

Selecting **Edit** > Undo is one way to erase notes from measures. Sometimes you will want to remove notation from measures after you have done several other tasks. To remove notation from measures when **Edit** > Undo is not an option:

1. Select the measures where you want to delete the notation. Use click and Shift-click to highlight multiple measures.
2. Press the Delete key on the keyboard or choose **Edit** > Delete (Clear).

Be careful! Deleting everything from the pickup measure will clear it and turn it into a complete bar. The better option is to reenter the notes one by one in the pickup bar.

Recording the Variation

Now try part two of this example—the "Carnival of Venice" variation printed below. First, examine the music to determine the notation (quantization) level.

Variation

To reset the quantization level:

In the above example, the quantization level must be reset because there are sixteenth and thirty-second notes and triplets.

1. Select **Notes** > Flexi-time Options.
2. Click the Notation tab at the top of the window.
    a. Change "Minimum duration" to a thirty-second note.
    b. Under "Allow these tuplets,"

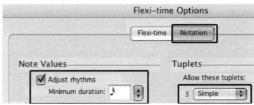

change the 3 to "Simple." This allows for triplets to be entered. Click OK to close the window.

3. Click on measure 1 of the second example. Record the "Carnival of Venice" variation (see the previous page).

The following is the printout that I got after several tries:

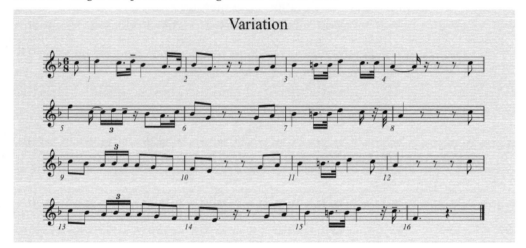

Your example will have printed differently, but this shows that, when there are many rests in the music, Flexi-time will do a fair-to-middling job of transcribing. You could go in and edit all of the errors, but I've found that by the time I edit out all of the mistakes, I could have entered in everything more quickly in step time from the beginning.

This brings up a good point. You may use different entry tools for various parts of a piece. I would have chosen Flexi-time for the melody of "Carnival of Venice" and step entry with MIDI for the variation.

> When you see triplets and lots of rests, it will most likely be faster to enter the notes using MIDI or alphabetic entry.

Complete the variation in the way most expedient way. Compare the final notation to the previous page.

Changing Note Beaming

In the example below, some of the beams have been manually adjusted.
This is done through the third Keypad layout (shortcut: F10). To adjust the beaming in measures 9 and 13:

1. Select the second eighth note, the B♭.
2. Advance to the third Keypad layout by clicking the + on the Keypad or using the shortcut F8.
3. Select the number 8 on the Keypad to attach the note selected to the notes to its left and right.
4. Repeat the above steps in measure 13.

Beaming Across Rests

In measures 3 and 11, some notes are beamed over rests. This is a bit trickier to accomplish than beaming to and from notes that are adjacent.

1. Select the note to the right of the rest.
2. Make sure you're on the correct page of the Keypad (page 3).
3. Press the number 9 on the Keypad.
4. Press the left arrow key two times to select the B natural to the left of the rest.
5. Press the number 7 on the second Keypad to join the note beams.
6. Repeat the above steps to beam the notes over rests on beat 4 of measure 3 and beat 2 of measure 11.

That was a lot of work. Congratulations! By the way, have you saved lately?

Changing Tempos for Playback

It is possible to change tempos in a piece for playback, for example, setting the first example (measures 1 through 16) to play at 72 and the variation to play back at another tempo, 110.

The melody tempo was set during score setup. It should already be at 72.

To set a new tempo for the variation:

1. Select the pickup measure of the variation.
2. Select **Create** > Text > Metronome Mark.
3. Right-click (CTRL-click on a Mac with a one-button mouse) and select a quarter note.
4. Type a period to create a dotted quarter note.
5. Type "110."
6. Press Esc.

Select the first measure of the piece and press the Play button. The tempo should start at 72 and immediately change to 120 at the beginning of the variation—assuming you haven't been dragging that tempo slider!

Hiding Objects (Tempo Markings, Notes, Etc.)

It is possible to hide objects (or any other note or marking) in Sibelius. In this example, the tempo markings can be hidden:

1. Select the metronome marking in measure one.
2. Select **Edit** > Hide or Show > Hide or use the shortcut: Shift-⌘-H (Mac); Shift-CTRL-H (Win).
3. To show characters that have been hidden so they are visible on screen but will not print, select **View** > Hidden Objects.

Printing

After the notation has been entered and edited, select **File** > Print to print a copy of the completed "Carnival of Venice" melody and variation.

Diatonic Transposition

Changing the diatonic transposition of a score is one of the amazingly easy things to do in Sibelius. When a melodic sequence takes place, this can be helpful. It is also handy to change melodies from one tonality to another, such as major to minor, major to Dorian, etc. This example takes you through the steps to change the melody from major to minor tonality.

1. Select **File** > Save As and name the new file something different from the major version: "CarnivalMinor."
2. Be sure the Transposing Score icon is selected. You should be viewing the part transposed, or in the key of F major.
3. Select the entire score. Remember the shortcut? It's ⌘-A (Mac); CTRL-A (Win). Or use the menu: **Edit** > Select > Select All.
4. To move all the notes diatonically down a third to D minor, press the down arrow on the computer keyboard three times.

Since that took all of a few seconds, let's try one other powerful feature Sibelius offers, the Selection feature. Since we are moving to D minor, let's change all of the Cs to C#s. You could go through the score, select each note, and press the sharp on the Keypad. However, if there were many Cs in the score, this would take some time.

Selecting Noncontiguous Items

It is possible to select noncontiguous items in Sibelius. To do this, you must hold down ⌘ (Mac); CTRL (Win) and click on the desired items: in this case, all of the Cs.

1. Press Esc.
2. Click on the notehead of the C in bar 10.

3. Hold down ⌘ (Mac); CTRL (Win) and click all of the other C noteheads in the piece to select them.
4. With all of the Cs selected, click on the # on the Keypad. Voilà! All Cs are now C#s.

Changing the Notation Preferences

When you set Preferences in Sibelius, they are retained even after you close the program. Since most music that you enter with Flexi-time will not be transposed parts like this example, I recommend that you change back to the default settings for note input.

1. Mac: select **Sibelius** > Preferences > Note Input; Win: select **File** > Preferences > Note Input.
2. Under Transposing Staves, check "Input sounding pitches." Like all Preferences settings, this will remain even after you shut down Sibelius.

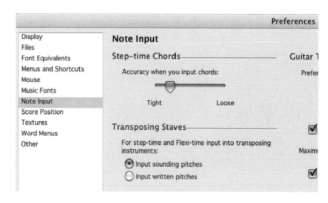

Summary

This chapter focused on entering music in real time using Sibelius's Flexi-time tool including how to:

- set up the score
- create an instrument name in the upper left corner of the score
- switch between concert and transposed scores (when using transposing instruments)
- add a specific number of bars to the score
- insert a time signature into a score and turn off cautionary time signatures
- create two sets of bar numbers in the same document
- lay out the page for two separate examples on a single page
- add a title in the middle of a score
- enter notes in real time with Flexi-time
- set up your MIDI keyboard
- change note beaming and beaming across rests
- change tempos for playback
- hide objects
- create a diatonic transposition of a score

Review

1. Keep practicing with Flexi-time. It takes time to become proficient, and the feature can be helpful with some types of notation.

2. Use Sibelius's Reference manual and Help menu to review the setup and features of Flexi-time.

3. Watch the tutorial video that summarizes all of the note entry options in Sibelius: Select **Help** > Tutorial Videos. Then click on #3, "Inputting notes."

4. Compare the two types of entry tools that have been covered so far: step-time (Chapters 2–4) and Flexi-time (Chapter 5). Which do you find easiest to use? Remember, you do not have to pick just one. Use the fastest method for the particular piece of music you're entering.

SECTION II

Grand-Staff and Small-Ensemble Scores

Simple Piano Arrangement
(Musical Example: "Come Back to Sorrento")

In this example, you'll create a two-staff piano part with chords and chord diagrams. Begin by looking over the score to identify new areas to be addressed. A major part of this chapter is dedicated to entering notation via the MIDI keyboard.

Come Back to Sorrento

The new skills in this chapter include:

- creating a piano staff
- deleting extra measures
- creating a key change
- first and second endings and repeat signs
- entering notation via Flexi-time with two hands
- listening to the playback with Live Playback turned on and turned off
- adding piano pedal markings
- inserting text on specific pages
- entering piano fingerings
- entering chord diagrams
- creating a clef change
- adding handbells used in score via plug-in
- orchestrating an arrangement using the Arrange feature

www.sibeliusbook.com

 You may find it helpful to have a printed copy of this example for reference. You can download the finished file from the *www.sibeliusbook.com* Web site. The file name is *Chapt6Sorrento.pdf*. After you download and open the file, print it out and keep it close by for reference.

Setting Up the Score

For this example, the piano score will be created with a custom House Style created from the Manuscript Paper examples provided by Sibelius.

1. Select **File** > New, or from the Quick Start screen choose "Start a new score."
2. With the New Score menu on the screen, type the letter P to quickly move to the P section under Manuscript Paper.
3. Select Piano. Click Next.
4. In the House Style window, choose Keyboard Opus (Times).
5. In the Main Text Font pull-down menu, select Times New Roman. This is a fast way to change the fonts in a piece before the score is even created.
6. Click Next.
7. Set the Time Signature to 3/4 and select the Tempo text: Andante.
8. Click Next.
9. Under Key Signatures, click the Minor keys button and select D minor (one flat).
10. Click Next.
11. In the Score Info screen, enter the following:
    a. Title: "Come Back to Sorrento"
    b. Composer/Songwriter: "Ernesto de Curtis"
    c. Lyricist: [leave blank]
    d. Copyright: "Copyright © 2006 by Tom Rudolph"
12. Click the Previous button and double-check that all the information is correct. Don't be in a hurry at this stage. Mistakes are much easier to fix here than in the score. Return to the final page and click Finish.

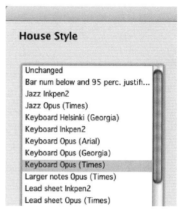

Your score should look as follows:

Adding Custom Titles, Credits, and Instrument Name

This example has some additional text to add at the top including a subtitle, arranger, and instrument name.

1.   Click inside the first bar to select it.
2.   Select **Create** > Text > Subtitle.
3.   Type the subtitle: "(Torna A Surriento)."
4.   Click on the composer's name: Ernesto de Curtis.
5.   Press the up arrow about 16 times to move it up. Use your eye to place it so it is not colliding with other text.
6.   Select **Create** > Text > Composer.
7.   Type: "arr. Tom Rudolph."
8.   Cick in bar 1 to select it.
9.   Select **Create** > Text > Special Text > Instrument Name at top left.
10. Type: "Solo Piano."
11. Press Esc.
12. Move the text to match the printout below. This example has a subtitle and chord diagrams, so you'll need a little more room at the top of the page.

Deleting Extra Measures

In this example, Manuscript Paper was used to generate the piano part. Sibelius automatically created 63 measures and filled an entire page. Since "Sorrento" has a total of 37 measures, measures 38 to the end must be deleted.

1. Show the measure numbers by selecting **View** > Staff Names and Bar Numbers.
2. If you don't see the entire page on your monitor, zoom out so you do: ⌘ (Mac); CTRL (Win) and press the minus key (–) above the letter P.
3. Select bar 38. You can manually go to it or use the jump to bar option by selecting **Edit** > Go to Bar. Or use the shortcut: Option-⌘-G (Mac); Alt-CTRL-G (Win).

4. Enter 38 in the "Bar number" window. Click OK.
5. Hold down the Shift key and click on the final barline in measure 63 at the bottom of the page.
6. Press the Delete key on the keyboard. Remember that measures cannot be deleted unless there is a double box around them. The other way to access the double box is by holding down ⌘ (Mac) or CTRL (Win) and clicking inside the desired measures.

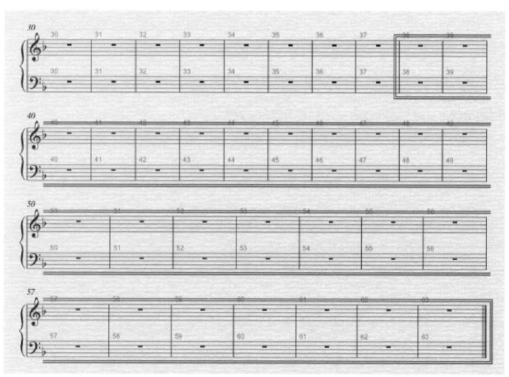

Formatting a Specific Number of Bars per Line

You can do the measure formatting after all the notation, text, chords, and so forth are entered. However, it can also be done at the beginning stages of entry. Looking at the final printout, notice that all of the systems are four bars per line with the exception of the second system where there are five measures. Here are the steps:

1. Press Esc.
2. Select the barline at the end of bar 4. Press Return (Mac); Enter (Win).
3. Select the barline at the end of bar 9. Press Return (Mac); Enter (Win).

Since the rest of the piece is 4 bars per system, let's use the plug-in.

4. Click inside bar 10. Hold down the Shift key and click inside the last bar, bar 37.
5. Select **Plug-ins** > Other > Make Layout Uniform.

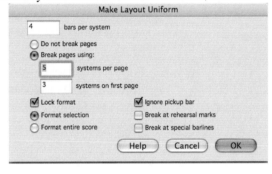

   a. In the Make Layout Uniform dialog box, make sure "Format selection" is selected.
   b. Click the button next to "Do not break pages."
   c. Enter five systems per page and three systems on the first page.
   d. Click OK.

Adjusting the Space Between All Staves

In this example, there needs to be more room between staves for the chord diagrams. The fastest way to change the space between staves is by adjusting the settings in Engraving Rules.

1. Select **House Style** > Engraving Rules.
2. Click on Staves.
3. Change the spaces between systems to 15.5. "Space" refers to the space between two lines on a staff. You can experiment with different space settings.
4. Under Justification, "Justify staves when page is at least 100% full" is the recommended setting.

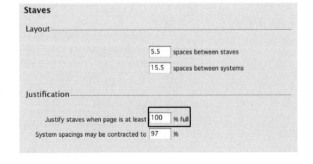

 Before using the mouse to drag staves, use the Engraving Rules as described above. You can quickly set the proper distance between all the staves in a score. Then, if you have to move one or more individual staves, you can click and drag them with the mouse.

Page 2 Titles

Next, add a title that will only print on pages after page 1. This is especially helpful in long pieces with several pages.

1. Click inside the lines and spaces of bar 26 to select it.
2. Select **Create** > Text > Other System Text > Header (after first page).
3. Type: Come Back to Sorrento.
4. Press Esc.

About Page Numbers

You will notice that Sibelius automatically created a page number at the top left corner of the second page. Page numbers will automatically update on every page. You will also notice that you can't click and drag or edit page numbers with the mouse. They are designed to appear on every page. You can turn them off or change their style by going to **House Style** > Engraving Rules > Page Numbers.

Saving the Engraving Rules Settings for Later Use

Any time you create a blank score setup that you're likely to reuse in the future, save the settings so they will appear in the Manuscript Paper options in the future. To accomplish this:

1. First, save the Sorrento file you have created so far. Select **File** > Save and name it "Sorrento." An important shortcut to memorize when using Sibelius, and just about every other computer program, is the shortcut for saving: ⌘-S (Mac); CTRL-S (Win).
2. Next, save the file with a different name. Select **File** > Save As and name it something like "Piano leadsheet chord diagrams."
3. To delete all the titles at the top of the page, just delete the first measure. All the titles are connected to measure 1. Hold down ⌘ (Mac); CTRL (Win) and click inside the lines and spaces of measure 1. Press Delete.
4. Select **File** > Export > Manuscript Paper.
5. You will get the following dialog box. Click Yes.

Now, when you create a new score, this will appear as one of the options.

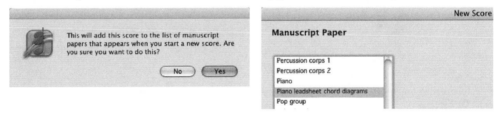

Returning to the "Sorrento" Score

To return to the file you saved named "Sorrento," select **File** > Open Recent File > Sorrento.

Entering a Key Change

There is a key change in measure 10.
To enter it:

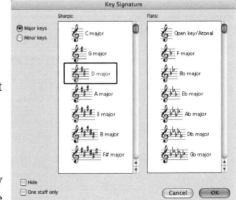

1. Press Esc.
2. Type the letter K (all by itself) or select **Create** > Key Signature.
3. Click the Major keys button.
4. Select D major, two sharps.
5. Click OK.
6. Click inside measure 10 to enter the key change. (You can also select bar 10 before step 2 above; then it will be automatically entered into the selected measure).

Entering First and Second Endings

There are three basic steps for entering the first and second endings. The easiest way to adjust the various markings so they display correctly is to enter the repeat barline, then the second ending, and then the first ending.

1. Click the barline at the end of bar 8 to select it.
2. Select **Create** > Barline > End Repeat.
3. Press Esc.
4. Click inside bar 9 to select it.
5. Type the letter L for line, or select **Create** > Line.
6. Under "System lines," select the second ending graphic. Click OK.

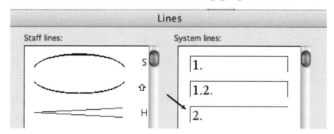

7. After the second ending bracket is inserted in the score, click on the number 2 to select it.
8. Use the right arrow key to move the bracket to the right, past the repeat bar.
9. Click inside the lines and spaces in measure 8 to select it.
10. Type the letter L.
11. Under "System lines," select 1 for the first ending and click OK.

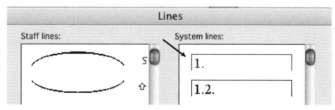

12. The left handle is automatically selected. Press the left arrow on the keyboard to move the left bracket slightly to the left. It should line up just inside the thick line of the repeat bar.

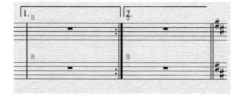

Entering Notation with Two Hands Using Flexi-time

In Chapter 5, Flexi-time was introduced. In this example, you will try playing with both hands together to simultaneously enter notation in the treble and bass staves. If you feel this is above your keyboard-playing skills, you can record each hand (staff) separately using Flexi-time. You can also choose to enter the notation in step time, as reviewed in Chapters 2–4. If you would like to try playing both the left-hand and the right-hand parts at the same time, read on!

Split Point Options

Flexi-time settings were initially discussed in Chapter 5. The additional consideration in this chapter is telling Sibelius how to split the music into the proper staves. There are two options: let Sibelius try to automatically pick a split point—a specific note that tells the program to put the notes above it in the treble staff and those below it in the bass staff—or determine the split point ahead of time. I experimented with both options and found that with this particular example, selecting a split point ahead of time required the least editing later. The problem comes in the first four measures of "Sorrento." If you choose a split point of middle C (referred to as C4), the D in measure 3 will be placed in the treble, not bass staff. However, a quick scan of the entire piece will reveal that this is the only bar that will not split correctly. So set a split point of C4, play the section in, and then go back and edit the measures that did not notate properly.

The first step is to set the Flexi-time options:

1. Select **Notes** > Flexi-time Options.
2. Change "Introduction" from the default of 1 bar to 2. Two bars of introduction allow you to get the feel of the beat, especially in 3/4 and 2/4 time.
3. Be sure "Record up to" is set to 0 (zero). If there is any other number in this box, that many additional measures will be added to the end of the score.
4. Set the "Flexibility of tempo" setting to None. Therefore, you will have to play in time with a metronome click.

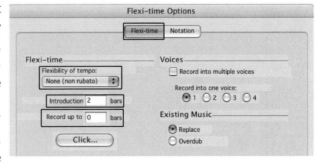

5. Uncheck "Record into multiple voices."
6. Click the Notation tab at the top of the window.
7. Make sure the value in the "Adjust rhythms" box is set to an eighth note, since this is the smallest rhythmic value in the piece.
8. Under "Split point between two keyboard staves," click the Fixed button and set it to C4 (middle C).
9. Since there are no triplets in the piece, set all of the tuplets to None. (If there are triplets with notes all the same value, select Simple. If some triplets included different rhythmic values, choose Moderate. If there are rests and other nonstandard notation in triplets, select Complex.)
10. Click OK to close the Flexi-time Options Notation window.
11. Be sure all the MIDI messages are unchecked.
12. After making the changes, close the Flexi-time Options window by clicking OK.

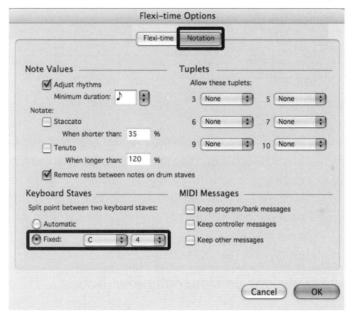

You do not have to use any one entry method for an entire piece. You could step enter with the MIDI keyboard for a few measures, switch to Flexi-time for a few more, then go to entering via the alphabetic typing method. Use the method that is best for the particular piece or phrase.

www.sibeliusbook.com

If you would like to begin at this point in this chapter, go to *www.sibeliusbook.com* and download the Chapter 6 files. To start at this point, open the file *Chpt6Sorrento1.sib*.

Entering Notation with Flexi-time and Two Hands

Remember to play legato when you are entering with Flexi-time. This will help reduce the number of rests. Start by recording the first seven bars of the piece.

1. Press Esc.
2. Click inside bar 1 in the treble (top) staff to select it.
3. Hold down the Shift key and click inside measure 1 of the bass clef.
4. Click the red Record button on the Playback toolbar, or use the shortcut: Shift-⌘-F (Mac); Shift-CTRL-F (Win). Wait for two bars before starting to play the first seven measures.

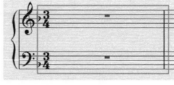

5. Press the space bar to stop after recording the first ending. During recording, Sibelius will repeat automatically to the first measure because of the repeat sign.
6. Look at the notation you just entered. How did you do? If there are a lot of mistakes, undo the recording and slow down the tempo by dragging the slider on the Playback toolbar.

Changing Note Durations on Noncontiguous Notes

You may have entered some of your left-hand bars with incorrect rhythms. A common problem while entering is eighth notes with eighth rests rather than a quarter note value. You can prevent this from happening if you play more legato. However, the wrong notes can be corrected pretty quickly.

1. Select any eighth notes that should be quarters. Hold down ⌘ (Mac); CTRL (Win) and click on all of the eighth notes that should be quarters. Click directly on the notehead.

2. Press the number 4 (quarter note) on the keypad to turn them *all* into quarters. Pretty cool, huh?

Moving Notes from One Staff to Another

Because of the split point, there will be several measures with problems. Anytime a D is played on the second space above the staff in the bass clef, since the split point is C4, several Ds will be notated in the treble clef. This will occur several times in the piece, starting in measures 3 and 7.

To move the notes:

1. Press Esc.
2. Select just the Ds in the treble staff. Hold down ⌘ (Mac); CTRL (Win) and click on the D noteheads that need to be moved—on beats 3 and 4 of bars 3 and 7. Only the Ds should be highlighted.
3. Press the Delete key to remove the Ds from the score in the treble clef.
4. Select all of the B♭s in the bass clef that need to be edited. Hold down ⌘ (Mac); CTRL (Win) and select them all.
5. Press the number 3 along the top of the keyboard to add a third above every note selected (another one of those cool things that Sibelius can do).

The other option is to select one note at a time and play the correct notes on the MIDI keyboard, in this case a B♭ and a D. However, since many of the changes are similar, the computer keyboard is the fastest way to enter the correct notes.

Since bar 8 is identical to bar 9, just copy it:

1. Select bar 8 by clicking inside the lines and spaces.
2. Hold down Option (Mac) or Alt (Win) and click inside bar 9. This will copy the selection to bar 9.

Back to Flexi-time Recording

Go to the key change in measure 10. This time, let's experiment with the Flexi part of Flexi-time.

1. Select **Notes** > Flexi-time Options.
2. Under "Flexibility of tempo," select "Low (poco rubato)." Sibelius will now try to follow your tempo should you slow down or speed up a bit. This setting can be useful when sight-reading something. Do not, however, make sudden changes in tempo.
3. Press Esc.
4. Click inside the top staff in bar 10.
5. Shift-click inside the bass clef in measure 10 to select both staves.
6. Type Shift-⌘-F (Mac) or Shift-CTRL-F (Win) to start recording, or press the Record button in the Playback window. Listen to the two-bar introduction and start recording in measure 10. Remember to play in the key of D major. Play legato and try to enter the rest of page 1 of "Sorrento" using Flexi-time.

Respelling Accidentals

One of the problems when entering with a MIDI keyboard or keyboard controller is that often notes are not spelled enharmonically correct. For example, the B♭ in measure 21 was entered as an A♯. To change the A♯ to a B♭:

1. Select the A♯s in bar 21. Hold down ⌘ (Mac) or CTRL (Win) and click on all three A♯s. Click directly on the noteheads so only the noteheads are selected.
2. Press Return (Mac) or Enter (Win) to respell the accidental, or use the menu: **Notes** > Respell Accidental.

Automatic Split Point

For the last sixteen measures, try the automatic split point option in Flexi-time to see how you like it. Sibelius tries to guess the split point. In some cases, this can be the way to go. In others, you'll want to set the split point ahead of time. Experimenting with the settings is recommended. There is no one preferred entry method.

1. Select **Notes** > Flexi-time Options.
2. Click the Notation tab.
3. Under Keyboard Staves, click the button next to "Automatic."
4. Click OK.

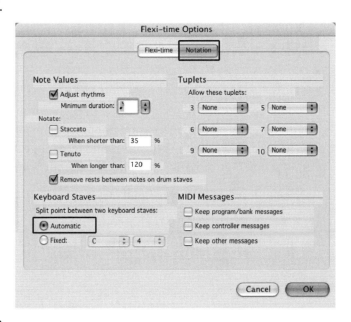

5. Press Esc.
6. Select the top staff in measure 22.
7. Hold down Shift and select the bottom staff in measure 22. Note that the last chord is rolled. Don't play it that way when you are recording. Rather, play it block and then go back and add the chord roll marking later.

8. To start recording, use the shortcut: Shift-⌘-F (Mac); Shift-CTRL-F (Win).

How does your printout look? Even with the automatic split point activated, when I entered these measures, there were about as many errors as before, when a fixed split point was set. I'd set the split point ahead of time, especially when playing from a printed score. If improvising, the automatic split point is usually best.

Use your editing skills to correct any wrong notes.

www.sibeliusbook.com

If you would like to start this chapter at this point, go to *www.sibeliusbook.com* and download the Chapter 6 files. Open the file *Chpt6Sorrento2.sib*. It will have all the notes and markings entered to this point.

Entering a Clef Change

In measure 36, there is a clef change before the last three eighth notes.

1. Press Esc.
2. Type the letter Q or select **Create** > Clef ...
3. Select the treble clef.
4. To enter it, click on the A on beat 2, the note *before* the clef change.

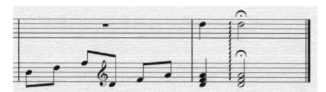

Proof-Listening via the Mixer

Now that your notes are entered and edited, listen to the piece to check for any wrong notes you might have missed. So far, we have run Playback just by clicking Play (or pressing the space bar). Sibelius also has a helpful mixer.

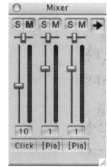

1. To display the Mixer, select **Window** > Mixer or press the letter M all by itself.
2. You may need to extend the window to see all of the different staves in the mixer. Click on the hash marks in the left corner of the mixer window and stretch the window to the right.
3. You can control the volume of the playback from this screen by dragging the sliders for each staff. Note that there is a slider for the click and for each of the treble and bass staves.

Live Playback

Sibelius can play back exactly what you played or disregard the subtleties of your playing and play back the exact notation on the screen. When Live Playback is on, it only recognizes the dynamics played during the recording.

Since Live Playback is on by default, when you press Play after entering music with Flexi-time, you will hear what you actually played, including any slight variations in tempo, dynamics, etc.

To turn Live Playback on or off, access this option from the Play menu. If Live Playback is checked, it is turned on.

Entering the Rolled Chord Marking

1. Select the half note chord on beat 2 of the last bar (37). Click on the noteheads so they are the only item selected.
2. Press the letter L for lines, or select **Create** > Lines.
3. Select the vertical squiggly line (rolled chord marking).
4. Click OK.
5. Once the marking is in the score, drag the handle upward into the treble staff.

Cautionary Accidentals

In bar 25, in the bass clef, a cautionary accidental is needed. To enter it:

1. Press Esc.
2. Select the F♯ in bar 25 by clicking on the notehead.
3. Be sure the Keypad is on the screen (**Window** > Keypad).
4. Press F12 to go to the fifth Keypad layout, or click on the double-flat icon in the top right corner of the Keypad window.
5. Press the Enter key on the Keypad to select the parentheses. You may also click on the parentheses using your mouse.

Cautionary Accidentals Plug-In

There is a plug-in for checking an entire score for places where cautionary accidentals are needed. This can save a lot of time, especially in a long piece of music.

1. Since plug-ins can't be undone, save your score first: **File** > Save.
2. Select **Plug-ins** > Accidentals > Add Cautionary Accidentals.
3. The Plug-ins warning about not being undoable will appear. Click Yes.

4. There are no changes recommended to the default settings in the Add Cautionary Accidentals dialog box. Look it over so you know what to expect.

5. Click OK.

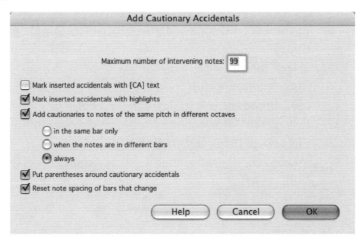

Sibelius searches the entire score and looks for places where cautionary accidentals would typically appear, places them in the score, then highlights the selections for easy reference. When I ran the plug-in it found two notes to change, both in bar 10.

To remove highlights:

The plug-in added highlights to indicate where cautionary accidentals were added. You will want to delete these. Time for another plug-in.

1. Select **Plug-ins** > Other > Remove All Highlights.

2. Click OK. No more highlights.

Entering Chord Diagrams

There are two ways to go about entering the rest of the markings in the score. One is to do all of the like items from beginning to end and then go back and enter another kind of marking. This can be an effective strategy. The other option is to enter all of the markings as you go along. Either way works. However, with Chord Diagrams, it may be fastest to get them all done and then go back and enter the other markings. Entering Chord Diagrams using the menu is a slow process in Sibelius, so using Copy and Paste really helps.

Remember the keystroke for a chord symbol from Chapter 3? If you do, pass Go and collect $200! If you forgot, it is located in the **Create** > Text menu. Go ahead, look it up to see if you were right. To create a single chord, the shortcut is ⌘-K (Mac); CTRL-K (Win). However, for this example, we want the chord name and the guitar fret diagram.

1. Press Esc.
2. Select the first D in bar 1 in the treble staff.
3. Select **Create** > Chord Diagram, or use the shortcut Shift-K.
4. In the Chord Diagram dialog box, select D next to Chord.
5. Select "minor."
6. Choose a fret option from the several provided. If you are not sure which one to use, choose the one in the upper left corner.
7. Be sure that "Show chord symbol" is checked in the bottom left corner.
8. Click OK or press Return/Enter.

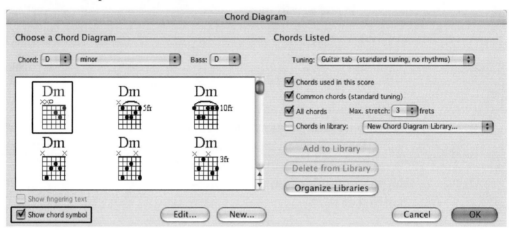

These steps are required each time you want to enter a chord diagram; there are no shortcuts. Therefore, I recommend you enter a few of the chords and then use Copy and Paste to copy them to other locations.

Remember how to copy anything in Sibelius? If something is highlighted, hold down Option (Mac); Alt (Win) and click in the desired location. Let's add one more key into the mix, because we want to copy the chord diagram and place it in the desired location. To do this, hold down Shift-Option (Mac); Shift-Alt (Win).

> Holding down Option (Mac); Alt (Win) allows you to copy the selected item(s) to another place in the score. Holding down Shift-Option (Mac); Shift-Alt (Win) will copy the item to the same location. This is helpful when copying chords and other symbols.

Copying Chord Diagrams

Since the Dm chord diagram repeats several times, copy and paste it as follows:

1. Select the Dm chord diagram if it is not already selected.
2. Hold down Shift-Option (Mac); Shift-Alt (Win) and click anywhere above the first beats of measures 4, 6, and 8.

3. In bar 8, the diagram will collide with the first ending. As soon as you enter it, press the up arrow on the computer keyboard to move it above the first ending line. Don't worry if your chord collides with the blue bar numbers that are displayed for reference via the View menu.
4. Select the first G eighth note in measure 3.
5. Press Shift-K to access the Chord Diagram dialog box.
6. Enter G minor and press OK.
7. Hold down Shift-Option (Mac); Shift-Alt (Win) and click on the first note in bar 5.
8. Enter the A7 chord in measure 7. See if you can remember the steps. The A and 7 are entered separately in the Chord Diagram dialog box.

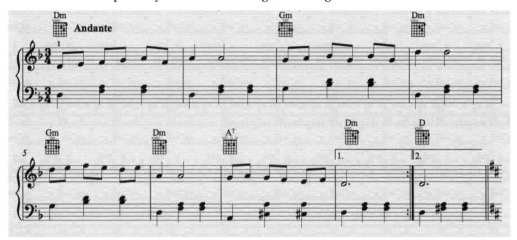

Enter the chord diagrams in measures 9 through 16. Use your new copy and paste skills for D, Em, and A7, since they repeat quite a bit.

Moving Selected Chord Diagrams Above the Repeat Marks

To move the chord diagrams up above the first and second endings:

1. Press Esc.
2. Click on the chord diagram in the first ending measure.
3. Hold down ⌘ (Mac); CTRL (Win) and click on the chord in the second ending measure. Just the chords in both measures should be selected.
4. Press the up arrow on the keyboard 11 times or until they just clear the top of the repeat lines.

 Shift-click (click on the left item and then hold down shift and click the last item) when you want to copy all markings in a measure. Use ⌘ (Mac) or Ctrl (Win) click when you want to select individual items in a measure.

Entering Chords with an Alternate Bass

There are a couple of examples when chords require an alternate bass. To enter the Gm/B♭ (G minor with a B♭ bass) in bar 21:

1. Select the D quarter note in measure 21.
2. Press Shift-K.
3. Select G, minor, and next to Bass, select B♭.
4. Click OK or press Return/Enter.

Enter the rest of the chord diagrams in measures 33 though 37. Use copy and paste to save time. Most of the chords on the second page have already been entered on page one. Enter just the chords. The rest of the markings (slurs, fermata, rit., etc.) will be entered later in this chapter.

Now make a final pass through the notation and add all of the other markings. This includes expressions, tempo markings, crescendos, piano pedal markings, ritards, and fermatas. Most of these have been entered in previous examples, with the exception of piano fingerings, "rit…", and pedal markings.

Moving All of the Chord Diagrams up Slightly

There will be some collisions of slurs and the chord diagrams. Since there is plenty of room above the staff, move up all of these slightly. Here's a quick way to do this:

1. Select **Edit** > Select > Select All or use the shortcut: ⌘-A (Mac); CTRL-A (Win).
2. Select **Edit** > Filter > Chord Diagrams.
3. Press the up arrow on the computer keyboard a couple of times to move all of the diagrams up slightly.

 You can always reset the position of anything that is selected. For example, if you already dragged some chord diagrams and wanted them to return to the original default positions, select the desired chords and select **Layout** > Reset Position.

Entering Piano Fingerings

Next, enter the piano fingerings in the first eight measures. There is a special text for fingerings in Sibelius.

1. Select the first D eighth note in bar 1.
2. Select **Create** > Text > Other System Text > Fingering.
3. Type the number 1 and press Esc.
4. Use the down arrow to move it below the chord diagram.

Like the chord diagrams, it will be a lot of mouse clicking to select the fingering text, so use Copy and Paste to copy them and double-click to change the fingering as needed. Once you enter one fingering, use Copy and Paste to create all the others.

5. With the number 1 still selected, hold down Option (Mac); Alt (Win) and click the mouse above the first note in bar 3. Use the arrow keys to adjust the positioning.
6. Hold down Option (Mac); Alt (Win) and click the mouse above the first note in the bass clef, bar 1.
7. Double-click on the number 1 you just copied to edit it.
8. Delete the number 1 and change it to a 5.
9. Use the arrow keys to move it below the staff (or drag it with the mouse).
10. Hold down Option (Mac); Alt (Win) and click the mouse below the second note in the bass clef, measure 1.
11. Double-click on the number 5.
12. Delete the number 5, then type 1 and then Return (Mac) or Enter (Win), and type a 3. The result should be a stacked 1 and 3.
13. Use the arrow keys to align it with the number 5.
14. Use the same steps to enter the fingerings in bars 3, 4, 5, 6, and 7.

15. Enter the fingerings on the left side of bar 36.

Entering and Flipping Slurs

Slurs were introduced in Chapter 3. To extend a slur:

1. Click on the first note of the slur, press the letter S (all by itself), or select **Create** > Lines and select the slur.
2. Press the space bar five times to extend the slur.

To flip a slur:

3. With the slur highlighted, press the X key on the keyboard or select **Edit** > Flip.
4. To edit the height of a slur, with it selected, use the up or down arrows on the computer keyboard or drag it with the mouse.

Enter a *p* marking in measure 1 and an *mf* marking in measure 6.

1. Select the note.
2. Type ⌘-E (Mac); CTRL-E (Win). Right-click (CTRL-click on a Mac with a one-button mouse) and select the appropriate marking. (See Chapter 4.)

Entering Crescendos and Decrescendos (Hairpins)

These were introduced in Chapter 4.

1. Select the first note and press the letter H for Hairpin, or select **Create** > Lines and choose the crescendo.
2. Press the space bar to extend the hairpin.
3. To enter a decrescendo, hold down the Shift key and type H. Press the space bar to extend it.

Entering the Fermatas in Bars 32 and 37

Fermatas were introduced in Chapter 4.

1. Select the notes in measures 32 and 37 by clicking on the notehead in measure 32. Then hold down ⌘ (Mac); CTRL (Win) and select the notehead in measure 37.
2. With the Keypad on the screen, go to the fourth Keypad (F11) and select the fermata.

Piano Pedal Markings

There are a variety of piano pedal markings, all located in the Lines menu. You will select the appropriate line and then use the arrow keys or mouse to extend or shorten them. This takes a little time, as most pedal markings need to be inserted separately and aligned by hand.

Enter the piano pedal markings in measures 10 through 14:

1. Press Esc.
2. Select the D in the bass clef on the first beat of measure 10.
3. Press L (for the Lines menu) or select **Create** > Lines.
4. Scroll down the "Staff lines" column and select:

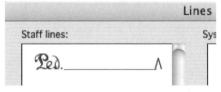

5. The marking will be inserted in the score. Click and drag the right side of the marking so the ^ lines up under the first note in bar 11. You must click directly on the ^ to extend the line.
6. Press Esc.
7. Click on the D quarter note on the first beat of measure 11 in the bass clef.
8. Type L for the Lines menu.

9. Select the pedal marking below. Click OK to select it.

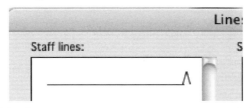

10. After it is entered in the score, use your mouse to extend the right side so the ^ lines up under the A on the first beat of bar 12.

11. Click on the left side of the line and drag it to the left so it lines up with the first pedal marking you entered.

12. Repeat the above steps and place another line under measure 12.

13. In bar 13, select the pedal marking:

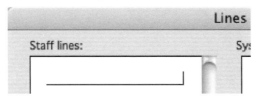

14. Using your new skills, enter the rest of the pedal markings in measures 14 through 26 and the final measure, 37.

Entering the "Rit…" Marking

The "Rit…" marking in bar 36 also comes from the Lines menu.

1. Select bar 36 in the treble staff.
2. Type L for Lines.
3. From the "System lines" column, select: rit. _ _ _ _
4. Use the arrow keys or mouse to adjust the location.

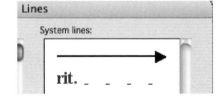

Entering Tempo Markings

The initial tempo marking of Andante was entered in the New Score window. To enter Meno mosso in bar 22:

1. Select the first eighth note, D, in bar 22 in the treble staff.
2. Select **Create** > Text > Tempo.
3. Right-click (CTRL-click on a Mac with a one-button mouse) and select "Meno mosso" from the menu. Click Esc.
4. Drag the "Meno mosso" to the right so it does not collide with the chord diagram and/or slur.

Congratulations! You have entered a lot of new items in Sibelius. You should save, then print (**File** > Print) your score and compare it to the printouts on page 97 and 98 of this chapter.

More Sibelius Tips and Tricks

www.sibeliusbook.com

Each chapter will introduce you to some fun, time-saving, and simply cool Sibelius features.

If you would like to start this chapter from this point (boy, will you miss a lot!), then download the Chapter 6 files from *www.sibeliusbook.com*. Open the file *Chpt6Sorrento3.sib*.

Handbells

There is a handy plug-in for those who compose music for handbells. Even if you don't envision yourself writing for handbells, you will learn a couple of handy page layout tips.

1. First, select **File** > Save As and make a copy of your file. Call it "SorrentoBells."
2. Select **Plug-ins** > Composing Tools > Show Handbells Required.

Handbells scores include all the notes required so the handbells players can get out what they need for the piece. Watch Sibelius perform its magic before your eyes! Here is what it creates:

This measure does need some editing to make it look more like traditional handbells scores:

3. Press Esc.

4. Click on the 23/4 bar and hide it: select **Edit** > Show or Hide > Hide or use the shortcut: Shift-⌘-H (Mac); Shift-CTRL-H (Win).

5. Next, hide the dotted half rests in both staves. Press Esc. Hold down ⌘ (Mac); CTRL (Win), and click on every dotted half rest, right on the rest to select it. Be sure only the rests are selected.

6. Hide them all at once using the shortcut: Shift-⌘-H (Mac); Shift-CTRL-H (Win).

Moving One Staff System

The handbells measure should look like it is floating above the rest of the music. The first step is to move it up and then indent the system on each end.

1. Press Esc.
2. Click inside the top staff in the handbells bar.
3. Shift-click the bass staff so they are both selected.
4. Hold down the Shift key and drag the selected systems up toward the top of the page. Holding down Shift tells Sibelius to move only the selected staff or staves.

Indenting Staff Systems

1. Press Esc.
2. Click on the left barline inside the lines and spaces of either staff.
3. Two handles should appear. Click and drag the handles slightly to the right.
4. Click on the barline at the end of the bar, inside the lines and spaces. You may need to click slightly to the right of the barline to make the handles appear.
5. Click one of the two handles and drag the staff to the left.

Here is the basic look you are shooting for:

Sibelius has many of the common markings (symbols) used in handbell music already built in. To access the handbell graphics and many others, press the letter Z all by itself, or select **Create** > Symbol. Page down to the Handbells section of the Symbols dialog box. Click a marking to select it and enter it in the desired measure.

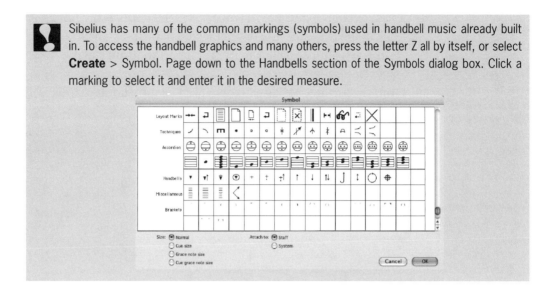

Orchestrating an Entire Arrangement Using the Arrange Feature

Sibelius has a fabulous feature called Arrange. It is actually an orchestration tool that is very, very powerful. We'll use it to orchestrate this piano arrangement for an entire ensemble.

Removing Selected Items: Chord Diagrams

In order to create an arrangement, the chord diagrams should be deleted.

1. Since we are going to make changes to the Sorrento master file, select **File** > Save As and name the new file "SorrentoArrange.sib."
2. Select **Edit** > Select > Select All, or use the shortcut: ⌘-A (Mac); CTRL-A (Win).
3. Select **Edit** > Filter > Chord Diagrams.
4. Press the Delete key to remove just the chord diagrams.

Using the Arrange Feature

The Arrange feature uses source material that is copied to the computer's clipboard. This material can be orchestrated into a new file or the existing one. For this example, the Arrange feature will be used to create a band arrangement in a new file.

1. In the Sorrento file, select bars 1 through 16. Be sure to include both the treble and bass staves (use click and Shift-click).
2. Select **Edit** > Copy or use the shortcut: ⌘-C (Mac); CTRL-C (Win).
3. Select **File** > New.
4. Under Manuscript Paper, select "Wind Band."
5. Click Finish.

6. Zoom out of the new file so you can see the entire score on the page.
7. Click in the first measure of the Piccolo part (top staff).
8. Hold down Shift and click in the Tuba part (bottom staff).
9. Select **Notes** > Arrange.
10. From the Arrange Styles window, select "Band Standard (mixed)."

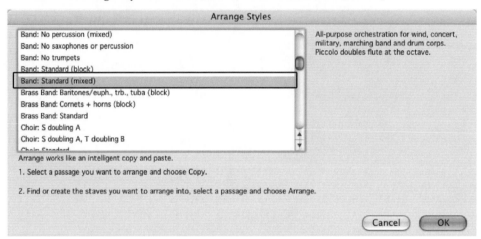

11. Click Yes to "Do you want to go ahead with arranging this passage?"

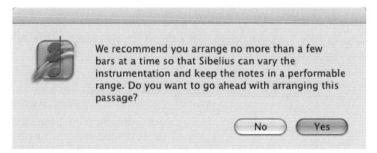

Check out the orchestration that Sibelius created. This can be a time-saving technique. You might want to try out some different Arrange Styles. Perhaps apply one to the first eight measures, another to measures 9 through 16, and so forth. You can also edit anything that is created by the Arrange feature or enter/arrange your own composition.

Don't worry about the individual parts right now. That will be covered in the next chapter (Chapter 7).

Summary

This example included the following Sibelius skills:
*   set up the score using Manuscript Paper
*   move the top staff down to make room for the titles
*   add custom titles, including page 2 text
*   delete extra measures
*   format a specific number of bars per system for the entire document

- add space between staves via Engraving Rules
- save as Manuscript Paper
- enter a key change
- enter first and second endings
- enter music via Flexi-time with two hands
- change the Flexi-time options
- remove notes from one staff and enter them in another
- respell accidentals
- enter a clef change
- playback via the Mixer
- turn Live Playback on and off
- enter a rolled-chord marking
- add cautionary accidentals one at a time or all at once via the plug-in
- remove highlighted notes via the plug-in
- enter, copy, and move Chord Diagrams
- enter Chord Diagrams with an alternate bass
- move all Chord Diagrams via the filter
- enter and copy piano fingerings
- enter and flip slur markings
- enter expressions, crescendos/decrescendos, and fermatas
- add piano pedal markings
- enter "Rit…" marks
- enter tempo markings
- add Handbells Used via the plug-in
- move and indent staves
- remove selected items via the filter
- create an arrangement using the Arrange feature

Review

1. Try entering other two-hand examples using Flexi-time. Experiment with the various settings and see which ones work best for you.
2. Try some other Arrange Styles. Experiment with different styles for various groups of instruments and styles. Go to Sibelius Reference via the Help menu for some more ideas on how to use this powerful feature.
3. Experiment with the Chord Diagrams. You can create your own diagram or edit existing chords. These can also be saved into a custom library.

7

Woodwind Quintet and Scanning (Musical Example: "The Easy Winners")

This is an arrangement of "The Easy Winners" by Scott Joplin, scored for woodwind quintet. This chapter introduces some new situations presented by multistave scores, as well as entering music via scanning.

2

The Easy Winners

The Easy Winners

133

Topics and skills new in this chapter include:

- scanning
- editing music with PhotoScore Lite 4.1.2
- importing a scanned file into Sibelius
- editing a scanned file in Sibelius
- use of filters for copying and pasting elements
- using the Copy Articulations and Slurs plug-in
- using the Mixer window
- using the Kontakt Player
- using Dynamic Parts
- changing the Text Style for parts
- creating a House Style for parts
- copying the Layout between parts
- repositioning objects in the parts
- navigating between individual parts and score
- closing a file with both score and part windows

This chapter introduces a new method of note entry, loading printed music using a flatbed scanner.

www.sibeliusbook.com

If you have a scanner, download the file from the book Web site (*www.sibeliusbook. com*). Download the Chapter 7 Folder. In the folder is the file *TEWScore.pdf.* You should print this file and scan it using your scanner. The steps for this are detailed in this chapter. Your scanner may produce different results, and the version of PhotoScore you use is also a factor. If your results differ greatly from the examples here, download the graphic files and use them for the editing.

If you do not have access to a scanner, there are graphics files on the web site as well. Click on Chapter 7 and download the files. They are large files and will take some time to download. Macintosh users should download the tiff files; Windows users should download the .bmp files. Use what you learn in this chapter to fix the errors in your own scans.

Scanning the Score

First you'll need to print the example to be scanned. I recommend this over using the printed example in the book, as it may not scan properly.

1. Open the file *TEWScore.pdf* in Sibelius (downloaded from *www.sibeliusbook.com*)
2. Print all three pages.
3. Quit Acrobat.

Power up your scanner and launch the scanner's software. Most music can be scanned with a resolution of 300 dots per inch (dpi) but if the music is particularly small, increase the resolution to 400 dpi.

For multipage projects, begin with a single test page to verify that the scan resolution is sufficient. If PhotoScore Lite successfully opens it, you can safely scan the rest of the document.

All music must be scanned as grayscale or black-and-white, not color.

The example (*TEWScore.pdf*) was scanned with an HP Officejet 6110 All in One, so all the screenshots are particular to that scanner. Your scanner will have similar settings, but they may be arranged differently.

1. Check that your scanner's image type is set for black-and-white or grayscale.
2. Check that the resolution is 300 dpi.
3. Make sure the resulting graphics file will be a Tiff file for Macintosh users or a .bmp file for Windows users.

 Black-and-white scan files will be smaller than grayscale files, so if disk space is an issue, definitely go with black-and-white for all music scanning.

With the scanner setup complete, take the printed score for "The Easy Winners" (*TEWScore.pdf*) out of the printer tray so you can begin creating the very file you just printed out. Yes, when you think about it, it's a bit silly, but you will learn some cool stuff in the process.

1. Place page 1 of the score face down on the scanner's bed. Be sure it is facing the right direction. Some scanners automatically create a preview scan; if your scanner provides this feature but it is not automatic, get a preview now.

The Lite version of PhotoScore, that comes with Sibelius, has a twelve-staff limit, but the original music has fifteen staves per page. The workaround is to scan the page in two stages, selecting the top two systems and scanning them, then selecting the bottom system and scanning it separately. The grayed-out options are available only in the full version of PhotoScore. For more information on the features of the full version, go to *http://www.neuratron.com*.

2. Drag the scan area box to include the first two systems on page 1.

3. Begin scanning. If you are asked to name the resulting scan file, name it "TEWpg1_1."

At this point, check the file with PhotoScore Lite.

1. Locate the PhotoScore Lite application on your hard drive and launch it. This should have been installed when you installed Sibelius. If you don't find the application, go back to your Sibelius install disk and install it.
2. In PhotoScore Lite, select **File** > Open, and locate the file *TEWpg1_1* on your hard drive.
3. Select it and click Open.

If you were successful, you will see the first two systems of "The Easy Winners." If your file does not open, recheck the scanner's settings and try the scan again.

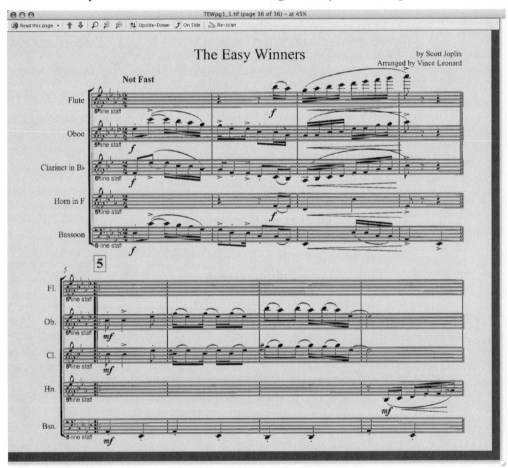

Return to the scanning software and continue scanning the first page.

1. Drag the scan area box to include only the last system on page 1.
2. Begin scanning. Name the file TEWpg1_2.
3. When finished, remove page 1 from the scanner and place page 2 face down on the glass.
4. Repeat the scanning process from page 1, selecting the top two systems and naming that file TEWpg2_1.
5. Select the bottom system on page 2 and scan it, naming the file TEWpg2_2.
6. Remove page 2 from the scanner and place page 3 face down on the glass.
7. Repeat the two-part scanning process, naming the first file TEWpg3_1 and the second file TEWpg3_2.
8. Once all the pages have been successfully scanned, quit the scanning software.

Opening a File in PhotoScore Lite

The next phase of the process is importing the tiff or .bmp graphics files into PhotoScore Lite. If you scanned in files, you've already begun this process with the test page; return to PhotoScore Lite and await Further Instructions. If you are importing the graphics files downloaded from the Web site, the next three steps are for you only.

1. Locate the PhotoScore Lite application on your hard drive and launch it.
2. In PhotoScore Lite, select **File** > Open, and locate the file "TEWpg1_1" on your hard drive.
3. Select it and click Open.

Further Instructions

1. Select **File** > Save As and name the file "TEW Scan.opt."

The music displayed in the PhotoScore window is still just a graphic. The next step is to have PhotoScore "read' the graphic file and create a music notation file.

2. Click the "Read this page" button in the scan file window's menu bar. This will bring up the Neuratron PhotoScore Preferences dialog box.

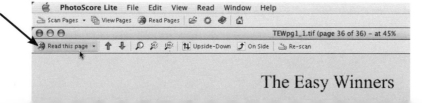

3. Under the Accuracy heading, choose "Read One Voice per Staff Only," since there is no polyphony in this example.

4. Click Read.

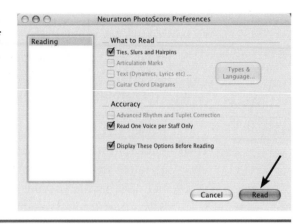

An Introduction to the PhotoScore Lite Interface

The first window displayed in PhotoScore is called the Scanned Page window. Once the reading process is complete, a second window, the Output window, appears. This window displays PhotoScore's reading of the graphics file, and it is where you will do any corrections before handing the file over to Sibelius. The white highlight strip follows the cursor as you move across the window. When a staff is highlighted white, it is editable. Drag the cursor slowly across the Flute staff, and notice that when it passes over any music symbol, a purple highlight appears. When editing music, always make sure that the item to be edited is highlighted before clicking on it. As you dragged the cursor, you probably also noticed another window in the upper right corner of the screen whose display seemed to be tracking the cursor movement. This is the Full Detail View window. It does follow the movement of the cursor, but it is displaying the same location in the Scanned Page window. Use Full Detail View to quickly check a scan error against the original file. A version of the Sibelius Keypad is in the lower right corner of the window. You'll use this for any notation editing. Anything musical not done with the Keypad can be found in the Create menu.

PhotoScore marks staves it recognizes with thick blue lines in the Scanned Page window. Occasionally a scan might produce a staff that PhotoScore isn't sure about. These will be marked with a thin blue line and may need further attention or rescanning. Any rhythmic problems will be highlighted with a red box, making them easy to spot. Above the upper right corner of the box is an indication of how many rhythms are over or under the amount set by the time signature. Missing elements will require a closer look. With a little experience, you will know what things generally fool PhotoScore and pay special attention to those elements.

Making Corrections in a Scanned Document

Start proofreading the music staff by staff, checking it against the original as displayed in the Full Detail View window. The first issue is the key signature for the Clarinet and Horn staves. The notes are in the correct place for the instrument, but PhotoScore Lite does not understand the concept of transposing instruments. It will allow for different key signatures to be placed on different staves, but it will not play them back properly via MIDI. This is the first item to fix.

Fixing Key Signatures for Transposing Instruments

The Clarinet needs a key signature of B♭ and the Horn needs a key signature of E♭.

1. Move the cursor to the third staff of the first system, the Clarinet part, so the key signature is highlighted. Right-click (CTRL-click on a Mac with a one-button mouse) to select it. The Key Signature dialog box will appear.
2. Type 2 in the text window or select 2 from the pop-up menu. The Flat button is already selected since the indicated key is a flat key.
3. Click OK. The key signature for the Clarinet is now B♭.
4. Move the cursor down to the Horn staff and repeat steps 1 through 3, but enter 3 for the number of flats. Press Esc when finished.

The same fix will be required on every system of the piece. These elements can be copied and pasted to all subsequent occurrences using the same keystroke shortcuts as in Sibelius.

Before you go on, please note that some of the problems encountered here are specific to my scan; your scans may require different corrections. Consult the PhotoScore help menu for any problems not covered here.

PhotoScore did not recognize the repeat bar at the beginning of the second system and has created a barline instead. The resulting new measure has no notes in it, and that's what the program has flagged. This barline must be deleted and replaced with the Start Repeat barline. There is also a rhythmic problem in the Bassoon part to remedy.

1. Position the cursor over the barline to be deleted in the Flute staff and click to select it.
2. Press the Delete key.

The barline will disappear on all staves, leaving only the red box around the first measure of the Bassoon staff.

Entering Notation in PhotoScore Lite

Drag the cursor over the area outlined by the red box, watching the display in the Full Detail View window to locate the problem. The indication above the right corner of the box is that the bar is an eighth note short of the required two beats. The eighth note rest on beat 1 should be an A♭ quarter note. Note entry in PhotoScore is the same as mouse input in Sibelius (see Chapter 1).

1. Select the eighth rest on beat 1 of the Bassoon part.
2. Press the Delete key.
3. Click the [♩] key on the Keypad or press the 4 key on the numeric keypad. The cursor will change to an arrow to indicate that something will be entered at the next mouse click.
4. Position the arrow in the approximate position of the first beat of the measure, with the tip in the first space of the staff, and click to enter the quarter note. If your aim was a little off, press Esc, then click on the note and drag it to the first space.
5. Press Esc twice.

Entering a Repeat Barline in PhotoScore Lite

The last correction on this page is replacing the repeat barline at the beginning of the second system.

141

1. Right-click (CTRL-click on a Mac with a one-button mouse) just to the right of the key signature in the top staff of the second system to place the repeat.

2. Select Barline > Start Repeat from the contextual menu. The cursor will switch to an arrow.

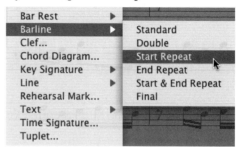

3. Click in that same cursor position to enter the repeat bar and press the Esc key.

Do not worry about the spacing while in PhotoScore. Sibelius will fix spacing problems when it opens the file. Take a good look at the rest of the music on the page to make sure everything else is in order. This would be a good time to save the document.

Loading Additional Pages

When scanning a multipage document, it is possible to link scanned pages in PhotoScore so the program understands that they are all part of the same score. There are several advantages to linking the files at this time. PhotoScore will follow the time signature(s) throughout the document, whereas loading the continuing pages separately will result in every measure being boxed in red because there is no time signature in the first measure of the page. PhotoScore will play back, via MIDI, all the pages as one continuous file (only a minimal advantage here since it can't properly transpose the score). PhotoScore can name the staves and apply those names to all staves that are linked together. Lastly, when the time comes to hand the score off to Sibelius, the piece will be imported as one file.

The three-page score is broken up into six scanned files. It is time to load the rest of the files into PhotoScore. Open them in the correct order, to ensure that when they're collectively sent into Sibelius, they get configured correctly as one continuous piece of music.

1. Select **File** > Open.
2. Select the graphic file *TEWpg1_2* and click Open.
3. Select **Read** > Place at End of Score to both read the scan and join it with the previous page(s).
4. Click Read in the Preferences dialog box. PhotoScore reads the file and creates another output window.

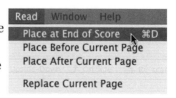

5. Repeat steps 1, 2, 3, and 4, loading the rest of the graphic files in order.

When you are finished, the Page display in the upper left corner of the window will display "6 of 6." You can navigate to any page by using the up and down arrows to the right of the page display.

Assigning Instruments to Staves

It is possible to add staff names to the score; these instrument assignments will transfer to Sibelius, allowing it to select the proper instruments for playback when the document is imported after editing. It is also helpful to have the staves labeled while editing in PhotoScore.

1. Use the page selection arrows to return to page 1.
2. Move the cursor to the left of the first staff in the first system.
3. Right-click (CTRL-click on a Mac with a one-button mouse) to select Instruments from the contextual menu.

4. In the Instruments dialog box, Staff 1 is already selected. Click the Rename button.

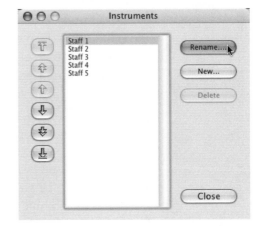

5. In the Rename Instrument dialog box, the Woodwind family is already selected. Choose Flute in the Available list.

6. Click Rename. Flute now appears in the instrument dialog box.

7. Select Staff 2 in the Instruments dialog box and click the Rename button.

8. Select Oboe from the Available list and click Rename.

9. Continue down the list, naming the Clarinet in B flat, Horn in F, and Bassoon staves. When naming the Bassoon staff, the Rename Instrument dialog box will still be displaying the Brass family even though Woodwind appears to be selected in the Section list. Click on Woodwind and the proper list will appear in the Available window.

10. Click Close in the Instrument dialog box after the Bassoon staff is named.

The staves of the score are now named properly, including the abbreviated names on the continuing systems, for all six pages. If you press the Play button at the top of the window, you'll hear the score playback on those instruments, minus the proper transpositions. For that you will need the full version of PhotoScore, or you can just wait until the score is imported into Sibelius. Before that happens, there are five more pages that need some corrections.

> Always import all the pages of a scanned score before assigning instruments to staves.

Fixing Page 2

The Clarinet and Horn key signatures await you: fix them first to get them out of the way.

1. Use the page navigation arrows to move down to page 2.
2. Repeat the steps for changing the key signature of the Clarinet and Horn staves.

There is one notation error to correct, a missing tie in the last measure of the Clarinet staff.

3. Position the cursor so the A quarter note on beat 1 of the Clarinet staff is highlighted.

4. Click to select it, and it will turn blue.

5. Click the key on the Keypad or press the Enter key on the computer's numeric keypad to enter the tie.

6. Press the Esc key to deselect the note.

When scanning scores, use the presence of a tie as a reason to check for any instruments playing the same rhythm that might be missing the tie.

Entering a Natural in PhotoScore

Do not worry about missing courtesy accidentals while in PhotoScore; they will be fixed in Sibelius. There is, however, a missing natural that must be fixed in the third measure, second beat of the Oboe staff.

1. Select the D sixteenth note at the beginning of the second beat in the third measure of the Oboe staff.

2. Click the ♮ key on the Keypad or press the 7 key on the computer's numeric keypad to enter the natural. Press Esc when finished.

3. Use the page navigation arrows to move down to page 3.

Fixing Page 3

A quick proof of this page turns up a few missing ties, once again in the Clarinet part. The end repeat bar is needed at the end of the fourth measure of the second system, and a double barline is needed at the end of the same system.

1. Begin by correcting the key signature on the Clarinet and Horn staves.

2. Repeat the steps for selecting a note and inserting a tie at the end of bar 3 in the first system and the end of bar 1 in the second system. Press Esc when you're finished.

The End Repeat barline and the double barline are inserted using the same basic procedure as for the Start Repeat barline, but since an existing barline is being modified, only the barline choices will be displayed in the contextual menu. The first and second ending brackets that appear over the measures will be added in Sibelius.

3. Right-click (CTRL-click on a Mac with a one-button mouse) on the barline at the end of the fourth measure in the second system

4. Select End Repeat from the contextual menu.

5. Move the cursor over one bar to the right and right-click (CTRL-click on a Mac with a one-button mouse) on the barline.

6. Select Double from the contextual menu.

The cautionary key signature will have to be entered at the end of the system after the double barline.

7. Position the cursor in the empty section of the Flute staff, to the right of the double barline you just added.

8. Right-click (CTRL-click on a Mac with a one-button mouse) and select Key Signature > Major Keys > D♭ from the contextual menu. The cursor will change to an arrow.
9. Click in the same space where you just clicked to enter the key signature.
10. Repeat steps 8 and 9 in the Oboe and Bassoon staves.
11. Repeat steps 8 and 9 for the Clarinet staff, entering E♭ for the key signature.
12. Repeat steps 8 and 9 for the Horn staff, entering A♭ for the key signature.
13. Use the page navigation arrows to move down to page 4.

Fixing Page 4

Begin corrections on this page by correcting the key signatures on the Clarinet and Horn staves, remembering to set the new key in the text box or pop-up menu.

Page 4 begins with a Start Repeat barline that, as on page 1, has been read as a regular barline with an empty measure preceding it.

1. Repeat the steps found in the "Fixing Page 1" section above for deleting the unnecessary barline and replacing it with the Start Repeat barline.
2. Use the page navigation arrows to move down to page 5.

Fixing Page 5

Begin corrections on this page with the key signatures on the Clarinet and Horn staves. Page 5 contains three measure overloads in the Oboe staves, indicated by the red boxes. All are dotted sixteenth notes that should be regular sixteenth notes, and each instance is at a different place in the measure.

1. Select the last note in measure 4, first system, of the Oboe staff.
2. Click the 　.　 key on the Keypad, or press the decimal key on the computer's numeric keypad to remove the dot.
3. Move down to the first measure of the Oboe staff in the second system. The same problem has occurred with the first sixteenth note on the second beat in the measure.

4. Repeat steps 1 and 2 to remove the dot.

5. Go to the third measure of the Oboe staff and repeat steps 1 and 2 to fix the dotted sixteenth note in that measure.

6. Move the cursor through each staff to locate all the missing ties. Use the Full Detail View window to check the original. After selecting the first note, hold down the ⌘ key (Mac) or the CTRL key (Win) and continue moving through the score, highlighting and selecting notes that require a tie. I count ten notes that require a tie.

7. When all the notes are selected, click the ⌐ key on the onscreen Keypad or press the Enter key on the computer's numeric keypad to enter all the missing ties simultaneously. Press Esc when finished.

8. Use the page navigation arrows to move down to page 6.

Fixing Page 6

The final page of the scan has some new twists and some old, favorite problems. When you open the graphic file, you may see the following warning. My advice is to continue and see if any problems do develop. In this case, the staff in question read better than some of the other staves on the page. If you do get an unusable page, rescan it.

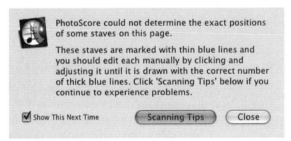

Once more, begin by correcting the key signatures on the Clarinet and Horn staves. Starting with the Flute staff, there is a missing dot in the second measure and a misread dynamic mark that has resulted in a dotted whole note in the last measure.

1. Select the D♭ eighth note in beat 1 of the second measure.

2. Click the ⬚.⬚ key on the Keypad, or press the decimal key on the computer's numeric keypad, to enter the dot.

3. Select the dotted whole note in the last measure.

4. Press the Delete key.

There are two ties missing in the staff as well. You can fix them now or use the ⌘ key (Mac) or the CTRL key (Win) to select all the notes on this page requiring a tie later.

Breaking a Beam in PhotoScore Lite

A beaming break is needed in the first measure of the Oboe staff.

1. Move the cursor to highlight and select the B♭ that starts the second beat of the Oboe staff.
2. Click the ▶ key on the Keypad two times, or press the + key on the computer's numeric keypad to select the Beams/Tremolos layout on the Keypad.
3. Press the ⊏ key on the Keypad or the 7 key on the computer's numeric keypad to correct the beaming.

There is a missing accidental on the first note in the fourth bar of the Oboe part.

4. Select the G♭ sixteenth note on beat 1 in the fourth bar of the Oboe part.
5. Click the ♮ key on the Keypad or press the 7 key on the computer's numeric keypad to enter the natural. Press Esc when finished.
6. Return to the first Keypad layout.

Entering a Rest in PhotoScore Lite

The clarinet is missing a sixteenth rest at the beginning of the first measure and a tie at the end of the second measure.

1. Click the ♪ key and the ⁊ ⁊ key on the Keypad or press the 2 and 0 keys on the computer's numeric keypad. The cursor will change to an arrow.
2. Position the cursor in the blank space preceding the B♭ sixteenth note on beat 1 in the staff and click to enter the rest.
3. Press Esc twice.

The Horn staff contains one more dotted sixteenth note. Repeat the steps from the page 5 fixes above to eliminate the dot.

4. If you've left the ties until later, now is later, so add as needed.
5. Enter the End Repeat at the end of the third measure. Review the steps in "Fixing Page 3" above if you need a refresher.

Time for a final save of the file. Now you will export the file to Sibelius, where the next phase of reconstructing "The Easy Winners" will take place.

Exporting from PhotoScore

There are three ways to export the scanned file to Sibelius, if your versions of PhotoScore and Sibelius are the same (Sibelius 4 and PhotoScore Lite or Pro 4). If you are still using an earlier version of PhotoScore, option 3 is the only one available. I recommend upgrading to the latest version of PhotoScore before continuing.

Option 1. A Sibelius icon will be visible in the menu bar in PhotoScore. To open the file in Sibelius, simply click the icon.

Option 2. Select **File** > Send to > Sibelius.

Option 3. Save and close the file in PhotoScore Lite. Launch Sibelius and choose the "Open another file" option. Select the scanned file and open it.

All three options will lead you to the Open PhotoScore File dialog box.

1. Under "Play using this device," select a playback device. Use the computer's internal synthesizer for now. Later in this chapter I will explain how to use the Kontakt Silver or Gold Player.
2. Check the "This is a transposing score" box.
3. Click the "Let Sibelius choose instruments" button.
4. Click OK.

Sibelius will open the file and from this point on, it will be just like any other Sibelius file created by the program.

Transposed Score or Concert Score

Sibelius understands that this is a transposed score and will play it back properly, but if you want to view it in concert pitch, that is easily done. In the toolbar is a button that you might think will put your piece into the key of Bb. Click on it with the mouse and it will toggle the score to Concert pitch. Click it again to return to a transposed score.

You can also toggle the score from the computer keyboard. The shortcut is Shift-⌘-T (Mac); Shift-CTRL-T (Win).

While concert scores are easier to use when writing and proofing, a transposed score shows the notes as they will appear in the parts. When it comes to positioning dynamics and text around these notes, transposed scores leave less work to be done when preparing parts for printing. That said, it is a personal preference, and you have the choice to do what suits you best.

Editing the Score in Sibelius

There is much work still to do, but it all begins with saving the file as a Sibelius document.

Select **File** > Save As and name the file "The_Easy_Winners."

Time to assess the situation and develop a plan of attack. Since the usual Quick Start process has been circumvented, there is no title, credits, tempo indication, or copyright text entered. All of the performance information, dynamics, and phrase markings will need to be entered, along with rehearsal numbers and ending brackets. The system bracket needs to include all five staves. The page formatting must be changed to get the score back to three pages. The good news is the score plays back properly now. The plan will be to start at the page level and work down to system issues, then finish with staff additions. Since everything to be added must be properly positioned, it is easier to place the little things properly when the big things are set first.

www.sibeliusbook.com

If you prefer to start at this point in the chapter, go to *www.sibeliusbook.com* and download the Chapter 7 folder. Open the file "7TheEasyWinners1.sib."

Re-creating the System Formatting

When a scan is imported, it may have some layout quirks. The recommended course of action is to clear all the formatting, and then re-create the scan by adding the system and page breaks individually, or by using the Make Layout Uniform plug-in.

1. Use the shortcut ⌘-A (Mac) or CTRL-A (Win) to select the whole document.
2. Use the shortcut ⌘-Shift-U (Mac) or CTRL-Shift-U (Win), or select **Layout** > Format > Unlock Format.

The example will now take up two pages and one system of the third page. Refer to the original example at the beginning of the chapter or the printout to aid in the reconstruction. Look for multiple systems with the same number of measures in them. This is an opportunity to use the plug-in to format several systems at once.

3. Select bars 1 through 16. Only one staff need be selected for the plug-in to work.
4. Select **Plug-ins** > Others > Make Layout Uniform.
5. With 4 already entered for "bars per system," enter 3 in the "systems per page" field, as well as the "systems on first page" field.

Make Layout Uniform

4   bars per system

○ Do not break pages
● Break pages using:

3   systems per page

3   systems on first page

☑ Lock format   ☑ Ignore pickup bar
● Format selection   ☐ Break at rehearsal marks
○ Format entire score   ☐ Break at special barlines

(Help)   (Cancel)   (OK)

6. Click OK.

The rest of the document alternates between a system of five measures and a system of four measures. These will need to be done individually.

7. Select the double barline at the end of bar 21 and press the Return/Enter key.
8. Select the barline at the end of bar 25 and press the Return/Enter key.
9. Select the barline at the end of bar 30 and press the Return/Enter key.

The last two systems should be okay, as the default spacing creates a system of four measures and a system of five, respectively. With the layout set, lock it so nothing moves during the rest of the editing.

10. Use the shortcut ⌘-A (Mac) or CTRL-A (Win) to select the whole document.
11. Use the shortcut ⌘-Shift-L (Mac) or CTRL-Shift-L (Win), or select **Layout** > Format > Lock Format.
12. Press Esc.

If time is not a factor, try not to leave just a few measures at the top of the last page of a document. Full pages give the document a professional look. Achieving this may involve spreading out or tightening up some systems. In my experience it's most often the latter. This does take some time, but it is one more detail in making your work look like professional engraving.

Creating Title and Page Text

Sibelius has a lot of text categories, and it is important to be aware of all of them and enter text properly so the program handles it properly. Since the title is usually created during the Quick Start process, it is something you'll rarely enter otherwise.

1. Select **Create** > Text > Title. Click at the top of page 1 and a blinking cursor will appear.
2. Type "The Easy Winners" and press Esc.

The Composer text is just below the title in the same menu.

1. Select **Create** > Text > Composer.
2. Click on the page, and the cursor will appear on the right margin above the music.
3. Type "by Scott Joplin" and press the Return key. Type "Arranged by Vince Leonard" and press Esc. It will turn purple.
4. Click on the Composer text, hold the button down, and drag it above the Flute part. Leave some additional room for the accent and slur that will be added later.

If you are creating this piece in a classroom or lab setting, repeat the above steps, selecting Lyricist instead of Composer, and type "Entered by (your name)."

The tempo indication rounds out text at the top of the first page of the score. Tempo is located in the Text submenu under Create as well, but there is a shortcut, so take advantage of it.

1. Use the shortcut Option-⌘-T (Mac); Alt-CTRL-T (Win) and click above the time signature to get the blinking cursor.
2. Type "Not Fast."
3. Press Esc twice when finished.

Move to the bottom of page 1 where the copyright notice will be added. Again, begin with the Create menu, but you'll be digging a little deeper this time.

1. Select **Create** > Text > Other System Text > Copyright.
2. Click on the page and the blinking cursor will appear at the bottom of page 1.
3. Type "Copyright © [Option-G (Mac) or CTRL-Shift-C (Win)] 2006 by Vince Leonard" and press Return.
4. Type "All Rights Reserved" and press Esc twice.

Copyright © 2006 by Vince Leonard
All Rights Reserved

Move over to the top of page 2 to add the continuing page header.

1. Select **Create** > Text > Other System Text > Header (after first page).
2. Click on the second page and the blinking cursor will appear.
3. Type "The Easy Winners." Press Esc twice when finished.

The page adjustments are complete. The next step is system adjustments. The bracket must extend down to the Bassoon, the repeat brackets need to be inserted, and rehearsal numbers need to be added. At this point the piece is no different than a piece that was played in or step entered.

 Any time the word "complete" enters your mind, it should immediately be followed by "save."

Editing the System Bracket

1. Click on the system bracket. It turns purple.
2. Click on the bottom end of the bracket and hold the mouse button down. Drag the bracket down to underneath the Bassoon staff and release the mouse button.
3. Press Esc.

This is a global change, so you will not have to do each system individually.

Adding the Repeat Endings

Ending brackets are no different in a score than in a single-staff or grand-staff document. They only need to be entered on the top staff to apply to all parts. It is possible to display them on several staves of larger scores, but only one occurrence is necessary here.

1. Click on bar 20.
2. Press the L key to access the Lines selection dialog box.
3. Select the first ending bracket from the right column.
4. Click OK.
5. Select the handle on the right side of the bracket and drag it to the left, so it is over the thick barline. The goal is to have a small gap between the first and second ending brackets.

6. Press the Esc key.
7. In bar 21 click on the first note, then Shift-click on the last item in the measure, the eighth rest.
8. Press the L key to access the Lines selection dialog box.
9. From the System Lines list on the right, select the second ending bracket with the open right end.
10. Click OK.
11. Use the right arrow key on the keyboard to nudge the second ending to the right a little if the right end of the first ending and the left end of the second ending are overlapping.

 The reason for selecting the music in bar 21 rather than the whole measure as usual has to do with a little quirk in Sibelius 4. When the first ending was inserted in bar 20, the right end of the bracket extended beyond the end of the measure. If I had entered the second ending by selecting the whole measure, the top line of the ending bracket would have extended into bar 22. This would have become a problem in all of the parts, where the ending bracket would extend over a system break onto the next system. The same problem can be found in hairpins that extend past the barline. This issue is on the list to be fixed in a future update of Sibelius.

12. Select the Flute staff in bars 36 and 37.
13. Press the L key and select the first ending bracket. The bracket will cover as many measures as selected.
14. Drag the right end of the bracket back so that it is over the thick barline.

15. Select bar 38 and enter the second ending bracket. Adjust the bracket positions so they do not touch. Press Esc when finished.

Creating Boxed Measure Numbers

You can place boxed rehearsal letters simply by selecting the desired measure and using the shortcut ⌘-R (Mac) or CTRL-R (Win) (see Chapter 4). If you prefer bar numbers instead of letters, all you have to do is make one small change in Engraving Rules so the same keystroke combination creates boxed bar numbers.

1. Select **House Style** > Engraving Rules.
2. Select "Rehearsal Marks" in the left column.
3. Under the Appearance heading, choose "Bar number" and click OK.

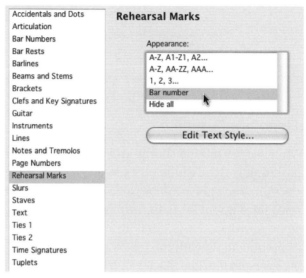

4. Select measure 5.
5. Use the shortcut ⌘-R (Mac); CTRL-R (Win) to enter the boxed rehearsal number.
6. Select and add the boxed rehearsal number in bars 13 and 22.
7. Press Esc when finished.

Staff Edits

The system adjustments are complete. It is now time to turn your attention to the performance information required on each staff. Entering performance marks in a score means only one thing: there are a lot of them, and they all have to line up neatly and not collide with the music or one another.

Adding Cautionary Accidentals

There is one last detail in correcting notes: adding any cautionary accidentals to the score. There is a plug-in to handle this task, but it works only staff by staff. If you ever want a cautionary accidental to appear in another staff to nip any confusion in the bud, it must be entered manually.

1. Select **Plug-ins** > Accidentals > Add Cautionary Accidentals.
2. No changes are necessary, so click OK. Any notes affected will be shaded in yellow.

3. Click OK.

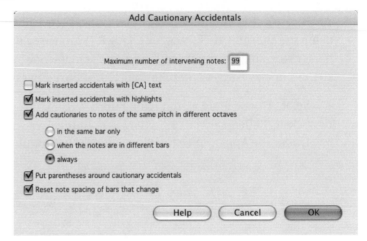

Adjusting Key Signature Positions

While we are talking sharps and flats, there is a little problem with the positioning of the cautionary key signature at the end of measure 21. The key signature appears to be right-justified, so the right end of the vertical stack lines up rather than the left side as normal. This situation did not come up when the original arrangement was created, so it must have something to do with the file being scanned. No matter what the cause, the problem must be fixed.

- Select the key signature on the Flute staff and press the left arrow key on the computer keyboard one time. The key signature will left justify at the correct position.

Entering Articulations in a Score

Have the printout you created for scanning handy or the printed example at the beginning of this chapter marked, as you will be referring to it frequently while you add articulations, dynamics, and slurs.

When adding performance information, I always begin with marks closest to the notes and work outward so articulations are first in line. A lot of you are probably looking forward to clicking each individual note and selecting the correct articulation from the keypad, but we will not be entering them that way here! Please try to contain your disappointment. There are several methods, and each will be demonstrated. All should find their way into your regular bag of tricks as the situation requires in your future work.

If you are at the end of the piece, use the Navigator window to return to the beginning or use the shortcut Option-⌘-G (Mac) or Alt-CTRL-G (Win) and type 1 for the bar. Click OK and press Esc. You can also press the Home key on the computer keyboard.

Adding Articulations to a Vertical Stack of Notes

The first method is to select a vertical column of notes that require an articulation.

1. In bar 1 of the Oboe staff, click on the E♭ eighth note on the first beat.
2. Shift-click on the E♭ eighth note in the Bassoon staff, also on the first beat.
3. Click the  key on the Keypad (at the top of the Keypad).

The staccato mark is entered for all three notes.

4. Repeat the selection procedure for the second eighth note in the bar and enter the accent.

Adding Articulations to Noncontiguous Notes

In the second measure you can take it one step further.

1. ⌘-Click (Mac); CTRL-click (Win) on all the noteheads requiring an accent, all the sixteenth notes in the first beat of the bar. Six notes should be selected, as indicated by the blue noteheads.
2. Click the > key on the Keypad computer's numeric keypad.

The notes to which you apply articulations can be non-contiguous. This requires a lot of precise clicking, so I'd suggest limiting yourself to notes that are visible on the screen or other small group so you don't mis-click and accidentally deselect five minutes' worth of notes.

3. Use ⌘-click (Mac) or CTRL-click (Win) to select the notes needing staccato dots in the second measure to add them.

Adding Articulations to Entire Measures Vertically

In measure 4, every note needs an accent.

1. Click on the Flute staff in bar 4 so the whole bar is selected.
2. Shift-click on the Bassoon staff in bar 4 so that all staves are selected.
3. Click the > key on the Keypad.

This method also works horizontally.

1. Select bar 5 of the Bassoon staff.

2. Shift-click in bar 11 of the Bassoon staff, so that all measures between 5 and 11 are selected.
3. Click the · key on the keypad.

Your repertoire now contains five ways of inputting articulations:

- during note entry
- selecting individual notes
- selecting vertical stacks of notes
- selecting noncontiguous groups of notes
- selecting whole measures vertically or horizontally

Entering Slurs in a Score

You've already learned how to enter slurs, and the fact that this is a score does not change the process at all. The trick is learning how many you *don't* have to enter. Begin by entering the slurs on the most active part that has the most in common with other instruments playing at that passage in the score. On page 1 of the score, the most active part is the Oboe.

1. Enter the slurs for the Oboe staff in bars 1 through 12.
2. Click the C eighth note in the Oboe staff on the first beat of measure 1.
3. Shift-click the A♭ eighth note on the down beat of measure 4, also in the Oboe staff.

4. Select **Edit** > Filter > Slurs. Only the slurs will remain blue.
5. Option-click (Mac); Alt-click (Win) on the D eighth note on the Clarinet staff in measure 1 to paste the slurs.
6. Press Esc.

To make the slur in measure 1 go above the staff:

7. Click on the slur in bar 1 to select it.
8. Press the X key to flip the slur above the staff.

The slur over the staff in bars 3 and 4 needs to have a slightly higher arc to clear the last sixteenth-note beam at the end of bar 3.

9. Click on the slur in bar 3 to select it.
10. Press the up arrow key on the computer keyboard one time to add arc to the slur.

Moving out from most active to least active, copy the slurs needed for the Flute.

11. Click on the B flat sixteenth note in measure 2 of the Oboe staff to select it.
12. Shift-click the A flat eighth note on the down beat of measure 4, also in the Oboe staff.
13. Repeat step 4 above to filter the slurs.
14. Paste them into the Flute part.
15. Flip the slur in measure 3 and readjust the text for the credits if necessary.

This method is not limited to copying and pasting one staff at a time. Look at the slurs on the last two sixteenths in measure 2. It is possible to select both the Oboe and Clarinet staves and copy both slurs and past them into the Horn and Bassoon staves.

1. Select the last two sixteenth notes in the Oboe and Clarinet staves.
2. Filter the slurs.
3. Option-click (Mac); Alt-click (Win) the F sixteenth note in the Horn staff to paste the slurs.
4. Finish the slurs in the Bassoon part for bars 1 through 4.

You may be looking at this example and thinking it would be really cool if you could have done the same thing with the articulations that you just did with the slurs. Sibelius can take you a step further and copy either or both at the same time using a plug-in. Measures 5 through 10 will serve for this demonstration, but the articulation needs to be entered first.

5. Enter the articulation in the oboe staff for bars 5 and 9.

 The next steps involve a plug-in whose actions are not undoable using the Edit menu's Undo command. Save before using plug-ins or completing any action that is not undoable. Then if you make an error, it is easy to close without saving, then reopen the document without losing any other work.

Using the Copy Articulations and Slurs Plug-in

1. Select bar 5 through the B flat in beat 1 of bar 11 of the Oboe staff.

2. Select **Plug-ins** > Notes and Rests > Copy Articulations and Slurs. Click Yes in the alert dialog box.

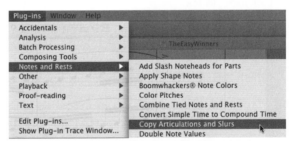

3. In the "Choose an action" menu, choose "Copy to clipboard."
4. Click OK. The slurs and articulations are now copied.

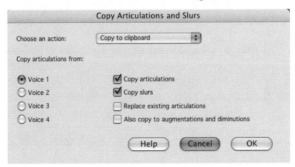

5. Click OK.

6. The alert dialog box lists the steps for two different options. I want option 2. Click OK to return to the Copy Articulations and Slurs dialog box.

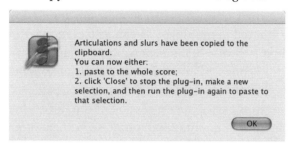

7. Click Close. Clicking OK at this point would enter the articulations and slurs anywhere in the score where a rhythmic match is found. A powerful feature, but not what I want.

8. Select the same region in the Clarinet staff, bar 5 through the first beat of 11.

9. Select **Plug-ins** > Notes and Rests > Copy Articulations and Slurs.

10. From the "Choose an action" menu, select "Paste to selection."

11. Click OK. The slurs and articulations will be pasted into the selected region. The plug-in dialog box will appear again. Click Cancel.

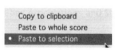

Refer to the completed example and use all of the techniques you just learned to finish all the articulations and slurs for the rest of the piece. Refer back to the tutorial steps if you are not sure about a specific technique or step.

Entering Expressions and Techniques in a Score

Entering Expressions in a score is all about copying and pasting. Expressions cannot be entered in multiples, as can articulations. However, they can be very easily copied without the use of filters or a plug-in. There are two possibilities for pasting copied text in the score: Option-click (Mac) or Alt-click (Win) or Shift-Option-click (Mac) or Shift-Alt-click (Win). The former method pastes the expression at the location of the cursor. The latter pastes the expression at the same proximity to the note as the original, and is helpful in maintaining a precise vertical line when copying text in scores. You are free to use whichever method you prefer. The Shift-Option-click (Mac) or Shift-Alt-click (Win) method will be used here.

1. Enter the forte in the first measure of the Oboe staff.
2. Press Esc once. The blinking cursor will disappear, but the Expression will still be highlighted.
3. Use Shift-Option-click (Mac) or Shift-Alt-click (Win) and click on the first note in the Clarinet staff to paste the Expression.
4. Repeat the paste in the Bassoon staff in measure 2 for the entrance of the Flute and Horn.

Continue through the score, entering Expressions and Techniques using copy and paste wherever possible.

Entering Hairpins in a Score

Hairpins (crescendos and decrescendos) are reproducible much like the Expressions that often precede and/or follow them. Once entered, they can be copied by selecting one individually and using the Copy and Paste commands, or any number of them can be copied at once using a filter.

1. Select all the sixteenth notes in bar 3 of the Flute staff.
2. Press the H key to enter the hairpin for the passage.
3. Click the hairpin to select it.
4. Use the shortcut Shift-Option-click (Mac) or Shift-Alt-click (Win) to paste the hairpin at the first sixteenth note in bar 3 of the Oboe staff.
5. Continue pasting this hairpin to the rest of the instrument parts in bar 3.

 When entering hairpins close to a barline, it is easier to stop a little short and drag the end closer to the barline than to have the hairpin extend past the barline and have to drag the end back.

6. Continue entering the hairpins and use the copy-and-paste method when appropriate.

Cleaning Up the Space Between Staves

There are times when the space between the staves fills up, and collisions occur. One such instance is in bar 3 between the Flute and Oboe staves. To clean this up, move the hairpin up closer to the Flute staff.

1. Select the hairpin under the Flute staff.
2. Use the up arrow key on the computer keyboard to nudge it up as close as possible to the staff without touching it. About eight or nine keystrokes should do it.
3. Select the slur over the Oboe staff.
4. Use the down arrow key on the computer keyboard to reduce the height of the slur's arc. This time, use six or seven keystrokes.

Taking the time to clean up situations like this will make your scores easier to read at any size. Continue through the score and look for any other places where a nudge will help clean up the space between staves or fix a spot where a collision occurs.

System Dividers (Optional)

When more than one score system is on a page, some publishers choose to add system dividers, two thick lines at the left and right ends of the space between systems. I did not use them in "The Easy Winners" score, but if you want to add them to your version, here are the steps.

1. Select **House Style** > Engraving Rules.
2. Select Instruments in the left column.
3. Under the System Separators heading, enter 5 for the number of staves.
4. Check the "Draw right separator" box.
5. Click OK.

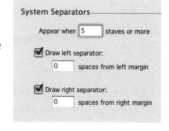

Tempo Settings for Playback

With all the elements entered, it is finally time to hear a playback, but before you press the Play button, a word about tempo. The Tempo slider in the playback controls is set for $\quarternote = 120$, a blistering pace for Joplin. The Tempo slider is not the most precise controller for setting a tempo, so it may be difficult to get it exactly right. Sibelius will read metronomic markings input using Tempo text entries, but there is none in the current tempo indication. There are times when a writer will not want to indicate an exact tempo but some basic decision has to be made, just to hear a reasonable play-back. The solution is to create a second tempo indication with a metronomic marking in it and either hide it altogether or have it displayed only on the score.

1. Press Esc and select bar 1 of the score.
2. Use the shortcut Option-⌘-T (Mac) or Alt-CTRL-T (Win) to create a new tempo indication.
3. Click on the page to activate the blinking cursor if it doesn't appear.
4. Use the shortcut ⌘-4 (on the keypad) (Mac) or CTRL-4 (Win) (on the computer keypad) to enter the quarter note, or right-click (Mac and Win); CTRL-click (on a Mac with a one-button mouse) and select it from the pop-up list.
5. Type "= 84" to complete the marking. Press Esc once.
6. Nudge with the up arrow key, or drag the mark above the existing "Not fast" indi-cation. It must remain vertically aligned with the beginning of the music to take effect from the start.
7. Use the shortcut ⌘-Shift-H (Mac); CTRL-Shift-H (Win) to hide the new tempo indication.

Now you have the best of both worlds—a tempo setting that is not a visible tempo setting.

The Mixer Window

Playing back scores is not only a useful tool for proofing the piece but also provides instant feedback for those who wish to experiment. Recently there has been a great leap in the quality of sounds available for playback. Acoustic instrument samples mar-keted by Gary Garritan and East West/Quantum Leap offer new levels of realism for composers creating demos or mock-ups. Playing back ensemble scores will ultimately lead to an exploration of placing the instruments on the virtual stage using the Mixer window.

• Press M on the keyboard to display the Mixer window if it is not visible.

The Mixer window is divided into two sections. On the left are the controls that resem-ble a mixing console. Each staff in the score is assigned a channel. Every Sibelius file has one slider (the first) reserved for a Click track. The right side of the window con-tains instrument-specific settings. Click on the instrument name below each fader to see the settings for that specific instrument.

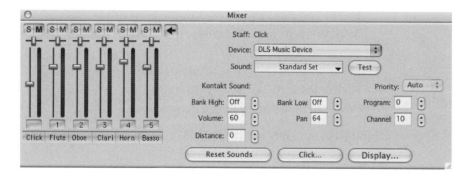

Panning

Panning is the placement of sounds in a stereo field. In order to hear the full effect of this part of the lesson, listen to the playback on stereo speakers or headphones. The woodwind quintet sets up in a U shape with either the Bassoon or the Horn in F at the center. The Flute and Oboe are to the left of center, the Clarinet and Horn or Bassoon (depending on which instrument is centered) to the right of center. The instruments Sibelius creates already have panning applied, but the positions match their placement in an orchestra.

1. If the Mixer window is not currently displayed, press the M key to display it.
2. Click on Bassoon below the sixth fader. The number displayed above the name is the MIDI channel. The settings for the Bassoon will appear on the right side of the Mixer window.

Bassoon staff Pan slider

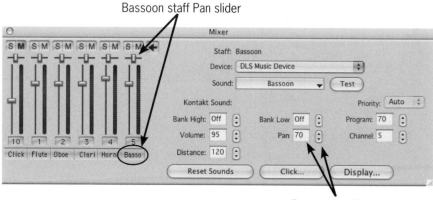

Pan number field and arrow

3. Use the Pan slider to center the Bassoon. The value of the Pan setting should read 64 (the center point in the MIDI 0-to-127 numbering system). The number can also be entered by using the up and down arrows next to the Pan setting box or by typing the number into the number field.
4. Select Horn in the Instrument strip. The settings to the right will change to indicate the Horn's default settings.

5. Use any of the Pan controls to position the Horn to the right of the Bassoon. Use increments of ten for starters; this can be adjusted to your own taste later. Set the Pan value of the Horn to 74.
6. Use any of the Pan controls to position the Clarinet at 84.
7. Set the Oboe to 54 and the Flute to 44.
8. Press the Play button in the Playback window to listen to the piece.

If you wish to make any adjustments, make them and try playing the score back again.

Playback Using Kontakt Silver or Gold Instruments

It's time to take MIDI playback up a few notches using Kontakt Silver or Gold. This section will show how to load instruments into the Kontakt Player, so Sibelius can use them instead of the computer's internal synth or sound card for playback.

1. Select **Play** > Playback and Input Devices.
2. Under the Device heading, select Kontakt Player. Windows users, click Yes; Mac users, just click on the word Kontakt. Windows users: always ensure that only one device has the word Yes selected. Clicking on the word No will make it turn to Yes.
3. If you have multiple sound sets that use Kontakt Player, check under the Sound Set heading to make sure Kontakt Gold or Silver (depending on which you own) is indicated.
4. Click OK.

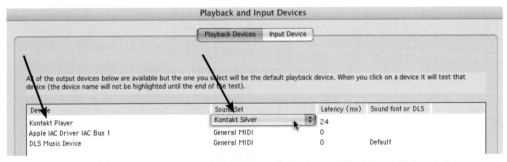

5. In the Mixer window, click the Reset Sounds button. Sibelius will load the correct sounds into the Kontakt Player. Click Yes if a dialog box appears.

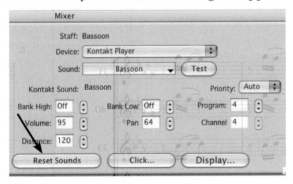

6. To view the Kontakt Player, select **Window** > Kontakt Player, or use the shortcut Option-⌘-O (Mac); Alt-CTRL-O (Win). The graphic below is the Gold Player. The Silver Player differs only in the number of slots for sounds: eight instead of Gold's thirty-two.

7. Press Play in the Playback window. There will be a short pause while each of the instrument samples are loaded into the computer's RAM. Once selected, these samples will be automatically loaded when the file is opened, or (if you are work-ing with multiple files open) when the file is reselected. Sibelius dumps the sam-ples when switching files to save RAM usage on your computer.

Time to save.

www.sibeliusbook.com

If you prefer to start at this point in the chapter, go to *www.sibeliusbook.com* and download the Chapter 7 folder. Open the file *7TheEasyWinners2.sib*.

Dynamic Parts

Now that all the kinks have been hammered out in playback, it is time to ready "The Easy Winners" for an unsuspecting live ensemble to reveal the secret of Dynamic Parts (no, they are not called Dynamic Parts just because they have dynamic marks in them).

1. In the toolbar at the top of the screen, click on the Dynamic Parts menu, where Full Score is currently selected. A pop-up menu will appear with each instrument in the score listed.
2. Select Flute from the menu.
3. From the Zoom menu, select Fit Page.

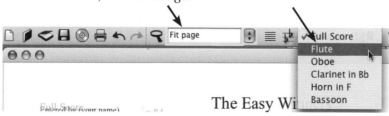

The Flute part (like all the other parts in the score) was created at the time the document was created. When creating a document, you can view parts at any time by selecting them from the menu, or by selecting a measure and hitting the shortcut letter W. Hitting W again toggles between a part and the full score.

Color My Part

Looking at the Flute part, a few differences from viewing the score will be obvious. The part window uses a different paper texture than the score to visually enhance the difference between the two. Some objects will be colored orange to indicate that they are in a different position than where they were placed in the score. The following is a demonstration of how objects are linked between score and parts.

1. Select the hairpin beneath measure 3 of the Flute part. This had to be moved to avoid a collision with the slur in the Oboe part.
2. Select **Layout** > Reset Position to return the hairpin to its default entry position under the staff.

The hairpin will turn orange to indicate that it is no longer in the same position as it is in the score. Sibelius will be able to track the object in case it is altered in some way.

3. Press the W key. This brings the score window to the front from any part window.
4. Select the left side of the hairpin in measure 3 of the Flute staff once to select it, and once more to display the handle on the closed end.
5. Drag the left end of the hairpin to the start of the second beat of the measure.
6. Press the W key to return to the Flute part. The hairpin there has matched the shape but has not moved from its new vertical position.
7. Use the shortcut ⌘-Z (Mac); CTRL-Z (Win) to undo the change. The slur reverts to its original length.
8. Press W to return to the Score window. The slur has reverted to its original length here at the same time.

It is possible to drag an object too far away from the score position and break the link. Should you do this, a red dashed line will appear between the object and the position to which it was originally attached. If not corrected, any changes made to the score would not be reflected in the part, because Sibelius no longer recognizes it as belonging to the place where the change was made.

Are You in a Hurry?

Take the time to select each of the five parts from the Dynamic Parts menu and look at their condition. Except for some collisions with the text at the top of the page, all could be printed and on the player's music stand right now. Those collisions might take a whole minute to clean up, so these parts could be on the stand in the time it takes the quintet to get ready to play. I could end the chapter here and send you off to round up a quintet to play the piece, but there are a few finer points of page layout and positioning that are worth knowing. Return to the Flute part and begin taking the parts to the next level.

Just as with the score, it helps to look over all the parts and make decisions about what elements need tweaking and how you will accomplish each task. More space is needed between music in the top staff and the tempo and credits text in several parts. I'd like to have rehearsal numbers beneath every bar. The copyright text looks a little too large in the part and the page size itself looks different than the score. Each part will likely contain a few items that need to be repositioned, due to score placement requirements.

Check to make sure the page size for the parts is correct. In the example, even though the score was set to letter size, all of the parts were set to A4. This is an anomaly due to the score starting life as a scan.

1. Use the shortcut ⌘-D (Mac); CTRL-D (Win) to view the Document Setup dialog box.
2. Under the size heading, select "Letter" from the "Page size" pop-up menu.

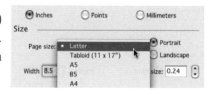

Changing the Measure Number Display for Parts

I have found few greater time savers in rehearsal than having bar numbers on every measure. My preference is to have them underneath the staff on the left side of the measure.

1. Select **House Style** > Engraving Rules.
2. Select Bar Numbers in the left column.
3. In the "Bar number frequency" list, choose "Every bar." "Center range on multirest" becomes active and checked at the same time.
4. Check "Show at start of sections."
5. Click the "After clef" button.
6. Check "Show range of bars on multi-rests."
7. Click the Edit Text Style button.

Sibelius allows bar numbers to be a different size in the parts.

8. Under the size heading, change Parts to 9 using the pop-up menu or by typing "9" in the number entry field.
9. Click the "Vertical Posn" tab.

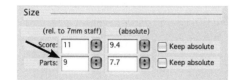

10. Under the Multiple Positions heading, uncheck "Top staff."
11. Click OK twice.

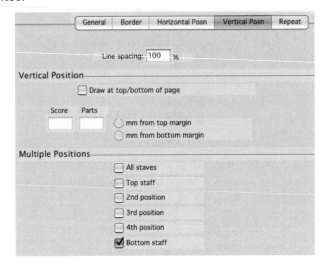

At this point there should be no bar numbers displayed at all.

12. Select **House Style** > System Object Positions.
13. Select "Below bottom staff." Both "Flute" and "Below bottom staff" should be highlighted. Do not uncheck "Flute" and click OK—Sibelius will likely crash!
14. Click OK.

The bar numbers are now displayed below the staff at the beginning of every bar, with

the exception of a multirest, where it is centered under the bar. Selecting both options in System Object Positions has had the unwanted effect of duplicating the tempo and boxed measure numbers, so they display both above and below the staff. Both objects will require one last tweak.

15. Select **House Style** > Edit Text Styles.
16. Select "Rehearsal marks" and click Edit.
17. Click the "Vertical Posn" tab.
18. Under the Multiple Positions heading, uncheck all but "Top staff."
19. Click OK.
20. Select Tempo in the Edit Text Styles list.
21. Repeat steps 17, 18, and 19 above and click OK to return to the Flute part.

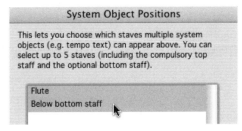

Moving Header Text

Before moving the Composer text, take note of its position in relation to the title. The names are just under the baseline of the title text. This is standard practice in the publishing industry. When the Composer text is raised, raise the title as well, so it is still above the top name.

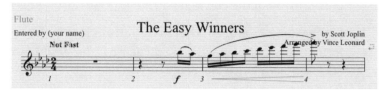

1. Click anywhere on the Composer text to select it.
2. Drag it toward the top of the page so it clears the accent over the A in the music.
3. Press Esc to deselect the text.
4. Select the title text and drag it up so its relative position to the credits is the same as before the credits were raised.

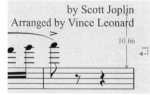

> If you want to see the distance amount displayed, as in the above graphic, select **View** > Rulers > Selection Rulers to display them.

Changing the Number of Measures on a Line

Sibelius does carry any system breaks made in the score over to the parts. These breaks may or may not be correct for the part layout. Manually entered system breaks are indicated by a blue arrow icon at the end of the system with the break. In the Flute part, these can be found at the end of bars 12 and 25. In the Flute part, I want to move bar 22 down to the system below, where the system break has created a three-measure line. I also want to move bar 18 down one system.

1. Select the double barline at the end of bar 21. This will also work if the repeat bar is selected.
2. Press the Return (Mac); Enter (Win) key or Select **Layout** > Break > System Break.

Sibelius has given me a "two for the price of one" bonus here. In addition to moving bar 22, bar 18 has moved down to fill out that system in the same process. There is an orange arrow at the end of bar 21 to indicate the manual system break just entered.

In measures 29 and 30, there is a hairpin leading to a forte that is colliding with the measure number of bar 30. At a quick glance this could be confused for a mezzo forte, so some space needs to be put between objects for clarity.

1. Select the hairpin, then Shift-click the forte to select both objects.
2. Use the shortcut Shift-⌘-P (Mac); Shift-CTRL-P (Win) to reset the objects to their default positions.
3. Press Esc when finished.

The vertical repeat brackets over the end repeat bar in the bottom system need a little gap between them.

The copyright text seems a bit large and draws too much focus when reading the bottom staff. Sibelius allows text to be set to a different size for score and parts. This is done using "Edit Text Styles" in the House Style menu.

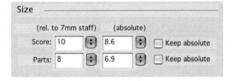

Changing Text Size in a Part (Part 2)

This is the same procedure used earlier with the bar numbers, only applied to the copyright. Any text type can be set for two sizes. This will be more of an issue in larger ensemble scores where there is a greater difference in size between score and parts.

1. Use the shortcut Option-Shift-⌘-T (Mac); Alt-Shift-CTRL-T (Win) to open the "Edit Text Styles" window.
2. Select Copyright from the list and click Edit.
3. Under the Size heading for Parts, select 8 from the pop-up menu or type "8" into the number entry field.
4. Click OK, and click Close.

Take It to the House

This chapter illustrates a key to working with Sibelius: developing the mindset of doing a task as few times as possible by using one of the copy-and-paste functions. Having to perform the same task to change the bar number display in every score might make you think twice about doing it at all, especially if you're close to deadline. This is an ideal situation for creating a House Style for parts. A House Style can be imported into any document, including this one, for the other four parts left to edit.

1. Select **House Style** > Export House Style.
2. Enter a name for the style, one you will recognize and remember.
3. Click OK to save.

171

Navigating Between Parts

With the Flute part done, it is time to move on to the Oboe part. Before returning to the Dynamic Parts menu to select the Oboe, try the following shortcut.

1. Use the shortcut Option-⌘-~ (Mac—the last key is the tilde key (pronounced TILL-day) in the upper right-hand corner of the keyboard) or CTRL-Alt-Tab (Win) to move to the next part below in score order. Using this shortcut allows you to toggle from dynamic part to dynamic part.

Now import the House Style just created.

2. Select **House Style** > Import House Style.
3. Select the House Style you just created from the list and click OK.

The Oboe part's appearance changes in several ways: the page size has been reset to letter, rehearsal numbers are now on every measure, and the layout of the music has compressed to six lines. I liked the layout of the Flute part and how it filled up the page, even though there was a seven-bar gathered rest at measure 5. If I could only copy that layout and then adjust where needed—back to the Flute part!

4. Use the shortcut Shift-Option-⌘-~ (Mac) or Shift-Ctrl-Alt-Tab (Windows) to move to the next part above in score order. Now you are back to the flute part.

Copying Layout Between Parts

Sibelius allows for the copying of layouts between parts using the Parts window.

1. Use the shortcut Option-⌘-R (Mac) or Alt-CTRL-R (Windows) to display the Parts window. It may also be selected using the Windows menu or the Parts window button on the toolbar at the top of your Sibelius screen.
2. Select Oboe in the Parts window list as the part you are copying to.
3. Click the Copy Part Layout button, third from left, at the bottom of the Parts window. Click Yes.
4. Use the shortcut Option-⌘-~ (Mac); CTRL-Alt-Tab (Win) to return to the Oboe part.

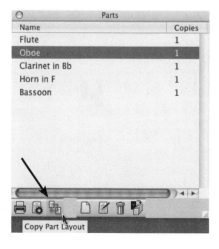

There are some new icons on the Oboe part, orange opposing arrows over each bar-line. This is a result of copying the layout and serve as an indication that those bars are to be kept together. It does not mean the layout cannot be changed.

Creating More Oboe Room

Job one will be moving the tempo text above the accent over the C in bar 1.

1. Select the tempo text.
2. Drag it above the accent, so it clears it with a little room to spare. The hidden metronome marking can remain where it is, since it is hidden and will not print.
3. Select the "Entered by" text.
4. Drag the "Entered by" text up, so that it is midway between the Oboe instrument name and the tempo text.

Grouping Measures into a System

The Oboe part now resembles the Flute part. In a few places, however, that is not a good thing. Some systems have too many measures and some could have more. The Oboe part differs in several ways: the seven measures' rest that the Flute had at bar 5, fewer notes at bar 22, and fewer ledger lines all around. I want to keep measure 5 where it is, so the beginning of the repeat is at the start of a line, rather than move it up to the first system. I also want to keep the first and second endings where they are, and reposition the music in between those points.

1. Select bars 11 through 16.

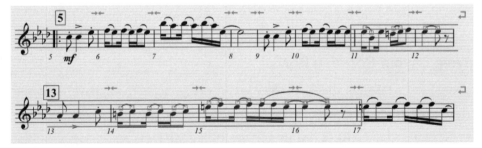

2. Select **Layout** > Format > Make Into System.

 When selecting a command using the menus, always look for a shortcut for the command, so that next time you can bypass the menu.

Measure 17 is left on a system of its own, but not for long.

3. Select bars 17 through 21.
4. Use the shortcut Option-Shift-M (Mac); Alt-Shift-M (Win) for grouping the selected measures into a system.
5. Select bars 22 through 26.

6. Use the shortcut Option-Shift-M (Mac); Alt-Shift-M (Win) to group the measures into a system.

The Oboe layout is complete. Since there were few problems with spacing between the Oboe and Clarinet in the score, only a few of the expressions had to be repositioned, and none of them looks noticeably out of position now. If you would like to check, try this technique.

1. Use the shortcut ⌘-A (Mac) or CTRL-A (Win) to Select All.
2. Select **Edit** > Filter > Expression Text.
3. Use the shortcut Shift-⌘-P (Mac) or Shift-CTRL-P (Win) to reset the position to the default. Any moved expressions will return to their "correct" position.
4. Repeat steps 1 through 3, selecting Hairpins from the Filter menu to adjust their position back to the default.

Pop Quiz

Didn't anyone tell you there would be quizzes? What is the shortcut to move down to the Clarinet part?

1. Use the shortcut Option-⌘-~ (Mac) or CTRL-Alt-Tab (Win) to move to the Clarinet part. (Okay, who peeked?)
2. Import the part House Style created on p. 171.

The Clarinet and Oboe parts are nearly identical, more so than the Flute and Oboe. Copying the layout will save a lot of time here. How do you copy the layout?

1. Use the shortcut Shift-Option-⌘-~ (Mac) or Shift-CTRL-Alt-Tab (Win) to return to the Oboe part.
2. Select "Clarinet in B♭" in the Parts window.
3. Click the Copy Layout button at the bottom of the Parts window.
4. Use the shortcut Option-⌘-~ (Mac) or CTRL-Alt-Tab (Win) to return to the Clarinet part.

Extra Credit

For extra credit, review the steps for grouping measures into systems, as the Clarinet part is a little more active at bar 22.

1. Select bars 26 through 30.
2. Select **Layout** > Format > Make into a system or use the shortcut Option-Shift-M (Mac) or Alt-Shift-M (Win) to group the measures into a system.
3. Select bars 31 through 34.
4. Use the shortcut Option-Shift-M (Mac) or Alt-Shift-M (Win) to group the measures into a system.
5. Select bars 35 through 39.

6. Use the shortcut Option-Shift-M (Mac) or Alt-Shift-M (Win) to group the measures into a system and press Esc when finished.

A Few Fine Points

The tempo text is too high, as is the "Entered by" text. The position was copied from the Oboe part, where it was adjusted. Use the Reset Position command to move it down to the default position.

The cautionary key signature at the end of bar 21, the very one repositioned in the score earlier in this chapter, needs to be repositioned again. This is probably a bug in the software; perhaps it will be fixed by the time you read this, but it is fixable.

1. Select the key signature.
2. Press the right arrow key three times to move it to the right, away from the double barline.
3. Press Esc when finished.

There is a dynamic in bar 33 that should be moved down.

4. Select the mezzo piano in bar 33 and move it straight down, so it is below the baseline of the bar number. This has to do with the music as well as the proximity of the bar number.

That concludes the Clarinet part. Time to see how well you know the process. For the Horn part, there will be a list of what needs to be done; if you need to review the steps, review them from the previous parts.

The Horn Part

1. Move to the Horn part.
2. Import the House Style.
3. Return to the Clarinet part.
4. Copy the layout from the Clarinet part.

Developing an Eye for Music

Over the course of your musical training you've "developed an ear" for music, the sort of critical listening that helps you rehearse an ensemble, separate players you like to listen to from those you don't, and for writers, make you able to notate what you hear in your head. As you create more and more music to print, you will begin to develop an eye for notation. Learn to examine each part you create as if you were the player. The time you spend tweaking parts now will save you time in rehearsal, which is always a valuable commodity. The Horn part has a lot of opportunities for tweaking the position of expressions. There is even a collision between a bar number and an accidental in bar 20 to clean up. Use your eye as a potential player to tweak as you see fit. You can compare your score to the file posted on the Web site.

You've Finally Hit Bottom

It is time for the final exam on parts editing for "The Easy Winners." Everyone relax, it's an open-book final. Format and edit the Bassoon part on your own. Refer to the order and procedures as needed.

The Dynamic Part

The idea behind Dynamic parts is not just creating them within the same file as the score. More importantly, these parts are always linked to the score so any changes, edits, additions, or deletions made there will instantly be amended in the parts. To illustrate this, add the following text to the score.

1. Press the W key to return to the score.
2. Double-click the "Enter your name" text on the first page, and enter your name.
3. Press Esc when finished.

The rest of the text will all be Technique text.

4. In bar 5 of the Oboe part, enter "lead."
5. Press Esc once and tweak position if necessary. Press Esc again to deselect the text.
6. In bar 13 of the Oboe part, enter "no lead."
7. Press Esc once and tweak position if necessary. Press Esc again to deselect the text.
8. In bar 21 of the Horn part, enter "melody" over the E♭ sixteenth note in the second beat.
9. Press Esc once and tweak position if necessary. Press Esc again to deselect the text.
10. In bar 25 of the Bassoon part, enter "bring out" over the second beat.
11. Press Esc once and tweak position if necessary. Press Esc again to deselect the text.
12. In bar 26 of the Horn part, enter "no lead" at the beginning of the bar as Technique text.
13. Press Esc once and tweak position if necessary. Press Esc again to deselect the text.
14. In bar 29 of the Flute part, enter "melody" over the accented A♭ sixteenth note in the second beat.
15. Press Esc once and tweak position if necessary. Press Esc again to deselect the text.

16. In bar 21 of the Horn part, enter "melody" over the E♭ sixteenth note in the second beat.
17. Press Esc once and tweak position if necessary. Press Esc again to deselect the text.
18. Check each part and tweak the position of the text as needed.

Printing Score and Parts

Since the score and parts are in two different windows, one print command will not cover printing both at the same time.

Printing the Score

1.   Press W to make the score window active.
2.   Use the shortcut ⌘-P (Mac) or CTRL-P (Win) to print the score.

<table>
<tr><td>

Printing the Parts, Option #1

1.   Select **File** > Print All Parts.

</td><td>

Printing the Parts, Option #2

1.   Press W to return to the Parts window.
2.   Click the Print Parts button at the bottom of the Parts window.

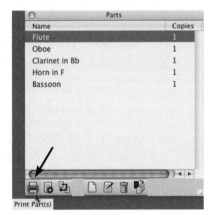

</td></tr>
</table>

End of Term

When you are closing a file with both score and parts, there is more than one window to be closed. Using the Close command or shortcut will close only the active window, not the whole document.

1. Select **File** > Close All, or use the shortcut: Option-⌘-W (Mac); Alt-CTRL-W (Win).

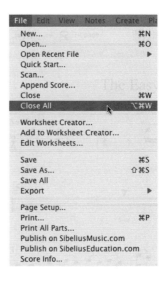

Summary

In this chapter, you learned how to import a graphics file into PhotoScore Lite, proofread and edit it, then import it into Sibelius.

In PhotoScore Lite, you learned how to:

- set up the scanner
- scan the file
- open the scans in PhotoScore Lite
- read the scans with PhotoScore Lite
- load pages to create a single document
- make corrections to the document
- assign instruments to staves
- edit beaming
- export the edited document to Sibelius

In Sibelius, you learned how to:

- open a file from PhotoScore Lite
- work with a transposed score
- format systems
- create title text
- create credit text
- create copyright text
- edit system brackets
- add first and second endings

- create boxed measure numbers
- add cautionary accidentals
- adjust key signature positions
- add articulations in a score
- enter slurs in a score
- use the Copy Articulations and Slurs plug-in
- enter and copy expressions and techniques in a score
- enter and copy hairpins in a score
- clean up space between staves
- enter system dividers
- enter tempo text
- work with the Mixer window
- playback a score with Kontakt Silver or Gold
- work with dynamic parts
- create a House Style for the parts
- copy the layout from one part to another
- change the measure number display in the parts
- change text size and position in the parts
- print the score and parts

Review

1. Try scanning some of the earlier examples in the book and re-creating them.
2. To further hone your scanning and editing skills, try downloading and scanning the Brahms Intermezzo in A major used in Chapter 9 of this book.

8

Vocal Score with Percussion
(Musical Example: "Wassail Song")

This chapter deals with entering lyrics, entering polyphony, and creating percussion parts. Begin by looking over the score to identify new areas that will be addressed.

This arrangement Copyright © 2006 by Tom Rudolph

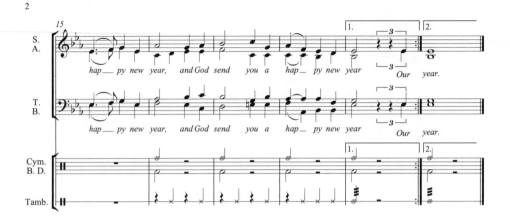

Verse 3:

We are not daily beggars
That beg from door to door,
But we are neighbor's children
Whom you have seen before.
¦Love and joy...

Verse 4:

Good master and good Mistress,
As you sit by the fire,
Pray think of us poor children
Who are wandering in the mire.
¦Love and joy...

Verse 5:

We Have a little purse
Made of raching leather skin
We want some of your small change
To line it well within.
¦Love and Joy...

Verse 6:

Call up the Butler of this house,
Put on his golden ring;
Let him bring us a glass of beer,
And the better we shall sing,
¦Love and joy....

- creating custom space between selected staves
- entering and hiding a Meter Change
- editing the staff (instrument) names
- adding a tempo marking
- entering notation in separate voices for polyphony
- turning on note voice colors
- hiding rests
- transposing within the score
- entering lyrics in lines 1 and 2
- copying and pasting lyrics via the filter
- adjusting the horizontal position of all lyrics
- resetting default lyric positions
- entering block lyrics at the end of the score
- importing a graphic into the score
- entering notation into percussion parts
- using and altering drum (percussion) maps
- saving custom percussion maps for later use
- moving voice 2 to voice 1
- saving lyrics as a text file via a plug-in

Setting Up the Score

For this example, there is no exact match in the Instruments list, so the goal is to get as close as possible. For example, there is no Soprano/Alto option, so you will choose Soprano and then alter it after the score is created. Similarly, it is important to choose the closest match to the percussion instruments. As in previous chapters, taking your time during the score setup process is a good habit to get into.

1. If Sibelius is not already open, launch it.
2. Select **File** > New.
3. In the New Score window, from Manuscript Paper choose "Blank," then click the "Add Instruments" tab.
4. Under Family, click "Singers."
5. Under the Instrument column, select "Soprano" and click "Add to Score." You can also just double-click on the word "Soprano" to add it to the score.
6. Double-click on the word "Tenor" to add it to the score.
7. Under Family, select "Percussion and Drums."
8. In the instruments list, double-click Drums.
9. Double-click Tambourine.

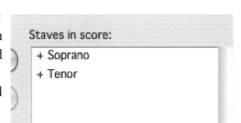

You need to be sure the staves are in the proper score order. The Percussion staff needs to be moved down.

10. Under "Staves in score," click on Tambourine to select it and click the Down button (not the down arrow) until the Tambourine is at the bottom of the score.
11. Click on Drums and click the Down button to move it below the Tenor staff. Your list should look like:

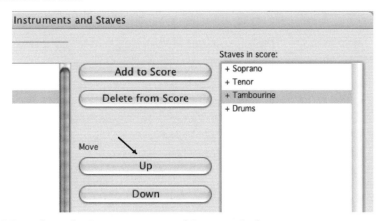

12. Click OK to close the Instruments and Staves window.
13. Click Next.

14. Under Manuscript, select "Vocal Opus (Times)." This choice is being made because the Times font is the smallest font and the recommended one when entering several verses of lyrics. Click Next.

15. Under Time Signature, select 6/8.

16. Under Tempo, check the box next to "Metronome mark."

17. To select a dotted quarter note value, first select the quarter note from the pull-down menu. Then go back and select the dot at the bottom of the same list. A dotted note requires selecting the duration first and then the dot.

18. Enter the tempo of 100 under "Metronome mark."

19. Click Next.

20. Under Key Signature, select E♭ major (three flats) and click Next.

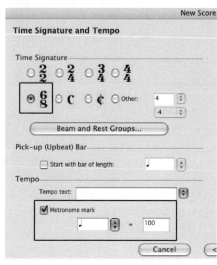

21. In the score info page, enter the following:

    a. Title: Wassail Song

    b. Composer/Songwriter: Traditional

    c. Lyricist: entered by [your name]

    d. Copyright: This arrangement Copyright © 2006 by Tom Rudolph

22. Wait, don't press Finish! Click the Previous button to be sure all the entries are correct. You know by now that this is the best way to save time creating a score in Sibelius. After you have reviewed the previous pages for accuracy, return to the last New Score page and click the Finish button.

The score should look as follows:

That was a lot of work! Before going on, save the file:

23. Select **File** > Save.
24. Name the file "WassailSong" and save it in a folder that you will remember.

Adding the Arranger Text at the Top of the Score

1. Click the word "Traditional."
2. Hold down ⌘ (Mac); CTRL (Win) and press the up arrow twice to move up the word.

 Holding down the ⌘ (Mac); CTRL (Win) key gives you larger movements than just pressing the up or down arrow key. Use just the arrow keys for fine movements and the ⌘ (Mac); CTRL (Win) keys with the arrows for larger movements.

3. Click inside the first bar in the Soprano part to select it.
4. Select **Create** > Text > Composer.
5. Enter the text: Arranged by Tom Rudolph.
6. Click Esc. The text will be highlighted. Use the left and right arrow keys to make any positioning adjustments to the text if needed.

Adding a Group of Bars (Measures)

There are a total of 21 bars in this arrangement of "Wassail Song." Therefore, 16 bars need to be added to the score.

1. Press Esc.
2. Click inside any measure (bar) to select it.
3. Select **Create** > Bar > Other or use the shortcut: Option-B (Mac); Alt-B (Win).
4. In the Create Bars dialog box, enter the number 16 and click OK. You can also use the shortcut: ⌘-B (Mac); Alt-B (Win) 16 times to add the additional bars.

Custom Bars per System (Line)

The final version of this piece has a custom number of bars per line. This can be set either at the beginning or the end of the note entry process.

1. Check to see if "View Staff Names and Bar Numbers" is turned on in the View menu. If it is not, select it: **View** > Staff Names and Bar Numbers.
2. Select the barline at the end of bar 4. It will turn purple.
3. Press the Return/Enter key to create a system break or select **Layout** > Break > System Break.
4. Select the barline at the end of bar 10. Press the Return/Enter key to create a system break.
5. Select the barline at the end of bar 16. Press the Return/Enter key to insert a system break.

Custom Space Between Staves

In scores it is often desirable to set custom distances between staves. For example, the Tambourine staff can be moved closer to the Snare staff to make more room between systems.

1. Press Esc.
2. Select the entire Tambourine staff by triple-clicking on any of its measures. Be sure the triple-click worked and every system is selected. If you double-click, only one system will be selected.
3. Hold down the Shift key and drag the staff upward with the mouse. For fine-tuning, hold down Option (Mac); Alt (Win) and press the up (or down) arrow.

The adjustment to the spacing of the Tambourine staff should have the following effect.

 To return the position of a staff to the default setting, first select the staff and then select **Layout** > Reset Space Above (or Below) Staff. If you want to move down more than one staff, triple-click the top staff that you want to move. Hold down Option-⌘ (Mac); CTRL-Alt (Win) and press the down arrow to move down all of the staves that are below the one selected.

Entering a Meter Change

This example has a nonstandard time signature change in measures 8 and 9. These partial measures sometimes occur in choral and older scores. In order to make this happen in Sibelius, you must apply some creative problem-solving skills. Essentially, you are going to insert a time signature change to create the illusion of the partial measure and then hide the real time signatures. The hiding step will take place later in this chapter, after the notation has been entered. First, create the custom time signatures:

1. Press Esc.
2. Select bar 8.
3. Press the letter T for time signature or select **Create** > Time Signature.
4. Check the box Other and enter the time signature of 3/8 for measure 8. Click OK.
5. Press Esc.
6. Select measure 9.
7. Press the letter T for time signature.
8. Click the box next to Other and enter the time signature of 1/2 for bar 9. Click OK.
9. Press Esc.
10. Select measure 10.
11. Press the letter T.
12. Select Cut-Time.

You should have the following time signatures in bars 8, 9, and 10:

Entering a Double Barline in Measure 8

1. Select the barline at the end of measure 8. It will turn purple.
2. Select **Create** > Barline > Double.

It is possible to hide or delete time signatures. Since we are going to delete the time signatures in these measures, there must be notation in the measures.

Entering the Repeat Bar and First and Second Endings

1. Select the barline at the end of bar 20.
2. Select **Create** > Barline > End Repeat.
3. Select bar 21 so the entire bar is selected.
4. Press the letter L for line or select **Create** > Line.
5. Under the right-hand System Lines column, select the second ending mark and press OK to enter it into the score.
6. Click on the number 2 of the second ending just entered.
7. Hold down ⌘ (Mac); CTRL (Win) and press the right arrow key once to move the marking slightly to the right.
8. Click inside bar 20 to select it.
9. Press the letter L for lines.
10. Under the System Lines column, select the first ending mark and press OK to enter it.

11. The end of the first ending is automatically selected when entered so there is no need to click on it to select it. To move it to the left, hold down ⌘ (Mac); CTRL (Win) and press the left arrow key once.

The endings should resemble the following:

Editing the Staff (Instrument) Names

There are two staff names that appear automatically in scores and are determined by the Engraving Rules default settings. There is the full staff name that appears on page 1 before the first system only, and the short or abbreviated name that appears before every subsequent system in the score. To view the default settings, select **House Style** > Engraving Rules > Instruments. I usually leave the default settings for this as they are. It is good to know where they are controlled, in case you want to make changes.

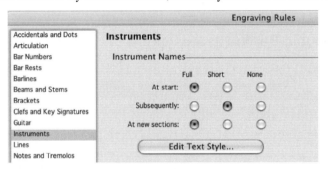

To change the full Instrument (staff) Names:

1. Go to bar 1.
2. Double-click on the word Soprano to the left of the first system to select it.
3. Press Return/Enter and type: "Alto."
4. Press Esc.
5. Double-click on the word Tenor.
6. Press Return/Enter and type: "Bass."
7. Press Esc.
8. Double-click on the word Drums.
9. Press the Delete key and type: "Sus. Cymbal."
10. Press Return/Enter and type: "Bass Drum."
11. Press Esc.
12. Tambourine is OK as is. So no changes to this staff are required.

To change the short or abbreviated Instrument (staff) Names:

1. Go to bar 5.
2. Double-click on the S to the left of the second staff system.
3. Press Return/Enter and type: "A."
4. Press Esc.
5. Double-click on the T.
6. Press Return/Enter and type: "B."
7. Press Esc.
8. Double-click on Dr.
9. Delete it and type: "Cym."
10. Press Return/Enter and type "B.D."
11. Press Esc.
12. No need to change the Tamb. abbreviation.

The score names should now appear:

Long names: Short names:

Changing the Clef in the Tenor/Bass Part

1. Press Esc.
2. To change a clef, press the letter Q or select **Create** > Clef. (Why the letter Q? If you press just the letter C, the note C will be entered, so Sibelius uses the letter Q for clef changes.)
3. From the Clef dialog box, select the Bass Clef and click OK. The cursor will turn blue.
4. In measure 1, click right on top of the existing treble clef in the Tenor/Bass part to change it to a bass clef. Be sure to click on the existing clef itself or Sibelius might think you want a clef change starting in a bar other than 1.

Entering a Tempo Marking in Measure 9 (That Will Also Play Back Properly)

In order to enter a tempo change that will affect the playback, you must enter tempo text.

1. Click inside bar 9 of the Sop/Alto staff to select it.
2. Select **Create** > Text > Tempo, or use the shortcut: Option-⌘-T (Mac); CTRL-Alt-T (Win).
3. Right-click (CTRL-click for Mac users with a one-button mouse) and select the quarter note value.
4. Again right-click and select the period from the pull-down menu.
5. Press the space bar, then the equal sign (=) on the computer keyboard. Then press the space bar again.
6. Right-click (CTRL-click for Mac users with a one-button mouse) and select the half note value from the submenu. Then press the Esc key when you're done.

Congratulations! You've just completed the score layout portion of this example.

☺ **Have you saved lately?** ☺

www.sibeliusbook.com

Save your work by selecting **File** > Save or using the shortcut: ⌘-S (Mac); CTRL-S (Win).

To start at this point in the chapter, go to *www.sibeliusbook.com* and download the Chapter 8 files. Open the file name *Chpt6WassailSong1.sib*.

Polyphony = Voices

After the score is formatted, it's time to enter the notation. In this "Wassail Song" arrangement, there are two polyphonic parts in each of the top two staves and in the top percussion staff. You can identify polyphony when there are two independent parts on one staff: one with stems up and one with stems down. Piano and vocal parts frequently have polyphony in one staff. Sibelius can handle four polyphonic voices in each staff, but it's rare to need more than two voices at any given time. With "Wassail Song," only two voices are needed: voice 1 for stems up and voice 2 for stems down. Up until now, every example in Sibelius was entered using voice 1. If only one voice is present, the stems move up or down according to the placement position on the staff.

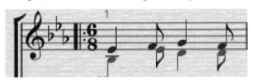

Homophonic Harmony = Only One Voice

There are times when music is written with more than one note at a time. This was introduced in Chapter 3. When the notes are homophonic, they are entered in the same voice. Below is an example of two notes in one voice, or homophonic music, that was inputted in Chapter 3.

 Voices Rules to Remember

- Every staff has a potential of using up to four voices. So, for the top staff, Soprano will be voice 1 and Alto, voice 2. In the second staff, Tenor will be voice 1 (*not* voice 3!) and Bass will be voice 2. In the top percussion staff, Sus. Cymbal will be voice 1 and Bass Drum will be voice 2.

- Only on rare occasions will you need a third or fourth voice. This sometimes occurs in very complex piano and guitar music and some drum set parts.

- Voices display in separate colors. Voice 1 displays in dark blue, voice 2 in green, voice 3 in orange, and voice 4 in pink.

- In scores, and even within chords, voices can be changed by choosing a note in the score you wish to change, then clicking on the number at the bottom of the Keypad; or by selecting **Edit** > Voice and then the desired voice.

Entering Notation in Voices

The first step when working with voices is to turn on the voice colors. This is quite helpful. These colors by default will not print; they are for onscreen reference only. Select **View** > Note Colors > Voices. Thereafter, a note turns to its voice color when you select it in Sibelius. You can print your score in color if desired. Turn on the "Print in Color" option in the **File** > Print window.

Entering Notation in Voices Options: Step Time and/or Flexi-Time

Previous chapters dealt with the specifics of the various Sibelius note-entry options. They each require a set of steps when entering separate voices. Remember, you don't have to use only one entry method. You might enter the Soprano in step time and then the Alto using Flexi-time. Step-time entry includes typing the letter names on the computer keyboard or playing in one note at a time with a MIDI keyboard. If you prefer to enter with Flexi-time, you will have to make changes to the Flexi-time settings before entering a different voice. In the steps that follow, each option is listed. Choose the method of entry best for you.

Choose one of the following methods to enter voice 1.

Entry option 1: entering the Soprano part in step time (playing one note at a time on a MIDI keyboard or using alphabetic entry):

1. Press Esc.
2. Click inside bar 1 to select it. It will be outlined by a blue box.
3. Press the letter N for notation or select **Notes** > Input notes.
4. Be sure Voice 1 is selected. This is the default voice. If it is not selected, click voice 1 with the mouse on the bottom of the Keypad or use the shortcut: hold down Option (Mac); Alt (Win) and press the number 1 on the main computer keyboard, above the Q key.
5. Enter the notation for voice 1 from the beginning to the end of the arrangement (see next page). Remember that the stems will flip only if another voice is present.

Entry option 2: entering the Soprano part using Flexi-time (playing a MIDI keyboard in time with a metronome):

1. Select **Notes** > Flexi-Time Options or use the shortcut: Shift-⌘-O (Mac); Shift-CTRL-O (Win).
2. Set the Flexi-time options as you prefer. I set "Flexibility of tempo" to Low, "Introduction" to 1 bar, and "Record into" voice 1.

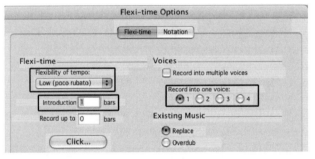

3. Click the Notation tab and set the notation level to an eighth note.
4. Click OK to close the Flexi-time Options window.
5. Select the first bar of the score.
6. Press the Record button on the Playback controls or use the shortcut: Shift-⌘-F (Mac); CTRL-Shift-F (Win). Listen for the number of bar(s) of the introduction and start playing the Soprano part.

Using your note entry method of choice, enter the Soprano part for the entire piece.

To enter the quarter note triplet in the first ending:

1. Enter the E half note on beat 1.
2. Select a quarter note value and press 0 on the Keypad to enter a quarter rest on beat 3.
3. Press ⌘-3 (Mac); CTRL-3 (Win).
4. Enter the quarter rest and then an E quarter note to complete the triplet.

Entering the Alto Part

Entry option 1: Step-time entry: typing letter names or entering one note at a time using a MIDI keyboard:

1. Select bar 1.
2. Press the letter N for notation or select **Notes** > Input Pitches.
3. Select voice 2 by clicking on the number 2 on the Keypad or via the shortcut: Option-2 (Mac); Alt-2 (Win). The cursor will turn green, as notes entered in voice 2 are indicated by the color green.

Entry option 2: Flexi-time entry:

1. Select **Notes** > Flexi-time Options or use the shortcut: Shift-⌘-O (Mac); Shift-CTRL-O (Win).
2. Under Voices, "Record into one voice," choose 2. Click OK.
3. Click inside bar 1.
4. Start recording by pressing the red Record button on the Playback controls or use the shortcut: Shift-⌘-F (Mac); Shift-CTRL-F (Win).

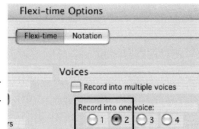

Alto Part:

Hiding the Rests in the First Ending

When voices are entered like this, each voice will display rests. Typically in finished notated scores, there is only one set of rests in a measure. Therefore, you will want to hide the two voice 2 quarter rests in the first ending.

Before hiding rests:

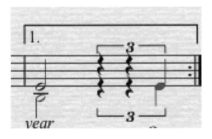

After hiding rests:

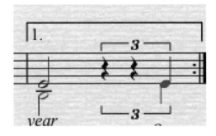

1. Enter the quarter note triplet in measure 20. Click in measure 20 to select it. Press the letter N. Choose voice 2 from the Keypad. Enter the quarter rest. Then press ⌘-3 (Mac); CTRL-3 (Win). A triplet bracket will appear. Enter the second rest and then the E quarter note.

2. To hide the two quarter rests, select the lower rests in voice 2. Click on one rest, hold down ⌘ (Mac); CTRL (Win), and click the second rest.

3. Select **Edit** > Show or Hide > Hide, or use the shortcut: Shift-⌘-H (Mac); Shift-CTRL-H (Win).

Entering the Tenor Part, Bars 1 Through 13

Next, enter the tenor and bass parts up to the first two beats of measure 13. Don't go past 13, since the next phrase can be copied directly from the Soprano/Alto parts.

1. Select the first measure in the Tenor part so it is outlined by a single square blue box.
2. Press the letter N for Notation.
3. If you are using Flexi-time, check the Flexi-time Options (**Notes** > Flexi-time Options) and be sure voice 1 is selected. If you are step-entering the part, select voice 1 from the Keypad.
4. Enter the notation for bars 1 through the first two beats of bar 13.

Entering the Bass Part, Bars 1 through 13

Now enter the bass part using Voice 2.

1. Press Esc.
2. Select the first measure in the Tenor/Bass part.
3. Press the letter N for Notation.
4. Select voice 2 (see step 3 in "Entering the Tenor Part" for specifics).
5. Enter the notation for bars 1 through the first two beats of bar 13.

 What if you entered the music in the wrong voice? You could delete it and start over, but there is an easier way. Just select the notes you entered in the incorrect voice. Then select the desired voice on the Keypad. That will instantly change the notes from one voice to another. Be sure to select the notes before selecting the desired voice.

Copy/Paste, Transpose

The Tenor/Bass parts, starting on beat 3 of bar 13 through the end of measure 16, are the same pitches, one octave lower than the Soprano/Alto part in the same measures. Assuming you have already entered the Soprano/Alto parts, the steps to copy and transpose are as follows:

1. Press Esc.
2. Click on the G notehead on beat 3 in the Soprano/Alto part in measure 13.
3. Hold down the Shift key and click on the last quarter note in measure 16.

4. To copy the part to the Tenor/Bass part, hold down Option (Mac); Alt (Win) and click the mouse on beat 3 in the bass part, measure 13.

5. The paste is in the wrong octave. To transpose it down an octave, with the notes still selected, hold down ⌘ (Mac); CTRL (Win) and press the down arrow key. You can also press the up and down arrow keys by themselves to move the selection step by step in either direction.

Enter the rest of the notation in the Tenor/Bass part. Remember, the Tenor is in voice 1 and Bass is in voice 2.

Play back the entire score to proof-listen to the four voice parts. Turn back to page 179 and press the Play button.

Hiding the Time Signatures in Measures 8, 9, and 10

Back at the beginning of the chapter, we entered the 3/8 and cut-time signatures to create nonstandard-looking measures. After the notes have been entered, these can be deleted.

1. Select the 3/8 time signature in measure 8.
2. Press the Delete key.
3. In the dialog box "Do you want the subsequent bars to be rewritten," click No. (If you click Yes, Sibelius will assume you wish to return to the previous time signature in the score.)
4. Select the 1/2 time signature in measure 9.
5. Press the Delete key.
6. In the dialog box "Do you want the subsequent bars to be rewritten," click No.
7. Press the letter T for Time Signature.
8. Select cut-time and click OK.
9. Check inside bar 9.
10. In the dialog box "Do you want the subsequent bars to be rewritten," click No.
11. Select the cut-time marking in bar 10.
12. Press Delete key.
13. In the dialog box "Do you want the subsequent bars to be rewritten," click No.

You should now have a custom-looking score that will play back properly as well.

☺ **Have you saved lately?** ☺

www.sibeliusbook.com

To start at this point in the chapter, go to *www.sibeliusbook.com* and download the Chapter 8 files. Open the file name *Chpt8WassailSong2.sib*.

Entering Lyrics: Two Verses and Block Lyrics

Chapter 3 introduced lyrics. This example has two verses and block lyrics at the end. You'll learn how to enter lyrics in italics and enter a second verse.

Wassail Song

entered by [your name]

Traditional
Arranged by Tom Rudolph

Lyrics Line 1

1. Select bar one in the Soprano/Alto part.
2. Click on the E♭ in the Soprano part. Be sure you are in voice 1.
3. Press ⌘-L (Mac); CTRL-L (Win) or select **Create** > Text > Lyrics Line 1.
4. Enter the lyrics in the top line (line 1) above. For a syllable break, press dash (-). To enter a melisma (also called a word extension), press the space bar. Enter the lyrics, line 1, up until measure 8.

Initially, the lyrics will be a bit too close to the staff. Don't worry about it at this point as you will enter the line 1 and line 2 lyrics and then move them together. That will be covered a bit later in this chapter.

To enter the verse lyrics in italics:

5. Select the G on beat 1 of bar 9.
6. Use the shortcut ⌘-L (Mac); CTRL-L (Win) or select **Create** > Text > Lyrics Line 1.
7. Enter the word "Love" in bar 9.
8. After the lyric is entered, drag-select the word to highlight it.
9. Use the shortcut ⌘-I (Mac); CTRL-I (Win) to italicize the selection. From now on, the lyrics entered will appear in italics. By the way, if you press the same shortcut again, the lyric will turn back to normal text.

There are several ways to change lyrics into italics. First, select one or a group of lyrics. You can select one lyric by clicking on it. To select a group of lyrics, select the bar or bars and then choose **Edit** > Filter > Lyrics. After the desired lyrics are selected, open the Properties window: **Window** > Properties. Click the Text tab. You can select from a variety of styles using the pull-down menu. If you select Lyrics (chorus), the lyrics will be in italics with the proper size and font.

10. Enter the rest of the lyrics for the refrain in italics (bars 16 through 21).

Lyrics Line 2

The second line or verse of lyrics must be selected with a different shortcut or menu option. Sibelius can enter up to five lines of lyrics under each staff. Each specific line of lyrics is selected from the Create menu. Lyrics lines 1 and 2 are located in **Create** > Text. Lyrics lines 3 through 5 and lyrics above the staff can be selected via **Create** > Text > Other System Text.

To enter Lyrics Line 2:

1. Click the E♭ in measure 1 of the Soprano/Alto part.
2. Select **Create** > Text > Lyrics Line 2 or use the shortcut: Option-⌘-L (Mac); CTRL-Alt-L (Win).
3. Enter the second line of lyrics in measures 1 through 8 (previous page). Use the dash (–) for syllable breaks and the space bar for lyrics over several notes (melismas).

Copying Lyrics Using the Filter

It is a snap to copy lyrics from one staff or instrument to another. The Filter option should be used. If you select a bar in Sibelius, everything is selected: notes, lyrics, articulations, etc. It is possible to filter out specific items to copy and move. This is a powerful option, and once understood, it opens up many time-saving techniques.

To copy lyrics in bars 1 through 8:

1. Press Esc.
2. In the Soprano/Alto part, only select bars 1 through 8. Click in bar 1, then hold down the Shift key and click in bar 8. All eight bars should be surrounded by a blue box.
3. Select **Edit** > Filter > Lyrics to select just the lyrics.
4. To copy the lyrics to the Tenor/Bass part, with the lyrics selected, hold down Option (Mac); Alt (Win) and click on the first note in the Tenor part in bar 1.

To enter and copy the lyrics in measures 13 through 21 in the Tenor/Bass part:

5. Enter the lyrics in the Tenor/Bass part, measures 11, 12, and 13 up to beat 1. Be sure to enter them as Lyrics Line 1 and make them italics.

Copy the lyrics from the Soprano/Alto part from measure 13, beat 3 through the end of the piece.

6. In the Soprano/Alto part, select bar 13, beat 3 through bar 21 (use Shift-click to select bar 21).

7. Select **Edit** > Filter > Lyrics.

8. To copy the selection, hold down Option (Mac); Alt (Win) and in the Tenor/Bass staff, click on beat 3 in bar 13.

Entering Slurs

Now that the notation is entered, go back and enter the slurs in each of the parts. There are slurs in bars 15, 16, and 19. Notice that there are slurs in each voice.

1. In measure 15, click on the upward stem of the A on beat 1. When you click on the stem, Sibelius will recognize the appropriate voice, in this case voice 1. Since these are unison notes, the noteheads are placed on top of each other.

2. Press the letter S for Slur.

3. Click on the down stem of the same note in bar 15. This will select voice 2.

4. Press the letter S for Slur.

5. Repeat these steps in bars 16 and 19.

Moving Lyrics

Sibelius does a good job of aligning the lyrics in most cases. However, in this example the Alto part is on the low side and the notes and stems collide with some of the lyrics. This is not the case in the Tenor/Bass parts, so they can be left alone.

To move down the Soprano/Alto lyrics:

1. Triple-click in any bar of the Soprano/Alto part to select the entire part. Check to be sure the triple-click worked. If not, try it again until the entire Soprano/Alto staff is selected.
2. Select **Edit** > Filter > Lyrics. Both the line 1 and line 2 lyrics will be selected.
3. Press the down arrow multiple times until the lyrics are below the stems of the Alto part. You'll need to click the arrow about ten times. You can also hold down ⌘ (Mac); CTRL (Win) and press the down arrow key for larger movements.

Resetting the Lyrics Position

It is also possible to reset the default positions of notes, text, and lyrics. This is sometimes the best option when you have made multiple changes and **Edit** > Undo is not an option. To reset the lyrics to their default position:

1. Select the measure or measures, or the entire piece.
2. Select **Layout** > Reset Position to return the lyrics to their default positions.

Entering Block Lyrics

In most vocal selections, additional lines of lyrics are added at the end of the score. This song has four additional verses that are added at the end as block lyrics.

1. Go to page 2 and select the Tambourine part, bar 17.
2. Select **Create** > Text > Other System Text > Block Lyrics.
3. Type "Verse 3:".
4. Press Esc.
5. Drag the words for verse 3 below the staff.
6. Double-click on verse 3.
7. Press Return/Enter two times.
8. Enter the rest of the lyrics for verse 3 (see below).
9. Press Return/Enter two times and type the text for verse 4.

> **Verse 3:**
> We are not daily beggars
> That beg from door to door,
> But we are neighbor's children
> Whom you have seen before.
> Love and joy…

Verse 4:
Good master and good Mistress,
As you sit by the fire,
Pray think of us poor children
Who are wandering in the mire.
Love and joy…

Changing the Size and Style of Block Lyrics

Block lyrics default to a point size of 9.8, and are in a normal text font (this kind of text defaults to using Times New Roman). To change the size and style:

1. Open the Properties Window: **Window** > Properties.
2. Select the words "Verse 3."
3. Click the Text tab to open it.
4. Change the font size to 12.2.
5. Click the box to the left of the letter B (for bold) to change the text to bold.
6. Select the text: "Verse 4."
7. Change the font size to 12.2.
8. Click the box to the left of the letter B (for bold) to change the text to bold.

To enter verses 5 and 6 as block lyrics:

1. Select the Tambourine part, measure 19.
2. Select **Create** > Text > Other System Text > Block Lyrics.
3. Type "Verse 5:".
4. Click Esc.
5. Drag verse 5 below the staff. Line it up with the verse 3 text. There is also a function in Sibelius to do this automatically: select several objects and select **Layout** > Align in a Row.
6. Enter the lyrics for verse 5.
7. Press Return/Enter two times and type the text for verse 6.
8. Review the above steps and change the font size to 12.2 and the verse captions to bold.

Verse 5:
We Have a little purse
Made of raching leather skin
We want some of your small change
To line it well within.
Love and joy…

Verse 6:
Call up the Butler of this house,
Put on his golden ring;
Let him bring us a glass of beer,
And the better we shall sing,
Love and joy....

Importing a Graphic File

Graphic files of virtually any kind can be imported into Sibelius. The program installs with some music clipart. For this example, you will import one of the graphic clipart files that Sibelius supplies.

1. Select **Create** > Graphic.
2. Navigate your way to the Sibelius folder that was created when you installed Sibelius. This will be found on your hard drive.
3. Once you have selected the Sibelius folder, click on the Example Scores folder.
4. Inside the Example Scores folder, select Graphic Files.
5. Select the file *Classical guitar.tif.*
6. The cursor is now loaded with the graphic. Click on the score in between the verses to paste the guitar graphic. Once a graphic file has been inserted into a score, you can click on it and use the bottom right-hand corner handle to resize it with the mouse.

Verse 3:

We are not daily beggars
That beg from door to door,
But we are neighbor's children
Whom you have seen before.
¦Love and joy...

Verse 4:

Good master and good Mistress,
As you sit by the fire,
Pray think of us poor children
Who are wandering in the mire.
¦Love and joy...

Verse 5:

We Have a little purse
Made of raching leather skin
We want some of your small change
To line it well within.
¦Love and Joy...

Verse 6:

Call up the Butler of this house,
Put on his golden ring;
Let him bring us a glass of beer,
And the better we shall sing,
¦Love and joy....

Congratulations! That was a lot of work.

☺ **Have you saved lately?** ☺

www.sibeliusbook.com

To start at this point in the chapter, go to *www.sibeliusbook.com* and download the Chapter 8 files. Open the file name *Chpt6WassailSong3.sib.*

Percussion Parts and Drum Maps

Before entering the notation in the percussion parts, review the following information on how percussion staves (instruments) are formatted so you understand how they function before creating your own.

Sibelius uses "percussion maps" that assign sounds and percussion notation to specific lines and spaces. A percussion map also assigns playback information so that a snare sounds like a snare and a bass drum like a bass drum.

The easiest way to enter percussion notation is to use the New Score setup and choose a percussion staff that most closely fits your needs. Since this step was taken at the beginning of this chapter, percussion map assignments have already been made by Sibelius.

Accessing Percussion Sounds

The next decision is how to enter the percussion sounds. The easiest entry method that I have found for percussion is using a MIDI keyboard. That is what I recommend. It is possible to enter percussion sounds by mouse clicking or typing letter names. These will be covered later in the chapter.

Sibelius gives you two options when entering with a MIDI keyboard. You can play the MIDI drum pitch or play the staff note that the percussion sound is assigned. I prefer to play the MIDI note. The MIDI percussion note assignments are a standard set of sounds that are built into every MIDI keyboard that is GM (General MIDI) compatible. Most keyboards are.

Entering the Tambourine Part via MIDI Pitches

To get an idea of how this works, enter the first part of the tambourine part in measures 10 through 14. In this case, the Tambourine is located on the F♯ below middle C, or pitch number F♯3. It can also be located by the MIDI note number 54. The MIDI note number for middle C is 60.

To set the preferences:

1. Mac: Select **Sibelius 4** > Preferences > Note Input;
   Win: Select **File** > Preferences > Note Input.
2. Under Percussion Staves, check "The MIDI device's drum map."

Percussion Staves

Step-time and Flexi-time input convert the note you input into a different pitch and notehead on the staff. This is defined in:

○ The staff type
⦿ The MIDI device's drum map

The standard GM map is below. See if you can find the Tambourine sound in the middle of the fourth system.

Caution: press Esc before playing on a MIDI keyboard to practice. Otherwise, notes may be entered into the score.

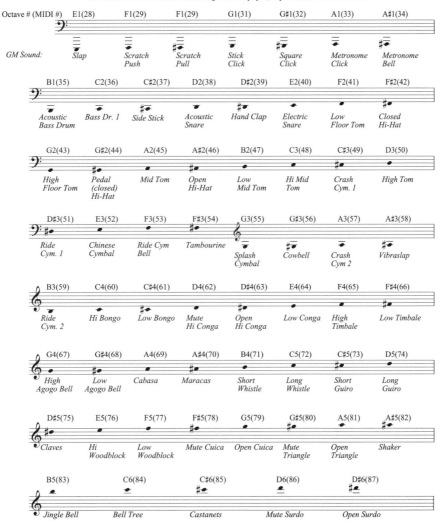

General MIDI (GM)
Percussion Note Assignments

GM Percussion sounds: Assign to MIDI channel 10
Notes below E1 and above D#6 are not assigned. When played, no percussion sound will be heard.

 You can go to *www.sibeliusbook.com* and download the above file. It was created in Sibelius and is file *GMPercussion.sib* in the folder Chapter 8. Print it out and use it for reference as you enter your percussion parts. I created this file using a lot of the techniques in this chapter, including custom time signatures, hiding time signatures, and changing the notehead type to stemless notes. I used a plug-in to automatically name the notes with the MIDI number: **Plug-ins** > Text > Add Note Names. Cool stuff!

1. Select bar 10 in the Tambourine part.
2. Press the letter N.
3. Select the quarter note value on the Keypad.
4. Press the number 0 to enter a quarter rest.
5. Play the note F♯3 on the MIDI keyboard.
6. Since the next two bars are identical, press Esc, then select the completed bar 9.
7. Press the letter R (for repeat) on the keyboard two times.
8. Enter the rest of the notation in bars 13 and 14. Play the note F♯3 (MIDI note 54).

Entering the Tambourine Part with a MIDI Keyboard Using Staff Pitches

Let's experiment with another option: telling Sibelius that you are entering the actual staff pitches for the part. In this case, the Tambourine, like any one-line percussion part, is placed on third line B in the treble staff. First, be sure that Sibelius is set correctly for entering the note on the actual staff line or space. If you use this technique, you should imagine that the percussion staff is a treble clef in terms of reading pitches. With this one-line staff, imagine that this is the third line B line.

1. The first step is to set the preferences for this option: Mac: Select **Sibelius 4** > Preferences > Note Input; Win: Select **File** > Preferences > Note Input.
2. Under Percussion Staves, choose "The staff type" and click OK.

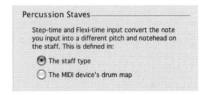

3. Select bar 17.
4. Press the letter N.
5. Select the quarter note value on the Keypad.
6. Press 0 to enter a quarter rest.
7. Play the note B4, or the B above middle C, on the MIDI keyboard.
8. Enter the rest of the notation in bar 17. Play B above middle C to enter the tambourine pitch.
9. Select bar 17 and press the letter R to repeat it in bar 18.
10. Enter the notation in bar 19.

To enter the rolled half note in bar 18:

11. Be sure the cursor is in bar 20, the first ending.
12. Select a half note on the first page of the Sibelius Keypad. Don't play this into the score just yet.
13. Click on the third page of the Keypad and select the roll (the shortcut is 3 on the computer's numeric keypad).
14. Play the note B above middle C to enter the tambourine note.
15. Follow the above steps and enter a whole note and roll in the second ending, bar 21.

Percussion Maps Revealed

The percussion maps in Sibelius are preprogrammed. If you understand how, you will be better able to work with them. Let's look at the map that is used when the Tambourine part is selected in the New Score setup.

1. Select **House Styles** > Edit Staff Types.
2. In the Edit Staff Types dialog box, under Category, click "Percussion."
3. Select "1 line (tambourine)."
4. Click Edit.

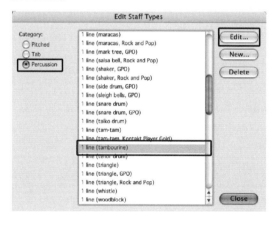
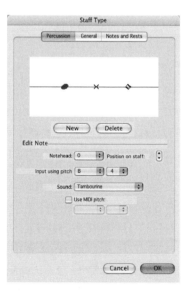

Notice that this percussion map only has one assigned note, the B line on the treble staff. There are three types of noteheads that are assigned to this line—normal noteheads, X noteheads, and diamond noteheads. All of these will play back a tambourine sound. When you use a MIDI keyboard to enter the pitches, the correct X notehead appears. However, when you click the mouse to enter the note or type the letters, Sibelius enters a normal notehead. If that is what you want, no change is needed. However, if you want an X or diamond notehead, you will have to manually change it in the score. The steps for making changes to percussion maps (noteheads and playback sound) will be explained later in this chapter.

Entering Tambourine Notes via Mouse or Alphabetic Input

If you have a MIDI keyboard, use it to enter percussion parts. Choose either the staff or MIDI note entry option and stick with it. If you don't have a MIDI keyboard and need to enter percussion parts with the mouse or alphabetic input, read on.

When you enter notes in a percussion part with the mouse or alphabetic input, you need to understand how the percussion maps work. Since the tambourine percussion map has three noteheads, Sibelius will enter a normal notehead when you click the mouse or use alphabetic input. If you want an X or diamond notehead, you must change it after the notes have been entered. Let's experiment. You'll put some pitches in measure 15 of the Tambourine part and then delete them.

To enter percussion pitches via mouse or alphabetic entry:

1. Select bar 15 of the Tambourine part.
2. Press N for Notation.
3. Select the quarter note value on the first page of the Keypad.
4. Press the letter B on the computer four times to enter four quarter notes.

These notes will be entered as normal noteheads. They will play back properly, because the percussion map was designed to play back a Tambourine sound for all three types of noteheads on the B line. To change the quarter notes into X noteheads:

5. Press Esc.
6. Select bar 15 of the Tambourine part, the bar where you just entered the four quarter notes.
7. To change the notehead, open the Properties window by selecting **Window** > Properties.
8. Click the arrow next to the Notes tab to open it.
9. Select the X notehead option.
10. Since this bar is not in the arrangement, select the bar and press the Delete button to remove the notes from the measure.

 There is a shortcut for changing noteheads. Once you memorize that 0 = normal; 1 = X, and 2 = diamond, you can change these by selecting the note or notes you want to change and then use the shortcut: Shift-Option (Mac); Shift-Alt (Win), followed by the appropriate number along the top of the computer keyboard (not the numeric keypad).

Entering the Bass and Cymbal Parts in the Same Staff in Voices

The Bass/Cymbal part requires the use of voices. Since the Cymbal has stems up, it will be entered in voice 1. The Bass drum part with stems down will be entered in voice 2.

The most common drum map is the drum set or drum kit. It includes most of the percussion notes in the GM percussion map. The easiest way to enter percussion parts is by playing the actual note on the MIDI keyboard. Sibelius will put these pitches on the proper line or space as programmed by the percussion map. See page 203 for the complete list of percussion notes.

To enter via the MIDI device drum map:

The best part about using MIDI input via the drum map is you don't have to concern yourself with how the Sibelius map is organized. Just play the correct pitch on the keyboard (see the GM chart on page 203) and Sibelius assigns it to the proper staff position and notehead following the recommendations of the Percussive Arts Society (in Norman Weinberg's book, *Guide to Standardized Drumset Notation*).

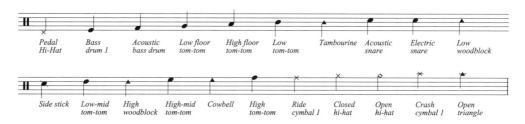

The percussion parts can be entered in step time or using Flexi-time.

1. Check the Preferences to be sure that the MIDI device drum map is selected: Mac: **Sibelius 4** > Preferences > Note Input; Win: **File** > Preferences > Note Input.
2. Under Percussion Staves, check "The MIDI device's drum map."
3. Start by entering the Bass drum part. Since the stems are down, the part should be entered in voice 2.
4. Click inside measure 1 of the cymbal/bass drum.
5. Press the letter N.
6. Select voice 2 by pressing the number 2 on the onscreen Keypad, or use the shortcut: Option-2 (Mac); Alt-2 (Win). Be sure to press the 2 above the "W" key, not the one on the computer's keypad.
7. Select a dotted quarter note on the Keypad by selecting the quarter note value and then clicking the dot.
8. Play C two octaves below middle, pitch C2 on the keyboard.
9. Enter the entire Bass drum part in voice 2.

To enter the Cymbal part using the MIDI device drum map:

1. Press Esc.
2. Select bar 2 of the Bass/Cymbal part.
3. Press the letter N.
4. Select voice 1 on the Keypad (stems up).
5. Select the dotted quarter note value on the Keypad.
6. Press 0 (zero) to enter a dotted quarter rest.
7. Select a dotted quarter note.
8. Play D♯3 below middle C or MIDI note number 51, which will play back as a ride cymbal. The percussion map assigns this to the top line of the staff.
9. Enter all of the Cymbal part in voice 1.

The Drum Set Map Revealed

The drum set map is complex. There are many different percussion sounds assigned, and it can be confusing to comprehend at first. Let's check it out and see if we can make some sense of it.

1. Select **House Style** > Edit Staff Types.
2. Click Percussion and then choose "5 lines (drum set)."
3. Click Edit.

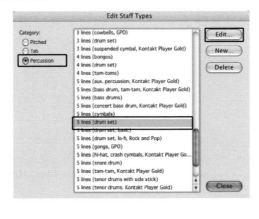

For example, for a ride cymbal, you must play F♯5 (top line of the treble staff) to get the proper sound and X notehead. Here's how to experiment: click on the X notehead on the F, top line of the staff in the Staff Type window. You will hear the percussion sound, and the "Input using pitch" will change. This refers to the staff method of entering percussion. To play in pitches using this method, you would have to change the input option in the Sibelius Preferences to Staff Type. You would play F above middle C for a bass drum and F♯, the top line of the treble staff, for a ride cymbal. I find this method more confusing than using the MIDI map, but you can choose the one you like best. Rather than switching back and forth, pick one and stick with it. This whole issue is confusing enough as it is.

To enter the bass and cymbal parts using mouse or alphabetic note entry:

If you do not have a MIDI keyboard, then you have to enter notes by clicking or typing letters. For practice, reenter the first two measures of the Bass/Cymbal part.

1. First, clear the measures by selecting bars 1 and 2 and pressing the Delete key.
2. Select Bar 1 to enter the Bass drum part.
3. Press the letter N for Notation.
4. Since the part has stems down, select voice 2 on the Keypad.
5. Select a dotted quarter note value and press the letter F on the computer keyboard three times to enter the Bass drum. Since there is only one sound assigned to this space, the correct sound and notehead is entered.

Now enter the Cymbal part:

6. Select bar 2.
7. Press the letter N for notation.
8. Select voice 1 on the Keypad (stems up).
9. Choose a dotted quarter note, then press 0 (zero) on the Keypad to enter a rest.
10. Select the dotted quarter note value.
11. Enter the F dotted quarter note by pressing the letter F.
12. It is entered in the wrong octave. To move it up an octave, press the up arrow seven times or use the octave shortcut: ⌘ (Mac); CTRL (Win) and press the up arrow key.
13. To change the notehead to an X, open the properties window: **Window > Properties**.
14. Open the Notes tab and select number 1, X noteheads. You can also use the shortcut: Shift-Option (Mac); Shift-Alt (Win) and press the number 1 on the main computer keyboard.

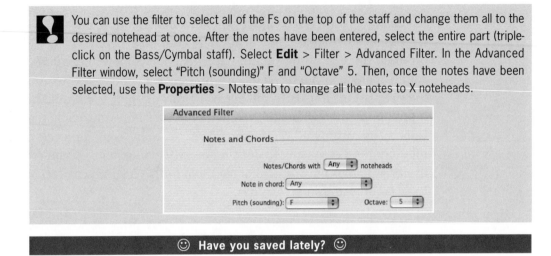

You can use the filter to select all of the Fs on the top of the staff and change them all to the desired notehead at once. After the notes have been entered, select the entire part (triple-click on the Bass/Cymbal staff). Select **Edit** > Filter > Advanced Filter. In the Advanced Filter window, select "Pitch (sounding)" F and "Octave" 5. Then, once the notes have been selected, use the **Properties** > Notes tab to change all the notes to X noteheads.

☺ **Have you saved lately?** ☺

Editing Drum Maps

It is possible to change or customize drum maps. I recommend using the default settings as much as possible for consistency (and sanity!). However, there may be times when you want to customize a drum map. Perhaps you may want to change the location of a particular sound on the staff or add a sound. For this example, we will move the ride cymbal from the F line on the treble staff down to the E space.

1. Select **House Style** > Edit Staff Types....
2. Under Staff Type, select Percussion and then "5 line (drum set)."
3. Click Edit.
4. Click on the F, X notehead on the top line of the staff.
5. To move it down to the E space, next to "Position on staff" under Edit Note, press the down arrow (not the down arrow on the keyboard).

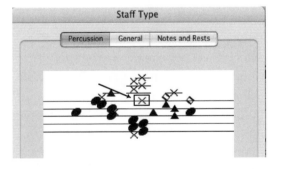

To delete a note from a map:

1. In the Percussion Staff Type window, select the notehead you want to delete.
2. Click the Delete button in the Percussion Staff Type window (not the Delete key on the computer keyboard).

To add a new sound and notehead to a percussion map:

1. In the Percussion Staff Type window, select the desired sound and notehead.
2. Click the New button.
3. Click the mouse on the staff where you'd like to add the new sound.

Saving Custom Percussion Maps for Later Use

If you find yourself making custom changes to maps on a regular basis, then it is a good idea to save your map as a custom House Style. We have done this in previous chapters with measure numbers and fonts. The steps are the same.

1. After making the desired changes to the percussion map, select **House Style** > Export House Style.
2. Give it a name you will remember, something like: "Tom's Custom Drum Map."
3. Click OK.

Now when you start a new score, this will appear as a House Styles option. You can also import this custom drum map from **House Style** > Import House Style.

 If drum/percussion maps gets you confused (as they do most people), consider using a series of one-line percussion staves. Most of the percussion instruments that have a single name, such as snare drum, bass drum, tambourine, and so forth come with a one-line staff. If you select them from the Instruments window in Sibelius, each sound will be assigned to the third line, B, on the treble staff. You won't have to worry about multiple percussion sounds being assigned to the same staff line or space.

That was a lot of work for sure! Save your example and print it out. Percussion maps can be dangerous to your mental health. ☺

More Sibelius Tips and Tricks

www.sibeliusbook.com

To start at this point in the chapter, go to *www.sibeliusbook.com* and download the Chapter 8 files. Open the file name *WassailSong4.sib*.

Combining Voice 2 with Voice 1

Sibelius includes many helpful options for dealing with voices. For example, you can combine any voice with another, moving the contents of voice 1 to voice 2. This will change the notation from polyphonic to monophonic, as if you played it in one voice when you entered it.

1. Select the first bar of the Soprano/Alto part. All the notes will be selected and will be blue and green, respectively.
2. Choose voice 1 on the Keypad (the number 1 at the bottom of the onscreen keypad). All the voice 2 notes are now joined with voice 1.

Changing a Homophonic Passage to Polyphonic

This can be helpful in a variety of applications, such as when you open MIDI files (see Chapter 13).

1. Select measure 1 of the Soprano/Alto part that you changed using the above steps.
2. Select **Edit** > Filter > Bottom note. This selects just the bottom notes of the passage.
3. On the keypad, select voice 2 (the number 2 at the bottom of the onscreen keypad). Voilà! Instant voices. In this case, it is back to the original.

Printing This Example on One Page

It is possible to reduce the print size of the music to reduce the number of pages to one. The size of the notes and text will decrease, and Sibelius will reformat the measures per system. This can be helpful when trying to reduce the number of pages in an example.

1. Select **Layout** > Document Settings or use the shortcut: ⌘-D (Mac); CTRL-D (Win).
2. If you prefer inches, make sure it is checked at the top left corner of the dialog box that appears, and change "Staff size" to 0.16 (4.1 millimeters) using the down arrow.

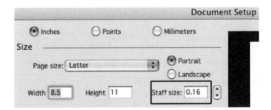

To tighten up the spacing on the page, adjust the justification as we have done in previous chapters:

3. Select **House Style** > Engraving Rules.
4. Select Staves.
5. Change "Justify staves when page is at least" to "90% full."

You will have to drag the extra verses to the middle of the page. They moved to the left, as they are attached to measures that were moved to the left when the size was reduced.

6. Select **Save** > Save As and rename the file.

Saving Lyrics in a Separate File

There is a handy plug-in to save the lyrics from a Sibelius score. Perhaps you would like to make a vocal sheet for a singer (since some don't read music well anyway), and you want to include just the lyrics.

1. Select **Plug-ins** > Text > Save Lyrics.
2. You will get the warning about plug-ins. Click Yes.
3. Sibelius will automatically save the lyrics to a folder on your hard drive. Make a mental note of the location and click OK.

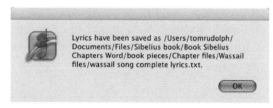

4. You can open this text file in any word processor such as Microsoft Word.

Summary

This chapter showed you how to:

- set up the score with percussion
- add the arranger text to the top of the score
- add a group of measures
- format custom measures per line
- set custom space between staves
- enter a meter change
- create custom barlines: double, first, and second endings
- edit the first and second ending positions
- edit the Staff (Instrument) full and abbreviated names
- change the starting clef of the Tenor/Bass part
- enter a tempo marking in bar 9 for playback
- understand how to notate polyphony (voices)
- use voices rules
- enter notation in different voices
- turn on voice colors
- enter voices in step time and Flexi-time
- hide rests in selected voices
- transpose passages within the score
- hide time signatures
- enter two lines (verses) of lyrics
- copy lyrics using the filter
- enter slurs
- move lyrics

- reset the lyrics position
- enter block lyrics
- change the size and style of block lyrics
- import a graphic file
- access percussion maps
- understand how percussion maps work
- enter notation into percussion parts using alphabetic, step time with MIDI, and Flexi-time entry
- work with percussion maps: deleting, adding, and saving
- combine voices 1 and 2
- change a homophonic passage to a polyphonic one
- reduce the staff size of this example so it will all fit on one page
- save lyrics as a separate file via the plug-in

Review

1. Read/review about lyrics in Sibelius Reference, found in the Help menu (**Help** > Sibelius Reference).
2. Experiment with the lyric slur plug-in that automatically applies slurs to notes with lyrics (**Plug-ins** > Text > Add Slurs to Lyrics). It tends to work better in duple meter and not as well in triple meter.
3. Practice setting up your own custom percussion maps. Export them as custom House Styles for future use (**House Style** > Export House Style).
4. Extract the two percussion parts as separate parts. These steps were covered in Chapter 7.

9

Advanced Piano Arrangement
(Musical Example: "Intermezzo in A Major"
by Brahms)

Intermezzo in A major - Op. 118, No. 2

Johannes Brahms

Entered by (Your Name)

New topics and skills covered in this chapter:

- cross-staff notation
- splitting a chord across two staves
- entering tuplets with no number
- changing stem directions
- cross-bar beaming

- altering tuplet appearance
- changing the staff size
- creating a split-system coda
- creating arpeggio lines
- changing the font style and size
- moving accidentals

Piano music can produce some of the most complex music notation situations around. Since its invention, composers have been stretching the boundaries of what the instrument and the player can produce. Polyphony will be the main challenge in this chapter; with lines crossing staves, melodies that are part of the accompaniment, and crossing voices, there are a lot of choices to make concerning what notes get put where. But, before donning our engraver's hat, a file must be created.

1. Launch Sibelius.
2. Select the desired Playback and Input Devices if any change is required.
3. In the Quick Start dialog box, select "Start a new score" and click OK.
4. In the Manuscript Paper selection list, press the letter P on the keyboard to move alphabetically down the list to P, then select "Piano."

A representation of the page to be created appears in the window on the right side of the dialog box. The page size and orientation are correct for the example, so no change is needed.

5. Click Next to continue setting up the file.

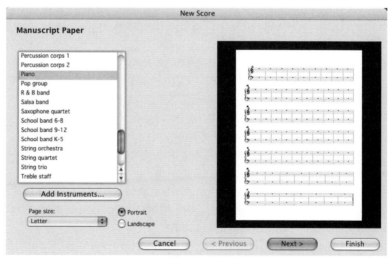

218

In the House Styles selection list, locate the options for Keyboard. There are three different music fonts available: Helsinki, Inkpen2, and Opus. The font in parentheses after the music font is the font used for all text in the file, other than dynamics. The menu underneath the selection list will allow the text font to be changed, so if you have a favorite or required font to use, make the selection here.

6. Select "Keyboard Opus (Times)."
7. Click Next.
8. Under the Time Signature heading, click the 3/4 button.
9. Under the "Pick-up (Upbeat)" Bar heading, check the box. The pick-up is a single beat, so no change is necessary for the duration.
10. Under the Tempo heading, select Andante from the pop-up menu, then click in the Tempo text field and type: "(space bar) teneramente."
11. Click Next.
12. Select A major for the Key Signature.
13. Click Next.

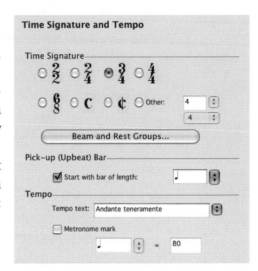

 The advantage to selecting at least part of the Tempo text from the menu is that a metronomic mark is also selected based on the tempo chosen. Even though the mark is not going to be displayed, the tempo is still used as the default playback tempo for the piece, so you will not have to enter any more Tempo text.

The final step in creating a new score is entering the text that will be displayed on the first page. It will also be on the title page, should the box under the copyright field be entered.

14. In the Score Info dialog box Title field, type "Intermezzo in A major—Op. 118, No. 2." Use the Tab key to advance to the next field.
15. In the Composer/Songwriter field, type "Johannes Brahms." Press Tab twice to skip over the Lyricist field.
16. In the Copyright field, type "Entered by" and your name.
17. Click the Finish button to create the file.
18. Save the file as "Brahms_Intmez_A."

Create Bars

The Intermezzo will require 86 bars, Sibelius has created 63, so 23 additional bars will need to be added to the piece.

1. Use the shortcut Option-B (Mac) or Alt-B (Win), to access the Create Bars dialog box.
2. Enter 23 for the number of bars to be created. The cursor will turn to the blue arrow.
3. Click in any bar of the piece, other than bar 1, to enter the additional bars.

The Anatomy of Polyphony

www.sibeliusbook.com

Before diving in, examine the full example at the beginning of this chapter, and download the completed file from the *www.sibeliusbook.com* Web site in the Chapter 8 folder (*9JBIntermezzo.pdf*). In Chapter 8 you followed a very simple formula: stems-up notes in Voice 1 and stems-down notes in Voice 2. While you will follow this rule of thumb here as well, the addition of cross-staff notation means you have some choices to make about the best way of entering a line of music. Here are some things to consider as you look over the finished version of the Brahms Intermezzo.

I will give you a bit more on specific situations as you follow the tutorial steps to enter the piece. These more general situations provide some basic rules for the next time you face a similar situation in your own work.

In bar 1 there is a cross-staff eighth note pattern. It looks like you should enter the first two eighths in Voice 2 and the sixteenth notes on beat 2 in the bass clef. The problem with that is Sibelius will not beam them together. Beaming is only possible between notes in the same voice entered on the same staff. As you will see in the Voice breakdowns later in this chapter, bar 1 of the bass clef has a quarter rest on beat 2 that will be hidden and the eighth notes entered in Voice 2 of the treble clef staff.

In bar 4, both staves have a Voice 2 line that does not last the full bar. It is not necessary to start at the beginning of the bar when entering notes in another Voice, only that there be a Voice 1 entry on the proper beat to select. That said, Sibelius needs to have a full bar for every Voice that is active so the appropriate number of rests will be entered to backfill the bar from beat 1. These rests will also be hidden, and I'll show you a quick method of hiding them later in the chapter.

In bar 29, treble clef staff, there is a third Voice needed for the G♯ dotted quarter note in the second beat. I could have switched the eighth note figure to Voice 1 of the bass clef staff but decided to leave it in the treble clef since it is the continuation of a figure already started in bar 25.

In bars 31 through 34, I avoid the use of a third Voice in the bass clef staff by cross-staffing the half note–quarter note figure from the treble staff. This will save a lot of rest entry and hiding, and keeps a single musical thought together in the same voice.

In bar 45 of the bass clef staff, the entire bar is entered in Voice 2 because of the cross-bar beaming required from the previous bar. The result is a whole rest entered in Voice 1 that requires hiding. Again I was following the pattern set up in previous bars based on stem direction for the bulk of the bars.

Landmarks

I find it a great help, when copying a piece rather than creating one, to enter any major landmarks before entering the music. They help keep you oriented and reduce the chances of a bar being skipped while copying. It will be easier to locate specific examples in the tutorial if each bar is numbered. This is not something I want for the final product, so I won't change the bar numbers that print.

1. Select **View** > Staff Names and Bar Numbers.
2. Enter the "Segno" in bar 16 using Repeat text.
3. Enter the "To Coda" indication and sign at the end of bar 45 using Repeat text.
4. Enter the Start Repeat bar in bar 49.
5. Enter the End Repeat bar at the end of bar 56.
6. Enter "piú lento" in bar 57.
7. Enter "Tempo primo" in bar 65.
8. Enter the double bar at the end of bar 83.
9. Enter the D.S. al Coda at the end of bar 83 using Repeat text.
10. Enter the 2/4 time signature in bar 86.

www.sibeliusbook.com

If you prefer to start at this point in the chapter, go to *www.sibeliusbook.com* and download the Chapter 9 folder. Open the file *9JBIntermezzo1.sib*.

The entry instructions in this chapter are for step entry using a MIDI keyboard. Begin with the treble staff, Voice 1 only. I will separate out each Voice to make clear what you actually need to enter and where. Be on the lookout for any enharmonic changes; you will have some to make.

Treble Clef: Voice 1

Entering Tuplets with No Number

In bar 73, there are triplets on beats 2 and 3. The beat 2 triplet is indicated only by the number. The triplet in beat 3 uses the old engraving practice of indication only by the presence of a beamed group of three notes. Sibelius is defaulted to display the number and the bracket, so a trip to the Tuplet dialog box is required to change the settings (turn off the bracket).

In bar 73 a tuplet number is required.

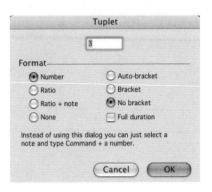

1. Enter the eighth rest.
2. Select **Create** > Tuplet.
3. Under the Format heading, click the Number button and the "No bracket" button, and click OK. Sibelius will enter future tuplets like this, so it'll need to be reset to the default when the number and/or bracket is required.
4. Continue entering the tuplet.

The next tuplet group requires no number.

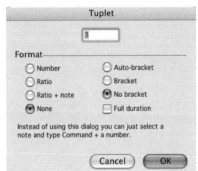

1. Enter the first note of the tuplet, the F♯, as usual.
2. Select **Create** > Tuplet.
3. Under the Format heading, click "None" and "No bracket," then click OK. This setting will remain in effect until it is changed or the file is closed.
4. Continue entering the notation.

In bar 79, the E♯s in beats 1 and 2 will have to be enharmonically shifted to F naturals.

1. Select the E♯ in beat 1.
2. ⌘-click (Mac) or CTRL-click (Win) and select the E♯ in beat 2.
3. Press the Return/Enter key to change the enharmonic. Then press Esc to deselect the notes.

Treble Clef: Voice 2

Sibelius will allow Voice 2 entries to begin anywhere in the bar. Just select a Voice 1 entry where you want to begin, but each Voice must have the correct number of beats for the whole bar. The rests will be filled in for you, but you must move or hide them as needed later. In the notation below, I used half rests in some bars. It is incorrect notation, but the rests will eventually be hidden and this creates one less item to hide. The whole rests shown (see next page) are defaults and do not need to be entered.

1. Select the first note in Voice 1.
2. Press the N key.
3. Use the shortcut Option-2 (Mac); Alt-2 (Win) to select Voice 2 and the cursor will turn green.
4. Begin note entry. Sibelius will handle the stem direction.

So you don't have to count ledger lines, the fourth note in bar 29 is an E.

Bass Clef: Voice 1

In all situations, a bar must contain as many beats as specified by the time signature. Enter rests, which you will hide later on, to fill any empty spaces.

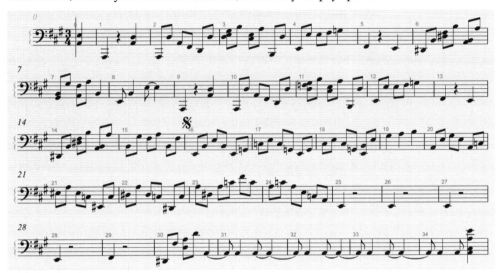

Be on the lookout for more beamed tuplets with no number beginning in bar 54.

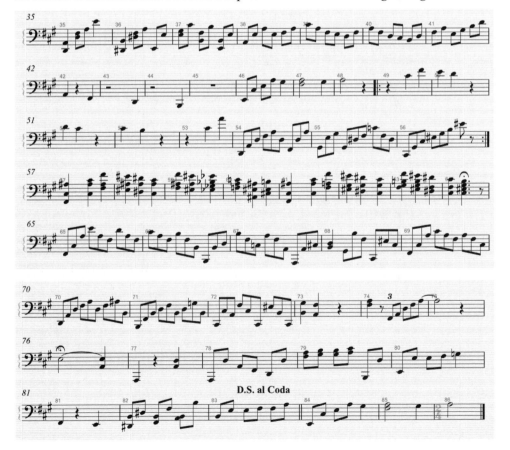

Bass Clef: Voice 2

Just as with the treble clef, Voice 2 entries, the whole rests should not be entered.

Whenever you encounter notes that are below the range of your keyboard, enter the note in the closest available octave, in this case, the octave above, then use the Octave Transposition shortcut, ⌘-Down Arrow key (Mac) or CTRL-Down Arrow key (Win).

In bar 49 you will need to repeat the steps for creating a tuplet with the number displayed, then reset it to display no number.

In bar 86 there is an octave where the bottom note is below the range of my MIDI keyboard. There are two choices for entering octaves in this situation. The first is the same method mentioned above, only entering both notes an octave higher, then using the Octave Transposition shortcut. The second is entering the top note and using the shortcut Shift-8 (the 8 along the top of the keyboard, not the keypad) to add the octave below. This command can also be accessed in the Notes menu, from the Add Interval submenu. There you can view the complete list of options available for adding any interval inside an octave.

One Small Voice (3)

There are a few spots where a third Voice is required. For this it is easier to go bar by bar.

1. Select bar 29.
2. Press N to enter notation.
3. Use the shortcut Option-3 (Mac); Alt-3 (Win) to enter notes in Voice 3.
4. Enter the dotted quarter rest and note.
5. Repeat steps 1 through 3 in bars 47, 60, and 85.

Bar 29 in the treble clef

Bar 47 in the bass clef

Bar 60 in the treble clef

Bar 85 in the bass clef

www.sibeliusbook.com

If you prefer to start at this point in the chapter, go to *www.sibeliusbook.com* and download the Chapter 9 folder. Open the file *9JBIntermezzo2.sib*.

Hiding Rests

With all the notes in place, it is time to hide all of the placeholder rests. In the treble staff, the first rest to be hidden is in bar 4, and the first Voice 2 rests that need to be visible are in bar 54.

1. Select bars 4 through 53 of the treble clef staff.
2. Select **Edit** > Filter > Advanced Filter; note the available keystroke for future use.
3. Under the View heading, select "Rests and Bar Rests."
4. Under the Find heading, uncheck "Notes and Chords" and check "Rest and Bar Rests."
5. Under the Voice heading, uncheck "1" and "4."
6. Click Select.

All the Voice 2 and 3 rests are selected, each highlighted in their color (green for Voice 2 and yellow for Voice 3).

7. Use the shortcut ⌘-Shift-H (Mac); CTRL-Shift-H (Win) to hide all selected rests.

Move on to the next region for hiding rests.

1. Select bars 56 through 68 of the treble clef staff.
2. Use the shortcut Option-Shift-⌘-F (Mac); Alt-Shift-CTRL-F (Win) to display the Advanced Filter dialog box.
3. All of the edits you made are unchanged in the dialog box, so click Select.
4. Use the shortcut ⌘-Shift-H (Mac); CTRL-Shift-H (Win) to hide all selected rests.
5. Select bars 74 to 83.
6. Repeat the above steps for selecting and hiding the rests.

In beat 3 of bar 74 there are rests in Voices 1 and 2. When the Voice 2 rest is hidden, the Voice 1 rest automatically returns to the center staff position.

Moving on to the bass clef staff, in addition to the Voice 2 and 3 rests, some Voice 1 rests require hiding.

1. Select bars 1 through 46 of the bass clef staff.
2. Repeat the steps for selecting and hiding the Voice 2 and 3 rests.
3. Use the shortcut Option-Shift-⌘-F (Mac); Alt-Shift-CTRL-F (Win) to display the Advanced Filter dialog box.
4. Under the Voice heading, check the 1 box.
5. Click Select.
6. Use the shortcut ⌘-Shift-H (Mac); CTRL-Shift-H (Win) to hide all selected rests.

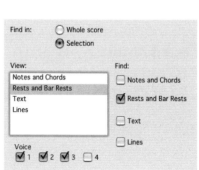

The Filter only selects rests that were entered, not the default rests provided by the program. For that reason the rest in bar 45 of the bass clef is still visible. It was added because there are Voice 2 entries in the bar. It can be hidden, but must be manually selected first.

7. Select and hide the rest in bar 45 of the bass clef staff.

In bars 45 through 76, the Voice 1 rests are necessary, so the Filter must be adjusted to only select the Voice 2 and 3 rests.

8. Select bars 45 through 76.
9. Use the shortcut Option-Shift-⌘-F (Mac); Alt-Shift-CTRL-F (Win) to display the Advanced Filter dialog box.
10. Under the Voice heading, uncheck the 1 box.
11. Click Select.
12. Use the shortcut ⌘-Shift-H (Mac); CTRL-Shift-H (Win) to hide all selected rests.
13. Select bars 77 through 85. The Voice rests need to be hidden, so the Filter must be adjusted again.
14. Use the shortcut Option-Shift-⌘-F (Mac); Alt-Shift-CTRL-F (Win) to display the Advanced Filter dialog box.
15. Under the Voice heading, check the 1 box again.
16. Click Select.
17. Use the shortcut ⌘-Shift-H (Mac); CTRL-Shift-H (Win) to hide all selected rests.

There are a few Voice 1 rests that will need hiding. They are in the bass staff in bar 49, beat 1, and in bar 75, beat 3. These will have to be done individually.

18. Select the Voice 1 rests and hide them.

This would be an excellent time to save the file.

Before beginning work on all the beaming and cross-staff work, step back and look at the document as a whole. The final positioning of some of these elements will depend on the final spacing of the piece, which needs a little refinement.

Select Fit 2 Pages from the Zoom menu. If this is too small on your monitor, choose the best size for viewing as much of the document as possible and still keeping it legible.

Page Layout

The good news is that the example fills two pages without stretching or shoehorning required. The bad news is that not a lot of space exists between the staves where you still must add and edit a lot of information. I will use the same "zoom in" formatting order as with "The Easy Winners": set the page first, then the system, and lastly the staves.

Judging the size and scale of the music on the computer screen is difficult. I recommend printing the example as it is and comparing it to any printed piano music you have in your collection or can find elsewhere, taking into account that it is most likely printed on a larger size page. Once you see how it compares in staff size and distance between staves and how those elements are controlled in Sibelius, you'll develop your own preferences and be able to execute them quickly.

Staff Size

When the music displayed on the screen begins to look very dense, you can let a little bit of light into the layout by reducing the size of the staff. The smaller size adds a little more white space between notes and creates a more open feel to the music. The less cluttered it looks, the easier it is to read.

1. Use the shortcut ⌘-D (Mac); CTRL-D (Win) to access the Document Setup dialog box.
2. Under the Size heading, change "Staff size" to 0.22. Click the down arrow next to the number entry field or type in the number.
3. Click OK.

The music has repositioned itself and there is room at the bottom of page 1 that will be put to good use in between the treble and bass staves as well as between systems. On the second page there is room for an additional system; so that allows you to change the number of bars on some systems where more room is needed. Before any definite decisions can be made about system spacing, let's see what bars will be on which system.

Entering System Breaks

Go through the piece system by system and see where some additional space may be needed. In creating this example, I reproduced an old engraving where some of the note positions differ from the Sibelius autopositioning placement. In some cases I like the Sibelius placement better than the original, but for the exercise, I will make this match the original.

The first system, bars 0 through 6, is fine. In the second system, there are some changes to make in bars 10 and 11. On both beat 3 of bar 10 and beat 1 of bar 11, the quarter note must be moved to the other side of the dotted eighth note. On beat 2 of bar 11 the eighth note must be moved to the other side of the quarter note to create a bit more space to work with on this system.

1. Select the barline at the end of bar 12.
2. Select **Layout** > Break > System Break.

Now there are six bars in the second system instead of seven. In the third system, bar 15 will require the same alteration on beat 2 as in bar 11. Make the system six bars as well.

3. Select the barline at the end of bar 18.
4. Press Return/Enter.

To give bar 29 more room, break the system after bar 31.

5. Select the barline at the end of bar 31.
6. Press Return/Enter.

This also has the benefit of placing the To Coda indication at the end of the system. Here are the page 2 changes.

7. Enter a system break after bar 51.
8. Enter a system break after bar 64.
9. Enter a system break after bar 76.

With the systems set, why not save the document before you tackle respacing the staves?

Separating the Coda

Sibelius provides a simple way to create a separation for the Coda that does not require a system break.

1. Select the double bar at the end of bar 83.
2. Select **Layout** > Break > Split System.

Locking the Layout

With the systems set, it is highly recommended that you lock the layout so there is no chance of an edit causing a bar to move on its own:

1. Use the shortcut ⌘-A (Mac); CTRL-A (Win) to select the entire document.
2. Use the shortcut Shift-⌘-L (Mac); Shift-CTRL-L (Win) to lock the format.

The opposing arrow icon will appear over the barlines and the system break arrows will now appear at the end of each system. A page break icon will be at the bottom of each page. The icon that resembles a split multirest symbol over the end of bar 83 indicates the split system.

Tools for Change

When moving elements around a virtual page, it can be difficult to understand just how far you are moving something. For just such circumstances, there are Rulers.

1. Select **View** > Rulers > Staff Rulers. There is a shortcut you can use in the future.

Now you can see the distance between the staves, systems, and page margins. If you want to go one step further, try using graph paper for the page texture. This will help when lining up text.

2. Select **Sibelius 4** > Preferences (Mac) or **File** > Preferences (Windows).
3. Select Textures in the left column.
4. Under the Full Score heading, select "Paper, graph" from the Paper pop-up menu.
5. Click OK.

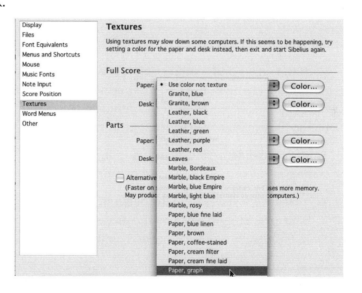

Changing the Distance Between Staves

More room is needed between the staves of the grand staff for all the up- and down-stemmed notes and cross-staff notes. The current distance is 7.6. I want to increase it to 10.5.

1. Use the Navigator window to position the page so you can see the first system in the piece and the Ruler numbers in the left margin.

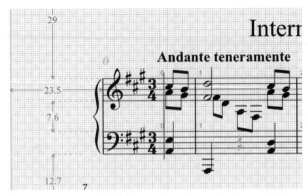

2. Triple-click the bass clef staff to select it for the whole piece.

3. Move the staves by holding down Option (Mac) or Alt (Win) and repeatedly pressing the down arrow key until the Ruler number hits approximately 10.5.

4. Press Esc to deselect the staff.

Save!

www.sibeliusbook.com

If you prefer to start at this point in the chapter, go to *www.sibeliusbook.com* and download the Chapter 9 folder. Open the file *9JBIntermezzo3.sib*.

Taking Measure

With the pages and systems set, it is time to go measure by measure and make any notational changes and add the performance information. To save flipping back to the beginning of the chapter to reference the completed example, download the completed file from the Web site and print it out for easy viewing (see page 219).

This is an excellent time to add cautionary accidentals to the piece, as they might have some bearing on positioning in the coming edits.

1. Select both staves from the beginning of the piece to bar 83. Do not select the Coda, since the plug-in will read the piece without repeats. Bar 84 will not be played after bar 83, so no natural is needed on the B eighth note in the treble clef.

 When adding cautionary accidentals with the plug-in, always process Codas separately. Any accidentals required in the first bar of the Coda will need to be added manually.

2. Select **Plug-ins** > Accidentals > Add Cautionary Accidentals and click Yes in the dialog box warning that this action is not undoable. Since you just saved the document, closing and reopening is the undo process for any action not affected by the ⌘-Z (Mac) or CTRL-Z (Win) command. (You did save, didn't you?)

3. Uncheck "Put parentheses around cautionary accidentals." (I also unchecked the highlight option for the screen shots used in this book.)

4. Click OK, then press Esc when the plug-in is finished.

Add Cautionary Accidentals

Maximum number of intervening notes: 99

☐ Mark inserted accidentals with [CA] text
☑ Mark inserted accidentals with highlights
☑ Add cautionaries to notes of the same pitch in different octaves
  ○ in the same bar only
  ○ when the notes are in different bars
  ● always
☐ Put parentheses around cautionary accidentals
☑ Reset note spacing of bars that change

(Help) (Cancel) (OK)

Beaming Alterations and Cross-Staff Notation

Both of these tasks are linked many times in this example, including the first instance of both in bar 2. I prefer joining the beams before cross-staffing the notes, but Sibelius allows you to work either way.

1. Select the A eighth note in Voice 2 of the treble clef on beat 2.
2. Select the Beaming Keypad by clicking the beam icon at the top of the Keypad or by pressing the + key (plus sign on the numeric keypad) two times. The Keypad will be color-coded green to indicate that a Voice 2 note is selected.

3. Click the [♭] key or press the 8 key on the numeric keypad.

To cross-staff the notes:

1. Select both the A and the F♯ eighth notes on beat 2 of bar 1.
2. **Select Notes** > Cross Staff Notes > Down a Staff.

The beam needs a little downward angle. To accomplish this, you will need to shorten the stem of the F♯ eighth note.

3. Select the stem of the F♯ eighth note.
4. Click and drag, or use the arrow keys to angle the beam down. The graph paper texture comes in handy here as well.

Changing the Horizontal Position of a Note

The D eighth note on beat 1, Voice 2 of this bar is positioned with accuracy at the middle of the first beat of the bar, and looks amazingly wrong. The offset required for the F♯ eighth note on beat 1 has no effect on the rest of the bar. The shorter distance between them creates an optical illusion that they might be sixteenth notes. Try wrongly moving the D eighth note a little to the right so it is spaced evenly between the F♯ and the A.

1. Select the D eighth note.
2. If the Properties window is not open in the Sibelius window, use the shortcut Option-⌘-P (Mac); Alt-CTRL-P (Win) to open it, or click the Properties button in the toolbar.

3. Click on the General tab in the Properties window so that its settings are displayed.
4. In the X value box, type 1. A positive number will move the note to the right.
5. Press Esc.

   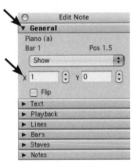

> Never reposition a note horizontally by dragging it. Always use the Properties X value box.

That completes the edits for bar 1. The slurs and other markings will be added later. Turn your attention to the bass clef staff in bar 2, where another beam needs to be joined.

1. Select the A eighth note on beat 2 of the bass clef staff in bar 2.
2. Select the Beaming Keypad by clicking the Beam icon at the top of the Keypad or by pressing the + key (plus sign on the numeric keypad) two times.
3. Click the 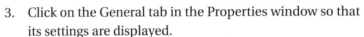 key or press the 8 key on the numeric keypad.
4. Press Esc.

Arpeggio Lines: Some Assembly Required

In the treble staff of bar 2, an arpeggio line is required.

1. Select the A half note.
2. Press the L key to access the Lines selection window.
3. Select the vertical squiggly line and click OK.

After clicking OK, you may wonder what happened to your arpeggio line. In this case it is just to the left of the barline underneath the staff.

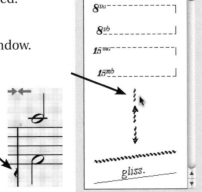

4. Select the arpeggio—it will turn blue—and drag it up next to the A half note.

5. Click on the arpeggio again. It will turn black and a handle will appear on the bottom of the shape.
6. Click and hold on the handle and drag it down so the resulting line is drawn through the first space of the staff next to the F♯ half note, then release the button.
7. Press Esc.

Bar 5 Edits

In bar 5 you have a chance to repeat the edits made in bar 1.

1. Select the A eighth note in Voice 2 of the treble clef.
2. Select the Beaming Keypad by clicking the Beam icon at the top of the Keypad or by pressing the + key (plus sign on the numeric keypad) two times.
3. Click the ♪ key or press the 8 key on the numeric keypad.
4. Select both the A and the F♯ eighth notes on beat 2 of bar 2.
5. Use the shortcut Shift-⌘-down arrow key (Mac); Shift-CTRL-down arrow key (Win), the keystroke for cross-staffing to the staff below.
6. Select the stem of the F♯ eighth note.
7. Click and drag, or use the arrow keys to angle the beam down.
8. Select the D eighth note in the second half of beat 1.
9. Open the Properties window.
10. In General Properties, type 1 in the X value box.

Bar 6 Edits

In bar 6 there are more Properties issues on beat 3 in the treble staff. The positions of the dotted eighth and quarter notes must be reversed. Move the dotted eighth note to the position of the quarter note first so the quarters can be used as a placement guide.

1. Select the C♯ dotted eighth note on beat 3.
2. In the General tab of the Properties window, click the down arrow button to the right of the X value box until the note is lined up with the Voice 2 quarter note, which is at 1.5.

> If you are not sure about the vertical alignment on the dotted quarter note, select the Voice 2 quarter note and flip the stem up (press X). When the stem for the dotted eighth aligns, the position is correct.

The dot for the dotted quarter note can also be manually repositioned. This will be a small move, but it will keep the quarter note closer to the dotted eighth.

3. Select the dot and drag it to the left so it is closer to the note. Leave enough space so that it is still clearly visible.
4. Select either one of the noteheads on the Voice 2 quarter note.

5. Click the up arrow button to the right of the X value box until the note is clear of the dot, which is at 1.65.
6. Press Esc.

Bars 9 and 10: Déjà Vu All Over Again

In bars 9 and 10 you have a chance to show what you know. Review the steps from bars 1 and 2 and the Properties change in bar 7 to make the alterations in these two bars. Here are two hints. The arpeggio line in bar 2 can be copied and pasted into bar 10 (steps to follow), and the A quarter note on beat 3 will need to go a little farther to the right (X value of 2.4 in the Properties window).

Copying a Line

A line can be copied using the same process as for copying an expression or technique. Select the line when copying and select the note to which it will be attached at the destination.

1. Select the arpeggio line in bar 2 and copy it.
2. Select the A half note in 10 and Option-click (Mac); Alt-click (Win) to paste the line, then press Esc.

Properties of Bar 11

Beat 1 features another dotted eighth and quarter note switch.

1. Select the dotted eighth note on beat 1 and move it to the left, -0.5.
2. Select the dots and move them closer to the note.
3. Move the quarter note G♯ to the right, 0.09.

The quarter note and eighth note in beat 2 also need to trade places.

4. Move the G♯ eighth note to the left, -1.65.
5. Move the quarter note to the right so there is a little separation between the notes and stems, 0.30.
6. Press Esc.

Bar 13 is the same as bar 5; review the steps for bar 5 if needed.

Bar 15 has something old on beat 2 and something new on beat 3. Just to keep it interesting, I've added a beam repositioning on beat 2.

1. Select the B♯ eighth note and move it to the left, -1.62.
2. Select the quarter note and move it to the right, 0.25.
3. Select the eighth note beam.
4. Drag the beam down a little so it does not crowd the E quarter note.
5. Select the Voice 2 A quarter note on beat 3 and move it to the left so it overlaps the A eighth notehead, -1.62.

Beaming 202

Bar 16 in the bass clef begins a stretch of eighth notes that are beamed in groups of four or six, including some cross-bar beaming. It is possible to change the beaming of multiple notes in a single click by ⌘-clicking (Mac) or CTRL-clicking (Win) the notes to be re-beamed.

1. Select the E eighth note on beat 2 in the bass clef.
2. ⌘-click (Mac) or CTRL-click (Win) on the C eighth note on beat 2 of bar 17.

3. Select the Beaming Keypad by clicking the Beam icon at the top of the Keypad or by pressing the + key (plus sign on the numeric keypad) two times.
4. Click the ⌐ key or press the 8 key on the numeric keypad to rebeam the selected notes.

Beaming Over the Barline

Creating a beam that connects notes across the barline is literally the same process you have been using in all the previous beaming instances in this chapter.

1. Select the C♯ eighth note on the downbeat of bar 18 in the bass clef.

2. Click the ⌐ key or press the 8 key on the numeric keypad.

That's all there is to it.

3. Select the C♯ eighth note on beat 2 in the bass clef and beam it to the previous group.

In the next system, put it all together and create all the beams in one click.

1. Select the A eighth note in Voice 2 on beat 2 of bar 19 in the bass clef.

> In situations where there are overlapping noteheads, click on the stem instead of the note to be sure that you're selecting the right voice.

2. ⌘-click (Mac) or CTRL-click (Win) on the following notes on the bass clef:
   - the B eighth on beat 3 of bar 19
   - the E eighth on beat 1 of bar 20
   - the F eighth on beat 1 of bar 21
   - the F eighth on beat 2 of bar 21
   - the D♯ eighth on beat 1 of bar 22
   - the D♯ eighth on beat 2 of bar 22
   - the A eighth on beat 2 of bar 23
   - the F♯ eighth on beat 3 of bar 23
   - the A eighth on beat 2 of bar 24
   - the C eighth on beat 3 of bar 24

   On the treble clef staff:
   - the G♯ eighth on beat 2 of bar 25
   - the C eighth on beat 3 of bar 25
3. Click the ♩ key or press the 8 key on the numeric keypad.
4. Press Esc.
5. Select all of the notes to be beamed in bars 26 though 31 and beam them with one click.

Cross-Staffing 202

Everything you just learned about selecting multiple notes for beaming also applies to selecting notes for cross-staffing. There is a pattern of cross-staff notes in the treble clef staff of bars 25 through 29 that are perfect for the one-click method.

1. Select the E eighth note in Voice 2, on beat 2 in bar 25.
2. ⌘-click (Mac) or CTRL-click (Win) the remaining two eighth notes in Voice 2 of the treble staff.
3. ⌘-click (Mac) or CTRL-click (Win) the last three notes in Voice 2 in bars 26, 27, and 28, and the last four notes in bar 29.
4. Use the shortcut Shift-⌘-down arrow key (Mac) or Shift-CTRL-down arrow key (Win).
5. Select and raise the eighth note beam in bar 28 so that it is above the natural sign on the G on beat 3.
6. Angle the beam down in bar 29.

Bar 29

Bar 29 needs a few other tweaks before moving on with cross-staffing and beam adjustment. The tie coming from bar 28 must be flipped. The dotted quarter note must be moved to the left and overlap the eighth note. Normally noteheads of different value are not overlapped, but the tie changes the equation. As currently notated, the player might assume a reattack of the A is called for since the tie is attached to the eighth note. The C♯ in Voice 1 is incorrectly downstemmed.

1. Select the tie in the treble clef staff.
2. Press the X key to flip the direction.
3. Select the dotted quarter note in beat 1 of the treble staff.
4. Under the General tab in the Properties window, use the down arrow button to nudge the dotted quarter to the left so it completely overlaps the eighth notehead, -1.5.
5. Select the C♯ quarter note in Voice 1, treble staff, and press the X key to change the stem direction.
6. Press Esc.

Bar 30

1. In the treble staff there is another arpeggio line. Repeat the steps for copying and pasting lines from the bar 10 edits above.
2. Join the eighth note beams between beats 1 and 2 in the bass clef staff.

Bars 31 Through 34

These bars contain cross-staffing that creates a stem collision problem in the bass clef staff. The solution to the problem is to move the upstemmed notes in the bass clef to the right so the stems no longer collide.

1. Select and cross-staff the treble clef, Voice 2 notes on beat 3 of bars 31 and 33 and on beat 1 of bars 32 and 34 and cross-staff them.
2. Select the A quarter note in the bass clef, beat 3.
3. Under the General tab in the Properties window, use the up arrow button to nudge the quarter note to the right, 0.50.
4. Select the eighth note on beat 1 of bar 32 in the bass clef and nudge it to the right by the same distance as the quarter note.
5. Repeat the above steps on the quarter note on beat 3 of bar 33 and the eighth note on beat 1 of bar 34.

Bars 35 Through 37

1. Join the beams as required in the treble clef staff.
2. In bar 36, nudge the G♯ in Voice 2 of the treble staff to the right so it is in the middle of the space between the beat 1 and beat 2 eighth notes, 0.4.

Bars 38 Through 47

1. Join eighth note beams as needed in the bass clef staff. In bar 39 you will see that beaming across both a barline and a system break is no different than any other beaming change in this chapter.
2. In bar 46, bass clef, the quarter note E on beat 3 requires a stem flip. Select the note and press the X key.

Splitting a Chord Over Two Staves

In bars 47 and 48 there is a partly cross-staffed chord. Sibelius does not handle this situation directly, but it can be reproduced with a little help from the Properties controls. In bar 47, the half notes in Voice 1 of the bass clef must have the stem direction changed, and be nudged to the right until the stem lines up with the D half note in Voice 2 of the treble staff to produce the effect.

1. Select the stem of the D half note in Voice 2 of bar 47 in the treble staff.
2. Drag the stem handle down so the handle is in the fourth space of the bass clef staff.
3. Select the half note in Voice 1 of the bass staff and flip the stem.
4. Under the General tab in the Properties window, use the up arrow button to nudge the  half note to the right. I recommend zooming in on this staff and bar so it is as large as possible on the computer screen. This will make it easier to see when the stems are in perfect alignment, which should be at 1.28 in the X value box.
5. Select the stem of the bass clef half note and drag the bottom end up so the stem ends at the second line of the staff.

There is one last detail to complete in the bass clef of bar 47.

6. Select the quarter note G♯ in Voice 1, beat 3 of the bass staff and nudge it to the left, away from the stem of the eighth note, -0.40.

In bar 48, the half notes in the treble staff need to trade places so that the octave A half notes line up vertically.

1. Select the stem of the A half note in Voice 2, treble staff.
2. Drag the stem's handle down so it ends in the fourth space of the bass staff.
3. Select the A in Voice 1 of the bass staff and flip the stem down.
4. Select the stem of the same note and drag the handle up so the stem ends in the middle of the third space of the bass staff. The handle will be in the middle of the first space when you select the stem.
5. Select the A half note in Voice 2, treble staff.

6. Under the General tab in the Properties window, use the down arrow button to nudge the half note to the left. Stop when the stem lines up perfectly with the A half note stem in Voice 1 of the bass staff, -1.66.
7. Select the E half note in Voice 1 of the treble staff.
8. Under the General tab in the Properties window, use the up arrow button to nudge the half note to the right, 0.40.

This bar also needs an arpeggio line. Enter a new line here, since the length must be adjusted even if the previous line was copied to this location.

1. Select the A half note in Voice 2, treble staff.
2. Press the L key to bring up the Lines selection window.
3. Select the arpeggio line in the Staff Lines selection list and click OK.
4. Select the arpeggio line and drag it up next to the A half note, midway between the note and the barline.
5. Click just underneath the line so the handle appears on the bottom.
6. Drag the line down until it extends just below the low A in Voice 2 of the bass staff.

Time to save!

www.sibeliusbook.com

If you prefer to start at this point in the chapter, go to *www.sibeliusbook.com* and download the Chapter 9 folder. Open the file *9JBIntermezzo4.sib*.

Bars 49 Through 56: Repositioning Rests

1. Enter the beaming changes for both staves in bars 49 to 56.
2. Select the quarter rest on beat 3 of bar 50 in the Bass clef.
3. Press the Up Arrow key on the computer keyboard three times.
4. Use the same process in bars 51, 52, and 53 to relocate the quarter rests there.
5. Select the quarter rest in bar 54, Treble staff, beat 3 and press the down arrow key one time.
6. Select the quarter rest in bar 55, Treble staff, beat 3 and press the down arrow key one time.

Bars 57 Through 64

This passage provides a little break, both musically and for you as engraver, from the flowing eighth note patterns that characterized the piece up until this point. That doesn't mean there are no eighth notes, and guess where you have to edit: the eighth notes in bar 60. This is a three-voice bar and requires a little of everything you've been doing so far in this chapter to sort out the overlapping notes.

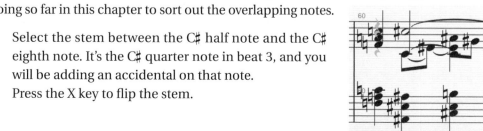

1. Select the stem between the C♯ half note and the C♯ eighth note. It's the C♯ quarter note in beat 3, and you will be adding an accidental on that note.
2. Press the X key to flip the stem.

3. Click on the downstemmed C♯ eighth note on the same beat.
4. Press the X key to flip the stem.
5. Select the A♯ eighth note in Voice 2, on beat 3.
6. Press the X key to flip the stem.
7. Press the ⬛ key or the 8 key on the computer keypad.
8. Press the ◀◀ key or the – (minus) key on the computer keypad to return to the first Keypad display.
9. Press the ♯ key or the 8 key on the computer keypad.

There are three tie-related problems to be resolved. The tie between the C♯ quarters must be flipped, the tie from the E♯ eighth note must be shortened, and the tie from the C♯ half note is lost in the eighth note stems and beam. The half note will have to move a little to the left so the stem does not collide with the eighth note stem.

10. Select the C♯ half note in bar 60.
11. Under the General tab in the Properties window, use the down arrow button to nudge the half note to the left, -0.40.
12. Click on the left end beam of the Voice 2 eighth notes on beats 2 and 3.
13. Drag the left end beam down so it just touches the fourth line of the staff.
14. Select the right end of the beam.
15. Press the up arrow key until the right end of the beam touches the top line of the staff.
16. Select the tie connected to the C♯ half note.
17. Press the up arrow key on the computer keypad two times.
18. Click the left end of the tie so the handle appears.
19. Nudge the end of the tie up until it clears the eighth note beam.
20. Select the tie between the C♯ quarter notes underneath the staff.
21. Press the X key to flip the tie.

The tie between the E♯s is a little tricky. The right end is on top of the C♯ quarter note, so if you try to select the slur you will get the note instead. The quarter note on beat 3 will have to be relocated temporarily.

22. Select the Voice 3 E♯ quarter note on beat 3.
23. Under the General tab in the Properties window, enter 3 for the X value and press the Tab key.
24. Select the right end of the tie from the E♯ eighth note and drag it to the left until it lines up with the tie from the C♯ below.
25. Select the relocated beat 3 quarter note.
26. In the Properties window, enter 0 for the X value and press the Tab key.

Moving Accidentals

There is a rare problem with the accidental placement in the bass staff on the down-beat of bar 58 and 60. The top accidental should be right next to the note.

1. Select the top sharp on beat 1 of bar 58 in the bass staff.
2. Use the shortcut Shift-Option-right arrow (Mac); Shift-Alt-right arrow (Win) to nudge the accidental to the right. Stop when the vertical lines line up with the accidental below.
3. Select the second sharp on beat 1 of bar 58.
4. Use the shortcut Shift-Option-left arrow (Mac); Shift-Alt-left arrow (Win) to nudge the accidental to the left. Stop when the vertical lines line up with the accidental below.
5. Select the bottom accidental on beat 1 of bar 58.
6. Use the shortcut Shift-Option-right arrow (Mac); Shift-Alt-right arrow (Win) to nudge the accidental to the right. Stop when the vertical lines line up with the accidental above.

The changes in bar 60 will have to be eyeballed since they will not line up or overlap at all. When the top and second accidentals are positioned, the bottom natural sign will require only a small nudge to the right.

7. Select the top sharp on beat 1 of bar 60.
8. Use the shortcut Shift-Option-right arrow (Mac); Shift-Alt-right arrow (Win) to nudge the accidental to the right.
9. Select the second sharp on beat 1 of bar 60.
10. Use the shortcut Shift-Option-left arrow (Mac); Shift-Alt-left arrow (Win) to nudge the accidental to the left.
11. Select the bottom accidental on beat 1 of bar 60.
12. Use the shortcut Shift-Option-right arrow (Mac); Shift-Alt-right arrow (Win) to nudge the accidental to the right.

Bars 65 Through 72

These bars make a great review of much of what you've done so far in this chapter. To help develop your engraver's eye, I've listed what needs to be done in each bar and leave it up to you to find and execute.

Bar 65: Flip stems and cross staff.

Bar 66: Flip stems, cross staff, join beam, angle beam, and move rest.

Bar 67: Flip stems, cross staff, join beam, angle beam, and move rest.

Bar 68: Flip stems, cross staff, join beam, and angle beam.

Bar 69: Flip stems, cross staff note and rest, join beam, raise beam, and move rest.

Bar 70: Join beam.

Bar 71: Join beam.

The treble clef cross-staffing in bar 72 requires an extra step. After you cross-staff the E♯ from the treble staff, the beam defaults to a stems-up and stems-down position.

1. Flip the stem direction on the last triplet group in the bass clef.
2. Select the left end of the eighth note beam and drag it above the staff. The default position would place the beam even with the first ledger line above the staff, an octave above the A. The stem, however, is on the wrong side of the notehead.
3. Press the X key to flip the stem direction.
4. Select the right end of the eighth note beam.
5. Angle the beam down so it touches the middle line of the treble staff.

Congratulations! You've done so well that you get a holiday for bar 73.

Bars 74 Through 76: Cross-Staffing Uphill

Begin with the Properties window X value repositioning of the quarter and half notes in the treble staff.

1. Select the A half note on beat 1 of bar 74.
2. Under the General tab in the Properties window, use the down arrow button to nudge the half note to the left, -1.68.
3. Select the E quarter note on beat 1.
4. Use the up arrow in the Properties window to nudge the quarter note to the right, 0.3.
5. Join the eighth note beams in bar 74 on the bass staff.

Up until this point in the Intermezzo, all of the cross-staffing has been from the treble to the bass staff. Reversing the direction only requires the substitution of the up arrow key on the computer keyboard for the down arrow key.

6. Select all the notes to be cross-staffed in bars 74 and 75.
7. Use the shortcut Shift-⌘-up arrow (Mac); Shift-CTRL-up arrow (Win).

It's okay if you feel a little winded—going uphill can be difficult, especially if you are at high altitude. There are a few details to clean up. The beams of the cross-staffed groups need to be angled to reflect

the contour of the line, the ties need to be flipped, and the placement of the tuplet number requires a change.

8. Select the tie from the A eighth at the end of bar 74.
9. ⌘-click (Mac); CTRL-click (Win) the tie from the A eighth at the end of bar 75.
10. Press the X key. Yes, you can do multiple flips with one keystroke. Kind of makes you want to do multiple flips; be careful, the folks at high altitude might still be winded.
11. In bar 74 of the bass staff, select the left end of the eighth note beam.
12. Drag it down toward the bass staff.
13. Select the right end of the tuplet beam.
14. Nudge it up toward the treble staff. Try to have the same stem length between the beam and F♯ in the bass staff and the beam and the A that is cross-staffed.
15. Select the tuplet number in beat 2 and drag it under the bass staff.
16. In bar 75, select the right end of the tuplet beam on beat 3 and nudge the end of the beam up toward the treble staff.

The tie from bar 75 into 76 extends a bit too far into the half note on beat 1 in the treble staff. Use the same tactic as in bar 60 to temporarily displace the half note so you can click on the tie's right end handle.

17. Select the Voice 2 half note in bar 76.
18. In the Properties window, enter 3 for the X value and press the Tab key.
19. Select the right end of the tie from the A eighth note and drag it to the left. To be on the safe side, drag it back across the barline.
20. Select the relocated half note.
21. In the Properties window, enter 0 for the X value and press the Tab key.
22. Select the right end of the tie and drag it to the right so that it ends just short of the A half note.

Bars 77 Through 81

If these bars look familiar, they should, because they are the same as bars 1 through 5 and 9 through 13. You should be ready to handle these on your own. Refer to those sections earlier in the chapter as needed.

Bars 82 Through 86: The Home Stretch

Bar 82 requires a single beaming change in the treble staff, from the eighth note in beat 2 to the dotted eighth in beat 3. Make it so.

The Coda should also look familiar. It is a repeat of bars 46 through 48, minus the pickup in bar 48. Refer to that section of the chapter and perform the same alterations here. Just for fun, there is a small difference in the bass staff of bar 85.

Time to save!

One More Trip Down Intermezzo Lane

Everybody board the bus as we journey back to the top of the piece for one more trip through the document. This time it will be to enter all the expressions, technique text, tempo text, and Coda-related indications. You should be well practiced in entering these by now, so there aren't instructions for every instance, but below are a few special situations that you may not have encountered before.

Bar 1: Slurs on Cross-staffed Notes

When entering slurs on cross-staffed notes, you may encounter some unusual behavior from time to time. As an example, in bar 1, the first slur entered positioned perfectly beneath the F♯ and D eighth notes. The slur entered on beat 2 appeared over the letter a and m in the tempo text. Magnetic slurs do not attach to cross-staffed notes, so some manual positioning of the slurs will be required. One option is to use nonmagnetic slurs, entered from the Lines selection window, but either way some manual positioning is required. The slur is impossible to select at the moment because of its proximity to the tempo indication. With the same technique used to edit the ties in the music, move the tempo mark, reposition the slur, then reposition the tempo mark.

1. Select the tempo mark and drag it up and away from the slur.
2. Select the left corner of the slur and drag it down so that is above the beam over the note (downbeat of beat 2).
3. Select the right end of the slur and drag it over the second eighth note.
4. Select the tempo mark and Use the shortcut Shift-⌘-P (Mac); Shift-CTRL-P (Win) to return the tempo to the default position.

 Use the mouse for the large moves and use the arrows to fine-tune the slur's position.

Two Slurs on a Note

On beat 3 of bar 2 in the treble staff, there are two slurs beginning on the same note. If you've input them both, you're looking at the situation shown. Once again there is the problem of overlapping objects and how to select and edit the one you want. My recommendation is to enter the outside  slur first, then drag the end or ends with the potential collisions out of the way before entering the inside slurs. Sorry, no selecting multiple noteheads and entering them all at once here.

Slurs Colliding with Stems

Any time stem directions are not at their normal position (in this case they are upstemmed because of Voice 2 music), there is a chance the slur may touch a stem. There are two ways of fixing this. It will be up to you fit the fix with the situation.

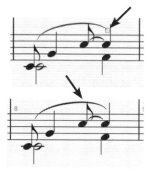

- Click on the end of the slur closest to the collision. Make sure the positioning handle appears before you try to edit the slur. Use the arrow key to nudge it up until the slur clears the stem.
- Select the slur and use the appropriate arrow key to increase the arc of the slur.

I chose to raise the right end of the slur.

Changing the Text Font Size

Since I've reduced the size of the staff, some of the Expression text looks a little too big. Here are the steps to change the size of any text entered in Sibelius.

1. Select the Expression.
2. In the Properties window, click the Text tab.
3. Click the down arrow to the right of the Size display to reduce the foot size. One click should do it in this instance.

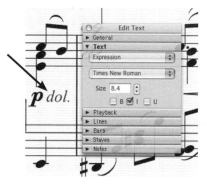

In the Intermezzo, I've reduced the size of all Expressions that are inside the grand staff. In Chapter 4 you changed the size of the To Coda sign. I did that in this piece as well.

The Properties window is also the place to change the type style. The legato mark in bar 25 was entered as a plain Technique text. I used the Properties Text window to italicize the text by selecting it and checking the I box.

Fine-Tuning Hairpin Length

When entering hairpins, the space bar can cover a lot of ground in extending the length, but occasionally falls short when precise placement of the end is desired. Any time the end is just a little short or a little long, use the right or left arrow keys on the computer keyboard to nudge the end the rest of the way. If you need to go back and change the length of a hairpin later, click on the end you want to edit so the editing box appears. Then adjust the length.

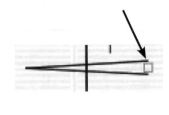

Raising the Bridge and Lowering the River

When two objects meet in the danger zone between staves, both may have to be adjusted a little to make the situation work. On beat 1 of bar 18, the downstemmed half note stem collided with the slur over the bass staff. Here the slur arc was reduced and the stem length was shortened to produce the final result.

There is no secret to getting the hairpins above the bar. Enter them below the staff and drag them up with the mouse.

Text Entry: Over or Under?

In Sibelius, the default formatting for Technique text is not italicized, but Expression text is. This will bring you to a choice if you encounter text over the staff that is italicized, and further, something that is in the Expressions menu. The choice is to enter the text as a Technique, then italicize it using the Properties Text window, or enter it as an Expression and drag the text to its new position above the staff. There are some possible ramifications with Technique-entered dynamics not playing back. It is up to you to choose which you'd rather do. To the player, they both look the same.

Sibelius has a lot of categories for text. The reason has to do with how the program positions and tracks each type. There are different font preferences for many of them, as well as different autoplacement controls, and different effects on playback. Ultimately, when the music is printed, it makes no difference, but to master the internal workings of Sibelius, learning all of the different categories of text is a must. At some point you may want to customize the font choice, appearance, or default placement to suit your own taste. Knowing what options are available in the program will help you become a true power user of Sibelius.

For the più lento indication, there is a ú character in the pop-up menu in both the Technique and Tempo text options. Access the list by right-clicking (CTRL-click on a Mac with a one-button mouse)) the blinking cursor. No need to hunt for the correct shortcut to produce the ú mark.

When entering text, you can select text from the pop-up menus, type it in manually, or both. It is also possible to make multiple selections from the pop-up menu. That is how I created the dynamic indication in bar 78.

System Lines

The dashed horizontal lines that follow a few of the ritards in the piece are System lines. Use the L key to access the Lines selection window and choose the dashed line from the right column. The line will appear above the staff. The line length is controlled by handles on each end, and they are accessed in the same way as a slur. I recommend you adjust the length while the system line is up and out of the way of any music or text. Once it is integrated with the rest of the music elements, it may be difficult to select the line for editing.

Enter the rest of the performance information. Using all of the information and techniques above, you will be able to match the look of the completed example shown at the beginning of the chapter. Examine every detail when something doesn't look the same. Details are what will separate average work from great work.

It is time to turn off the individual bar numbers and get a good look at the finished product.

- Select **View** > Staff Names and Bar Numbers. This toggles the display off.

MIDI Playback

Open the Playback window, if it is not already open, and play back the piece. Other than a good note check, it is not the best of performances, especially when notes begin to drop out on the second time through the repeated section. This is due to the decrescendo hairpins having a cumulative effect. To solve this problem, enter another piano dynamic marking inside the repeat in bar 49 and hide the mark so it is not visible. This will reset the MIDI numbers before the dynamics begin turning them down again. Use this technique anywhere you want to improve the dynamic performance of the piece around hairpins.

Summary of Chapter Steps

This chapter was no lullaby. This is a very complex piece that required a lot of editing. In creating the example, you learned to:

- create a grand staff file in 3/4 time with a pickup bar
- enter music in Voices 1, 2, and 3
- create tuplets with only the number displaying
- create tuplets with no number or bracket displaying
- hide multiple rests at the same time using the filter
- change the staff size
- separate a Coda
- lock the layout
- create cross-staff notation
- change beaming
- change beam angles
- use a plug-in to add cautionary accidentals
- use the Properties window to change the horizontal position of notes
- enter arpeggio lines
- copy lines to new locations
- reposition rests
- create multiple slurs originating from the same note
- adjust slur arcs
- move accidentals
- change the size of expression text
- change the length of stems
- play back the piece via MIDI

Review

1. Re-input the Intermezzo using only the summary list of procedures as a guide.
2. Find another solo piano work that presents similar challenges and enter it.
3. For further refining, download the MIDI files of the piece available on the Classical MIDI Archives Web site (*www.classicalarchives.com*). Analyze the performance and try to replicate it in your Sibelius file by adding tempo changes and dynamics. Hide those markings so they do not complicate the printed version.

SECTION III

Large-Ensemble Scores

10

Pop Ensemble with Guitar Tab
(Musical Example: "Pop Quiz"
by Vince Leonard)

The example in this chapter is representative of an arrangement you might find recording a track for a pop or R&B-style recording session, or a production music track recording. The first two pages of the finished score for "Pop Quiz" are shown below. The full-size version, printed out, will be easier to work with while completing the example.

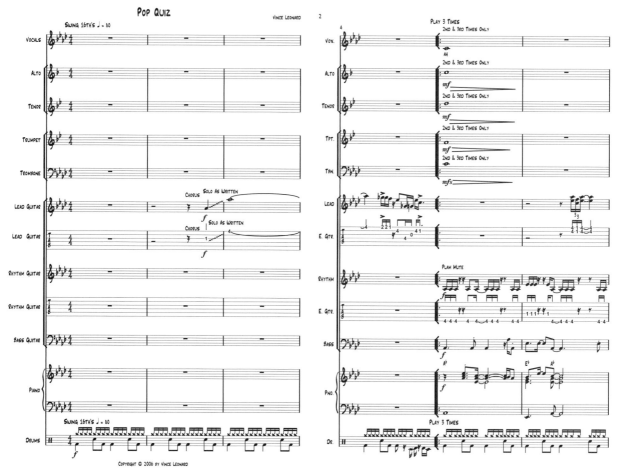

www.sibeliusbook.com

Before beginning this chapter, take the following steps:

1. Go to *www.sibeliusbook.com* and download the Chapter 10 files.
2. Open the completed file *10_PopQuiz.pdf* in Acrobat or other PDF viewer.
3. Print out the file (**File** > Print).
4. Keep the printout handy for reference throughout this chapter.

New in this chapter:
- adding staves to an existing score
- creating a score using the Inkpen2 font
- setting up Sibelius for written pitch input
- using the Mixer for muting staves during playback
- changing the instrument sounds used for playback
- setting up the Sibelius Rock & Pop Collection for score playback
- using the Add Drum Pattern plug-in
- filtering a single pitch on a staff for editing
- setting up Sibelius for note entry using a MIDI guitar controller
- inputting notes to a tab staff from the computer keyboard
- using the "Strummer" plug-in
- entering lyrics above the staff
- adjusting the baseline of lyrics
- entering altered bass chord symbols
- creating complex repeats
- doing multipass playback of parts
- calculating the duration of a piece with many repeats using Timecode display
- adding crescendo data to held notes
- creating a fade ending
- panning the ensemble using the Mixer window
- adjusting the reverb setting
- saving as an audio file
- creating an MP3 file using iTunes
- exporting from Sibelius to a MIDI/digital audio sequencer
- creating combined parts
- creating a piano/vocal part
- changing the staff size of a part
- changing the number of parts to print

Setting up and Adding Staves to the Score

In this example, you will add tab staves for both guitar parts already indicated in the score. Tab (short for "tablature") is a form of notation used predominantly for guitar parts but also for other fretted string instruments. It replaces the five-line staff with a staff consisting of the number of strings on the instrument. Numbers indicating the fret to be fingered replace noteheads. The combination of the two indicates the pitch of the note. The staff is usually accompanied with a traditional five-line staff depicting the same part indicated by the tab staff.

1. Launch Sibelius, or select **File** > New if the program is already running.
2. Select "Start a new score" from the Quick Start menu.
3. From the Manuscript Paper list, choose "R & B band."
4. Click the Add Instruments button.
5. In the Choose from list, select "Rock and Pop Instruments."
6. In the Family list, select "Electric Guitar."
7. In the Instrument list, select "Standard tuning [tab]."
8. Click the Add to Score button two times to add two tab staves to the score. They will appear on the top of the Staves in score list on the right.

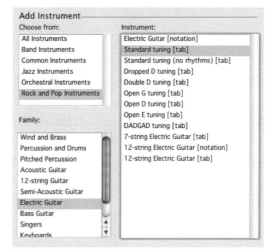

9. Select one of the tab staves in the Staves in score list.
10. Click the Down button so the selected tab staff is positioned under the Lead Guitar in the Staves in score list.
11. Select the other tab staff at the top of the Staves in score list.
12. Click the Down button so this tab staff is positioned above "Rhythm Guitar."

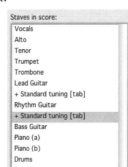

13. Click OK, then click Next.
14. In the House Styles list, select "Jazz Inkpen2" and click Next. The Inkpen font will give the music a hand-copied look.
15. Select 4/4 for the Time Signature. There is no pickup bar, so leave this option unchanged.
16. In the Tempo text box, type "Swing 16ths."
17. Check the Metronome box and set the tempo at quarter note = 80.
18. Review the above to make sure it is correct, then click Next.
19. Select A♭ Major for the key signature and click Next.
20. Type the Title: "Pop Quiz."
21. Type the Composer/Songwriter: "Lyrics and Music by Vince Leonard."
22. Type the Lyricist: "Entered by [your name]."
23. Type the Copyright information: "Copyright © 2006 by Vince Leonard."
24. Click Finish.

25. Use the shortcut: Option-B (Mac); Alt-B (Win) to access the Create Bars dialog box. Enter 18 in the dialog box to add eighteen measures to the score.
26. Click any measure other than the first measure to add the measures.
27. Press Esc.
28. Select **File** > Save As and name the document "Pop Quiz."

Entering the Barline Changes

Finish the score setup by adding the repeat bars.

1. Right-click (CTRL-click on a Mac with a one-button mouse) the beginning of bar 5 and select **Barline** > Start Repeat.
2. This loads the cursor and it will turn blue. Click on the beginning of bar 5 to add the repeat barline.
3. Press Esc.
4. Right-click (CTRL-click for Mac Users with a one-button mouse) the end of bar 24 and select **Barline** > End Repeat. This loads the cursor.
5. Click on the end of bar 24 to add the barline.
6. Press Esc.
7. Repeat steps 1 and 2 above to enter the repeat barlines in bars 25 and 32.
8. Right-click (CTRL-click for Mac users with a one-button mouse) the end of bar 16 and select **Barline** > Double. This loads the cursor.
9. Click on the end of bar 16 to add the barline. Press Esc.

Changing an Instrument Name in the Score

Both tab staves have the same name. To give each staff a unique name:

1. Double-click on the name of the first Electric Guitar tab staff on page 1 of the score. A blinking cursor will appear at the end of the name.
2. Use the shortcut: ⌘-A (Mac); CTRL-A (Win) to select the existing name. Press the Delete key.
3. Type "Lead TAB." Press Esc twice when finished.
4. Double-click the name of the second Electric Guitar tab staff. A blinking cursor will appear at the end of the name.
5. Use the shortcut: ⌘-A (Mac); CTRL-A (Win) to select the existing name. Press the Delete key.
6. Type "Rhythm TAB." Press Esc twice when finished.
7. Repeat steps 1 through 3 for the first E. GTR. staff on page 2 of the score to change the name on the continuing pages to "L. TAB."
8. Repeat steps 1 through 3 for the second E. Rhythm staff on page 2 of the score to change the name on the continuing pages to "R. TAB."

Page 1 Instrumentation   Continuing Page Instrumentation

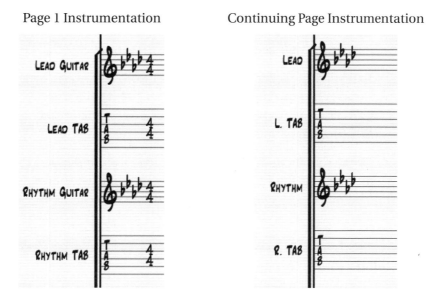

Entering Transposed Scores

In this example you will be copying the music for the four horn section parts from the finished example, which is a transposed score. This will require you to set the input to sounding pitches in the Sibelius Preferences dialog box, as was done in Chapter 5 while entering the Clarinet part.

1. Use the shortcut ⌘-, (comma) (Mac) or CTRL-, (comma) (Win) to access the Preferences dialog box, or use the Apple Menu (Mac) or the File menu (Win).
2. Select Note Input in the left column.
3. Under the Transposing Staves heading, click "Input written pitches." Click OK.

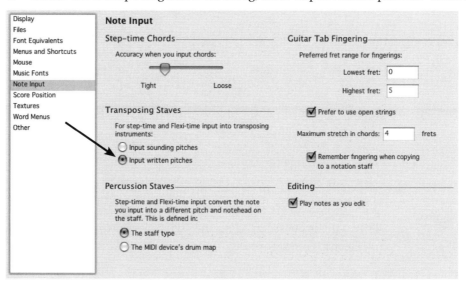

Guitarists will notice that the Tab Fingering preferences are also located in the Note Input dialog box. No changes will be made during this chapter, but this is where to find them if you want to make changes in the future.

To display the score with the proper transpositions: select **Notes** > Transposing Score or type Shift-⌘-T (Mac); Shift-CTRL-T (Win). You can also click the B♭ key signature icon at the top center of the screen.

The lessons in this book involve copying the examples to show the different features of the software. But for those who will create, not just copy music, your workflow may be a bit different. I'll add a few comments and procedures when appropriate in this and the next two chapters.

Changing Sounds in the Mixer Window

When the score was created, Sibelius automatically assigned General MIDI instruments for each instrument created. These sounds can be viewed and changed on the right side of the Mixer window. I prefer an Electric Piano sound for this piece instead of the default Acoustic Piano, as it sounds more appropriate for the style.

1. Press the letter M to display the Mixer window.
2. Underneath the number for channel 12, click on the word "Piano." The right side of the Mixer window will change to display the settings for the Piano (a) staff.
3. Click on the Sound pop-up menu.
4. From the menu, select Keyboards > Electric Piano 2 (5), and release the mouse button.

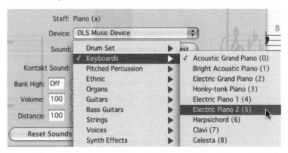

5. Repeat steps 1 through 3 above on channel 13 (the other Piano staff) to change the sound on the Piano (b) staff.

I also want to change the sounds used for both Guitar staves.

6. Repeat the process in steps 1 through 3 above to change Lead Guitar, channel 6, to "Electric Guitar (clean)."
7. Repeat the process in steps 1 through 3 above to change Rhythm Guitar, channel 8, to "Electric Guitar (muted)."

www.sibeliusbook.com

If you prefer to start at this point in the chapter, go to *www.sibeliusbook.com* and download the Chapter 10 folder. Open the file *PopQuiz1.sib*.

Using Sibelius Rock and Pop Sounds

This is an optional section for users who have purchased the Rock & Pop Collection of sounds for use with the Sibelius Kontakt Player. This is an add-on product available from Sibelius and not on the Sibelius 4 CD-ROM you used to install the software. For more information and a demo of the sounds, go to *www.sibelius.com/products/rock_ and_pop/index.html.* If you create a lot of music using the instruments contained in the collection, you will find an improved sound quality over the basic computer synthesizer sound.

If you do not own this package, skip ahead to the next section of this chapter: Hearing Instrument Sounds During Note Entry.

To access the sounds in the Rock & Pop Collection (after they have been purchased and installed), you must select Kontakt Player as the playback device for this file.

1. Select **Play** > Playback and Input Devices.
2. In the Devices column, select Kontakt Player. It will turn blue.
3. In the Sound Set column, click on Kontakt Gold. Select "Rock and Pop Collection" in the pop-up list.
4. Click OK to exit the dialog box.

5. You will see a warning dialog box suggesting that the sounds need to be reset. Click Yes.
6. In the Mixer window, click the Reset Sounds button. Sibelius will load the data from the samples into the computer's RAM and automatically assign instruments based on the instrument names of each track.

Just as with the internal synthesizer sounds, I want to choose some different, more appropriate sounds for the rhythm section. For these staves, choosing a new sound will result in loading audio sample data and creating a test sound.

1. Click Lead under channel 7.
2. From the Sound pop-up menu, select Electric Guitar > Electric Guitar [Stratocaster/Chorus].
3. Click Rhythm under channel 9.
4. From the Sound pop-up menu, select Electric Guitar > Electric Guitar [Stratocaster/Palm Mute].
5. Click Bass under channel 11.
6. From the Sound pop-up menu, select Electric Bass > Electric Bass [Precision/Slap].
7. Click Piano under channel 12.

8. From the Sound pop-up menu, select Keyboards > Fender Rhodes Mk2 [Phaser].

9. Select the second Piano channel, 13, and repeat step 11.

10. Click Drums under channel 14.

11. From the Sound pop-up menu, select Drums and Percussion > Drum Kit [Motown].

The new ensemble should now be loaded and ready to play when you begin entering notes.

Hearing Instrument Sounds During Note Entry

If you've been listening to computer playback while entering notation, you have been hearing sound generated by the computer's internal synthesizer. When a staff is selected, the sound for that staff will respond to all note entry commands. If you are entering notes from a MIDI keyboard or controller and need to work out a part before entering the notation into Sibelius, select the staff, then press the Esc key twice. Now you are free to play without entering any notes on the selected staff. You will hear the sound for the last staff selected until another staff is selected.

Creating the "Pop Quiz" Score: Tips for Note Entry

The composition of this piece started with an improvisation on a Korg Karma synthesizer. The Karma has an advanced accompaniment generator built in, so I am able to jam along with it while working out the basic composition. When I began writing the piece down, I had to re-create the drum pattern.

The groove I'm looking for has a swing sixteenth feel. Therefore, Sibelius must be configured to swing sixteenth notes.

To Set Swing Sixteenth Notes

1. Select **Play** > Performance or use the shortcut Shift-P to access the Performance dialog box.

2. Under the Style heading, click on "Rhythmic feel" and select Swing 16ths.

3. Click OK.

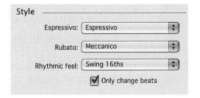

In the next phase of this lesson enter only the notes, leaving all the dynamics and text for later in the chapter.

Drum Set Notation

The basic pattern for the intro (bars 1 through 4) and verse (bars 5 through 16) is a four-bar pattern with a short fill in the last bar. The hi-hat is entered in Voice 1 (stems up); the snare, bass drum, and congas for the fill are in Voice 2 (stems down). Refer back to Chapters 8 and 9 for the steps to enter music in Voices.

1. Enter the sixteenth notes for the Hi-hat part in Voice 1 for bar 1, and stop after you enter the first measure. Press Esc twice.
2. Select the first sixteenth of the Hi-hat part and press N to begin the Voice 2 notation entry process.
3. Press Option-2 (Mac); Alt-2 (Win) or click the number 2 at the bottom of the Keypad to shift to Voice 2 for note entry.
4. Enter the Bass drum and Snare drum parts above. Press Esc when you are finished the bar 1 Drum part.
5. Select bar 1.
6. Press the R key three times to copy the pattern to bars 2, 3, and 4. The Voice 2 part for the third and fourth beats will be changed in the next set of steps.

There are two rhythmic variations of bar 4, one for the General MIDI drum kit and one for the kit used by the Rock & Pop Collection. The difference is in the position of the high conga drum in beats 3 and 4 of the Voice 2 fill. This is because each kit uses a different drum map. See Chapter 8 for more detailed information on drum maps.

General MIDI   Sibelius Rock & Pop Collection

7. Press Esc.
8. Select the quarter note Bass drum note on beat 3 of bar 4.
9. Select the eighth note from the numeric keypad.
10. Enter the Voice 2 part for the third and fourth beats of bar 4. Press Esc twice when finished.
11. Select bars 1 through 4 of the Drum part.
12. Press the R key three times to copy the pattern to bars 5 through 16.

The chorus drum pattern in bar 10 is a two-bar beat figure that repeats with variation in bar 22 and a fill in bar 24.

13. Enter the drum pattern in bars 17 and 18 found on page 6 of the printout. The first note of the Voice 1 part is a cymbal crash. The MIDI keyboard note to play is A♯.

14. Press Esc when you are finished entering each Voice

15. Select bars 17 and 18, then press the R key three times to copy the pattern to bars 18 through 24.

Bar 22 requires a fill to be entered on beat 1 in Voice 1.

16. Select the eighth rest at the beginning of bar 22 and press N to begin note entry.

17. Click the ♪ key on the Keypad or press 3 on the computer's numeric keypad.

18. Click the ▸ key on the Keypad or press + on the computer's numeric keypad to go to the second Keypad layout.

19. Click the ♪ key on the Keypad to set Sibelius to enter the grace notes.

20. Enter the two grace notes.

21. Click the ♪ key on the Keypad again to return to normal note entry.

22. Click the ◀◀ key on the Keypad or press – (minus) on the computer's numeric keypad again to return to the main Keypad layout.

23. Enter the eighth note for the tom on beat 1.

24. The first sixteenth note is the same A♯ cymbal crash used in bar 17. The G following it is the Hi-hat, and the beginning of the basic pattern again.

The drum fill in bar 24 replaces the entire Voice 1 part for the measure. The Voice 2 part requires deleting the snare grace note and quarter note from the fourth beat. Begin with the changes to Voice 2.

25. Select the snare drum grace note on beat 4 of bar 24—it will highlight green, and press the Delete key.

26. Select the snare drum quarter notehead on beat 4 of bar 24, it will highlight green—and press the Delete key.

It is not necessary to delete the current Voice 1 entries before entering the new drum fill. Enter the fill with the usual note entry process; the existing entries will be replaced as you enter the new notation.

27. Select the eighth rest on beat 1 of bar 24 and press N to begin note entry.

28. Enter the new Voice 1 drum fill.

29. Press Esc twice when finished.

Using the Add Drum Pattern Plug-In

To complete the Drum part, you will be calling on one of Sibelius's composition tools, the Add Drum Pattern plug-in. I wanted a Motown feel for the last section of "Pop

Quiz," so I imported one of the plug-in drum patterns and developed the composition around it.

1. Save the file (**File** > Save) before using the plug-in, as the results cannot be reversed using the normal Undo command.
2. Select bars 25 through 32 in the Drum Set staff.
3. Select **Plug-ins** > Composing Tools > Add Drum Pattern.
4. Click OK in the warning dialog box.
5. Under Style, select "R&B: Motown double-time (100-120 bpm)."
6. Under Options, uncheck "Start with intro bar (1 bar)."
7. Set the "Fillbreak bar count" to 8. This will place a fill in the pattern every eight bars. Since the section is only eight bars long, there will be only one fill bar.
8. Uncheck "End with outro bar" and click OK.

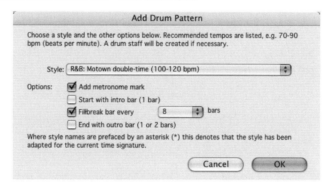

In addition to the drum pattern, the plug-in has provided a Tempo text indication of the new tempo at bar 25. This indication needs to be amended with a change from swing sixteenths to straight sixteenths.

♩ = 112

9. Double-click the Tempo text to get the blinking cursor.
10. Type "[space bar] Straight sixteenths" and press Esc twice.

These patterns can be used as is, or as a starting point for developing your own. Be aware that some patterns may sound different when using the Rock and Pop Collection sounds because of the different drum maps. For example, the Motown beat has a sixteenth note sleigh bell part that will play back using the computer's internal sounds, but there is no sound mapped to that key in the Rock and Pop Collection. I want to delete just that part of the pattern from the Drums staff.

Filtering a Single Note from a Staff

The Advanced Filter is an excellent tool for focusing in on very specific items in a score. To remove a single pitch from the pattern just entered via the Add Drum Pattern plug-in:

1. Select bars 25 through 31 in the Drums staff. There are no sleigh bell notes in bar 32, so don't select it.

2. Select **Filter** > Advanced Filter or use the shortcut: Option-Shift-⌘-F (Mac); Alt-Shift-CTRL-F (Win) to open the Advanced Filter dialog box.
3. Under Find In, choose Selection.
4. In the View list, select "Notes and Chords."
5. Under Find, check "Notes and Chords."
6. Under Voice, uncheck all but Voice 1.

Sibelius will now only look for a note or chord in Voice 1, but there are several notes, so you must be even more specific.

7. Under the Notes and Chords heading, set "Pitch (sounding)" to B in the pop-up list.
8. Select 5 in the "Octave" pop-up list.
9. Select sixteenth for "Note value" in the pop-up list.
10. Click Select.

Sibelius will only search for sixteenth note Bs in octave 5, right where the sleigh bell part is located.

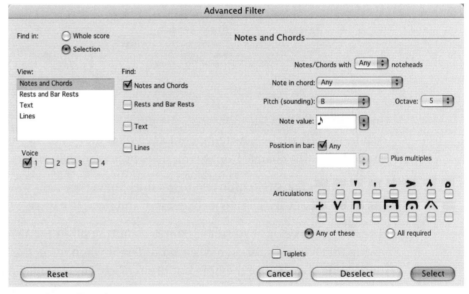

11. Press the Delete key.
12. Press P to hear the final drum pattern.

www.sibeliusbook.com

If you prefer to start at this point in the chapter, go to *www.sibeliusbook.com* and download the Chapter 10 folder. Open the file *10PopQuiz2.sib*.

The Piano

If you completed the Brahms example in Chapter 9, this piano part will be a piece of cake! The verse (bars 5 through 16) is a two-bar pattern that repeats, with a one-note variation in the right hand, even when the bass note drops down a third in bars 9 through 12. There are a few Voice 2 notes and a rest to hide in bar 5, but you're an old pro at hiding rests by now.

1. Enter bars 5 and 6 on page 2 of the printout, and then copy the right hand to 9 and 10.
2. Add the chord symbols to both and enter the left-hand notation in bars 9 and 10.
3. In bar 10, the fifth space E♭ on beats 1 and 2 must come down a fifth. Select the E♭ and use the down arrow key to lower it.
4. Copy the patterns as required in the original on pages 3 through 6 of the printout.

The chorus (bars 17 through 24) is also a two-bar pattern with a variation in the fourth bar of the phrase, and a turnaround to go back to the verse in the eighth bar. Remember to enter the chord symbols before copying. The Coda is a four-bar phrase with the first and third bars the same. Copy the whole thing to make eight bars.

5. Complete note entry for the Piano part.
6. Press P to hear the Piano and Drum parts.

Entering a Chord Symbol with an Altered Bass Note

The chord symbol in bar 10 on beat 1 has an altered bass note for the chord.

1. Enter the basic chord symbol E♭, then type or select the /, then enter the F. If you are typing, Shift-B will be converted to an Inkpen flat character.
2. Chords with long suffixes like the one in bar 24 can be either typed in or selected from the chord pop-up list.

> When inputting a piece as repetitive as this one, always look for sections that can be easily copied to other parts of the score. Complete the first occurrence with all articulations, dynamics, text, and chord symbols. Proof them both visually and aurally before copying so you don't multiply a mistake.

www.sibeliusbook.com

At this point, the basic foundation of the composition is entered. The composer now becomes arranger and orchestrator, adding details to fill out the track.

If you prefer to start at this point in the chapter, go to *www.sibeliusbook.com* and download the Chapter 10 folder. Open the file *10PopQuiz3.sib*.

The Bass

The bass part is where the left hand of the piano meets the bass drum pattern. It takes the rhythmic foundation of the bass drum and adds the harmonic foundation outlines in the piano. Look for opportunities to copy the left hand of the piano in the chorus and Coda.

Entering Notation from a MIDI Guitar

The following section is optional and is designed for those who would like to try to enter guitar parts, or any other parts for that matter, using a MIDI guitar controller. All you keyboard wizards can skip to the next section heading: Inputting Directly to a TAB Staff.

Before you can input anything from your guitar controller, such as the Roland GI-20 GK-MIDI Interface, Sibelius must be set to receive signal from the guitar. You also must set a different MIDI channel for each string.

1. Select **Play** > Playback and Input Devices.
2. Click the Input Device tab at the top of the dialog box.
3. Under the MIDI Guitar Channels heading, check "Input device is a guitar that outputs one MIDI channel per string."
4. Click the 6 button to indicate the number of strings on a MIDI guitar.

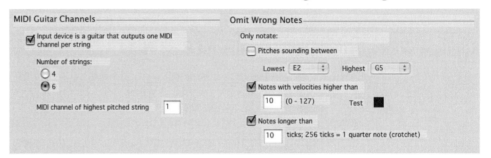

Depending on your playing technique, you may want to return to this dialog box to tweak the settings under the Omit Wrong Notes heading. Since the guitar is a hands-on instrument, it is very easy to accidentally create a note entry. Setting the sensitivity and even the range can eliminate entering notes by accident. This can also be affected by setting the sensitivity on the MIDI interface you're using.

5. Click OK.

When choosing a staff for a guitar part, remember that there are alternate tuning staves available in the Instruments and Staves dialog box. This chapter uses the Standard tuning staff.

 You can set a custom tuning for any tab staff and display the tunings in the score. For the steps and many more possibilities for guitar and tab staves, check out the Sibelius 4 manual in the Guitar notation and tab section.

Inputting Directly to a Tab Staff Using the Computer Keyboard

It is possible to input notes to the tab staff from the computer keyboard. Try this method for the first two measures of the Rhythm Guitar part.

1. Select the Rhythm tab staff in bar 5.
2. Press the N key to activate note entry. The caret will appear on the bottom line of the tab staff.
3. Click the ♪ key, or press 2 on the computer keypad.
4. Press the number 4 key on the main computer keyboard (not the numeric keypad).
5. Press the right arrow key. There is no automatic caret advance on tab note entry, except for rests, to allow for entry of chords.
6. Press 4 on the computer keyboard and press the right arrow key.
7. Repeat step 6.
8. Click the ♪♪ key, or press 0 on the numeric keypad to enter the rest. The caret will advance to the next entry position.
9. Click the ♪♪ key or press 0 on the numeric keypad to enter the rest.
10. Click the ♪ key or press 3 on the computer keypad.
11. Press 4 on the computer keyboard and press the right arrow key.
12. Click the ♪ key or press 2 on the computer keypad.
13. Press 4 on the computer keyboard, then press the ⌢ key or the Enter key on the numeric keypad.
14. Press the right arrow key.
15. Enter three more sixteenth notes using the number 4 on the computer keyboard.
16. Enter a sixteenth rest, then an eighth rest.
17. Enter two more sixteenth notes using the number 4 on the computer keyboard.
18. After advancing the note entry caret to the first beat of bar 6, press the up arrow key two times to move it to the third string.
19. Press the 1 key on the computer keyboard, then press the right arrow key.
20. Enter the next three notes on the third string, then press the down arrow key two times to return to the first string and enter the rest of the measure.
21. Select both measures, then copy and paste into the treble staff for the Rhythm Guitar part.
22. Use whichever method you prefer to enter the rest of the Rhythm Guitar part.

When you are finished inputting the Rhythm Guitar part, you will have to copy it to the other staff. So if you completed it using the treble staff, the music must be copied to the tab staff. Likewise, if you completed the part on the tab staff, it will have to be copied to the treble staff.

> When pasting from a treble staff, always check the tab staff to make sure there are no out-of-range notes. These will be indicated by a "?" in the tab staff for the note that is out of range. Consult the Sibelius 4 manual's "Guitar notation and tab" section for the procedure for changing the computer's tab assignments.

Using the Strummer Plug-in

The chords in the Lead Guitar staff in bars 17 through 24 would be strummed when played by a live player. Sibelius provides a plug-in to add this to the MIDI performance.

1. Select all of bar 17 and the first two beats of bar 18 in the Lead Guitar staff. Do not select any notes on the right side of a tie as the plug-in does not recognize ties.

2. Select **Plug-ins** > Playback > Strummer.
3. Under "Strum down every," click "strictly alternating." Click OK.
4. Select all of bar 19 and the first half of bar 20 in the Lead Guitar staff. Again, select only the first note of a tied group.
5. Select **Plug-ins** > Playback > Strummer.
6. In the "Strum chords of" value box, enter 3 since the last chord in the group selected contains only three notes.
7. Under "Strum down every," click "strictly alternating."

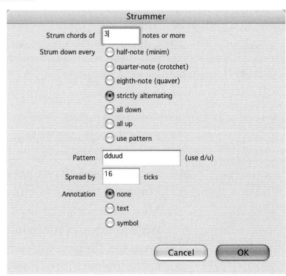

8. Click OK.
9. Select all of bar 21 and the first half of bar 22 and repeat the steps for applying the plug-in.
10. Select all of bar 23 and the first chord in bar 24 and repeat the steps for applying the plug-in.
11. Click OK and play back the piece to hear the results.

The Horn Section

For readers who have not spent their idle youth hanging out with pop groups, "horn section" is a common pop music term for any group of wind instruments in a pop band. I'll be using the term throughout the chapter to refer to the Alto Sax, Tenor Sax, Trumpet, and Trombone parts as a group. Before entering the horn section parts, check to make sure the score is displaying as a transposed score.

1. Enter the music for all four horn parts.
2. Enter all of the Technique text for the playing directions on the repeats, as well as the dynamics, articulations, and slurs. You will need to refer to your printout and you are on your own to enter the notation. This will be a good test of your Sibelius skills.

The Vocals

After you've entered the horn section parts, enter the vocal part only. There are a few Voice 2 lines in the chorus to be aware of. Enter only the lyrics for bars 9 through 13 and 25 through 32. Add the dynamics, slurs, and hairpins for these sections as well. In the next section you will finish off the vocal part with the chorus lyrics.

Lyrics Above the Staff

Entering lyrics should be a snap by now, if you worked through Chapter 3. In this chapter, we'll cover some other placements of lyrics that need to go above the staff in the chorus section of the tune, beginning in bar 17. In pop music, the chorus is the most repeated section of the song, not a vocal ensemble singing in the background.

1. Select the first note in the Vocals staff in bar 17, Voice 1. The note will turn blue when selected. Voice 2 notes will appear in green.
2. Select **Create** > Text > Other Staff Text > Lyrics Above Staff.
3. Enter the lyrics for the first four bars. Refer to your printout.
4. Press Esc.
5. Select the first downstemmed note in the Vocals staff in bar 17, Voice 2. It will turn green when selected.
6. Use the shortcut: ⌘-L (Mac); CTRL-L (Win) and enter the lyrics for the first four bars.

Copying Lyrics

Bars 21 and 22 are the same as 17 and 18. You can copy and paste both sets of lyrics at the same time.

1. Select bars 17 and 18.
2. Select **Edit** > Filter > Lyrics.
3. In bar 21, select the first eighth note (the B♭) on beat 3 to copy the lyrics.
4. Enter the lyrics for bars 23 and 24 to complete the entry of the lyrics.

Moving a Line of Lyrics

The downstemmed notes in bars 17 through 22 collide with the lyrics underneath the staff.

1. Select bars 17 through 22.
2. Select **Edit**> Filter > Lyrics to select all the lyrics in the selected bars, above and below the staff.
3. Select **Edit** > Filter Voice 2 Only. Now only the lyrics below the staff are selected.
4. Press the down arrow key to lower the lyrics. Continue pressing it until the lyrics are below the notes, but not touching anything in the Alto Sax staff.

If similar sets of lyrics still need moving in your score, use the steps above to make the necessary tweaks.

Copying Chord Symbols

You can rarely go wrong in providing the members of the rhythm section with the chord symbols. Armed with this information, they can take the parts you've written and add their own embellishments, or, more than likely, dump them entirely and create new parts, which they will, of course, insist are superior. It always helps if you got them the gig, or are signing their paychecks. Now, let's copy those chord symbols.

1. Select the Piano staff in bars 5 to 32.
2. Select **Edit** > Filter > Chord symbols.
3. Option-click (Mac); Alt-click (Win) the first note of the Rhythm Guitar part in bar 5.
4. Option-click (Mac); Alt-click (Win) on the first note in bar 5 of the Lead Guitar part.

In the chorus section and Repeat and Fade, the chord symbols will need to be raised to avoid colliding with notes or articulations. The process to move chords is the same as for moving lyrics.

1. Select the Piano part in bar 17 to 23.
2. Select **Edit** > Filter > Chord symbols.
3. Press the up arrow key until the chord symbols are above the articulations.
4. Repeat the process for the Bass part in the same bars.
5. Select bars 17 to 24 of the Lead Guitar part and repeat the process.
6. Select bars 25 through 32 of the Rhythm Guitar part and raise the chord symbols.

www.sibeliusbook.com

If you prefer to start at this point in the chapter, go to *www.sibeliusbook.com* and download the Chapter 10 folder. Open the file *10PopQuiz4.sib*.

Creating Complex Repeats

Sibelius can make thirty-two bars of music run until next New Year's Eve! True, you may gnaw though your computer's power cable in self-defense before then, but let that be a lesson to you about the power of music, played over and over. (Gnawing through any cable is expressly not recommended and may void your computer's warrantee, but that will be the least of your problems.)

In this section you will use Repeat text for both sections of the piece. The A–B section will be played a total of three times and the Repeat and Fade section will be played six times, with a fade out on the sixth time.

1. Select bar 5.
2. Select **Create** > Text > Other System Text > Repeat.
3. Type "Play 3 Times."
4. Press Esc.
5. Position the text over the start of bar 5 and press Esc again.

 When using text to define a repeat, it is important to have clear instructions for the performer. If I had entered "Repeat Three Times," some might play it three times, some might play it once, then repeat it three times for a total of four passes. My recommendation for a section that repeats more than two times is to use the word "Play" instead of "Repeat" in the text indication.

6. Select bar 25.
7. Select **Create** > Text > Other System Text > Repeat.
8. Type "Play 6 Times" and press Esc.
9. Position the text over the start of bar 25 and press Esc again.
10. Move the Tempo text inserted by the Drum pattern plug-in over the Repeat text.

Mean What You Say: Multiple Repeated Sections

Every part except the Piano has Technique text directions to play or not play on specific passes through each section. In this case, Sibelius needs a little more information in order to carry out those directions for MIDI playback.

1. Use the shortcut: Option-⌘-P (Mac); Alt-CTRL-P (Win) to make the Properties window active, if it is not already showing on the desktop.
2. Click the Playback tab.

The vocal and horn staves in bar 5 have the indication "2nd and 3rd Times Only."

3. Select the Vocals, Alto Sax, Tenor Sax, Trumpet, and Trombone staves in bar 5.
4. Under the "Play on pass" heading, uncheck the box under 1.
5. Advance to bar 9, and select bars 9 through 13 in the Vocal staff.
6. Repeat step 4, above, and disable playback on the first pass by unchecking the number 1 under "Play on pass."

The horn parts in this section call for playing on the third pass only.

7. Select from the Alto Sax in bar 9 to the Trombone in bar 14.
8. In Properties, under "Play on pass," uncheck the boxes under 1 and 2. This will disable playback on the first and second passes, and since there is a third pass, the section will play.
9. To check the settings, play back the first section of the piece.

The Repeat and Fade section beginning at bar 25 starts with only electric piano playing. Go through this section in the order of entry for each instrument. The drums will sneak in with the hi-hat in the fifth through seventh bars of the phrase and fill in to playing the pattern in bar 25 on the second time through. I have decided to use "Tacit 1st time" on both the drums and bass since they both will be entering later in the first phrase.

1. Select bars 25 through 28 of the Drum staff.
2. In the Properties window, under "Play on pass," uncheck the box under 1.
3. Select bars 29 through 31 of the Drum staff.
4. Select **Edit** > Filter > Voice 2 Only.
5. In the Properties window, under "Play on pass," uncheck the box under 1.
6. Select the first cymbal crash in bar 29, Voice 1, of the Drum staff.
7. In the Properties window, under "Play on pass," uncheck the box under 1.

That completes the Drum part. Time to set the playback for the Bass. The Bass also makes its entrance in bar 29 on the first pass.

8. Select bars 25 through 28 of the Bass staff.
9. In the Properties window, under "Play on pass," uncheck the box under 1.

Both guitar parts enter at the start of the second pass in bar 25. Since the tab staves are not playing back, it is not necessary to make any changes to them, but since it is easy to select the entire region, you might as well make both edits.

10. Select bars 25 through 32 of both the Guitar and Tab staves.
11. In the Properties window, under "Play on pass," uncheck the box under 1.

The Vocal part enters on the third pass.

12. Select bars 25 through 32 of the Vocal staff.
13. In the Properties window, under "Play on pass," uncheck the boxes under 1 and 2.

The four horn parts are the last to enter.

14. Select bars 25 through 32 of the Alto Sax through Trombone staves.
15. In the Properties window, under "Play on pass," uncheck the boxes under 1, 2, and 3.

How Long Has This Been Going On? Calculating the Total Performance Time of a Composition

With all of these repeats, it can be a little difficult to calculate just how long in time the composition is running. The Timecode display, normally used for scoring to picture, can come to the rescue and provide a running count of elapsed time as well as a total duration at the end.

1. Select **Play** > Video and Time > Timecode and Duration.
2. Under the Timecode heading, click "At start of every system."
3. Check the "Hide above first bar" box.
4. Under the Duration heading, check the "Duration at end of score" box.
5. Click OK.

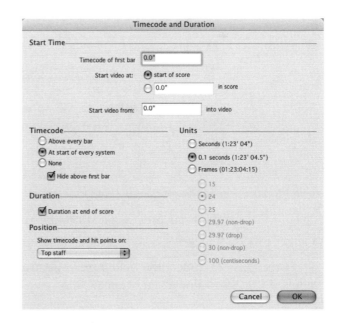

The Timecode display shows each pass of the repeated sections, with the first pass being the bottom number in the stack. Look for the total elapsed time at the bottom of the score under the right barline of the last measure. Here's how to get rid of the Timecode display if you don't want to print it when you are finished.

6. Select **Play** > Video and Time > Timecode and Duration.
7. Under the Timecode heading, click the None button, then click OK.

Hairpins and Whole Notes

There are a few places in the piece where crescendos or diminuendos occur on whole notes. Sibelius does not automatically generate volume changes for whole notes when playing back the score, but there is a plug-in for adding the necessary data.

1. Use the shortcut: Option-⌘-G (Mac); Alt-CTRL-G (Win) to access the Go to Bar dialog box.
2. Enter 5 for the bar number and click OK.
3. Press Esc to deselect the bar.
4. Since you are about to use a plug-in whose effects cannot be undone in the normal way (**Edit** > Undo), save the document.
5. Select from the Alto Sax to the Trombone staves in bar 5.
6. Select **Plug-ins** > Playback > Cresc./Dim Playback.
7. Click OK.

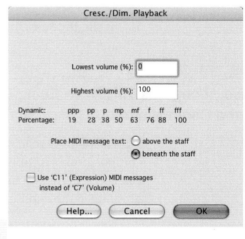

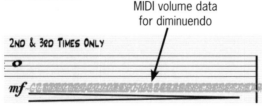

MIDI volume data for diminuendo

The resulting MIDI data will appear as hidden Expression text underneath the staff. This will not print, but if you still prefer not to see it on the screen, turn off Show Hidden Objects in the View menu.

1. Apply the Cresc./Dim. Playback plug-in to the Vocal staff in bar 25. Select bar 25, then Shift-click the first note of bar 26 so the whole tied group is selected.

The same process must now be applied to the other two crescendos in this section of the piece.

2. Select the held note beginning at the end of bar 26 and sustaining through the downbeat of bar 29.

In the next section of the chapter, you will add a fade out. Since the crescendo data will work against the fade data, you must select the crescendo data and set it to not play back on the sixth pass.

3. Click on the beginning of bar 25.
4. Shift-click on bar 32.

5. Select **Edit** > Filter > Expression Text to select the crescendo data, as well as the dynamic indications positioned above the staff.
6. In the Properties window, Playback tab, under "Play on pass," uncheck the box under 6.

 Whenever you are making changes to MIDI controller data, be aware of any controller requiring resetting before the next entrance of the part. This is especially true in bar 5, where the horns fade to nothing on the second and third passes. Since the plug-in uses MIDI controller 7 data for the diminuendo, it is controller 7 that needs to be reset to full value, which is 127. Since this is text we don't need to see, Sibelius provides a method of entering it and hiding it at the same time. Enter the message in bar 7, so it is close (without being too close) to the event the message is undoing. For more information, consult the Syntax heading in the MIDI messages section of the Sibelius manual.

Resetting the MIDI controller 7 value

1. Select bar 7 of the Alto Sax staff.
2. Use the shortcut ⌘-T (Mac) or CTRL-T (Win) to enter the text as Technique text.
3. Type "~C7,127." Syntax is essential. The tilde symbol will tell Sibelius to hide any text that follows it. C7 (case is important for the C) indicates the MIDI controller number and, following the comma, 127 is the value to which controller 7 should be reset.
4. Press Esc once, then ⌘-C (Mac); CTRL-C (Win) to copy the text.
5. Shift-Option-click (Mac); Shift-Alt-click (Win) bar 7 of the Tenor Sax staff to paste the text.
6. Repeat step 5 for the Trumpet and Trombone staves in bar 7.

The Fade

On the sixth pass through the Repeat and Fade section, I want the whole piece to fade down to nothing, just as most pop song recordings do. This is, once again, a job for Properties.

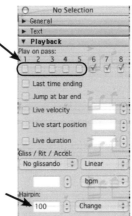

1. Select the first note of the Vocal staff in bar 25.
2. Use the shortcut Shift-H to create a decrescendo hairpin.
3. Press the space bar until the hairpin extends to the end of bar 32.
4. Click on the hairpin to select it.
5. Under the Playback tab in Properties window, under "Play on pass," uncheck the boxes under the numbers 1 through 5.
6. Farther down the window, under Hairpin, change the percentage to 100. Changing this number to 100 percent allows the decrescendo to go all the way down to silence.

276

7. Repeat the steps above for every staff until all the staves in the score have an eight-bar decrescendo that will take effect on the sixth repeat of this section. The Drums staff will need two hairpins, one for each voice. Make sure you select the first upstemmed note and attach the Voice 1 hairpin, then select the first down-stemmed note for the Voice 2 hairpin.

There is one more step required for the Drums to properly fade out. Since this section of the Drums was generated by the plug-in, it has one element that the rest of the Drum part does not: Live Playback Velocities. This is data that comes from the notes being played into Sibelius using Flexi-time. The Live Playback Velocities are overriding the hairpin data that is trying to fade the Drum part. If you used Flexi-time to play in any other parts of this section, you will have to use the next set of steps on those staves as well.

8. Select bar 25 of the Drum staff and then Shift-click bar 32 to select the entire passage entered by the Add Drum Pattern plug-in.

9. In the Properties window, under the Playback tab, uncheck the "Live velocity" box.

10. If you have entered any of the other parts in the score using Flexi-time, repeat step 9 for those parts.

MIDI Playback

From time to time as the composition came together, I listened to single parts or combinations of parts, to make sure that each was as I heard it and they were interacting to create a good groove. In the audio recording world this is done by soloing, or muting, a specific track or group of tracks. In Sibelius this can be done in two ways. The easiest way to make a single staff play back is to select any measure of that staff and press the letter P to begin playback.

1. Select any measure of the Drums staff.
2. Press P to begin playback.
3. Listen to a few bars so you can see that only the Drums are playing back. Press the space bar to stop it.

This method also works when multiple staves are selected. Noncontiguous staves can be selected by ⌘-clicking (Mac); CTRL-clicking (Win) the desired staves.

1. Select any measure of the Piano staff.
2. Shift-click the Rhythm Guitar staff so the Piano, Bass, and Rhythm Guitar staves are all highlighted.
3. Press P and listen to a few measures so you can see that only the selected staves are playing.
4. Press the space bar to stop playback.
5. Press Esc to deselect the staves.

The Mixer Window

You can hear the playback of the score while you are working by simply pressing the Play button. However, for more fine-tuning and control, the Mixer window is a better option.

- If the Mixer window is not displayed, press the M key.

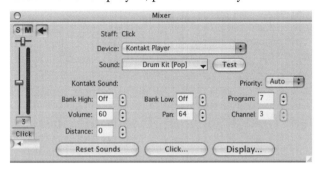

The above window shows only the click track in the Tracks section. The window can be expanded to display more instruments. The only limit is the size of your monitor and what is practical to display while you are working on a score.

- Mac: To expand the Mixer window, select the tab in the lower right corner of the dialog box and drag to the right.

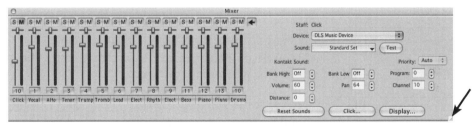

- Windows: Drag the left or right side of the Mixer window to expand it.

Muting Channels in the Mixer Window

Above each channel strip are two buttons, labeled S for solo and M for mute. Clicking a staff's Solo button will play back only that staff. (Yes, you can solo more than one staff at a time.) Clicking a staff's Mute button will silence that staff during playback. Since the two tab staves will be duplicates of the Lead and Rhythm Guitar staves, there is no need to have them both enabled for playback.

1. Open the Mixer window, if it is not already visible on the desktop, by pressing the letter M.
2. In the Mixer window, click the M button above the second Lead channel and the second Rhythm channel. The buttons will turn blue to show that they are active and the staves are muted.

278

3. Click the S (Solo) button above the Vocals channel and the two Piano channels.
4. Press the space bar, or P, to start playback. You will hear the Vocals and Piano only.
5. Listen to several measures to hear both parts, then press the space bar again to stop playback.
6. Click the M and S buttons again to reset to all staves playing back.

> The choice to mute tracks or solo tracks depends on the number of tracks that need a Mute or Solo button pressed. Usually the 50 percent mark is the dividing line, which in this piece would be five. If I wanted to hear only three tracks in "Pop Quiz," I'd solo those three, since that is less work than muting seven. If I wanted to hear seven, I'd mute the three I didn't want to hear, since that is also less work than soloing seven tracks.

Starting Playback from a Specific Place in the Score

As you progress through a score, especially when you are creating it, you only want to hear playback of the section you are focused on at the time. For example, when working on the chorus of "Pop Quiz," I would do the following.

1. Select bar 16.
2. Press the Y key. This moves the playback (green) line to the selected point in the score.
3. Press the space bar to begin playback, and press it again to stop playback after bar 24.

This method doesn't entirely work in this piece due to all the repeats. You can only select a measure to begin playback, not a specific time in the repeat passes. Here is where the Timecode display can be a big help.

1. Locate the time for the beginning of the repeat and fade section at bar 25, 3 minutes and 12 seconds.
2. Click on the slider in the Playback window and drag it.
3. Watch the time indication in the Playback window as you drag the slider. Target time is 3:12 for the start of the section. I'd rather start a little early than a little late. In this case, 3:11 is just fine to begin playback.

Panning

If the sound of the ensemble is dull, it may be due to all the instruments coming from the center of the stereo field. Using the panning slider or number entry field, you can give your virtual musicians a little elbow room. Panning is short for "panoramic" and is used to move various instruments to the left or right of the stereo field. Think of panning as the place on the stage where the various musicians are performing. In a symphony orchestra, the violins are typically on the left of the stage, so they would be panned slightly left. The basses are on the right of the stage, so they would be panned slightly right. A full explanation of panning is beyond the scope of this book, so consult texts on digital audio and mixing for more information.

1. Activate the Mixer window if it is not already displayed (press the letter M).
2. Select the Piano in the channel name strip.
3. Drag the pan slider to the left.

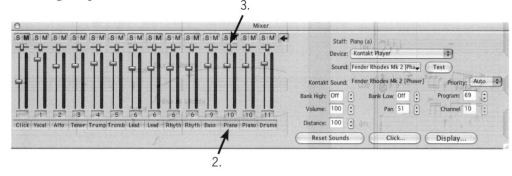

4. Pan the Piano and Vocals slightly to the left of center.
5. Pan the Guitars and four horn parts slightly to the right of center, leaving the Drums and Bass in the center of the mix.

The ensemble should now be spaced out as shown in the graphic below.

Left		Center		Right
Vocals	Electric Piano	Bass/Drums	Guitars	Saxes Brass

Working with the Rock & Pop Collection Sounds

This section is for owners of the Sibelius Rock & Pop Collection of sounds, but if you have Garritan Personal Orchestra Sibelius Edition, follow along, since that package operates using the same window. If you don't fall into either category, skip ahead in this chapter to the next section: Saving as an Audio File on page 281.

The sounds included with the Rock & Pop Collection are samples, not from the synthe-sizer in your computer. For them to work properly, Sibelius must load them into the Kontakt Sample Player. Sibelius remembers which sounds are needed for each file and loads them when the file is opened.

1. Select **Window** > Kontakt Player or use the shortcut: Option-⌘-O (Mac); Alt-CTRL-O (Win) to display the Kontakt Player window.

In this window you can view the sounds that are loaded for the file. The Pan and Volume settings on the right side of the window are linked to the sliders in the Mix window.

If you have multiple files open at the same time and each is using Kontakt Player samples, switching files will cause one set of sounds to be dropped and the newly selected files' sounds to be loaded. This causes a small delay as the new samples load. If you wish to avoid this delay each time you switch, change the default playback device back to your computer's synthesizer.

The Sound of Troubleshooting

Occasionally, when switching back and forth between files that use the computer's sounds for playback and files that use Kontakt Player sounds, you may find that the Kontakt sounds are not properly loaded. If you open a file and do not hear the sampled sounds during note entry or playback, try the following steps.

1. Make sure you haven't accidentally muted the sound output of your computer. Sometimes we overlook the obvious.
2. Press the Esc key twice to make sure that nothing in your score is selected by mistake.
3. Select **Play** > Playback and Input Devices.
4. Reselect Kontakt Player as the playback device.
5. Reselect Rock & Pop Collection as the Sound Set and click OK.
6. Press the space bar, or Play in the Playback window, to begin playback. Pressing the Reset Sounds button in the Mixer window also works, but you will have to repeat the steps for changing the piano and guitar sounds from p. 259 after the sounds are loaded.

You will see a succession of "Working" boxes like the one shown on the next page as each sound used in the score is loaded. Playback will begin when all sounds are loaded.

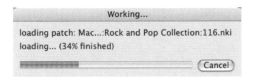

Reverb Settings

When designs for computer music notation programs began, there were probably only about two people who envisioned the need for reverb settings, and they were in the wrong meeting. Yet, here we are, able to create with a computer and speakers (headphones optional) what it used to take a computer, a mixer, a hardware reverb, an amplifier, a pair of speakers, and several hundred feet of permanently tangled wiring to accomplish. Reverb is the number one effect, a term used for any type of sound processing, for taking a piece of music and making it sound like a "real recording." The bad news is it also is the number one drain on computer processor power. Should you experience problems with playback such as the sound dropping out, stuttering, or other things you can't explain, try turning the Reverb off to see if the problem goes away.

To Turn off the Reverb Setting

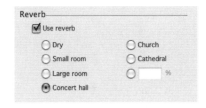

1. Reverb can be found in the Performance dialog box, accessed by typing Shift-P.
2. Click the Dry button, then OK, and try playing back the score again.

Saving as an Audio File

This book and Sibelius in general is about the written form of the musical language, but the audio form travels a bit better and can easily be appreciated by all. Sibelius provides the ability to create an audio file of the MIDI playback if you are using Kontakt Silver or Gold, or the Rock & Pop Collection. GPO Sibelius Edition falls in the same category as the sounds just mentioned, but the internal synthesizer of your computer does not. If you are using a mix of Kontakt and internal synthesizer sounds, you must convert to all Kontakt sounds for saving as audio. Saving files as audio files can be helpful in a wide variety of applications, such as sharing Sibelius files in audio format to burn CDs and post on Web sites.

1. Check to make sure that Kontakt Player is properly configured and selected as the playback device.
2. Make sure the playback slider is all the way to the left side, and its time display is set to 00:00'00. Sibelius will give you a warning message if this is not set properly. Sibelius begins to create the audio file from wherever the playback indicator is located.

3. Select **File** > Export > Audio.
4. Name the file. Mac files will be in aiff format, thus the .aif extension. Windows users will create .wav files.
5. Click Save.

Creating an MP3 File Using iTunes

If you want to create an MP3 file, you will need another software program to do the conversion, as currently, Sibelius 4 does not support saving in this format. There are many options that will convert CD-quality audio to MP3. One of the most popular is Apple Computer's iTunes, which is a free program for Mac and Windows computers. People usually don't complain about *FREE*! If you don't have iTunes on your computer, download if from *www.apple.com/itunes*.

1. Launch iTunes.
2. In iTunes, type ⌘-, (comma) (Mac) or CTRL-, (comma) (Win) to open the Preferences window.
3. Click the Advanced icon in the top row.
4. Click the Importing tab.
5. From the Import Using pop-up menu, select MP3 Encoder.
6. Click OK.
7. Drag the audio file's icon to the library window and release the mouse button to import the file, or select **File** > Import, select the file, and click OK.

Exporting from Sibelius to a MIDI Sequencer

Notation programs can be used as starting points for compositions that will be ported to a sequencer for adding additional parts or recording. The file must be saved as a Standard MIDI file to be opened by a sequencer program. When the file is exported, Sibelius creates a MIDI file with the repeats "written out," so to speak. When played back by a software sequencer, the piece is the correct length with the proper entrances made on the second, third, and fourth passes, and even retains the fade out ending. If you are using Kontakt, the playback device must be reset to the internal synthesizer of your computer before creating the MIDI file to ensure that it is created correctly.

 If you prefer to start at this point in the chapter, go to *www.sibeliusbook.com* and download the Chapter 10 folder. Open the file *10PopQuiz5.sib*.

Dynamic Parts Too

When creating parts for the studio, I stick to the four-bars-to-a-line format. In smaller song recording sessions, I won't worry so much about measure numbers on every bar. The piece is short and with all the repetitions, players will likely refer to each section by form rather than number; for example, first verse, third chorus, etc.

The Vocals part is a bit of a mess at the moment. In the steps below, use the Make Layout Uniform plug-in to create a "4 bars to a line" layout. But before you go and Select All, take another look at the part. When the plug-in creates a layout, it considers a gathered rest as one bar. The result with all bars selected will not be what I want, it will be the classic "what I told the computer to do."

1. Select bars 17 through 32.
2. Select **Plug-ins** > Other > Make Layout Uniform.
3. With "4 bars to a line" indicated, click OK.
4. Select the repeat sign at bar 5 (actually the end of bar 4) and press Return.
5. Tweak the positions of the Repeat and Technique text in bars 5 and 25. Also, adjust the Expression text in bar 25.

6. Review the steps for repositioning a group of lyrics on page 270 and lower the lyrics below the staff a little in bars 17 through 24.

The four horn section parts are very similar to the Vocals, so copy the layout from the Vocals.

1. Activate the Parts window (**Windows** > Parts).
2. In the Parts window, click on Alto, then Shift-click on Tenor so both are highlighted in blue.
3. Click the Copy Part Layout button at the bottom of the Parts window.

4. Advance to the Alto Sax part using either the Dynamic Parts menu or the shortcut: Opt-⌘-~ (Mac); CTRL-Alt-Tab (Win).
5. Tweak Expression, Technique, and Repeat text positions as needed.
6. Properly position the fall symbol in bar 26.
7. Advance to the Tenor Sax and repeat steps 5 and 6.
8. Advance to the Trumpet and repeat steps 5 and 6.
9. Advance to the Trombone and repeat steps 5 and 6.
10. Advance to the Lead Guitar five-line staff part and complete the steps below.

Creating Combined Parts

I want the Guitar parts to contain both the five-line staff and the tab staff.

1. Select the top Lead Guitar staff in the Parts window.
2. Click the Staves in Part button at the bottom of the window.
3. In the Staves in Part dialog box, select "Lead tab" in the Staves Available list.
4. Click the Add to Part button.
5. Click OK.

With both staves combined, all that's left is the layout.

1. Select the whole Lead Guitar part.
2. Select **Plug-ins** > Other > Make Layout Uniform.
3. For "bars per system," 4 should already be entered.
4. Click "Break pages using."
5. Enter 4 for "systems per page."
6. Enter 4 for the systems on first page.
7. Click OK.

A little more space is needed between the staves of each system. When you want to change the staff or system positioning from the default, use engraving rules to change the page justification setting. This is the setting that expands partially filled pages to fill the whole page. Its effect may prevent the changes made to the staff and system distances from being properly displayed.

1. Use the shortcut Shift-⌘-E (Mac); Shift-CTRL-E (Win) to access the Engraving Rules dialog box.
2. Select Staves in the left column.
3. Under the Layout heading, enter 11 for the "spaces between staves".
4. Enter 15 for the "spaces between systems."
5. Under the Justification heading, change "Justify staves when page is at least" to 100 percent full.
6. Click OK.
7. Tweak the text positions as needed.

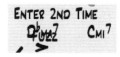

Staves

Layout

| 11 | spaces between staves |
| 15 | spaces between systems |

Justification

Justify staves when page is at least | 100 | % full
System spacings may be contracted to | 95 | %

There is overlapping text in bar 25. It may be impossible to select some specific text without moving what is over it.

1. Select the D♭ma7 chord symbol and drag it to the right, then press Esc.
2. Select the word "Fuzz" and position it to the left of the repeat sign.
3. Select the D♭ma7 chord symbol and use the shortcut: Option-Shift-⌘-P (Mac); Alt-Shift-CTRL-P (Win) to reset it to the score position.

ENTER 2ND TIME

In parts with chord symbols, you must always be on the lookout for chord symbol collisions like the ones in bars 28 and 32.

1. Select the B♭ eighth note on beat 3 of bar 28.
2. Use the shortcut Shift-Option-right arrow key (Mac); Shift-Alt-right arrow key (Win) to nudge it to the right, away from the A♭/C chord symbol on beat 2.
3. Repeat steps 1 and 2 in bar 32.
4. Advance to the Rhythm Guitar five-line staff part.

The Rhythm Guitar part is, well, more rhythmic than the lead part, so it will be spread out a bit more. First, it must be combined with the tab staff.

1. Select the top Rhythm Guitar staff in the Parts window.
2. Click the Staves in Part button at the bottom of the Parts window.
3. In the Staves in Part dialog box, select "Rhythm tab" in the Staves Available list.
4. Click the Add to Part button.
5. Click OK.

You need to make one adjustment to the current measures-per-system layout.

1. Select the Repeat/Enter bar at the end of bar 24.
2. Press Return to add a system break.

The final page layout will be five systems on the first page and four systems on the second and third pages.

1. Use the shortcut Shift-⌘-E (Mac); Shift-CTRL-E (Win) to access the Engraving Rules dialog box.
2. Select Staves in the left column.
3. Under the Layout heading, enter 11 for the "Spaces between staves."
4. Click OK.

Now for the page breaks:

5. Select the end barline of bar 14.
6. Use the shortcut: ⌘-Return (Mac); CTRL-Enter (Win) to enter a page break.
7. Select the End Repeat bar at the end of bar 24.
8. Use the shortcut: ⌘-Return (Mac); CTRL-Enter (Win) to enter a page break.
9. Reposition the text and chord symbols as needed.
10. Click on bar 15 of the tab staff.
11. Shift-click on bar 32 of the tab staff to select it for pages 2 and 3.
12. Drag the tab staff down to create more room between the staves and fill up the available room at the bottom of the page.
13. Reposition the text over bar 5 and bar 25.

The bass part is as straightforward as they come:

1. Select bars 5 through 32.
2. Select **Plug-ins** > Other > Make Layout Uniform.
3. With 4 entered in the "bars per system" box, click "Do not break pages."
4. Click OK.
5. Reposition the text in bars 5 and 25.
6. Reposition the Eb/Bb chord symbol on the third beat of bars 28 and 32.

Creating a Piano/Vocal Part

The same method used to combine the guitar staves can also be used to create a Piano/Vocal part so the singers can accompany themselves while learning their parts. Giving the same part to the pianist will allow him or her to give starting notes to the singers during rehearsal or before recording.

1. Advance to the Piano part using the shortcut or Dynamic Parts menu.

2. Click the Staves in Part button.
3. In the Staves in Part dialog box, select Vocals in the Staves Available list.
4. Click the Add to Part button.
5. Click OK.

Creating a Cue in a Part

It also would be a good idea to cue the guitar solo intro for the piano player, since the bass note in bar 5 completes the musical thought of the guitar intro.

1. Press W to return to the score.
2. Select the Lead Guitar part in bars 2 through 4.
3. Copy and Paste it into the treble staff of the Piano part.
4. Select bars 2 through 4 of the Piano, treble staff.
5. Select **Edit** > Hide or Show > Show in Parts.
6. Press W to return to the Piano/Vocal part.
7. Delete the Clean text.
8. Enter "Guitar Cue" over the first note of the cue as Technique text.
9. Press Esc.
10. Select **Edit** > Hide or Show > Show in Parts.
11. Use the up arrow key to move the text over the "Solo As Written" indication.

To reduce the size of the notes to cue size, return to the Keypad. If you've hidden it, make it active again by selecting the Window menu or clicking the button on the toolbar.

1. Select bars 2 through 4 of the Piano treble staff.
2. Click the ▶ key on the Keypad to move to the second Keypad.
3. Click the ⚲ key or press Enter on the computer keypad.
4. Press Esc twice.
5. Return to the first Keypad.

Changing the Staff Size of a Part

When a part looks as dense as this Piano/Vocal does, it usually looks a lot better with a little reduction applied to staves. Sibelius allows for each part to have a different staff size.

1. Use the shortcut: ⌘-D (Mac); CTRL-D (Win) to access the Document settings for the Piano/Vocal part. If inches is not selected as the unit of measurement at the top of the dialog box, select it.
2. Click the down arrow to the right of the "Staff size" field to lower the staff size to 0.24 inches.
3. Click OK.

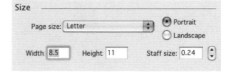

With staves just a bit smaller, it will be easier to fit the part on two pages.

1. Use the shortcut: ⌘-A (Mac); CTRL-A (Win) to select the entire part.
2. Select **Plug-ins** > Other > Make Layout Uniform.
3. With 4 bars per system entered, click "Break page using."
4. Enter 4 for "systems per page."
5. Enter 4 for "systems on first page."
6. Click OK.

This part will show the flexibility available in page layout. On page 2 of the Piano/Vocal, you can add space between the vocal and top piano staves to allow more room for the lower vocal line. You will also add space between the second and third systems to allow more room for all the text at bar 25.

1. Select both piano staves from bar 17 to 24.
2. Hold down Shift-Option (Mac); Shift-Alt (Win) and press the down arrow key to create the needed space between the chord symbols and the lyrics.
3. Press Esc twice when finished.
4. Select all three staves of the third system, bars 25 through 28.
5. Hold down Shift-Option (Mac); Shift-Alt (Win) and press the down arrow key to create additional room for the text at bar 25.

There are a few more tweaks to make, which should be familiar by now: positioning tempo text, dynamics, tweaking lyric positions, and fixing chord symbol collisions. Make them all, then save the document.

Drums

The drum part has a few issues that arise with MIDI playback-oriented parts versus parts specifically written for a live player. Having the drummer listen to an audio file would help. The fills in bars 4, 8, 12, and 16 use congas, so an alternative fill will have to be worked out by a set drummer. The part in bars 25 through 32 came from the plug-in and was altered to remove some notes. This has left a few individual sixteenth notes that will be confusing to read. Here is how to fix them.

1. Select the first sixteenth rest in Voice 1, beat 1 of bar 25.
2. Click the ♪ key on the first Keypad or press 3 on the computer keypad.
3. Click the . key on the Keypad or press the . (decimal) key on the computer keypad.

Now the rest is a more readable dotted eighth. In bar 26 there are four sixteenth rests in Voice 1, beat 1. They need to be converted to quarter rests.

4. Select the first sixteenth rest in bar 26.

5. Click the key on the first Keypad or press the 4 key on the computer keypad.
6. Continue editing the sixteenth rests in bars 27 through 31.

The layout of the Drum part will be four bars to a line for the first six systems, then three bars to a line for two systems and two bars on the bottom system.

7. Select measures 1 through 24.
8. Select **Plug-ins** > Other > Make Layout Uniform.
9. With 4 bars per system entered, click "Do not break pages."
10. Click OK.
11. Select bars 25 through 32.
12. Select **Plug-ins** > Other > Make Layout Uniform.
13. Enter 3 for the bars per system and click OK.

This part could also do with a little staff size reduction, just as you did with the Piano/Vocal part.

1. Use the shortcut ⌘-D (Mac) or CTRL-D (Win) to access the Document settings for the Drums part.
2. Click the down arrow to the right of the "Staff size" field to lower the staff size to 0.24.
3. Click OK.
4. Reposition the text as needed.

One last adjustment remains to be made on all parts, if you haven't already spotted it and fixed it. The combined part names all collide with the "Entered by" text at the top left corner of the page. Make the adjustment now.

Managing Ensemble Parts Windows

When working with orchestrations for larger-size ensembles, you may reach a point where the computer slows down due to the number of windows Sibelius has open. If you feel a noticeable lag in response, try closing the windows of parts that are finished.

> Remember, when working on parts with multiple windows open on the desktop, there is a Close All command to close all windows when closing a file, as well as a Save All command for saving all open windows.
>
> If you have the Parts window on the desktop, you can open any part by double-clicking its name in the Parts window list.

Printing Multiple Parts

You are ready to print out "Pop Quiz," but there still is one last trick to learn. You've combined a few parts, so there is no need to print either tab part. However, three copies of the Piano/Vocal part are needed for the singers and pianist. This can all be set up in the Parts window so one print command will create parts for the entire ensemble.

1. Activate the Parts window (**Windows** > Parts).
2. Select "Vocals, Piano."
3. Option-click (Mac) or Alt-click (Win) on the number in the Copies column.
4. Press the Delete key to delete the number currently in the entry field.
5. Type "3" and press Esc.

Since I'm giving the two vocalists a Piano/Vocal, I don't need to print the part with just the Vocals staff.

6. Select Vocals.
7. Option-click (Mac) or Alt-click (Win) on the number in the Copies column.
8. Press the Delete key to delete the number currently in the entry field.
9. Type 0 and press Esc.
10. Repeat steps 7 through 9 for the Lead tab and Rhythm tab staves.

If you don't want to commit this to paper, feel free to skip the final step.

11. Select **File** > Print Parts.

Transposing a Score

In "Pop Quiz," you've learned to deal with inputting music for transposing instruments, but there is one nontransposing instrument that will be the reason behind a lot of transpositions: singers. A common situation you will encounter, especially in vocal music, is the need to change the key of the piece to accommodate the singer. Depending on the size and direction of the interval of the move, this may be a simple procedure or a time-consuming rewrite if instruments suddenly go out of range. For example, I'll transpose "Pop Quiz" down a whole step to Gb.

1. Select **File** > Save As and rename the piece "Pop_Quiz_Gb" so there is no confusion with the original file.
2. Press W to return to the full score of "Pop Quiz."
3. Use the shortcut: ⌘-A (Mac); CTRL-A (Win) to select the whole score. Don't worry, the Drums staff will not transpose.
4. Use the shortcut Shift-T, or select **Notes** > Transpose to access the Transpose dialog box.
5. Click the down button.
6. With Major/Perfect selected for the type of interval, select 2nd from the pop-up menu for the actual interval.
7. Make sure "Transpose key signatures" is checked.

8. Uncheck "Use double sharps/flats," unless you like reading them.
9. Click OK.

With the score now in G♭, it is time to search for any notes that have drifted off the low end of an instrument or have drifted into a more difficult range.

10. Select **View** > Note Colors > Notes Out of Range, if it is not already turned on, to help in locating notes that will need octave adjustment or rescoring.

The only problems with the score in G♭ seem to be both guitars and the bass. With the guitar tab staves, it is best to delete the existing information and recopy the parts in the new key so Sibelius can reassign strings to make it easier to play. I won't go step by step through this version to tweak it, but it will make a good review of the editing skills you've learned in this chapter. Check for lyrics that may need to be repositioned; Technique, Expression, and Repeat text that needs to be sorted out; and chord symbol collisions. Don't forget to check the parts for any additional adjustments required.

Summary

In this chapter, you learned to:

*   add staves to an existing score
*   create a score using the Inkpen2 font
*   enter repeats and barline changes using the contextual menu
*   change the instrument name on the first page and continuing pages
*   set up Sibelius for written pitch input
*   use the Mixer for muting staves in MIDI playback
*   change the instrument sounds used for playback
*   set up the Sibelius Rock & Pop Collection for score playback
*   enter a multivoice drum set part
*   use the Add Drum Pattern plug-in
*   filter a single pitch on a staff for editing
*   set up Sibelius for note entry using a MIDI guitar controller
*   input notes to a tab staff from the computer keyboard
*   use the Strummer plug-in
*   input transposed parts to transposed staves
*   enter lyrics above the staff
*   copy lyrics
*   adjust the baseline of lyrics
*   copy chord symbols
*   create complex repeats
*   do multipass playback of parts
*   calculate the duration of a piece with many repeats using Timecode display
*   add crescendo data to held notes
*   create a fade ending

- start playback from a specific place in the score
- pan the ensemble using the Mixer window
- review the Reverb setting
- save as an audio file
- create an MP3 of that file using iTunes
- export from Sibelius to a MIDI sequencer
- edit the Dynamic Parts layout
- create combined parts
- create a piano/vocal part
- add cues to a part
- change the staff size of a part
- change the number of parts to print
- transpose the piece into a new key

Review

1. Try creating the example using only the summary list, above.
2. Try creating a different arrangement around the existing piano part using the R&B band template.
3. Rearrange the piece for a different instrumentation.
4. Try transposing the piece into a more remote key and reworking any problems that result.

11

Big Band Score
(Musical Example: "Joshua Variations",
arranged by Vince Leonard)

www.sibeliusbook.com

In this chapter, you will create a seven-page big band score. You will copy a piano reduction, also referred to as a sketch, that I created, and use a variety of copy and paste tools throughout. In order to complete this chapter, you must download two files from the *www.sibeliusbook.com* Web site.

Preparing to Start This Chapter (Don't Skip These Steps!)

1. Go to the *www.sibeliusbook.com* Web site.
2. Download the Chapter 11 folder.
3. After you download the Chapter 11 folder to your hard drive, open it and open the Sibelius file *11JoshuaSketch.sib*.
4. Print out the sketch file *11JoshuaSketch.sib* for reference (**File** > Print). Leave the file open on your computer. It will be needed later in this chapter.
5. In the Chapter 11 folder, open the Sibelius file *11JoshuaScoreComplete.pdf*.
6. Print the entire score of seven pages. Keep the printout near you for reference. This is what you will create in this chapter.
7. Close the *11JoshuaScoreComplete* file and quit Acrobat.

File: *11JoshuaSketch.sib*. This should be open in Sibelius on your computer.

The above part is the sketch or piano reduction from which you will work to create a big band score. You will be working from this sketch and using the Sibelius Arrange feature to orchestrate a complete arrangement.

New in This Chapter

- creating a big band score
- creating a landscape format score
- changing the staff size
- changing Opus text to Inkpen in Tempo text indications
- entering a metric modulation
- copying from one file to another
- creating staff transposition changes for instrument doublings
- changing the default range
- entering caesuras
- entering slash notation
- entering single-bar repeats
- entering a two-bar repeat
- changing parts from landscape to portrait orientation
- copying the Trumpet part for drum set cues
- copying the Bass part for the Bass Drum part
- adjusting the score horizontally
- adjusting the staves of a score vertically
- using Multiple Part Appearance to reformat all parts at once
- changing the default placement of articulations
- changing the multirest symbol

Setting Up the Score

Before you can orchestrate, you'll need some score paper, virtually speaking. In this example you will use a landscape format score. Sibelius is able to support multiple orientations, including portrait and landscape, as well as multiple page sizes in scores or parts. The terms "portrait" and "landscape" refer to whether the score or part is oriented vertically or horizontally. A page with landscape orientation is horizontally oriented. Therefore, it is wider than it is tall. So far in this book, every example has been entered and printed in portrait style. It is possible to create scores in either format, at page sizes limited only by your printer. There are some more expensive printers that can print $11'' \times 14''$ or larger. The number of staves in a score will determine whether portrait or landscape should be used.

Selecting landscape orientation for the score will result in the parts also being set up as landscape. The parts orientation will be changed to portrait later in the chapter.

Creating a Blank Big Band Score

1. Launch Sibelius and from the Quick Start screen select "Start a new score," or if Sibelius is already open, use the shortcut: ⌘-N (Mac); CTRL-N (Win).
2. From the Manuscript Paper list, select "Big band."
3. Next to the Page Size selection list, click the Landscape button. The page display window on the right will change to landscape to reflect the new page orientation.
4. Click Next.

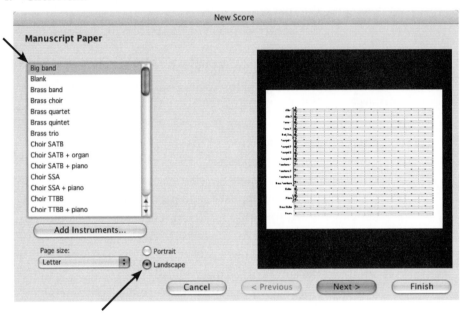

5. From the House Styles list, select "Jazz Inkpen2" and click Next.
6. Set the Time Signature to 4/4.
7. In the "Tempo text" field, type "Swing."
8. Check the Metronome mark box and enter "112" for the quarter note value.
9. Click Next.
10. Click the "Minor keys" button and select C minor for the key signature.
11. Click Next.
12. In the Score Info window, enter the Title: "Joshua Variations".
13. Enter the Composer/Songwriter: "Arranged by Vince Leonard."
14. Enter the Lyricist: "Entered by [your name]."
15. Enter the Copyright: "© 2006 by Vince Leonard."

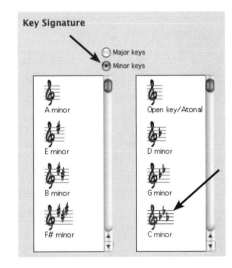

16. Click the Previous button to review the above. Return to the final New Score setup page and click Finish.
17. Add 51 bars to the score for a total of 61 (**Create** > Bars > Other).

Transposing and Concert Score View

Be sure that the score is set to display as a Transposing Score. This can be selected via the menu: **Notes** > Transposing Score, or by clicking the transposing score button on the menu. If the button is highlighted, the score is in transposed view.

Changing the Staff Size

The score is a bit of a tight fit initially .To compensate for the page being shorter (landscape orientation is 11 × 8½ inches), the staff size should be reduced.

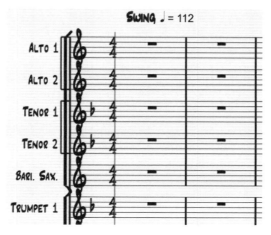

1. Use the shortcut: ⌘-D (Mac); CTRL-D (Win) to access the Document Setup dialog box or select **Layout** > Document Setup.
2. Select Inches at the top of the Document Setup window.
3. Next to the Size heading, use the down arrow button to reduce the staff to 0.15 inches.

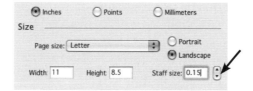

This number can be changed at any time, so if you feel you need more room, reduce it for less room between staves. Use the up arrow button to increase the staff size.

Adjusting the Page Margins

In addition to changing the staff size, moving the top and bottom page margins closer to the edge of the page will add a little extra space between staves. How close you can go to the edge of the page without losing any of the notation will depend on your printer. Some printers will print edge to edge; others may enforce a border on all sides of the page. Check your printer's documentation, or use good old trial and error to determine your printer's limits. Aesthetically, some white space around the margin is desirable so continuing page numbers, headers, rehearsal numbers, and other page text have adequate room.

1. In the Document Setup dialog box, under the Page Margins heading, be sure that Same is selected so any changes to the Right Pages margins will automatically update to match the Left Pages settings.

2. Change both the top and bottom Left Pages margins to 0.25 inches (6.3 millimeters). This adds approximately one inch more space to the score.

3. Click OK.

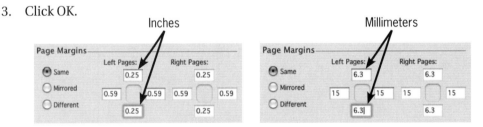

4. Save the file (**File** > Save) with the name Joshua Variations.

Entering the Time Signatures

There are several time signature changes in this piece, and it is important to add them before you begin the note entry process.

1. Select **View** > Staff Names and Bar Numbers.
2. Select bar 6.
3. Press the T key.
4. Click the 3/4 time signature button.
5. Click OK.
6. Select bar 8.
7. Press the T key.
8. Click the Other button.
9. Select 5 from the pop-up list for the number of beats, or type "5" into the number entry field to create a 5/4 time signature.
10. Click OK.

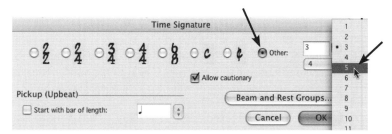

11. Repeat the above steps to enter the rest of the time signature changes for the piece: 3/4 time in bar 9; 4/4 time in bar 13; and cut time in bar 32.

Double Bars and Repeat Bars

A double bar is not necessary for time signature changes, but it is required for a key change. Double bars also make excellent landmarks for identifying phrases when entering music. Try entering barline changes via the contextual menus (right-click).

1. Press Esc twice to make sure nothing is selected.
2. Be sure bar 4 is visible.
3. Right-click (CTRL-click on a Mac with a one-button mouse) on any part of the score and select Barline > Double from the contextual menu. The cursor will change to an arrow and turn blue, indicating there's something to be inserted.
4. Click on the right barline of bar 4 to add the double bar.

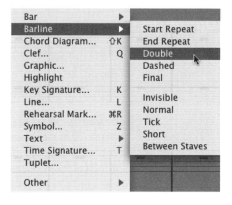

 You can click anywhere in the score, to get the contextual menu, but it is best to work close to the bar to which you want to add the barline.

5. Repeat steps 2 and 3 and enter a double barline at the ends of bars 15, 23, and 44.

Use the right-click method (contextual menus) to enter the repeats in bars 24 and 31.

6. To quickly advance to bar 24, use the shortcut: Option-⌘-G (Mac); CTRL-Alt-G (Win).
7. Press Esc to clear the selection.
8. Right-click (CTRL-click on a Mac with a one-button mouse) near bar 24 of the score, and select Barline > Start Repeat from the contextual menu. The cursor will change to an arrow, indicating there's something to be inserted.
9. Click on the left barline of bar 24 to add the repeat bar.
10. Follow the above steps to add the End Repeat bar in bar 31 (page 4 of the printout).

Changing Rehearsal Marks from Letters to Numbers

Rehearsal numbers default to letters in Sibelius. You may prefer to enter the rehearsal marks so the actual bar number is displayed rather than rehearsal letters. This needs to be set via the Engraving Rules setting for Rehearsal Marks.

1. Type Shift-⌘-E (Mac); Shift-CTRL-E (Win) to access the Engraving Rules dialog box.
2. Select "Rehearsal marks" in the left column.
3. Select "Bar number" in the Appearance list and click OK to close the Engraving Rules dialog box.
4. Select the left barline of bar 5 and enter the rehearsal number via the shortcut: ⌘-R (Mac); CTRL-R (Win).
5. Use the above shortcut to enter the rehearsal marks in bars 16, 24, 32, and 45.
6. Press Esc.

Metric Modulation

The tempo changes from a swing 4 feel to a fast 2 at bar 32. This should be indicated in the score with a quarter note-equals-half note mark over the time signature change.

For Sibelius to properly interpret it during playback, the tempo indication must be entered as Tempo text.

1. Advance to bar 32 and select the top staff of the score.
2. Use the shortcut: Option-⌘-T (Mac); Alt-CTRL-T (Win), or select **Create** > Text > Tempo to enter the tempo mark.
3. Right-click (CTRL-click on a Mac with a one-button mouse) on the blinking cursor to access the tempo pop-up list. Scroll down and select the quarter note value.

 All the note values in the pop-up list have shortcuts, and to help you remember them, each rhythm is assigned the same Keypad value. Just remember to use the number on the Keypad, not the numbers on the main computer keyboard along the top.

4. Press the space bar, type the equals sign (=), and press the space bar again.
5. Use the shortcut ⌘-5 (Mac) or CTRL-5 (Win), for the half note, or right-click the mouse again and select the value from the pop-up menu.
6. Press Esc.

Changing Tempo Text Fonts

The music note in the tempo indication in bar 1, and the music notes and metric modulation in bar 32 are still in the Opus Text font instead of Inkpen2 text. This can be changed in the Properties window.

1. Activate the Properties window if it is not already (select **Window** > Properties).
2. Double-click on the tempo Text in bar 1.
3. Drag-select the quarter note and the "= 112" so only they are highlighted.
4. In the Properties > Text window, click on the Font pop-up menu, currently displaying Opus Text, and select Inkpen2 Text font from the list.

The equals sign and number are a smaller font size, or point size, than the word Swing. Increase the size so they match.

5. Drag-select only the "= 112."
6. Click the up arrow next to the Size entry field twice to increase the size from 5.7 to 7.7.
7. Jump to bar 32 and repeat the steps to change both the quarter note and the half note to Inkpen2 Text font.

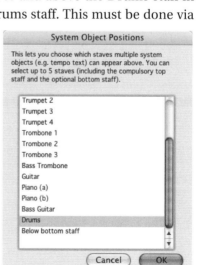

8. Using Tempo text, enter the rest of the tempo indications in bars 52 (Rubato) and 55 (Tempo half note = 100) (see page 7 of the printout).

Switching System Object Positions On and Off

The System Object Positions setting indicates on which staff or staves the rehearsal marks, tempo text, and bar numbers will appear. Since we selected the "Big band" Manuscript Paper at the beginning of this chapter, Sibelius automatically set the markings to appear above the top and bottom staves and above the Drums staff in the score. To save space, remove them above the Drums staff. This must be done via House Styles.

1. Select **House Style** > System Object Positions.
2. Scroll down until the Drums staff is automatically highlighted.
3. Shift-click on the highlighted Drums staff to deselect it.
4. Click OK.
5. Save and name the file "JoshVarBB.sib."

www.sibeliusbook.com

If you prefer to start at this point in the chapter, go to *www.sibeliusbook.com* and download the Chapter 11 folder. Open the file *11Joshua1.sib.*

Copy and Paste Between Sibelius Documents

If you started with Chapter 1 of this book, you've entered a lot of music up to this point. In consideration of all that work, here's a little bonus: I'll enter most of the music for you in this chapter. You will use the Joshua Variations sketch file you opened from the *www.sibeliusbook.com* Web site. This chapter will show you how to copy the notation from the sketch into the piano staff of the score file and then use the Arrange feature to create the complete orchestration.

There is an important procedural issue you need to be aware of before copying notation from one file to another. You must select the staves manually instead of using the Select All command. Using Select All will result in the music being pasted into the top two staves of the score since they are in the top two staves of the document in which they were created.

1. Select the Joshua Variations sketch file: **Window** > 11JoshuaSketch (you should have opened this at the beginning of this chapter).
2. Triple-click anywhere in the treble staff to select it for the entire score.
3. Hold down the Shift key and triple-click in the bass staff to select both staves for the entire score.
4. Use the shortcut: ⌘-C (Mac); CTRL-C (Win) to copy the notation.
5. Select **Window** > Joshua Variations, to make the score document active.
6. In the JoshVarBB score, select bar 1 of the Piano part, both treble and bass staves (click and shift-click).
7. Use the shortcut: ⌘-V (Mac); CTRL-V (Win) to paste the sketch into the Piano part of the score, or select **Edit** > Paste.

☺ **Have you saved lately?** ☺

 Keep the printout of the completed "Joshua" arrangement handy for reference throughout the rest of this chapter. I suggest you use a pencil to number the bars at the top of the score. This will save you time when looking up bars to compare with the instructions that follow.

About the Arrange Feature

The Arrange feature is an extremely powerful tool to create music in the ensemble of your choice. The Arrange feature can be applied in broad brushstrokes across an entire composition or phrase by phrase and staff by staff to provide more control over textural changes. Even if it does not give you the complete final result, it can be a helpful guide to finding the ideal orchestration.

I think of the Arrange feature as actually an Orchestration feature since it orchestrates the music you've entered for the instrumentation you select. It does not harmonize your music, realize chord symbols, add counter lines, substitute chords, or remove the need to study those subjects further if you need to use them. It does copy, split, and transpose notes into other staves to create an orchestration using the notation you've provided.

The big band arrangement in this chapter is "old school" as such arrangements go, which is just fine because the Sibelius Arrange feature is able to reproduce ensemble voicings made famous by Sammy Nestico, the Count Basie Orchestra, and others. This piece is excerpted from a longer arrangement, so it works well using different voicings from section to section.

Here is how to use the Arrange feature.
- Select a source region containing the music you wish to orchestrate.
- Copy it.
- Select the destination staves.
- Choose the Arranging Style, paste, and before you can say Sammy Nestico, your music is ready.

Orchestrating (Arranging) Bars 1 and 2

From here on, you will be using the big band score with the copied piano sketch inserted in the Piano part. So you don't get the files confused, I recommend that you close the sketch part. Select **Window** > 11JoshuaSketch and then **File** > Close to close the file.

1. Select **Window** > Joshua Variations so the big band score is active.
2. Select only bars 1 and 2 of the Piano's treble staff.
3. Use the shortcut: ⌘-C (Mac); CTRL-C (Win) to copy the selected bars.

Next, you must select a destination region.
4. Click on the Alto 1 staff in bar 1, then Shift-click on the Trumpet 4 part in bar 2.
5. Select **Notes** > Arrange or use the shortcut: Shift-⌘-V (Mac); Shift-CTRL-V (Win) to access the Arrange Styles list.

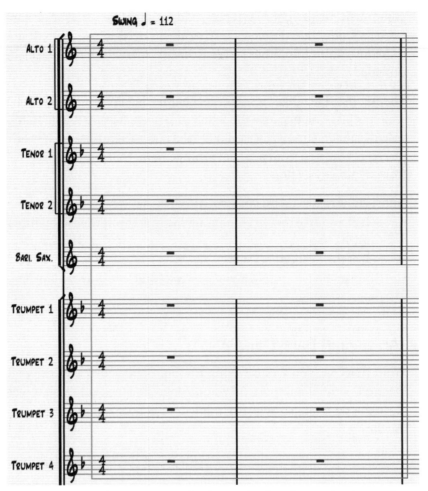

6. Scroll down the Arrange Styles list and select "Jazz: Nestico-style 1a mid (Trumpets & Altos)."

7. Click OK.

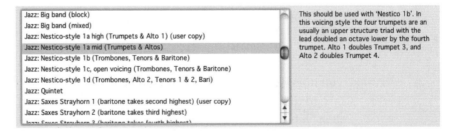

 When you select an Arrange Style, a description of how the style will orchestrate appears to the right of the selection list. Reading these descriptions can save you a lot of trial-and-error work in selecting the most appropriate style for the job at hand.

The four voices of the Piano staff have been split among the four Trumpet staves. The bottom two voices are doubled by Altos 1 and 2.

To fill out the ensemble, return to the Piano part and be sure the bass clef staff is visible.

8. Select bars 1 and 2 of the Piano's bass staff.
9. Use the shortcut: ⌘-C (Mac); CTRL-C (Win) to copy the notation.

10. Click on the Tenor 1 staff in bar 1, then Shift-click on the Bass Trombone part in bar 2.
11. Use the shortcut: Shift-⌘-V (Mac); Shift-CTRL-V (Win) to access the Arrange Styles list.

12. From the Arranging Styles list, select "Jazz: Nestico 1c, open voicing (Trombones, Tenors & Baritone)."

13. Click OK.

The results are a little different this time since there are only two notes in the original voicing from the Piano staff. Finishing this passage will require some good ol' copy and paste.

14. Select bars 1 and 2 of the Trombone 2 staff.
15. Option-click (Mac); Alt-click (Win) bar 1 of the Trombone 3 staff to paste the music.
16. Repeat the copy and paste steps and paste the Trombone 2 part into the Bass Trombone and Bari. Sax. staves.
17. Select bars 1 and 2 of the Trombone 2 staff.
18. Press ⌘-up arrow key (Mac) or CTRL-up arrow key (Win) to transpose the music up one octave.

The first two bars are complete—almost. The eighth note C that originated in the bass staff of the Piano has a tie hanging over into bar 3. This note is part of what will become a solo for the bass player. The horns are assigned to play a staccato note on the end of bar 2.

19. Select the C eighth note on beat 4 of the Trombone 1 staff.
20. Shift-click the C eighth note on beat 4 of the Bass Trombone staff.
21. ⌘-click (Mac) or CTRL-click (Win) on the C eighth note in the Tenor 1, Tenor 2, and Bari. Sax. staves.
22. On the first Keypad layout, click the ⌃ key or press the Enter key on the numeric keypad to remove the tie.
23. On the Keypad, click the > key to remove the accent.
24. On the Keypad, click the ∙ key to enter the staccato.

The notes now have the proper playing instructions, but octave Cs are a bit boring, so add a chord.

25. Select the C eighth note in the Tenor 1 staff and press ⌘-up arrow key (Mac) or CTRL-up arrow key (Win) to transpose it up an octave.
26. Repeat the above step for Trombone 1.
27. Select the C eighth note in the Tenor 2 staff and press the down arrow key (all by itself) to move it down a third, to A.
28. On the Keypad, press the ♮ key or press the 7 key on the numeric keypad to enter the natural.
29. Repeat steps 28 and 29 for the Trombone 2 part.
30. Select the C eighth note in the Trombone 3 staff and use the up arrow key by itself to raise it up a fifth, to G.
31. Select the C eighth note in the Bass Trombone staff and press ⌘-down arrow key (Mac); CTRL-down arrow key (Win) to transpose it down an octave.
32. Press Esc twice to clear the selection.

The horn parts are now finished in bars 1 and 2. As you can see, it is possible to use multiple styles in the same region, and there are usually some minor details that need attention after using the Arrange feature.

Arranging Bars 5 Through 14 (Pages 1 and 2 of the Printout)

In this section, the Alto 1 player will double on flute and the Tenor 1 player on clarinet.

Changing the Staff Transposition for Instrument Doublings

In the Alto 1 staff, insert a staff transposition change beginning at bar 5. When a staff transposition change is inserted and a change of key is required (such as going from Alto Sax to Flute), the change of key is always placed at the first bar where the new instrument begins playing.

1. Press Esc so nothing is selected.
2. Select **Create** > Other > Transposition Change.
3. Click OK in the Transposition Change dialog box. Since flute is a nontransposing instrument in the key of C, make sure the "written middle C sounds as" pitch is set at C, and "in octave no." is set at "4 (middle C)."
4. Click on the Alto 1 staff at the beginning of bar 5 to enter the staff transposition.

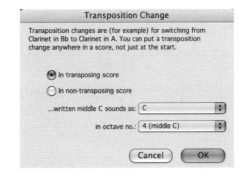

5. If the key signature appears a little to the right of the beginning of the measure, as in the graphic below, it must be moved over to the left of the barline or it will collide with the notation. With the key signature change highlighted, drag it to the left with the mouse or nudge it with the left arrow key.

The change affects bar 5, in this case, to the end of the piece. In this arrangement, the Alto 1 player will be changing back to Alto Sax in bar 15 (page 2 of the printout). This change will be made later in the chapter.

The next staff transposition change for instrument doubling will be the Tenor Sax 1 part. This part is changing to B♭ clarinet. Since both tenor sax and clarinet are B♭ instruments, no key signature change is needed. However, there is an octave change in the transposition that will affect playback.

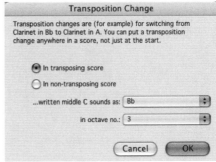

1. Select **Create** > Other > Transposition Change.
2. Change "written middle C sounds as" to B♭ using the pop-up list.
3. Change "in octave no." to 3 using the pop-up list.

4. Click OK.
5. Click on the Tenor 1 staff at the beginning of bar 5. No key signature will appear since both instruments are B♭ instruments. However, a blue box will appear on the staff to signify where the change begins. The blue box must be at the beginning of the bar just like a displaying key signature since it indicates the place in the measure where the staff transposition change takes effect.

To see the results of the changes, enter some notation.

1. Select bars 5 through 14 of the treble Piano staff.
2. Use the shortcut: Option-Shift-⌘-1 (Mac); Alt-Shift-CTRL-1 (Win) to select only the Voice 1 notes, or select **Edit** > Filter > Voice 1.
3. Option-click (Mac); Alt-click (Win) the Alto 1 staff to paste the selected music .

> If Sibelius is set to display red noteheads on out-of-range notes (**View** > Note Colors > Notes out of range), you will see a lot of red noteheads in the Alto 1 staff. Even though Sibelius understands the transposition change, it is still using the Alto Sax range to determine which notes are in range and which are not. Ignore the red notes when using staff transpositions for instrument doublings such as the ones used in this score.

For the Alto 2 and Clarinet parts, arrange (orchestrate) the notes in Voice 2, measures 5 through 8 (pages 1 and 2 of the printout).

4. Select measures 5 through 8 of the treble Piano staff.
5. Use the shortcut: Option-Shift-⌘-2 (Mac); or Alt-Shift-CTRL-2 (Win) to select only the Voice 2 notes, or select **Edit** > Filter > Voice 2.
6. Use the shortcut: ⌘-C (Mac); CTRL-C (Win) to copy the passage.
7. Select the Alto 2 and Tenor 1 staves in bars 5 through 8.
8. Use the shortcut: ⌘-Shift-V (Mac); CRTL-Shift-V (Win) to access the Arrange Styles dialog box.
9. Select "Jazz: Saxes Tenor 1 Lead." This will place the top note for the Clarinet in the Tenor 1 staff instead of the Alto 2 staff.
10. Click OK.
11. Select the Tenor 1 staff in bars 5 through 8.
12. Press ⌘-up arrow key (Mac) or CTRL-up arrow key (Win) to transpose the passage up one octave. The E pitches in bar 8 are the reason for the octave adjustment. They are out of the set tenor sax range, so Sibelius automatically adjusted the octave to put the notes in a better range.

> It is possible to use part of an Arranging Style's instruments. Even though the Tenor 1 Lead style is set to fill out all five sax staves, you can limit it by only selecting two staves.

Text Instrument Changes

With the instrument doublings entered, the next step is to let the player in on what's happening. Every instrument change should have two indications: one indicating which instrument to switch to and another where the new instrument begins. After the last saxophone bar, in this case the end of bar 2, enter a text indication to inform the player of the instrument change. Then, enter a text indication where the new instrument begins playing.

1. In the Alto 1 staff, select bar 3.
2. Use the shortcut: ⌘-T (Mac); CTRL-T (Win) to enter Technique text.
3. Type "To Flute" and then press Esc twice.
4. In the Alto 1 part, select bar 5.
5. Use the shortcut: ⌘-T (Mac); CTRL-T (Win) to enter Technique text.
6. Type "Flute" and then press Esc twice.
7. Repeat the above steps to enter the change to Clarinet on the Tenor 1 staff in bar 3.

Adding the text gives the player an indication of what is coming next and generates a MIDI patch (sound) change so the proper instrument is heard during playback.

8. In the Alto 1 staff, select bar 1.
9. Shift-click bar 1 in the Tenor 1 staff so the first three staves are selected.
10. Press the letter P (all by itself) to play back the selected bars.
11. Press Esc to stop playback.

Changing the Staff Transposition in Bar 19 (Page 3 of Printout)

In this arrangement, the woodwinds must change back to saxes, making their reentrance in bar 19.

1. In the Alto 1 staff, select bar 19.
2. Select **Create** > Other > Transposition Change.
3. Change "written middle C sounds as" to E♭.
4. Change "in octave no." to 3.
5. Click OK.
6. In the Tenor 1 staff, select bar 19.
7. Select **Create** > Other > Transposition Change.
8. Change "written middle C sounds as" to B♭.
9. Change "in octave no." to 2.
10. Click OK.

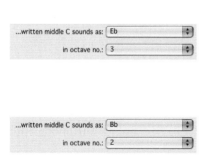

Sibelius cannot accept an instrument transposition change in the first measure of a score. If you want to begin a piece with an instrument double, you must select the proper staff for the initial instrument. You can edit the staff name as needed.

Finishing the Saxes in Bars 9 Through 14 (Page 2 of the Printout)

The most basic way to orchestrate is via good ol' copy and paste.

1. Select the Piano bass staff from the beginning of bar 9 through beat 1 of bar 14.
2. Option-click (Mac); Alt-click (Win) bar 9 of the Bari. Sax. staff.
3. Select bars 11 and 12 of the Bari. Sax. staff.
4. Option-click (Mac); Alt-click (Win) to paste the selection into bars 11 and 12 of the Alto 2 and Tenor 2 staves.

In bars 13 and 14, use the "Jazz: Saxes Tenor 1 Lead" Arrange Style, this time for three saxes.

5. In the treble Piano staff, select bars 13 through 14.
6. Use the shortcut: Option-Shift-⌘-2 (Mac); Alt-Shift-CTRL-2 (Win) to select only the Voice 2 notes.
7. Use the shortcut: ⌘-C (Mac); CTRL-C (Win) to copy the passage.
8. Select the Alto 2 through Tenor 2 staves in bars 13 through 14.
9. Use the shortcut: ⌘-Shift-V (Mac); CRTL-Shift-V (Win) to access the Arrange Styles dialog box.
10. Select "Jazz: Saxes Tenor 1 Lead."
11. Click OK.

Changing the Value of an Existing Note

The quarter note in bar 14 of the Bari. Sax. staff must be changed to a whole note to match the rest of the section.

1. Select the quarter note in bar 14 of the Bari. Sax. staff.
2. On the first Keypad, click the ▯ key, or press 6 on the numeric keypad. Any notes or rests in the beats occupied by the new rhythm are erased in favor of the new rhythm.

Adding the Performance Information (Page 1 of the Printout)

To complete this section for the saxes, enter the dynamics (expressions) for all the entrances. You have entered expressions many times before in previous chapters.

To enter an expression, select the note in the staff and use the shortcut: ⌘-E (Mac); CRTL-E (Win). Right-click (CTRL-click on a Mac with a one-button mouse) and choose the appropriate expression:

1. Enter a mezzo-forte for the Flute in bar 5.
2. Enter a mezzo-piano for the Alto 2 and Tenor 1 staves in bar 5, the Bari. in bar 9, and the Tenor 2 in bar 11.
3. Enter hairpins in bars 13 and 14 as shown in the graphic below.

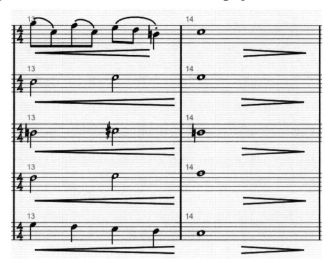

Muted Brass Markings (Pages 1 and 2 of the Printout)

In bars 13 and 14, double the Alto one octave lower in the Trumpet 2 in a Harmon mute.

1. In the Alto 1 staff, select bars 5 through 14.
2. Option-click (Mac); Alt-click (Win) bar 5 of the Trumpet 2 staff (doubling on Flute) to paste the music.
3. Use the shortcut: ⌘-down arrow key (Mac) or CTRL-down arrow key (Win) to transpose the passage down one octave.

Mute changes are entered in a similar fashion to the woodwind doubles. Give the player a mute indication at the end of the open passage and another indication of the required mute at the start of the muted passage.

1. In bar 3 of the Trumpet 2 staff, type "To Harmon Mute" as Technique text. Use the shortcut: ⌘-T (Mac); CTRL-T (Win).
2. In bar 5 of the Trumpet 2 staff, type "Harmon Mute" as Technique text.

The entered text will trigger a sound change to muted trumpet during playback.

Bars 9 through 12 in Voice 2 of the Piano staff will be assigned to the Trumpet 3 and 4 and Trombone 1 staves (see Chapter 8 for a detailed explanation of Voices).

1. Select bars 9 through 12 of the treble Piano staff.
2. Use the shortcut: Option-Shift-⌘-2 (Mac); Alt-Shift-CTRL-2 (Win) to select only the Voice 2 notes or select **Edit** > Filter > Voice 2.
3. Use the shortcut: ⌘-C (Mac); CTRL-C (Win) to copy the passage
4. Select the Trumpet 3 through Trombone 1 staves in bars 9 through 12.
5. Use the shortcut: ⌘-Shift-V (Mac); CRTL-Shift-V (Win) to access the Arrange Styles dialog box.
6. Select "Explode (user copy)" at the top of the styles list. (Explode simply takes a chord and assigns the notes to each of the target staves. The top note in the top staff, second note from the top in the second staff, and so forth.)
7. Click OK.

This section is played in cup mutes, so indications must be added to all three staves.

8. In bar 3 of the Trumpet 3 staff, enter "To Cup Mute" as Technique text by using the shortcut: ⌘-T (Mac); CTRL-T (Win).
9. In bar 9 of the Trumpet 3 staff, enter "Cup Mute" as Technique text.
10. In bar 11 of the Trumpet 3 staff, enter "Open" as Technique text.
11. In bar 9 of the Trumpet 3 staff, enter a piano dynamic as Expression text by using the shortcut: ⌘-E (Mac); CTRL-E (Win).

Use the Advanced Filter to copy all four indications to the Trumpet 4 and Trombone 1 staves.

12. Select bars 3 through 11 of the Trumpet 3 staff.
13. Use the shortcut: Option-Shift-⌘-F (Mac); Alt-Shift-CTRL-F (Win) to access the Advanced Filter dialog box or select **Edit** > Filter > Advanced Filter.
14. In the View list, select Text.
15. Under the Find heading, uncheck "Notes and Chords" and check "Text."
16. In the "Text style" list, scroll to Expression and select it.

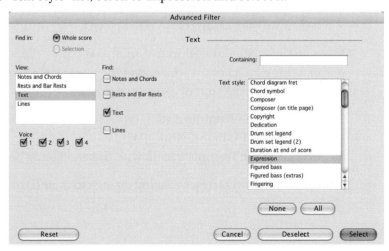

17. Scroll down to Technique and ⌘-click (Mac) or CTRL-click (Win) to select both Expression and Technique. Scroll up to be sure both items are highlighted (selected).
18. Click Select.
19. Shift-Option-click (Mac); Shift-Alt-click (Win) the Trumpet 4 staff to paste the text.
20. Shift-Option-click (Mac); Shift-Alt-click (Win) the Trombone 1 staff to paste the text.

The mute change will also work in these staves, but there is only one muted sound in the General MIDI patch list, a Harmon mute sound, so the mute changes will not be reflected in playback. All muted playback will be Harmon mute.

 When using mutes and instrument doubles in your scores, always be sure to give the player enough time to make the switch. Players can save time by placing an instrument or mute on their lap or the music stand, but time is still needed to physically make the change. Reed-to-flute changes require resetting of the player's embouchure, so a quick change to a demanding part may be difficult for players unless they have time to get themselves set. Lastly, try to avoid instrument or mute changes during page turns unless there are enough measures' rest to turn the page and get the new instrument or mute ready.

Bars 15 Through 23 (Pages 2 and 3 of the Printout)

Bars 15 through 23 are principally a *soli* for the brass section with some unison sax lines. Use the saxes that are not changing instruments to double some of the notes in the fortissimo chords for added punch. Use the Filter to select the specific Voice containing the passage to be arranged. One of the sax lines is entered in Voice 2 in bars 19 and 20; the other is in Voice 1 beginning on beat 4 of bar 21 and going through all of bar 22. Begin with the Voice 2 phrase.

1. Select bars 19 and 20 of the treble Piano staff (page 3 of the score).
2. Use the shortcut: Option-Shift-⌘-2 (Mac); Alt-Shift-CTRL-2 (Win) to select only the Voice 2 entries, or select **Edit** > Filter > Voice 2.
3. Use the shortcut: ⌘-C (Mac); CTRL-C (Win).
4. Select bars 19 and 20 in both the Alto and Tenor Sax staves.
5. Use the shortcut Shift-⌘-V (Mac) or Shift-CTRL-V (Win) to access the Arrange Styles list.
6. From the Arranging Styles list, select "Standard Arrangement" and click OK.

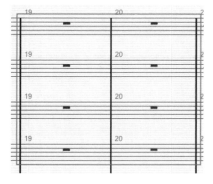

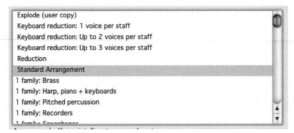

7. With the notes in place, add the articulations to all notes by selecting the entire sax section vertically and entering each articulation. In other words, select the note in the top staff, Shift-click the bottom staff note, and then choose the appropriate articulation on the Keypad.

8. Enter the dynamics (Expressions) in the Alto 1 staff. Once entered, you will copy and paste these Expressions to the rest of the sax staves.

9. Select the Alto 1 staff in bar 19.

10. Select **Edit** > Filter > Advanced Filter.

11. In the View list, select Text.

12. Under the Find heading, check the Text box.

13. In the Text Style list, scroll down and select Expression.

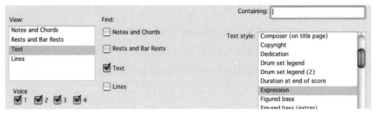

14. In the View list, select Lines.

15. Under the Find heading, check the Lines box.

16. In the "Staff Lines" list, scroll down and select the crescendo hairpin.

17. Click OK.

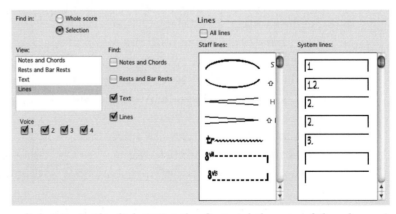

18. Option-click (Mac); Alt-click (Win) the first eighth note of the phrase in bar 19 of the Alto 2 staff.

19. Option-click (Mac); Alt-click (Win) on the first eighth note in each of the remaining sax staves and paste the dynamics to each.

Arranging a Phrase That Contains a Partial Measure

The sax line in bars 21 and 22 can be arranged using the same Arrange Style; however, since the phrase begins on beat 4 of the measure, there must be a corresponding fourth beat to select in the first destination measure.

1. Select the Alto 1 staff in bar 21.
2. Press N to enter notation and enter a half rest and two quarter rests.
3. Press Esc twice.

4. Select the unison line in the treble Piano staff beginning on beat 4 of bar 21 and continuing through all of bar 22.
5. Use the shortcut: ⌘-C (Mac); CTRL-C (Win) to copy it.

6. Click on the quarter rest on beat 4 of bar 21 in the Alto 1 staff.
7. Shift-click on bar 22 of the Bari. Sax. staff.
8. Use the shortcut: Shift-⌘-V (Mac); Shift-CTRL-V (Win) to access the Arrange Styles list.
9. Select "Standard Arrangement" from the list and click OK.

The unison line is copied to all five sax staves and adjusted down an octave where appropriate.

Big Band Brass

10. Select the treble staff of the Piano from bar 15 through 23.
11. Use the shortcut: ⌘-C (Mac); CTRL-C (Win) to copy it.
12. Click on bar 15 in the Trumpet 1 staff, then Shift-click in bar 23 of the Bass Trombone staff to select the entire Trumpet and Trombone staves.
13. Use the shortcut: Shift-⌘-V (Mac); Shift-CTRL-V (Win) to access the Arrange Styles list.
14. Select "Jazz Basie-style, brass only 1 (block)" from the Arranging Style list.
15. Click OK.

This Arrange Style option orchestrates the passage for all four trumpets, doubled one octave lower in the trombones. The Trumpet 1 part, and therefore the Trombone 1 part, has been lowered one octave according to the range that Sibelius considers best for the trumpet. This range is on the conservative side. Since most trumpet players will not admit to having an upper limit to their range, in their honor, transpose the Trumpet 1 part up one octave.

16. In the Trumpet 1 staff, select bars 15 through 23
17. Press ⌘-up arrow key (Mac); CTRL-up arrow key (Win) to transpose the selected bars up an octave.
18. Repeat steps 16 and 17 for the Trombone 1 staff.

A mute change indication is needed for the Trumpet 2 in bar 15. This is an exception to the practice of two indications for a mute change, since there is only one bar to make the change.

19. In bar 15 of the Trumpet 2 staff, enter "Open" as Technique text by using the shortcut: ⌘-T (Mac); CTRL-T (Win).

Changing the Default Instrument Range

You can change the default instrument range, which chooses the octave of a part. Making this change will also change the color of notes that are in or out of range.

1. Use the shortcut: Shift-⌘-P (Mac); Shift-CTRL-P (Win) to activate the Properties window or select **Window** > Properties.
2. Click the Staves tab.
3. Select the Trumpet 1 staff.
4. Use the pop-up lists to change the Comfortable range top and bottom notes to match the Professional range.
5. Select the Trombone 1 staff.
6. Repeat step 4 above and change the Trombone 1 and Bass Trombone Comfortable range to the Professional range.

Filling in the Saxes in Bars 15 Through 23

Navigate back to the top of the score to complete the sax parts for bars 15 through 23. The Alto 1 and Tenor 1 players will be changing instruments after bar 14, so they will not be able to play the fortissimo chords in bar 15; leave them out. The Alto 2, Tenor 2, and Bari. Sax. are available to play in bar 15 and can lend some added punch to those chords.

The Alto 2 doubles the Trumpet 4 part.

1. In the Trumpet 4 staff, click on bar 15 and Shift-click on the first quarter note in bar 16.
2. Option-click (Mac); Alt-click (Win) on bar 15 of the Alto 2 staff to paste the music.
3. Repeat steps 1 through 3 above and double the Trombone 2 part with Tenor 2.

The Bari. Sax. will act as the fifth trombone part. In situations where rhythms are the same but the pitches are different, use the Re-input Pitches function to save time. You should already have a selection on the clipboard that can provide the proper rhythms, with articulations and dynamic marks attached.

4. Option-click (Mac); Alt-click (Win) on the Bari. Sax. staff in bar 15 to paste the Trombone 2 part.
5. Press Esc.
6. Select the first eighth note on beat 4 of bar 15.
7. Use the shortcut: Shift-⌘-I (Mac); Shift-CTRL-I (Win) or select **Notes** > Re-input Pitches. A dashed cursor will appear.
8. Enter just the pitches by typing the letter names or playing them on your MIDI keyboard.
9. Press Esc twice to clear the selection.

In bar 19, both the Alto and Tenor 1 will need a text indication that this is once again a sax part.

10. Select the Alto 1 staff in bar 19.
11. Use the shortcut: ⌘–T (Mac); CTRL-T (Win).
12. Type "Alto Sax."
13. Press Esc twice.
14. Repeat the steps for the Tenor 1 staff, entering the text "Tenor Sax" in bar 19.

In bar 19, the Bari. Sax. will once again be playing fifth trombone. Use your preferred method of note entry to input the D dotted quarter note and C quarter note as shown in the graphic below.

15. Enter the notes in the Bari. Sax. staff, along with the articulation and dynamic mark.

Next, fill out bar 23 for the saxes. The Altos will double Trumpets 3 and 4 and the Trombones will double Trombones 1 and 2.

16. Click on the Trumpet 3 staff in bar 23.
17. Shift-click on the Trombone 2 staff in bar 23 to select all staves between the two click points.
18. Option-click (Mac); Alt-click (Win) on the Alto 1 staff in bar 23 to paste the four brass parts into the four sax staves.

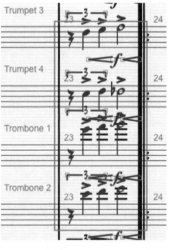

The last detail is the Bari. Sax. Once again it will play something different, copying the left hand of the Piano staff.

19. Select bar 23 of the Piano bass staff.
20. Option-click (Mac); Alt-click (Win) on the Bari. Sax. staff in bar 23.
21. With bar 23 of the Bari. Sax. still highlighted, press ⌘-down arrow key (Mac); CTRL-down arrow key (Win) to transpose the line down an octave.

The Bari. Sax. needs two hairpins and the dynamic mark to match the rest of the ensemble. Using the Advanced Filter feature, you can copy both elements at the same time.

22. Select the Tenor 2 staff in bar 23.
23. Select **Edit** > Filter > Advanced Filter.
24. In the View list, select Text.
25. Under the Find heading, check the Text box.
26. In the Text Style list, scroll down and select Expression.

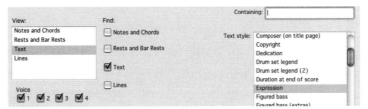

27. In the View list, select Lines.
28. Under the Find heading, check the Lines box.
29. In the Staff Lines list, scroll down and select the crescendo hairpin.
30. Click OK.

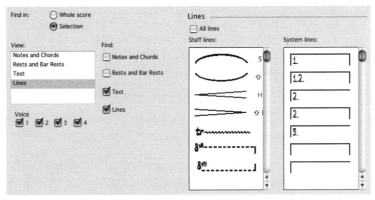

31. Option-click (Mac); Alt-click (Win) on the Bari. Sax. staff in bar 23 to paste the selection.

Entering Bars 24 Through 32 (Page 4 of the Printout)

Bars 24 through 32 is the solo section of the arrangement, and you get the chance to fly solo. In other words, there will be no steps to complete this section, so you will have to refer to previous sections of this chapter. This section combines some of the skills used in the last section along with the first and second time playback indications from Chapter 10.

Voice 1 in the treble staff of the Piano part contains the brass section. Use the same Arranging Style as in bars 15 through 23, "Jazz Basie-style, brass only 1 (block)."

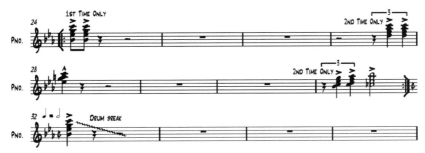

Taking a Big Fall (Fall Off)

The fall off in bar 32 playback has been turned off in the sketch document. The fall off is actually a glissando, so when the program sees this shape it looks for notes at the beginning and end of the mark. With a jazz fall off, there is no ending note, so the result will be a playback problem. So whenever you are using the glissando as a fall off, turn off the playback for all occurrences of the shape.

1. If the Properties window is not on the screen, activate it by selecting **Window** > Properties.
2. Select the fall off shape in bar 32 of the piano part.
3. Click the Playback tab.
4. Under "Play on pass," uncheck the box under 1.

Voice 2 Saxes

In bars 24 through 31 the saxes play a unison line, and one voiced chord in bar 31. This has been entered in the treble staff of the Piano staff in Voice 2. Follow these steps:

1. Copy only the Voice 2 notes in the piano treble staff, bars 24-31.
2. Paste to the saxophone parts.
3. After copying, delete the Voice 2 notes in the Piano treble staff, bars 24 through 31, before arranging the brass parts.

Here's a hint: bar 31 is the same as bar 23 except for the Alto and Tenor Saxes on the first two beats. Don't worry about who is soloing. That comes later in the chapter.

Bars 36 Through 44 (Page 5 of the Printout)

In bars 36 through 44, the trombones have a *soli* that shows off the versatility of the Arrange feature. There are unison sections, four-part harmony, and octave doubling all within the same section.

1. Select the bass staff of the Piano in bars 36 through 44.
2. Use the shortcut: ⌘-C (Mac); CTRL-C (Win) to copy the passage.
3. Select the Trombone 1 through Bass Trombone staves in bars 36 through 44.

4. Use the shortcut: ⌘-Shift-V (Mac); CRTL-Shift-V (Win) to access the Arrange Styles dialog box.
5. Select "Explode (user copy)" at the top of the styles list.
6. Click OK.

 The same results could have been achieved using several Arranging Styles. You could have used the "1 Family: Brass" or the "Nestico: Trombones Tenors and Bari" styles and, as long as only the Trombone staves were selected, only the Trombone staves would receive notes.

The treble clef staff of the piano in this section will be assigned to the saxes, with the trumpets doubling the chord punches in bars 37 and 38, scored up one octave.

1. Select the treble staff of the Piano in bars 37 through 44.
2. Use the shortcut: ⌘-C (Mac); CTRL-C (Win) to copy the passage.
3. Select the Alto 1 through Tenor 2 staves in bars 37 through 44.
4. Use the shortcut: ⌘-Shift-V (Mac); CRTL-Shift-V (Win) to access the Arrange Styles dialog box.
5. Select "Explode (user copy)" at the top of the styles list.
6. Click OK.
7. Select the Alto 1 through Tenor 2 staves in bars 37 and 38.
8. Option-click (Mac); Alt-click (Win) on the Trumpet 1 staff in bar 37 to paste the selection.
9. Use the shortcut: ⌘-up arrow key (Mac); CTRL-up arrow key (Win) to transpose the parts up one octave.

The Bari. Sax. will join the trombones in unison on the "Sing Sing Sing"-type bass line, starting in bar 43.

1. Select bars 43 and 44 in the Bass Trombone staff.
2. Option-click (Mac); Alt-click (Win) on bar 43 in the Bari. Sax. staff.
3. Enter an Expression dynamic (forte) in bar 43 (shortcut: ⌘-E [Mac]; CTRL-E [Win]).

To complete this section, some Expression and Technique text needs to be added. Copy them to the rest of the section using the Advanced Filter.

1. Use Technique text, ⌘-T (Mac) or CTRL-T (Win) and enter "Soli" in the Trombone 1 staff.
2. Use Expression text, ⌘-E (Mac) or CTRL-E (Win) and add a forte in bar 36.
3. Use the Advanced Filter to copy both Technique and Expression text to the rest of the section.

The trumpets need a mute indication along with a dynamic in bar 33.

4. In bar 33 of the Trumpet 1 part, enter "To Straight Mute" using Technique text.

5. In bar 37 of the Trumpet 1 part, using Technique text, enter "Str. Mute" and a mezzo forte above the staff. The abbreviation of straight (Str.) is common in jazz arranging.

6. In bar 38 of the Trumpet 1 part, using Technique text, enter "Open."

7. Use the Advanced Filter to copy both Technique and Expression text to the rest of the section.

The saxes only need a single dynamic in this section.

8. In bar 37 of the Alto 1 part, using Expression text, enter a mezzo forte.

9. Select the mezzo forte and copy it to the rest of the section.

Bars 45 Through 52 (Pages 6 and 7 of the Printout)

This section continues the quasi "Sing Sing Sing" treatment of the melody with the saxes playing the melody. The trumpets join the saxes in bar 51 leading to the fermata in bar 52. Bars 49 and 50 of the treble Piano staff is the one phrase that the Arrange feature does not handle seamlessly, since there are multiple voices. You will get close, but there will be some extra work to do on this section.

1. Select the treble Piano staff in bars 46 through 50.

2. Use the shortcut: ⌘-C (Mac); CTRL-C (Win) to copy the passage.

3. Select the Alto 1 in bar 46 through the Tenor 2 in bar 50.

4. Use the shortcut: ⌘-Shift-V (Mac); CTRL-Shift-V (Win) to access the Arrange Styles dialog box.

5. Select "1 Family: Saxophones" from the styles list.

6. Click OK.

The altos are correct and, other than the stem direction on beat 1 of Tenor 1, bar 50 is also correct. In bar 49, Tenor 1 has two notes instead of one. The tenors will need the unison notes for bar 46 through beat 3 of bar 49, so add that first.

7. In the Alto part, select bar 46 through beat 3 of bar 49.

8. Option-click (Mac); Alt-click (Win) on the Tenor 1 staff in bar 46 to paste the passage.

Use the Arrange feature to explode the Tenor 1 part to both tenors. However, you will have a problem with the high E in bar 46 being out of the instrument's comfort range. The comfort range can be adjusted on a staff-by-staff basis.

9. With the Tenor 1 staff still selected, if the Properties window is not on the screen, activate it (**Window** > Properties).
10. Select the Staves tab in the Properties window.
11. Under the Comfortable heading, change the range limits to match the notes under the Professional heading using the pop-up list.
12. Select the Tenor 2 staff and repeat step 13.
13. Select the Tenor 1 staff from bar 46 through all of bar 49.
14. Use the shortcut: ⌘-C (Mac); CTRL-C (Win) to copy the passage.
15. Select bars 46 through 49 of the Tenor 1 and 2 staves.
16. Use the shortcut: ⌘-Shift-V (Mac); CRTL-Shift-V (Win) to access the Arrange Styles dialog box.
17. Select "Explode (user copy)" from the Arranging Styles list.
18. Click OK.
19. Select the D♯ quarter note on beat 1 of Tenor 1 in bar 50.
20. Press the X key to flip the stem to the down position or select **Edit** > Flip.

In bars 49 and 50, I had to explode 51 and 52 separately in order to get the four-part chord to distribute correctly. I'd like to add a caesura after the fermata in bar 52. If I add it before using the Arrange feature, it will be copied to all the parts, saving me the time and trouble of manually entering it on all staves.

1. Click on any note of the chord under the fermata on beat 3 of bar 52.
2. Press Z (all by itself) to access the Symbol library.
3. Locate the caesura (sometimes called a cut) in the library. Find Articulation in the left margin, then the caesura in the third line of that section. There are two different caesuras in the library. The first looks hand-drawn, which fits best with the Inkpen look of this document, so click on it. The caesura will turn blue and the box around it will bold.
4. Click OK and use the right arrow key to move the mark to the right, away from the fermata. When it is clear of the fermata, use the mouse to drag it to its correct position.

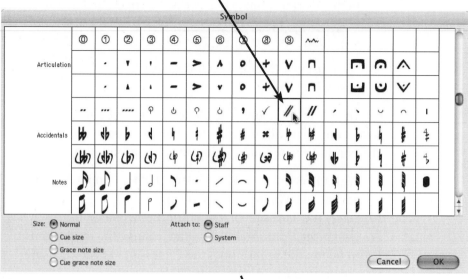

5. Repeat the steps to add a caesura to the bass staff in the Piano part. The caesura will remain selected in the Symbol window until you select another symbol or quit Sibelius.

Now, resume arranging.

1. Select the treble Piano staff from the beginning of bar 51 through the third beat of 52. The eighth notes on beat 4 will become a solo trumpet part.
2. Use the shortcut: ⌘-C (Mac); CTRL-C (Win) to copy the passage.
3. Select the Alto 1 through Tenor 2 staves in bars 51 and 52.
4. Use the shortcut: ⌘-Shift-V (Mac); CRTL-Shift-V (Win) to access the Arrange Styles dialog box.
5. Select "Explode (user copy)" from the Arranging Styles list.
6. Click OK.

The trumpets will double the saxes in this section, giving you two choices for filling in the trumpet staves. You could reselect bar 51 and all of 52 in the Piano and use the Arrange feature, then delete the fourth beat of 52 in the lower three trumpets, or copy the saxes, then copy the fourth beat from the piano to the Trumpet 1 staff. (Yes, life as a composer/arranger often hinges on such questions.) Let's choose the latter, as the simple copy and paste uses fewer keystrokes.

1. Select the four sax staves in bars 51 and 52.
2. Option-click (Mac); Alt-click (Win) on bar 51 in the Trumpet 1 staff to paste the passage.
3. Select beat 4 of the Piano treble staff in bar 52.

4. Option-click (Mac); Alt-click (Win) on the quarter rest on beat 4 of the Trumpet 1 staff in bar 52 to paste the eighth notes.

5. Select the first eighth and enter "Solo" as Technique text.

The trombones and bari sax continue to double the bass line until 51, where there is another multiple-voice situation. In this case, copy only the Voice 1 notes, leaving the single measure of Voice 2 for later.

1. Select the bass Piano staff in bars 45 through 52.
2. Use the shortcut: Option-Shift-⌘-1 (Mac); Alt-Shift-CTRL-1 (Win) to select only the Voice 1 entries or choose **Edit** > Filter > Voice 1.
3. Use the shortcut: ⌘-C (Mac); CTRL-C (Win) to copy the passage.
4. Click on bar 45 of the Bari. Sax.
5. Shift-click on bar 52 of the Bass Trombone.
6. Use the shortcut: ⌘-Shift-V (Mac); CRTL-Shift-V (Win) to access the Arrange Styles dialog box.
7. Select "Jazz: Nestico-style 1b (Trombones, Tenors & Baritone)."
8. Click OK.

The unison section is okay; however, this time the caesura did not copy in bar 52. Bar 51 needs some attention, but that was expected. Fortunately, the fixes in bar 51 are easy. In the trombones, copy the third and fourth parts up one staff to make room for the Voice 2 line, which will be copied to the Bass Trombone part. The Bass Trombone part should be copied to the Bari. Sax. staff.

9. Select the Trombone 3 and 4 staves in bar 51.
10. Option-click (Mac); Alt-click (Win) on the Trombone 2 staff in bar 51 to paste the selection.
11. Select the Bass Trombone staff in bar 51 and press the Delete key.
12. Select the bass Piano staff in bar 51.
13. Use the shortcut: Option-Shift-⌘-2 (Mac); Alt-Shift-CTRL-2 (Win) to select only the Voice 2 entries.
14. Option-click (Mac); Alt-click (Win) on the Bass Trombone staff in bar 51 to paste the Voice 2 line.

15. Use the shortcut: Shift-V to swap Voice 1 and 2.
16. Use the shortcut: Option-Shift-⌘-2 (Mac); Alt-Shift-CTRL-2 (Win) to select only the Voice 2 rest.
17. Press the Delete key.

Before copying bar 51 to the Bari. Sax., enter the missing caesuras in bar 52 so it can be copied at the same time. The Arranging Style used for this section did not copy the caesuras. Since placement of the caesuras is very time-consuming, the quickest fix is to rearrange this bar using the Explode arranging style for the Trombones, then copy the Bass Trombone part to the Bari. Sax. staff.

1. Select all four Trombone staves in bar 52.
2. Press the Delete key to clear the notation in these bars.
3. Select the bass Piano staff in bar 52.
4. Use the shortcut: ⌘-C (Mac); CTRL-C (Win) to copy the selection.
5. Select all four Trombone staves in bar 52.
6. Use the shortcut: ⌘-Shift-V (Mac); CTRL-Shift-V (Win) to access the Arrange Styles dialog box.
7. Select "Explode" from the Arrange Styles list.
8. Click OK.

Now copy the Bass Trombone part in bars 51 and 52 to the Bari. Sax. and fix both bars in one copy-and-paste operation.

1. Select bars 51 and 52 in the Bass Trombone part.
2. Option-click (Mac); Alt-click (Win) on bar 51 of the Bari. Sax. part to paste the selection.

The last beat of bar 52 begins a written Trumpet 1 solo and should be marked "Rubato" as Tempo text.

1. Select beat 4 of bar 52 in the Alto 1 staff. Clicking on any staff will do, but the text will appear at the top of the score, so it helps to have that Alto 1 staff on the screen for positioning purposes.
2. Use the shortcut Shift-⌘-T (Mac); Alt-CTRL-T (Win) to enter Tempo text.
3. Press Esc once, and use the right arrow key to nudge the text over beat 4 of the measure.
4. Press Esc again when you are satisfied with the position.

Time for a save!

Bars 53 Through 61

The last section features a written trumpet solo with the rest of the ensemble playing a supporting role. Begin with the Trumpet solo part.

1. Select the treble Piano staff in bars 53 through 60.

2. Use the shortcut: Option-Shift-⌘-1 (Mac); Alt-Shift-CTRL-1 (Win) to select only the Voice 1 entries.
3. Option-click (Mac); Alt-click (Win) on the Trumpet 1 staff in bar 53 to paste the passage.

For the last measure, the Trumpet 1 should play a high-register ad lib while the Trumpet 2 player ad libs with a plunger.

1. Select bar 53 of the Trumpet 2 staff.
2. Enter "To Plunger" as Technique text.
3. Press Esc twice when finished.

With the solo part completed, focus on the rest of the winds. Bars 53 and 54 are a rubato section with a chorale "pad" to arrange for the saxes and trombones. There is a Voice 2 part in measure 54 that will be an issue if you try to arrange both measures at the same time.

1. Select the bass Piano staff in bar 53.
2. Use the shortcut: ⌘-C (Mac); CTRL-C (Win) to copy the passage.
3. Click on the Alto 1 staff in bar 53.
4. Shift-click on the Bass Trombone staff in bar 53.
5. Use the shortcut: ⌘-Shift-V (Mac); CTRL-Shift-V (Win) to access the Arrange Styles dialog box.
6. Select "Jazz: Nestico-style 1d (Trombones, Alto 2, Tenors 1 & 2, Bari)" from the styles list.
7. Click OK.

Even though the style name only mentions Alto 2, it does enter notes in the Alto 1 staff.

8. Select the bass Piano staff in bar 54 and repeat steps 5 through 7 above, using the "Jazz: Nestico-style 1d (Trombones, Alto 2, Tenors 1 & 2, Bari)" Arranging Style to enter the notes in the sax and trombone sections for bar 54.

Bars 55 through 60 are a repeated two-bar phrase that builds harmonically. Use a simple cut and paste for the Voice 2 notes in the treble staff of the Piano.

1. Select the treble Piano staff from bar 55 through bar 60.
2. Use the shortcut: Option-Shift-⌘-2 (Mac); Alt-Shift-CTRL-2 (Win) to select only the Voice 2 entries.
3. Paste the selection in the Alto 1, Alto 2, Trumpet 3, and Trumpet 4 staves using the Option-click (Mac); Alt-click (Win) shortcut.

The notes in Voice 1 of the bass Piano staff will go to the Tenors and Trombones 1 and 2. The Voice 2 notes will go to the Bari. Sax., Trombone 3, and Bass Trombone. In this case, each Voice is a complete line, not part of something in another Voice. This is easier for the Arrange feature to handle properly.

1. Select the bass Piano staff from bar 57 through bar 60.
2. Use the shortcut: ⌘-C (Mac); CTRL-C (Win) to copy the selection.
3. Click on the Tenor 1 staff in bar 57.
4. Shift-click the Bass Trombone staff in bar 60.
5. Use the shortcut: ⌘-Shift-V (Mac); CRTL-Shift-V (Win) to access the Arrange Styles dialog box.
6. Select "Jazz: Nestico-style 1b (Trombones, Tenors & Bari)" from the styles list.
7. Click OK.

Each Voice has separated properly, but since there were only two voices, there are only two instruments in each section with music. The good news is that a simple copy and paste will get the result I want, and the task of moving the Voice 2 entries to Voice 1 has been handled.

The Saxes

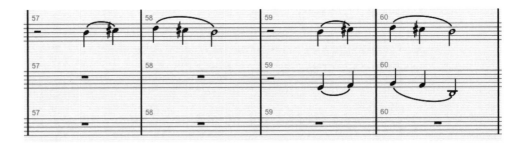

1. Select the Tenor 2 staff in bars 59 and 60 and paste it into the Bari. Sax. staff.
2. Select the Tenor 1 staff in bars 57 through 60 and paste it into the Tenor 2 staff.

The Trombones

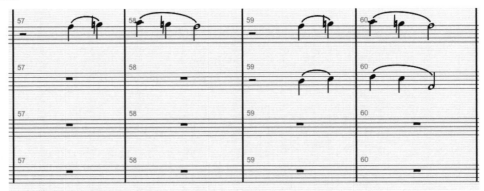

3. Select the Trombone 2 staff in bars 59 and 60 and paste it into the Trombone 3 and Bass Trombone staves.
4. Select the Trombone 1 staff in bars 57 through 60 and paste it into the Trombone 2 staff.

The last bar has a single chord to be voiced in the Saxes, Trumpets 3 and 4, and Trombones. The Arrange feature can orchestrate from more than one staff at a time. In this measure I will select both staves and explode them to the brass parts. The approach here is to orchestrate the brass first, then copy and paste to the Saxes.

1.   Select both staves of the Piano in bar 61.
2.   Use the shortcut: ⌘-C (Mac); CTRL-C (Win) to copy the selection.
3.   Click on the Trumpet 3 staff in bar 61.
4.   Shift-click the Bass Trombone staff in bar 61.
5.   Use the shortcut: ⌘-Shift-V (Mac); CTRL-Shift-V (Win) to access the Arrange Styles dialog box.
6.   Select "Explode" from the styles list.
7.   Click OK.

Sibelius has orchestrated the bar but added an extra measure to the piece.

8.   ⌘-click (Mac) or CTRL-click (Win) on the extra measure.
9.   Press the Delete key.

To finish the wind score, a little copy and paste for the Sax parts.

10. Select the Trumpet 3 staff in bar 61.
11. Shift-click the Trombone 2 staff in bar 61.
12. Copy the parts to the Alto and Tenor Saxes.
13. Copy the Bass Trombone part in bar 61 to the Bari. Sax. and raise it up one octave.
14. Save.

To start from this part of the chapter, open the file *11Joshua2* from the Chapter 11 folder that you downloaded from the *www.sibeliusbook.c*om Web site.

www.sibeliusbook.com

The Rhythm Section

In Chapter 10, I approached the rhythm section with an emphasis on playback. For this example I'll approach the rhythm section parts with the typical player in mind, meaning fewer written notes and more slash notation.

Guitar

Attention, everyone, I have an announcement to make: the free ride is over! You have to resume entering notes. Not just any notes, however: these will undergo a unique metamorphosis and emerge as slash notation. There are two types of slash notation: beat slashes that define the number of beats in a bar but do not indicate any specific rhythm for the player, and rhythmic slashes that indicate specific rhythmic values, but leave the actual chord voicing up to the guitar player.

To get slashes in the middle of the staff, enter notes on the pitch of the third line. That is, third line B for treble clef staves in concert pitch and third line D for bass clef staves. Transposing instruments will need to adjust according to the interval of transposition for the specific instrument. When the notes are converted to slashes, any accidentals are removed. Input single notes only, as multiple notes result in multiple slashes in both rhythmic and slash notation.

Guitar Part Rhythmic Slashes

1. Select bar 1 of the Guitar part and enter the notation, articulations, and rests for bars 1 and 2. Enter all Bs on the third line of the treble clef.
2. Press Esc twice to exit note entry.

3. Activate the Properties window if it is not already on the screen (**Window** > Properties).
4. Select bars 1 and 2 of the Guitar staff.
5. Click the Notes tab of the Properties window.
6. From the pop-up list at the top of the Notes pane, select item 4, rhythmic slashes or use the shortcut: Shift-Option-4 (Mac); Shift-Alt-4 (Win).

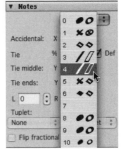

7. With the Guitar staff still selected, play back bars 1 and 2 by pressing the letter P. Notice that notes do not play once they have been converted to slashes. This allows you to mix slash and written parts in a score and hear only the written sections for proofing purposes.

Beat Slashes

Beat slashes are entered the same way rhythmic slashes are entered.

1. Select bar 5 of the Guitar staff and enter B♭ quarter notes on the third line for bars 5, 6, and 7.
2. Press Esc twice to exit note entry.

3. Select bars 5 through 7 of the Guitar staff.
4. With the Notes pane of the Properties window still open, select item 3, beat slashes, from the pop-up list or use the shortcut: Shift-Option-3 (Mac); Shift-Alt-3 (Win).

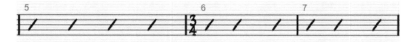

Both slash and beat notation can be used on individual notes, so they can be used in combination and with normal notation. For example, in bar 8, beats 1 and 2 require rhythmic notation, beats 4 and 5 use slash notation, and there is a standard quarter rest.

1. Select beats 1 and 2 of the Guitar staff in bar 8.

2. From the Notes pane of the Properties window, select item 4, rhythmic slashes, from the pop-up list or use the shortcut: Shift-Option-4 (Mac); Shift-Alt-4 (Win).
3. Select beats 4 and 5 of the Guitar staff in bar 8.

4. From the Notes pane of the Properties window, select item 3, beat slashes, from the pop-up list or use the shortcut: Shift-Option-3 (Mac); Shift-Alt-3 (Win).
5. Press Esc twice when finished.

Enter the complete Guitar part with all the slashes, notes, and dynamics that are required (see next page). Enter all the notes first and then convert to slashes or rhythmic notation as required.

The next step is adding the harmonic information (chords) to the guitar part.

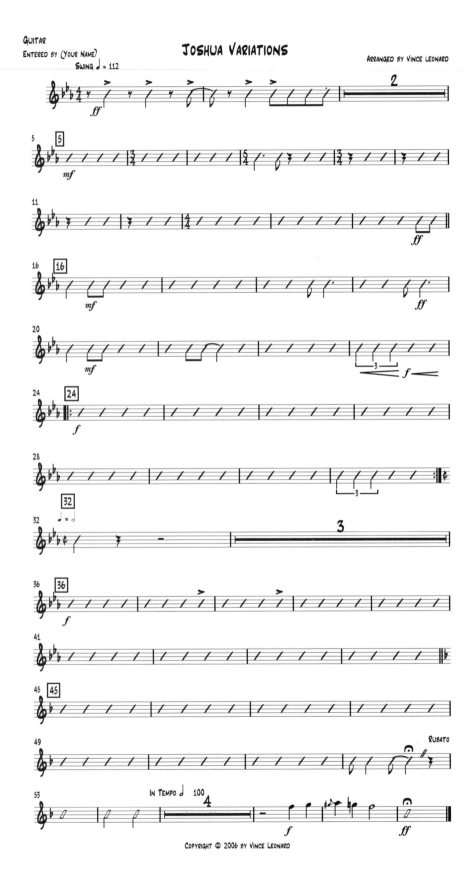

JOSHUA VARIATIONS

Chord Symbols

You've had some experience with chord symbols in Chapters 3, 6, and 10, so adding them is not new. However, some of the chord symbols in "Joshua" have complex alterations and will present spacing problems that will have to be handled manually. Sibelius does not factor chord symbol width into note spacing, so you must increase the available room on a system manually. Start back at the beginning of the Guitar part.

1. Click on the first slash note in bar 1 of the Guitar staff. It will highlight.
2. Use the shortcut: ⌘-K (Mac); CTRL-K (Win) to enter chords. A blinking cursor will appear over the selected note.
3. Type an uppercase G for the chord letter, or select G from the pop-up list by right-clicking to the right of the blinking cursor. Always use uppercase letters in chord symbols.

At this point you have several options. First look for the desired chord symbol in the pop-up list. If you don't find an exact match, assemble it piece by piece. Some items have shortcuts. As you frequent the list, take note of which elements have shortcuts assigned. Lastly, chord symbols can be typed in on the computer keyboard. Both chord entry approaches can be combined when necessary. Typing the G is less work than selecting it from the list; however, using the shortcut for the diminished circle (suffix) is faster than trying to locate the correct character to type.

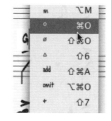

4. Use the shortcut: ⌘-O (Mac); CTRL-O (Win) to enter the circle suffix to indicate a diminished chord, or select the circle symbol from the pop-up list.
5. Type 7 to complete the first chord symbol (G°7).
6. Press the space bar twice to advance the cursor to the slash on beat 3 of bar 1.

 When entering chords, be aware that the space bar stops at notes or slashes and downbeats. Always visually check to make sure it is in the correct position before entering a chord symbol.

Entering a Chord Symbol with an Altered Bass Note

The second symbol in bar 1 on beat 3 will start a string of altered bass note chords.

1. Enter the basic chord symbol "F♯°7" then type, or select, the / and enter the G. If you are typing, Shift-# will be converted to an Inkpen sharp character.

 Altered bass chords are different from polychords, where the symbols are aligned vertically, with a horizontal line between them. To create polychord symbols, use the Chord Symbols as Fractions plug-in found in the Text submenu of the Plug-ins menu. Consult the Sibelius Reference guide for more details.

Below is the Guitar part with the chord symbols added. The spacing issues have already been adjusted for the purpose of readability.

2. Enter the rest of the chord symbols. They all can be typed in or entered from the pop-up list.

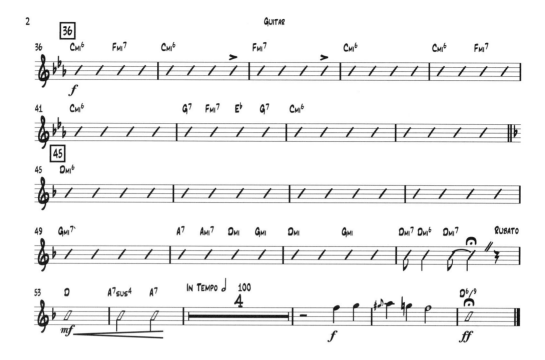

Bass

There are bass notes in the sketch, but not all of these will make it into the final part. Some are there to keep time as much as to complete the harmony for sketch playback. Give a professional bass player freedom to create: only indicate the actual pitches in places where exact notes are absolutely needed.

 If you want to enter specific notes in the Bass part for playback but want to display just chords and slashes, enter both notes and slashes in different voices. For example, enter the notes for playback in Voice 2, then hide them. Then construct the visual part with only chords and slashes in Voice 1. I advise removing any notes from the hidden part that will be doubling the same note in the visible part to avoid an annoying phasing sound during playback.

Enter the Bass part using the example on the next page as your guide, or use your printout of the entire score. Look for places where you can copy the chords and slashes from the Guitar staff to save time. If you do, you will find that once notes have been converted to slash notation, they do not transpose. However, they must be changed using the Re-input Pitches feature to enter Ds for the bass clef.

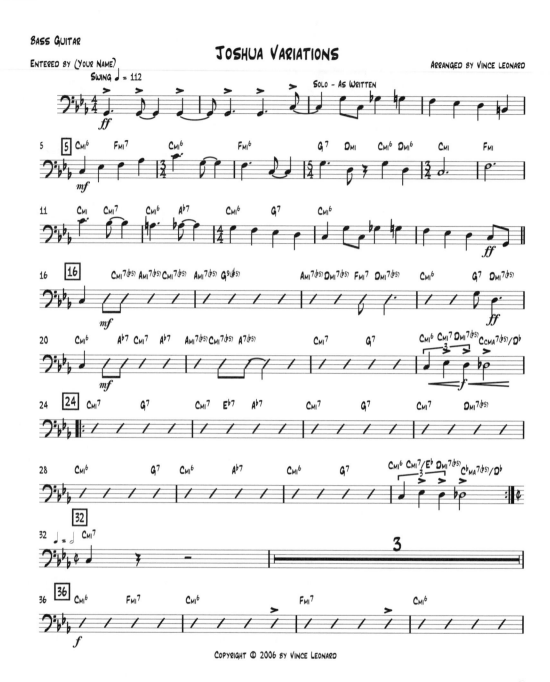

Piano

The Piano part is currently the sketch for the arrangement. It is not necessary to include all of this notation for the player. However, some of it will be used to create the final Piano part. Here are the steps to convert the sketch copy to a Piano part.

The following is a brief description of what to do, not all of the step-by-step instructions. You may need to reference these skills in earlier parts of this chapter or use the Sibelius Reference from the Help menu.

1. In bars 1 and 2, copy and paste the chord symbols from the Guitar part.
2. Delete the Piano bass staff part in bars 3 and 4.
3. In bars 5 through 8, copy the Guitar part to the Piano treble staff.
4. Transpose the Piano bass notes down one octave and reduce them to cue size in bars 5 through 8.
5. In bars 9 and 10 of the Piano part, swap Voices 1 and 2 in the treble staff, then select Voice 2 and delete it, leaving only the waltz accompaniment figure in both hands.
6. For bars 11 through 13, repeat steps 3 and 4 above.
7. Delete all entries currently in the treble Piano staff in bars 14 through 31.
8. Copy the Guitar part to the treble Piano staff in bars 14 through 31.
9. In the bass Piano staff, delete all notes in bars 14 through 22.
10. Delete all bass clef notes in bars 24 through 30.
11. Select bars 23 through 31 and transpose the bass notes down one octave, then change the notes to cue size.

12. Copy the chord symbol from the Guitar part in bar 32.
13. Delete all treble staff entries in bars 36 through 54.
14. Copy the Guitar part into the treble Piano staff in bars 36 through 54.
15. Delete the Bass staff in bars 36 through 42.
16. Leave the Bass line as is in bars 43 through 50.
17. Delete all entries in the Bass staff in bars 51 through 54.
18. In bars 55 through 60 of the treble staff, swap Voices 1 and 2, then delete the solo Trumpet part in Voice 2.
19. Use the Re-input Pitches feature to re-voice the chord in bar 61 in both staves.

2

PIANO

PIANO

3

Drums

Jazz drum parts tend to be more of a guide to the player than a literal part. The notation placed on the bottom line of the staff typically lets the player know what is happening in the rest of the ensemble so they can provide the correct style of accompaniment. The slash marks are typically placed in the center of the part and represent the beats per measure. At the top of the Drums staff is usually an ensemble cue. Try not to write out exact parts for the jazz drum set player. The information below is plenty for them and even that can be a challenge for young and inexperienced players.

Bars 1 and 2 of the arrangement are full ensemble with two different rhythmic ideas happening between the high and low instruments. For the drum set part, ensemble rhythmic cues are traditionally placed above the staff in cue size notation. There is a nice trick to creating these cues that will save entering information that already exists in the score and provide the slash notation at the same time.

Copying the Trumpet 1 Part for Ensemble Cues

The first task is copying a part with the rhythmic information part to the Drums staff.

1. Select bars 1 and 2 of the Trumpet 1 part.
2. Copy and paste them to the Drums staff.

3. Select bars 1 and 2 of the Drums staff.
4. Select **Plug-ins** > Notes and Rests > Make Pitches Constant.
5. Click OK in the Undo warning dialog box.

The Make Pitches Constant dialog box is divided into two parts. The top half will convert the trumpet part into ensemble cues while the bottom half will add the slashes in Voice 2.

6. Change "to this pitch" to G using the pop-up list.
7. Change "in this octave" to 5 using the pop-up list.
8. Check "Move rests together with the notes."
9. Check "Fill the selection with notes of the following properties."
10. Change "with this style of notehead" to "beat without stem" using the pop-up list.
11. Click OK.

Make Pitches Constant

This plug-in will transpose all the notes/chords in the selected passage to a single chosen pitch. You can choose to transpose only notes in a specific voice if desired.

Transpose notes in voice	1
to this pitch	G
in this octave	5
with this style of notehead	normal

☑ Move rests together with the notes

☑ Fill the selection with notes of the following properties.

Fill with notes in Voice	2
with this pitch	B
in this octave	4 (middle C)
with this note value	Quarter note (crotchet)
with this style of notehead	beat without stem

Cancel   OK

12. Select bars 1 and 2 of the Drums staff.

13. Use the shortcut: Option-Shift-⌘-1 (Mac); Alt-Shift-CTRL-1 (Win) to select only the Voice 1 entries or select **Edit** > Filter > Voice 1. (Use the number 1 on the main computer keyboard.)

14. Click the ▶ key on the Keypad or press the + key on the numeric keypad to access the second keypad layout.

15. Click the key or press the Enter key on the numeric keypad to change the notes to cue size.

16. Press Esc.

17. Select the slur in bar 2.

18. Press the Delete key to remove it.

The drummer should also know what is happening rhythmically in the lower ensemble. Enter this rhythm in the first space of the Drums staff.

19. Select the first slash in bar 1 of the Drums staff.

20. Type "N" for Notation.

21. Use the shortcut: Option-3 (Mac); Alt-3 (Win) to enter the notes in Voice 3.

22. Enter the rhythms in the Trombone part in bars 1 and 2 in the first space of the Drums staff. The notes and ties will need to be flipped. I prefer to flip them after they are all in rather than as each note is entered.

23. After the notation is entered, press Esc twice.

24. Select bars 1 and 2 of the Drums staff.

25. Use the shortcut: Option-Shift-⌘-3 (Mac); Alt-Shift-CTRL-3 (Win) to select only the Voice 3 entries.

26. Press X to flip the notes or select **Edit** > Flip.

27. Press Esc.

28. Click on the first tie in bar 1 on the second half of beat 2 in the Drums staff.
29. ⌘-click (Mac) or CTRL-click (Win) on the second tie going over the barline connected to beat 4. Make sure only the two ties are selected; they will both be yellow.
30. Press X to flip the ties. Of course, you could select each tie and press X to flip it. By selecting them both at the same time saves a step. Remember, time is money, right?
31. Press Esc.

Funny Symbols, Funny Cymbals

The Drums part in bars 3 and 4 uses Voice 1 for the upstemmed notes and Voice 2 for the downstemmed notes. This is the same approach used in all the polyphonic examples in previous chapters in this book.

The Roll indication on the snare drum in bar 4 can be added at the time of note entry or afterward. If the note has already been entered, select the note and in the third Keypad layout, click the ![key] key or press the number 3 key on the numeric keypad.

The Drums staff is set to display certain notes with X noteheads to indicate cymbals. This is via the drum map. (See Chapter 8 for more information on drum maps.) In measures 3 and 4, the Hi-hat should be played with the foot instead of with sticks. Caution: when entering the notes in Voice 2 of measure 3, the whole rest in Voice 1 will automatically be added.

1. Select bar 3 in the Drums staff.
2. Press N for Notation.
3. Use the shortcut: Option-2 (Mac); Alt-2 (Win) to enter notes in Voice 2 or click the Voice 2 number on the Keypad.
4. Enter the rest on beat 1.
5. Enter D (above middle C) for the Hi-hat. The default drum map layout uses treble clef pitches.
6. Continue entering the part in bars 3 and 4.
7. Press Esc twice.

The slash notation in bar 5 is entered with the same steps used in the Guitar part shown earlier in the chapter.

Copying Bass Notes for the Bass Drum

Since there is a strong relationship between the bass and the bass drum in the rhythm section, it is always good to let the drummer know about any specific rhythm patterns that the bass player is playing. In bars 6 through 8, use the same plug-in that was used for the trumpet cues in bars 1 and 2. You could not use this plug-in for the bass drum, since the plug-in cannot handle two pitches at the same time.

1. Copy and paste the Bass part for bars 6 through 8 into the Drums staff.
2. Select bars 6 through 8 of the Drums staff.
3. Select **Plug-ins** > Notes and Rests > Make Pitches Constant.
4. Click OK in the Undo warning dialog box.

If you haven't quit Sibelius since using this plug-in for bars 1 and 2, the settings will still be as you set them earlier in this chapter.

5. In the top half of the dialog box, change "to this pitch" to F.
6. Change "in this octave" to "4 (middle C)."
7. In the bottom half of the dialog box, make sure "with this style of notehead" is still set to "beat without stem."
8. Click OK.

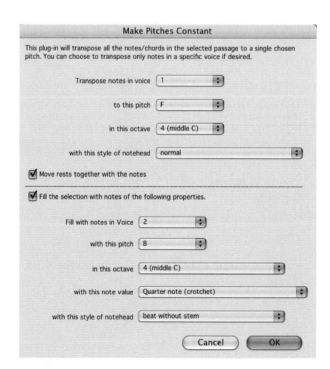

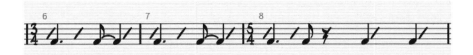

9. With the measures selected, type Shift-V to swap Voice 1 and Voice 2. That will take care of the stem direction issue.

Continue entering the Drums as shown in the graphic below, stopping at bar 33. If needed, review the steps for copying cues from the Trumpet part and converting them with the Make Pitches Constant plug-in. Remove all slurs from the cues and replace them with tenuto marks. In the measures with no cues, copy the slashes from bars 13 and 14.

Single-Bar Repeats

In bar 33, that staple of percussion parts, the single-bar repeat, makes its first appearance in this arrangement. Single-bar repeats are entered using the Properties window, so make it active if it is not currently on the desktop (**Window** > Properties).

> ! The single-bar repeats that are available from the Properties menu can only be entered in measures where no notation or rests have been manually entered. If you have a situation where you want to combine a repeat bar with other notation such as an ensemble cue, you can enter the repeat bar marking from the Symbols library (shortcut: letter Z).

1. Select bars 34 and 35.
2. Click on the Bars tab of the Properties window.
3. From the active popup list, currently displaying the number 2, select the single-bar repeat, number 1.
4. Enter the single-bar repeats in bars 37 through 44.
5. Resume entering the Drum part as shown below, stopping at bar 57 for the two-bar repeat, which will be covered next.

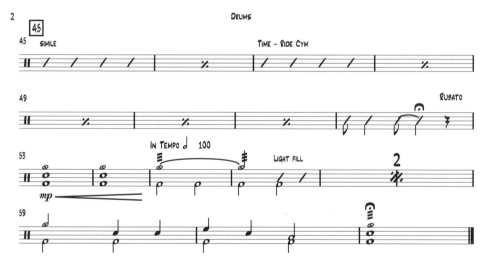

Two-Bar Repeats

Another popular shortcut in percussion parts is the two-bar repeat, indicating that the previous two measures are to be repeated.

1. Select bars 57 and 58 in the Drums staff.
2. In the Bars pane of the Properties window, select 0 for blank bars.

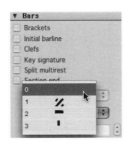

The actual repeat symbol must be added from the Symbols library.

3. Press Z (all by itself) to access the Symbols library.
4. Select the two-bar repeat symbol found in the top row of the library.
5. Click OK. The cursor will change to a blue arrow.

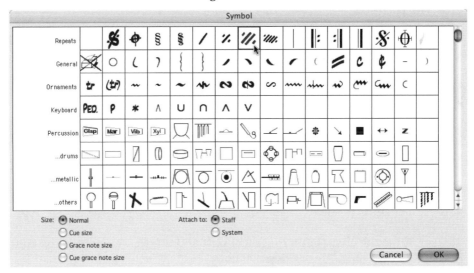

6. Click near the barline dividing the two blank measures. Center the symbol over the barline.

7. Enter the number 2 as Technique text above the Drums staff. Center it over the barline where the repeat symbol is located.

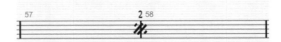

Make the number larger so it stands out from any other Technique text or other text that might be above the staff in the same area.

8. Click on the Text tab in the Properties window.
9. Increase the size of the text to 11.9 using the up arrow button.

10. Finish entering the Drum part.

www.sibeliusbook.com

☺ **Have you saved lately?** ☺

To start from this point in the chapter, open the file *11Joshua3.sib* from the Chapter 11 folder downloaded from the *www.sibeliusbook.com* Web site.

Chords for Horn Solos

With the rhythm section complete, it's time to go back and take care of the solo section and the trumpets in the last bar. The score has to be toggled back to concert pitch in order for the chords to be displayed in the correct key for the transposing instruments. The symbols are transposed when you toggle the score back to a transposed score.

1. Click the Transpose button in the toolbar or use the shortcut: Shift-⌘-T (Mac); Shift-CTRL-T (Win) to change the score display to concert pitch.
2. Navigate to bar 24 of the score.
3. Copy bars 24 through 31 of the Guitar part to the Bari. Sax. staff.
4. Use the Re-input Pitch feature to enter Bs so the slashes are on the middle line of the staff.

Copy the chords into the Alto 1 part and the Tenor 1 part so the conductor can switch or add soloists if needed.

1. In the Bari. Sax. staff, select bars 24 through 31.
2. Select **Edit** > Filter > Chord Symbols.
3. Paste the chord symbols to the Alto 1 and Tenor 1 staves.
4. Select the Alto 1 through Tenor 1 staves in bars 24 through 31.
5. Select **Edit** > Filter > Chord Symbols.
6. Select **Edit** > Hide or Show > Show in Parts.
7. Click the Transpose button in the toolbar or use the shortcut: Shift-⌘-T (Mac); Shift-CTRL-T (Win) to change the score display to transposed.

Cautionary Accidentals

Next, add the cautionary accidentals. This process will save you answering questions from players in every rehearsal, depending on the harmonic complexity of the piece. For example, if a C♯ is added in one bar, a cautionary accidental is placed around the C in the following bar. This could be done on a note-by-note basis or for a section or the entire score using the plug-in. Since you've been working on this chapter for at least a couple of hours so far, let's go the fast route with the plug-in.

1. Save the file: **File** > Save.
2. Use the shortcut: ⌘-A (Mac); CTRL-A (Win) to select the entire score.
3. Select **Plug-ins** > Accidentals > Add Cautionary Accidentals.
4. When you see the plug-in warning, click Yes; since you just saved you'll be able to close and reopen the file if there is a problem.
5. No changes are needed in the Add Cautionary Accidentals dialog box, so click OK. The inserted cautionary accidentals will be highlighted in a yellow box.
6. Press Esc.

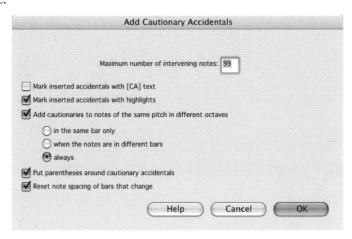

Score Adjustments: Horizontal

With all the elements on board, it's time to clean up the spacing issues as best you can. Sibelius usually handles note spacing well, but chord symbols are not considered in that spacing, so bars that contain a lot of chord symbols may present a problem. In this arrangement you only have to look as far as measure 2 to find a chord symbol log-jam. The chord symbols on beat 4 need a little space inserted between them.

1. Select the last eighth note slash in bar 2 of the Guitar part. (Any note on the desired beat will do.)

2. Hold down the Shift-Option keys (Mac) or the Shift-Alt keys (Win) at the same time and press the right arrow key repeatedly until there is sufficient room between the two chord symbols.

In places where more horizontal room exists, you can slide the chord symbols a little to the right or left rather than drag the notes for every collision. For example, in bar 16 the chord symbols on beats 3 and 4 can slide to the right to create some space after the symbol on the second eighth note of beat 2.

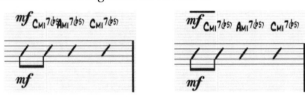

3. Click on each chord symbol and use the arrow keys to nudge it, or drag it with the mouse.

4. Continue through the score and fix any collisions using either of the above methods.

Score Adjustments: Vertical

Places to look for potential problems will be in the spaces between sections where low parts at the bottom of one staff meet high parts in the staff below. Repositioning some text or a dynamic can clear up some of these collisions. Others may require a staff to be repositioned. You can move an individual staff of a score or select a group of staves and move them all at the same time.

Look at the space between the Trumpet 4 and Trombone 1 staves in bars 15 and 16. Even with the dynamics offset to the left to avoid the high trombone notes, the articulations still collide. To fix this problem, borrow some space from somewhere else in the score where it is not needed.

353

1. Select the Trombone 1 staff and Shift-click on the treble staff of the Piano so that all the staves in between and including the Trombone 1 and Piano treble staff are highlighted.
2. Hold down the Shift-Option keys (Mac) or Shift-Alt keys (Win) and use the down arrow key to nudge the staves down until sufficient room opens up between the eighth note beam in Trumpet 4 and the accents in Trombone 1.

The only difference in moving staves is the number you select and the direction you move them. Hold down the same two keys, Shift-Option (Mac) or Shift-Alt (Win) when moving them. You can also drag the staves with the mouse, but nudging with the arrow keys will keep overcompensating to a minimum.

As you may have noticed, in the first two measures there are some vertical spacing issues with the chord symbols. You already learned how to adjust them in Chapter 10. You can adjust individual symbols by selecting and nudging or dragging them, or by selecting a region and using the Filter to single them out for nudging with the arrow keys. In measures where there are nothing but chord symbols, there is plenty of room to lower them as needed.

www.sibeliusbook.com

• Save and print the score when you are finished.

If you would like to begin at this point in the chapter, open the file *11Joshua4.sib* that was downloaded from the Chapter 11 folder from the *www.sibeliusbook.com* Web site.

Turn-Around Time for the Parts

Time to turn your attention to the parts and get them ready for the players. Remember way back at the beginning of this chapter when you created the big band score in landscape view? The parts should be printed in portrait view, so there are a few changes to be made. Start with broad, global changes to get every part to the same basic configuration, then go part by part to add the finishing touches.

1. Use the shortcut: Option-⌘-R (Mac); Alt-CTRL-R (Win) to activate the Parts window or click the icon on the toolbar.

2. From the Dynamic Parts window, select the Alto 1 part to highlight it.
3. Click the Multiple Part Appearance button at the bottom of the Parts window.
4. Click Yes to change all the parts.

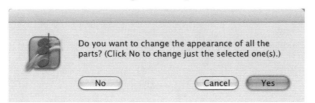

Document Setup

Next, change the page orientation back to portrait for all parts. This process is different in each OS so separate steps are provided for Mac and Windows computers.

The Mac steps are:

1. Activate the Parts Window: **Window** > Parts.
2. At the bottom of the Parts Window, select the Multiple Part Appearance icon.
3. In the Document Setup Tab, under "Page Size" click the Letter Button and then Portrait.
4. Click the Page Setup button.
5. Select the portrait page Orientation as well as the appropriate printer, if it not already selected.
6. Click OK.

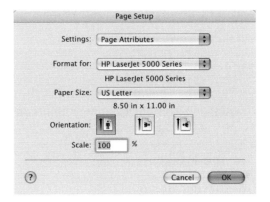

The Windows steps are:

1. Activate the Parts Window: **Window** > Parts.
2. At the bottom of the Parts Window, select the Multiple Part Appearance icon.
3. In the Document Setup Tab, under "Page Size" click the Letter Button and then select Portrait.
4. Click OK.

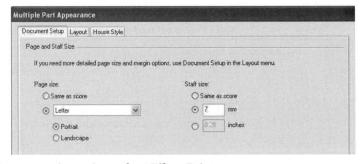

5. To set the page orientation select **File** > Print.
6. Click on the Properties Tab.

7. Click on Page Setup tab.
8. Select the portrait page orientation (settings will vary slightly depending on your printer make and model).

House Style Changes

Importing a House Style will change some settings, so it is imperative that you do this first.

1. Click the House Style tab at the top of the Multiple Part Appearance dialog box.
2. Click the Import House Style button.
3. Select My_Part_Style, or whatever name you gave the House Style you created in Chapter 7 (pp. 170–171), from the House Styles list.

Once the House Style is imported, the settings under the Bar Numbers heading will change to reflect the House Style's settings.

4. Under the Text heading, click the Edit Text Styles button.
5. Select "Title" in the Styles list and click the Edit button.
6. Change the Parts title size to 36 using the pop-up list or the number entry field.

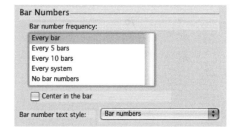

7. Click OK.
8. Select "Rehearsal marks" and click "Edit."
9. Click the Vertical Posn tab.
10. Under the Multiple Positions heading, uncheck all but the "Top staff" box.
11. Click OK.
12. Select Tempo in the Edit Text Styles list.
13. Repeat steps 10, 11, and 12 above and click Close to return to the Alto 1 part.
14. Click OK, and then click Close.

Page Layout

Use the layout controls to shape the systems and pages. Since this is a relatively short piece, you will not need a lot of power to format long parts with multiple page turns, but remember that you can make changes when you need to.

1. Click the Layout tab at the top of the Multiple Part Appearance dialog box.
2. Click the Auto Layout button.
3. Under the System Breaks heading, uncheck "Tempo text."
4. Uncheck "Use auto system breaks."
5. Click OK.

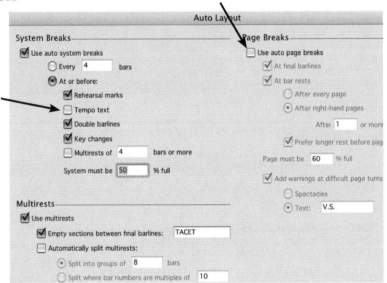

6. Under the Breaks heading, uncheck "Keep page breaks." This will transfer the page breaks used in the score to the parts.
7. Uncheck "Keep gaps before codas" since there is no Coda in this arrangement.
8. Under the Staves heading, change "Indent first system by" to 0 spaces, eliminating the indent.
9. Change "Justify staves when page is" to "90" % full. This prevents Sibelius from spreading out the staves on partly filled pages from top to bottom.
10. Under the Multirests heading, select Narrow from the Appearance list to steer clear of the key changes in the Alto 1/ Flute staff.
11. Click OK.

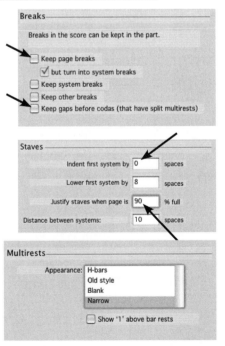

One last little tweak for the bar numbers:

12. Select **House Style** > Engraving Rules.
13. Select "Bar Numbers" in the left column.
14. Click the Edit Text Style button.
15. Under the size heading, change Parts to 9 using the pop-up menu or by typing 9 into the number entry field.
16. Click the "Vertical Posn" tab.
17. Under the Multiple Positions heading, uncheck Top Staff.
18. Click OK twice.
19. Select **File** > Save All.

Did Something Else Just Change?

You may have noticed that, up to this point, all the articulations are on top of the staff in this score. This is a convention found in hand-copied music. The philosophy is that they will be easier to read if they are all in the same place over the staff. The settings controlling the placement of this can be saved as part of a House Style. The House Style you just imported likely changed those settings. Here are the steps for changing them back, if you like.

1. Use the shortcut: Shift-⌘-E (Mac); Shift-CTRL-E (Win) to access the Engraving Rules dialog box.
2. Select Articulation in the left column.
3. In the "Always above" row, check the boxes for the staccato, tenuto, and accent.
4. Click OK.

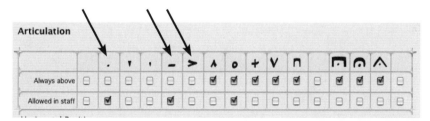

Reset to Score Position

There is a problem at the end of the first system due to the instrument change. There is a cautionary key signature change for the flute entrance in the next staff. This is the reason you changed the symbol used for the rest to the narrow H-bar symbol.

1. Select the E♭ key signature in the right margin of the first system.

2. Select **Layout** > Reset to Score Position or use the shortcut: Option-Shift-⌘-P (Mac); Alt-Shift-CTRL-P (Win).

Setting the Number of Bars per System

Use the four-bars-to-a-line approach for the parts, with each rehearsal mark beginning on a new system. Use the Make Layout Uniform plug-in to get in the ballpark, then manually clean up the minor details.

1. Select **File** > Save All. This saves both the score and part information.
2. Use the shortcut: ⌘-A (Mac); CTRL-A (Win) to select the entire Alto 1 part.
3. Select **Plug-ins** > Other > Make Layout Uniform.
4. Click OK in the Undo warning dialog box.
5. Click the "Do not break pages" button.
6. Check the "Break at rehearsal marks" box.
7. Click OK.

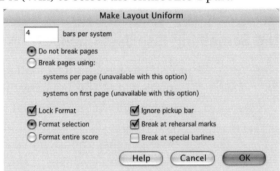

The three-bar-to-a-line phrases are allowed, but the one-bar rest by itself, bar 44, needs to be moved. It is the last of a nine-bar phrase and should be moved to the system above.

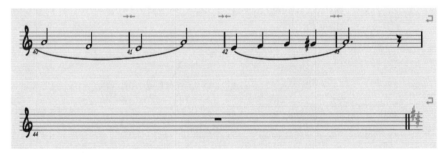

8. Select bars 40 through 44.
9. Select **Layout** > Format > Make into System, or use the shortcut: Option-Shift-M (Mac); Alt-Shift-M (Win).

Creating More Space in Individual Measures

There's a chord symbol pileup in bar 31. Since Sibelius does not adjust the spacing for chords, this same problem happens in several locations in the score. You can correct this with the same process you used to create space in bar 2 of the score (page 352).

1. In the Alto part, bar 31, select the note to the right of the collision, in this case the C half note.
2. Hold down the Shift-Option keys (Mac) or Shift-Alt keys (Win) and press the right arrow key repeatedly to make the selected measure larger.

3. When you have created sufficient space, select the chord symbol(s) and fine-tune their position. Chord symbols center themselves over their attachment point, but can be a little more left-aligned.

   Leave space between those two points when manually positioning chord symbols.
4. Continue through the Alto 1 part, adjusting the position of text, rehearsal marks, and any other element of the music that needs tweaking.

Copy Part Layout

With the layout of the Alto 1 part complete, transfer it to the rest of the wind parts.

1. In the Parts window, select the Alto 2 part and Shift-click the Bass Trombone part to select all the rest of the wind parts.
2. Click the Copy Part Layout button at the bottom of the Parts window.

3. Click Yes.

In less time that it takes to put the kettle on to make some tea, Sibelius has reformatted the rest of the wind parts. Isn't it time for a cup of tea yet? I can't work under these conditions!

4. Use the Next Part navigation shortcut: Option-⌘-` (Mac); Alt-CTRL-` (Win) to take a look at the Alto 2 part.
5. Clean up any positioning issues and move on down through the rest of the wind parts.

The Rhythm Section

The three parts that involve chord symbols will have plenty of positioning to be done, but begin by adjusting the measures per line.

1. In the Parts window, select the Guitar part.
2. Select the end bar of bar 8.
3. Press the Return/Enter key to break the system.
4. Select the end bar of bar 12.
5. Press the Return/Enter key.
6. Select the end bar of bar 35.
7. Press the Return/Enter key.
8. Select the end bar of bar 58.
9. Press the Return/Enter key.

Next, untangle the chords. In an individual part, I prefer to shift the note, since I'm not concerned about the spacing of the ensemble as a whole.

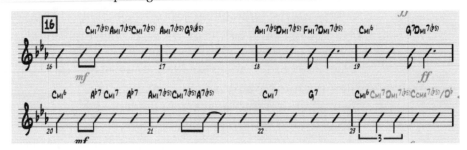

1. Move beats 3 and 4 of bar 16 to the right.
2. Move both notes on beat 3 of bar 18 to the right.
3. Move both notes on beat 3 of bar 19 to the right.
4. Move the chord symbols in bar 17 to the right to sit more directly over the slashes.

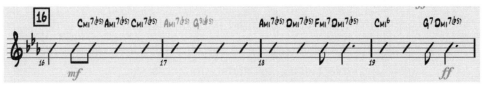

5. Use the same techniques, plus your own judgment, on the next system.
6. Give some attention to bars 31 and 52 to make sure they are well spaced.
7. Copy the layout of the Guitar part to the Bass part.
8. Move to the Piano part.

The Piano part presents some of the same issues as the Guitar part, with the added bonus of taking up an extra page thanks to the grand staff. Initially, I was not happy with how the systems are set on the page, so once you get the measures per staff and chord symbol spacing issues fixed, you can bring some (feng shui) harmony to the page as well.

10. Select the barline at the end bar of bar 8.
11. Press the Return/Enter key. You should get the line break at bar 12 as a bonus.
12. Clean up the chord symbols as you did with the Guitar part.
13. Fix any text and dynamic placement issues.
14. Drag the tuplet brackets down for the bass clef cues in bars 23 and 31.

To expand the Piano part to fill up the page, you need to add just a little more space between the top two systems. Then Sibelius will finish the job.

15. Select both staves of the second system on page 1 of the Piano part.
16. Hold down the Shift-Option keys (Mac) or Shift-Alt keys (Win) and press the down arrow key a few times (approximately two or three times, so type slowly) until the music expands to fill up the page.
17. Repeat the process by selecting the second system on page 2 and expanding the space until Sibelius takes over.

18. Repeat the process one more time on page 3.
19. Move down to the Bass part.

The Bass part will be a little closer to finished, thanks to your work on the Guitar part, but there will be some chord and text positioning to do.

20. Fix any chord symbol, text, or dynamic placement issues.
21. Move down to the Drums.

Finally, tonality takes a holiday. No more pesky chord symbols to space, just some text and rehearsal marks, and you are ready to print.

22. Select the end barline in bar 27.
23. Press the Return/Enter key.
24. Group bars 36 through 44 together as a system.
25. Select the end barline in bar 48.
26. Press the Return/Enter key.
27. Select the end barline in bar 52.
28. Press the Return/Enter key.
29. Select the end barline in bar 56.
30. Press the Return/Enter key.
31. Fix any text, rehearsal marks, or dynamic placement issues.
32. Select **File** > Save All.

The Very Optional Final Step

This step will produce a set of parts. I'll understand if you want to save a tree and skip printing the whole set. Perhaps print a few parts just to see what your handiwork looks like; perhaps you'll be pleased enough to hang them on the fridge.

33. Select **File** > Print All Parts, or open the specific part you want to print and use the regular Print command.

Summary

In this chapter you moved a lot of things from point A to point B. I hope it was a moving experience. ☺ You learned to:
* set up a landscape format score
* change the staff size
* enter various time signatures
* enter double bars
* enter repeat bars
* change Opus text to Inkpen in Tempo text indications
* copy and paste between Sibelius files
* use the Arrange feature
* change the staff transposition

- change the default range
- use the Advanced Filter
- use Properties for first- and second-time playback
- use Properties to disable playback
- enter text to change sounds during MIDI playback
- enter caesuras
- enter slash notation
- enter single-bar repeats
- enter a two-bar repeat
- enter chord symbols
- enter altered bass chord symbols
- copy the Trumpet part for drum set cues
- copy the Bass part for the Bass Drum part
- enter cautionary accidentals
- adjust the score horizontally
- adjust the staves of a score vertically
- use the Dynamic Parts feature
- use Multiple Part Appearance to reformat all parts at once
- change the default placement of articulations
- manually change the layout of individual measures

Review

1. Try giving one of your favorite melodies the variations treatment and take it through some different time signatures and styles.
2. Input a phrase of some piano music and try out some Arranging Styles on various ensembles.
3. Since this is a jazz arrangement, you might want to invest in the Garritan Jazz and Big Band Sound Library (*www.garritan.com/jazz.html*). If you do a lot of arranging in this medium, you will surely find it helpful when preparing playback files.

12

Orchestral Film Score (Musical Example: "Heartland" by Vince Leonard)

In this chapter, you will put together many of the skills learned in previous chapters and delve into the world of film scoring with Sibelius. You will also encounter many of the advanced score input and layout techniques that are possible.

New skills introduced in this chapter include:

- creating personalized Manuscript Paper
- creating multipart staves
- changing the default position of text
- changing the time signature display
- using the video feature
- entering trills and tremolos
- using Focus on Staves
- using GPO Sibelius Edition sounds

At the beginning of this chapter you see first page of the finished "Heartland" score. You will not be required to enter the entire example to complete the chapter.

Creating Manuscript Paper

In this example you will make changes to the basic manuscript paper in Sibelius and save that for use in future projects.

1. Launch Sibelius and from the Quick Start menu select "Start a new score," or select **File** > New if Sibelius is already running.
2. From the Manuscript Paper list, select "Orchestra, film."
3. Click the Add Instruments button.
4. In the "Staves in score" list on the right side of the window, scroll down to the very bottom.
5. Select both Guitar staves in the list, Guitar I and Guitar II. Click Guitar I to select it, hold down the Shift key, and click on Guitar II to highlight them both.
6. Click the Delete from Score button to remove these staves from the score.
7. You will get a warning that this will delete the staves from the score. Click Yes to delete the staves.

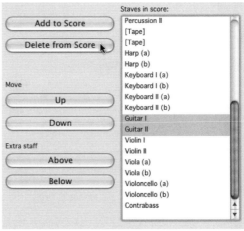

For this score, add an additional staff to Violin I and Violin II.

8. In the "Staves in score" list, select Violin I.
9. Under "Extra staff," click the Below button.

In the list, the Violin I you selected now has an (a) next to it, and below is a new staff labeled Violin I (b). Adding staves in this manner produces a different result from adding staves using the instrument list in the center of the dialog box. Extra staves are included in the same part, as opposed to being a separate part. This method bypasses the need to combine staves to create a single part, as you did with the Guitar parts and the Piano/Vocal part in Chapter 10. Staves created using the "Extra staff" buttons are indicated with letters in parentheses that follow the staff names in the "Staves in score" list.

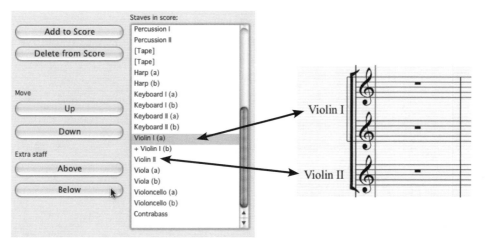

10. In the "Staves in score" list, select Violin II.
11. Click the Below button to add an extra staff to the part.
12. Click OK.
13. Click Finish.

Customizing the Score

My first preference is to bring down the staff size a bit. This adds a little more room between the staves for dynamics and other staff-specific text.

1. Use the shortcut: ⌘-D (Mac); CTRL-D (Win) to access the Document Setup dialog box or select **Layout** > Document Setup.
2. Be sure the measurement option is set to inches at the top of the screen.
3. Reduce the staff size to 0.18.
4. Click OK.

Changing the Rehearsal Marks

At this point, consider any other modifications that you would like to make to the score.

I prefer to use bar numbers as rehearsal marks, so make that change in the Engraving Rules dialog box.

1. Open the Engraving Rules dialog box (**House Style** > Engraving Rules) and select "Rehearsal marks" and in the Appearance list, click on "Bar numbers."

In large scores I also prefer to place the measure numbers on each bar of the score. I also would like to place them a little higher so they do not collide with the flute part in the top staff.

2. Select **House Style** > Default Positions.
3. Select "Bar numbers" in the scroll list.
4. Under Creating Object, change "Vertical position relative to staff" to 10 for the Score. Leave the Parts setting at 2.5.

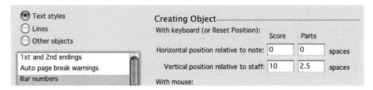

Next, change the type style and enclosure.

5. Use the shortcut: Option-Shift-⌘-T (Mac); Alt-Shift-CTRL-T (Win), or select **House Style** > Edit Text Styles to access the Text Style dialog box.
6. Select "Bar numbers" and click the Edit button.
7. Under Font, check the Bold box and uncheck the Italic box.
8. Under Size, change Score to 14.
9. Click the Border tab at the top of the dialog box.
10. Under Border Shape, uncheck the Circled box and check the Boxed box.
11. Click OK, and click Close to return to the score.

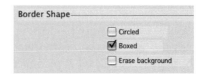

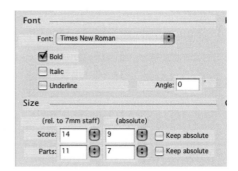

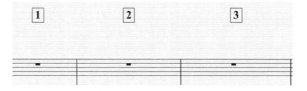

The above change to the bar numbers will make them collide with the title and credits at the top of the score, so their vertical position must be raised as well.

Changing the Default Position of Text

1. Select **House Style** > Default Positions.
2. Select Title from the scroll list.
3. Under Creating Object, change "Vertical position relative to staff" to 15 for the Score.

4. Select Composer from the scroll list and repeat step 3.
5. Select Lyricist from the scroll list and repeat step 3.
6. Select Header (after first page) and change the position to -5.

Make one last adjustment to lower the default position for Expression text entered in the score and in the parts where there is more room below the staff.

7. Select Expression from the scroll list.
8. Under Creating Object, change "Vertical position relative to staff" to 5.5 for the Score and 6 for the parts.
9. Click OK.

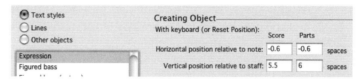

Making the Big Time (Signature)

Next, make the time signatures in the score easier to see and read by displaying larger numbers. They will be placed at key points in the score rather than on every staff.

1. Use the shortcut: Shift-⌘-E (Mac); Shift-CTRL-E (Win) to access the Engraving Rules dialog box.
2. Select Time Signature from the left column.
3. From the "Text style" list, choose "Time signatures (huge)."
4. Click OK.

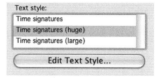

A Manuscript Paper Is Born

The changes that have been made so far are things that I want to display in most scores. To save time, we'll save it as Manuscript Paper. This was also introduced in Chapter 8.

1. Use the shortcut: Shift-⌘-S (Mac); Shift-CTRL-S (Win) to name and save the document. The name you enter will become the name of the Manuscript Paper you are about to create, so make sure it is descriptive, memorable, and at the same time pithy.
2. Type the filename "Orchestra My Film."
3. Select **File** > Export > Manuscript Paper.
4. Click Yes. The Manuscript Paper file has been created and will appear in the Manuscript Paper list when you begin a new score in the future.
5. Close the file by selecting **File** > Close.

Sibelius has added this file to the Manuscript Paper list, so let's go and use it.

6. Use the shortcut: ⌘-N (Mac); CTRL-N (Win) to create a new document.
7. Scroll down and select Orchestra My Film from the list.

The page size is currently set for tabloid. For those of you who don't have printers that can handle that size, I'll tell you how to make adjustments when it's time to print. Leave the size as tabloid for now. The House Style remains unchanged and the time signature and tempos will be determined later, so leave them alone for now.

8. Click Next three times to reach the Key Signature selection page.
9. Select A♭ Major for the Key Signature and click Next.
10. For the Title, type "Heartland."
11. For the Composer/Songwriter, type "Vince Leonard."
12. For the lyricist, type: "Entered by [your name]."
13. For the Copyright, type: "2006 by Vince Leonard."
14. Click Finish.
15. Save and close the file.

No Film Composers Were Harmed in the Writing of This Chapter

This chapter is not intended to be a clinic on the process of scoring to picture. There are many excellent texts on the subject for you to explore. The objective of this chapter is to show you how Sibelius can be used to score for video/film.

In creating this example, I began with a blank file and created the music to fit the visuals. Since the compositional process is not a part of the lesson, you will begin by completing note and text entry in the full score, then match the music to the video.

Due to the page size and the length of the orchestra score, I won't ask you to print and reenter the entire score.

www.sibeliusbook.com

1. Open your web browser and go to the book website: *www.sibeliusbook.com*
2. Download the Chapter 12 folder.
3. In Sibelius, open the file *12Heartland1.sib*. This file has everything entered except for a few bars, which you will complete in the next section.

Trills (Bar 48, Page 5)

With the *12Hearland1.sib* file open in Sibelius, advance to bar 48. The woodwinds and violins require a trill indication.

1. In the top Flute staff, select bar 48.
2. Type the letter L all by itself to access the Lines list or select **Create** > Lines.
3. Select the trill symbol from the "Staff lines" list.
4. Click OK.

5. The blue handle at the right end of the line is for length adjustment. Adjust the length of the trill line to fill the bar (see the graphic below) and position the shape so that it is above the notes.

6. Add trills to the bottom Flute staff, top Oboe staff, Violin I, Violin II, and Viola staves.

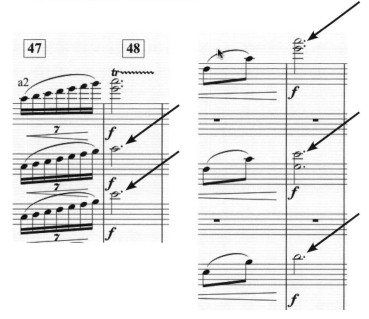

 If you prefer, you can select the trill from the staff list without first selecting a destination staff. Press Esc so nothing is selected. Press the letter L and select the trill. The cursor will turn blue, so click on the desired note to add the trill. You can also copy just the trill markings by selecting the trill and then Option-clicking (Mac) or Alt-clicking (Win) on the desired note.

Focus on Staves

Working on a score with a large number of staves can be very cumbersome, especially in trying to see the staves and navigate around the score. The Focus on Staves feature allows you to select any group of staves, contiguous or noncontiguous, and display only those staves on the page. When you are finished, you can use a shortcut to return instantly to the full score.

1. Select the top Flute staff.
2. ⌘-click (Mac) or CTRL-click (Win) the following staves so all are selected:

- the bottom Flute staff
- both staves of the Harp grand staff
- both staves of the Piano grand staff
- both staves of the Violin I part
- both staves of the Violin II part

3. Click the Focus on Staves button in the toolbar or use the shortcut: Option-⌘-F (Mac); Alt-CTRL-F (Win).

Focus on Staves

The entire score has been temporarily reduced to the staves selected, allowing you to work more efficiently with this group of staves. The selected staves compress to fill up the available room on each page, changing the number of systems on the page to three. Sibelius remembers this specific group of staves until you select another staff or group, allowing you to toggle back to the full score, then back to the Focus group without having to reselect the same staff or group of staves.

The group of staves selected happens to be the instruments that play tremolos in bars 53 through 56. This is a new skill.

Tremolos (Bars 53 Through 56, Page 5)

Tremolos are complex-looking bits of notation that are actually very simple to produce in Sibelius. To enter a tremolo, first divide its number of beats in half. In bars 53 through 56, the tremolos are all a half note in duration, which divide down to quarter notes.

1. Navigate to bar 53 of the Focus score.
2. Enter quarter notes for the downward tremolo part, along with the required rests and dynamic, for the top Flute staff, Harp, and Violin I in bars 53 through 56.

3. Enter quarter notes for the upward tremolo part, along with the required rests and dynamic, for Voice 2 of the top Flute staff, Voice 1 of the Piano, and Violin II in bars 53 through 56.

In the Flute staff, the voices will cross, but Sibelius will handle properly positioning the notes on beat 3.

4. Select all of the staves in bars 53 through 56.
5. On the Keypad, click the ▭ icon at the top of the window for Layout 3.
6. On the Keypad, click the ⌐ key, or press the Enter key on the computer's numeric keypad. This joins both notes as a tremolo group.

7. On the Keypad, click the ♪ key, or press 3 on the computer's numeric keypad. This sets the number of beams between the notes.
8. Press Esc.

Add Interval (Bars 63 through 69, Page 6)

In sections where the harmony interval is a constant, take advantage of the Add Interval feature to add the additional part. I want to harmonize the Flute soli passage in bars 63 through 69 with the Flute 2 playing a sixth below the Flute 1.

1. With the Focus group of staves still selected, navigate so the Flute part in bars 63 through 69 is visible on the screen.
2. Select the Flute staff in bars 63 through 69.
3. Type Shift-6 (use the numbers above the letter keys, not the numeric keypad), or select **Notes** > Add Interval > 6th Below to add the lower voice.

> Add Interval is especially useful for octave doubling in the left hand of keyboard parts when the notes go below the range of a five-octave MIDI keyboard. Enter the upper octave, then add the lower octave by selecting the passage and typing Shift-8 (the 8 above the letter U, not the 8 on the numeric keypad).

Entering Multiple Parts on the Same Staff

When two or more parts occupy the same staff in a score, some indication is required when entrances are made to tell each player who is playing what part, or, if there is only one note, if is it a solo or a unison part. Even if these parts will be separated during the part extraction process, the indications must be made on the score for the conductor.

1. Navigate to bar 29 of the Horn part. In this passage the 1st Horn plays bars 29 and 30 as a solo. This must be indicated so the 2nd Horn player, reading the same staff, does not play.

2. Using Technique text, ⌘-T (Mac) or CTRL-T (Win), enter "1st Solo" in bar 29.

3. The 2nd Horn enters in bar 31. Using Technique text, ⌘-T (Mac) or CTRL-T (Win), enter "tutti (all)" in bar 29. This mark not only tells the 2nd Horn to play, it also lets the 1st Horn know the solo passage is over.

4. The 3rd and 4th Horns have a unison note in bar 31. Using Technique text, ⌘-T (Mac) or CTRL-T (Win), enter "a2" (a due, pronounced *ah DOO-ay*) in bar 31. Marking the entrance unison, or with the abbreviation "unis.," is also acceptable.

When two parts become a unison part, use a2, or unis., to indicate that both players should continue playing. The exception to this rule is demonstrated in the Horn 1 and 2 staff, where the unison B♭ at the end of the bar is double-stemmed. Double-stemming is created by entering the same note in two different Voices.

5. Navigate to the Horn part in bar 81.
6. Select the unison B♭ at the end of beat 3 in bar 81 of the Horn 3 and 4 staff.
7. Using Technique text, ⌘-T (Mac) or CTRL-T (Win), enter the "a2."

No indication is necessary in places where there are two notes present, unless the voices are crossed and the lower part is on top of the higher part. See measure 60 of the Horn part as an example.

String instruments have the potential to play more than one note at a time, up to four in the right circumstances. This effect is not used in "Heartland." When more than one note appears in this orchestration, the section will divide in half when necessary. This must be made clear to the players in the form of a text indication. In "Heartland," the strings divide for a single measure in bar 48. The strings need a divisi indication, abbreviated to div., and an a2 in bar 49 to indicate the end of the divisi section.

1. Navigate to the Violin I and II parts in bar 47 through 49.
2. Using Technique text, ⌘-T (Mac) or CTRL-T (Win), enter "div." for both Violin I and Violin II in bar 48.
3. Using Technique text, ⌘-T (Mac) or CTRL-T (Win), enter "a2." for both Violin I and Violin II in bar 49.

Divisi Stave Parts

In the string section, the Violin I, Violin II, Viola, and Cello parts have two staves per part. This is to accommodate passages where there are divisi or divided parts too complex to read comfortably from the same staff. The main part should always be in the top staff and the lower staff only used when necessary. After the orchestration is completed, all unused bottom staves will be hidden in both the score and parts to conserve space.

When a divisi staff is used, each staff should contain a complete part for that system, so all parts that are not divided should be copied to the lower staff. This is so the player does not have to switch staves in mid-system.

1. Navigate to page 3, specifically to the Viola staves for that page. The Violas make a unison entrance in bar 21, then begin a divided section in bar 25.
2. Select the unison section, bars 21 through 24.
3. Copy and paste those four bars to the divisi staff below.

Now each staff contains a complete part for the section. I have taken care of all other places in the score where this situation occurs. This process will have to be revisited when you create the parts if the music does not fit onto systems in the same way as it does in the score.

Hiding the Divisi Staves

With the orchestration completely entered, hide the unused divisi string staves. If you left them visible, it would give the impression that only half the section is playing during the unison passages. These staves are just extensions of a single part, not parts unto themselves. Also, the space can be used in other places in the score. This process should be done carefully, going page by page, to make sure the correct staves are hidden.

1. Navigate to page 1 of the score with the complete string section visible on the screen.
2. Double-click anywhere on the lower staff of the Violin I part to select the staff for the entire system.
3. Select **Layout** > Hide Empty Staves.

The staff will disappear and a blue dashed line will appear between the Violin I staff and the top Violin II staff to indicate that a staff is hidden.

4. Double-click anywhere on the lower staff of the Violin II part.
5. Use the shortcut this time: Shift-Option-⌘-H (Mac); Shift-Alt-CTRL-H (Win) to hide the staff.
6. Continue using the process to hide the lower Viola and Cello staves.
7. Navigate to page 2 of the score and repeat steps 2 through 6 to hide the divisi staves.
8. Navigate to page 3 and hide the Violin I, Violin II, and Cello staves.
9. Navigate to page 4 and hide the Violin I and Violin II staves.
10. Navigate to page 5 and hide the Violin I, Violin II ,and Viola staves.
11. Navigate to page 6 and hide the Violin I and Violin II staves.
12. Navigate to page 7 and hide the Violin I, Violin II, and Viola staves.
13. Navigate to page 8 and hide the Violin I, Violin II, and Viola staves.
14. Navigate to page 9 and hide the Violin I, Violin II, and Viola staves.

Showing Hidden Staves

Just in case you want any of those hidden staves visible again for that new part you just worked out, here are the steps:

1. Navigate to page 1 of the score and place the string section on the screen.
2. Select bar 1 of the Violin I part. You can select anything in the system where you want to restore the hidden staff.
3. Select **Layout** > Show Empty Staves or use the shortcut: Shift-Option-⌘-S (Mac); Shift-Alt-CTRL-S (Win).
4. In the Show Empty Staves window, click the Deselect All button.
5. Select the staff you wish to show. If you want to show more than one, ⌘-click (Mac) or CTRL-click (Win) on the additional staves.
6. Click OK.
7. If you clicked OK but really want them hidden again, remember, **Edit** > Undo is your friend.

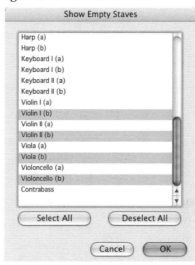

Multiple Percussion Parts on the Same Staff

1. Navigate back to page 1 of the score and show the Percussion parts on the screen.
2. Press M to activate the Mixer window, and scroll to the percussion channels.
3. Click the S (Solo) button for both percussion channels. Only these two staves will playback.
4. Press P to play back the percussion parts.

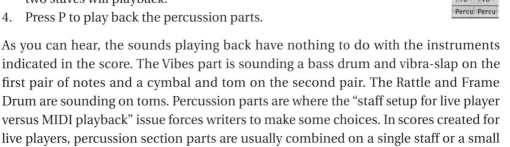

As you can hear, the sounds playing back have nothing to do with the instruments indicated in the score. The Vibes part is sounding a bass drum and vibra-slap on the first pair of notes and a cymbal and tom on the second pair. The Rattle and Frame Drum are sounding on toms. Percussion parts are where the "staff setup for live player versus MIDI playback" issue forces writers to make some choices. In scores created for live players, percussion section parts are usually combined on a single staff or a small group of staves depending on the complexity of the part and the size of the percussion section.

 Combining all percussion staves on a single percussion part or printing each staff separately will depend on the situation. Involved parts can be easier to follow when they are on their own staff. Lighter parts are more easily combined.

When setting up a score in Sibelius, there are special staves, which are already configured for playback, for most common percussion instruments (see Chapter 8). Using a staff for every percussion instrument can take up a lot of space in a large score, making the staves smaller and harder to read. Sibelius can track multiple nonpitched percussion instruments (placed on MIDI channel 10, which is reserved for nonpitched percussion), but in this score, the Vibes part placed on the percussion staff will play percussion sounds, not Vibes. To remedy this, the staff must be changed to a MIDI channel other than 10.

1. Select the first (top staff) Percussion channel in the Mixer window.
2. From the Sound pop-up menu, select Pitched Percussion > Vibraphone.
3. Also in the Mixer window, click the S (Solo) buttons for the Keyboard I staff.
4. Press P to play back the score again.

On this pass the Vibes do sound, but as you can hear against the Piano part, the part does not sound correctly, since the Percussion stave is set up to map notes to the correct General MIDI percussion sounds, not to handle chromatic pitches. Had I used a Vibes staff when I set up the score, I would not be able to hear correct playback of the Snare drum or Gong parts that share the staff later in the piece. The best solution for this project is to mute the percussion staves.

5. Click the M (Mute) buttons twice for both the Percussion I and Percussion II channels.
6. Click the S (Solo) buttons on both of the Keyboard I channels.

 To play back a complex score intended for live a performance after the score is finished, save the file under a different file name to create a playback-only version. Then add the required percussion staves to the score and copy and paste the percussion parts from the live section staves to the playback-ready staves. Some pitch adjustment will be required for the parts to sound properly. Use the Re-input Pitch feature or the Transpose feature to speed the process.

Always make sure the instrument is clearly indicated at every change of instrument. In a part, staff names from the score are lost.

Creating Boxed Staff Text

Use boxed text to draw attention to instrument changes in scores. Boxed text sets the changes apart from other expressions on the score so when a player scans the part, they can instantly see what to prepare and when those changes need to be made. The first instruments played by the percussionist have been entered in the score, but each instrument used needs to be entered as well.

1. Navigate to bar 15 on page 3 of the score, with the Percussion parts visible on the screen.
2. The Percussion II staff needs an instrument indication in this bar.
3. Select the Percussion II staff in bar 15.
4. Select **Create** >Text > Other Staff Text > Boxed Text.

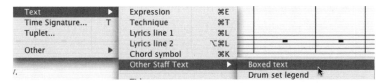

> Another way to access the many text styles in Sibelius is using the Properties menu. I usually enter text above the staff using Techinque text and below the staff using Expression text. Each text style has unique formatting such as boxed text, lyrics, etc. Every text style is accessible from the Properties menu. For example, to enter boxed text, you can enter Technique Text, open the Properties box, click on the Text tab to expand it and below text is a pull-down menu that lists every type of text style Sibelius offers. This can save time searching for text styles in the Create menus and submenus, which I find difficult to memorize.

5. Type "Large Gong," then press Esc.
6. Use the up arrow key to position the text over the "l.v." (let vibrate) indication, then press Esc.

Repositioning Individual Staves

With the unused string staves hidden, you'll notice that the score has been expanding to fill in the space between the top and bottom of the page.

1. Select "View 2 pages" from the magnification menu in the toolbar.
2. Position the Navigator window so the first four pages are visible.

The position of the white strip created by the Timecode display area is lower in the first three pages, showing how the score has expanded to fill up the space left when the string staves were hidden. Sibelius divides that space over the entire system, but there are a few places that require some individual adjustment.

There is a little more room needed between the bass staff of the Keyboard I and the treble staff of the Keyboard II parts on page 1. To accomplish this, move the Harp and Keyboard I parts up into the ample room occupied by the Timecode display.

3. Select bar 1 of the Harp treble clef staff, then Shift-double-click the bass clef staff of the Keyboard I staff to select all four staves for the entire system.

4. Use the shortcut: Shift-Option-up arrow (Mac); Shift-Alt-up arrow (Win) to raise the Harp and Keyboard I grand staves up until there are no collisions between the Keyboard I and Keyboard II staves.

5. Navigate to page 2 of the score.

6. Select the Harp and Keyboard I staves for this page and repeat the process of raising them so there are no collisions between the Keyboard I and Keyboard II staves.

Downloading the "Heartland" Video

You will need to download the "Heartland" video from the Web site *www.sibeliusbook.com*. It is available in small, medium, and large file formats to accommodate different ISP connection speeds. The larger files will be of higher quality.

www.sibeliusbook.com

1. Go to the *www.sibeliusbook.com* Web site.

2. Click on the Chapter 12 link.

3. Download one of the following video files. The larger the file, the longer it will take to download. Also, the larger the file, the better the video quality. If you have a dial-up connection, go with the 29.7 MB version. If you have cable or DSL, the medium or large files are an option.

Heartland_Large.mov (826.5MB)

Heartland_Medium.mov (60.6MB)

Heartland_Small.mov (29.7MB)

 If this is the first time you are working with video in Sibelius, take a few minutes to watch the tutorial video. Go to the Help menu and select Tutorial Videos, then select number 15, "Video." You can also access the tutorial videos from the Quick Start screen under Tutorial Videos.

1. To make the Video window active, if it is not already on the desktop, click on the Video button on the toolbar. The video screen will appear on the desktop.

2. You will need to see the Playback controls while you are working with Video, so be sure the controls are displayed on the screen. They can be turned on and off via **Window** > Playback Controls.

Loading a Video Into Sibelius

"Heartland" is a QuickTime file, identified by the .mov file extension. QuickTime is available as a free download for both Mac (*www.apple.com/quicktime/download/ mac.html*) and Windows (*www.apple.com/quicktime/download/win.html*) computers. Sibelius can load files in .avi, .mpg, and .mov formats on Macintosh computers. Windows Sibelius users can load .avi, .mpg, .wmv, and .mov files, the latter if Quick-Time is installed.

1. To load the Video file that you downloaded from *www.sibeliusbook.com* (Heartland_Small.mov, for example), select **Play** > Video and Time > Add Video.

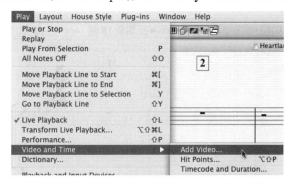

2. Locate the video file that you downloaded on your hard drive, select it, and click Open. The name of the video file will be displayed at the top of the video screen.

Adjusting the Size of the Video Window

Spend a few minutes getting familiar with the video screen.

1. Resize the video screen by clicking on the icons along the bottom left corner of the Video window. The first icon controls Hit Points, which we will discuss later in this chapter. Starting with the second icon, there are four window sizes ranging from a small window up to a full screen. Click each one to see how it affects the size.

2. To close out of the full-screen view, press Esc.

The slider to the right of the size selection boxes is for audio volume on the video. However, there is no audio in this file.

When you are working primarily with the video, expand the video window to as large a size as possible without negatively affecting computer performance. When working primarily with the notation and checking it against the video, use a smaller size so you can easily see the notation.

Playing the Video

Video playback is handled by the Playback controls. However, Sibelius will only play the video for the duration of the score. I have purposely entered a slow tempo at the start of the score so you will see the entire video when you play the file the first time.

"Heartland" is a four-minute-long video that depicts a day in the life of the Grand Teton National Park in Wyoming. The first step is to familiarize yourself with the video.

1. Turn down or mute the volume on your computer or MIDI keyboard so you do not hear any music for the first video playback.
2. Press the Play button and watch the video.

Playback will stop at the end of the video, or the last bar of the score, whichever comes first.

About Timecode and Hit Points

To begin matching the music to the video, you need to insert markers, called Hit Points, that identify important places in the video. The placement of these markers in the score will be based on time, not specific places in the music. As you work through this section, you will bring the Hit Points together with the desired locations in the music.

In the blank strip in the middle of the "Heartland" score are a string of numbers called Timecode. These numbers indicate the time, in minutes, seconds, and tenths of seconds, of the start of each measure. Elapsed time is where the time language of music, expressed in beats per minute, meets video, which is calculated in frames per second; the measuring device both sides can understand is time.

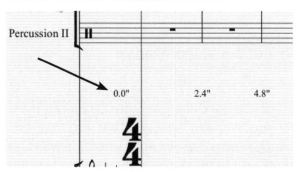

To make it easy to find a specific point in time, Sibelius is able to create markers (Hit Points) at specific places you select in the video. These points indicate exact moments in time in the video. You can then use time signature and tempo to create music that flows naturally to and from the Hit Points.

The location of the Timecode display is controlled in the Timecode and Duration dialog box (**Play** > Video and Time > Timecode and Duration) under the Position heading. Use the popup list to select the desired staff in the score. In the Orchestra Film Manuscript Paper, two blank staves (Tape) were added to the score to provide space for both the timecode display and hit points.

Entering (Creating) Hit Points

The first two elements in the video worth noting are the title screen and the first visual after the title screen.

Title

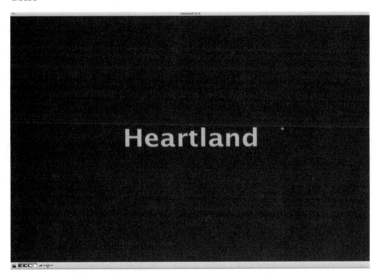

Pre-dawn (Snake River at Dawn)

Hit Points can be created during playback or while the video is stopped at a specific location.

Creating the First Hit Point

1. Click the rewind button on the Playback controls to go back to the beginning.
2. Move the pointer cursor with your mouse over the Hit Point button on the video screen so it will be close by when you want to create a Hit Point. Don't click the button, just leave the pointer close by.
3. Press the space bar to begin playback.
4. When the title screen appears, click on the Hit Point button to create the first Hit Point. Press the space bar to stop playback. If you want to try it again, Undo is your friend.

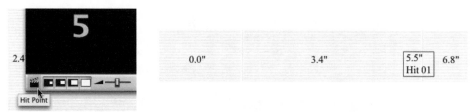

It is possible to "scrub" (move stepwise in tenth of a second intervals over a specific region of video) over a spot in the video in order to precisely place a hit point. To do this, stop playback in the area you want to place a marker and use the square bracket keys ([and]) on your computer keyboard. The left bracket moves backward in time and the right bracket moves forward in time.

Creating a Second Hit Point

1. Rewind to the beginning of the video.
2. Press the space bar to start playback.
3. Click the mouse button when the first picture, the Snake River at dawn, appears.
4. Press the space bar to stop playback.

Editing the Location of a Hit Point

If you find a Hit Point that is not as precise as you need it to be, the location can be edited in the Hit Points window.

1. Press the space bar to stop playback where you want the Hit Point.
2. Check the Time display in the Playback window.
3. Use the shortcut: Option-Shift-P (Mac); Alt-Shift-P (Win) to access the Hit Points dialog box.

4. Double-click on the number in the Timecode column and enter the number in the time display of the Playback window.
5. Click the mouse to deselect the number, and then click OK to return to the score.

Timecode	Bar.beat.100ths	Name
00:00'05.5"	2.3.45	Hit 01
00:00'08.4"	3.3.12	Hit 02

> Unless you watch the video clip enough times to anticipate each change, your Hit Point times will most likely be a little late due to the time it takes you to recognize the picture and click the mouse button, and the time it takes Sibelius to register the click and attach the Hit Point. Use the square bracket technique from the previous tip once you have determined where a Hit Point is needed.

Locating the Hit Points in the Score

The two Hit Points you just created will appear in a box, in the same line as the Timecode display in the score. Hit 01 (Hit Point 1) is the title screen and Hit 02 (Hit Point 2) is the first picture. Now you will need to locate the other important pictures in the video.

Each of the following pictures starts a section of the visual story. Insert a Hit Point where each of these begins. To view the pictures in color, download *hitframes.pdf* from the Web site.

1. Position the cursor over the Hit Point button in the Video window so it is close by. Press the space bar to resume playback.
2. Click the mouse button when you see each of the following frames.

Sunrise (The sun hits the high peaks)

384

Morning (Looking east across the valley)

Afternoon (Mt. Moran across Jackson Lake)

Aerials (Approaching Mt. Moran by air)

Sunset (Mt. Moran at dusk)

Last Shot (The Tetons at twighlight)

End

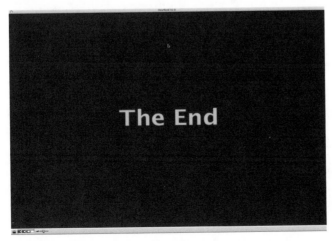

3. Press Esc to stop playback after the last Hit Point has been entered.
4. Play the video clip again from the beginning and check your Hit Points. Make edits as needed.

Naming Hit Points

After the Hit Points are entered, give each a descriptive name so you can locate them in the video.

1. Use the shortcut: Option-Shift-P (Mac); Alt-Shift-P (Win) or select **Play** > Video and Time > Hit Points to access the Hit Points list.
2. In the Name column, click each Hit Point and enter a name to identify each. Press Return/Enter after typing each name in the dialog box.
   a. "Title"
   b. "Pre-dawn"
   c. "Sunrise"
   d. "Morning"
   e. "Afternoon"
   f. "Aerials"
   g. "Sunset"
   h. "Last Shot "
   i. "End"
3. Click OK when finished.

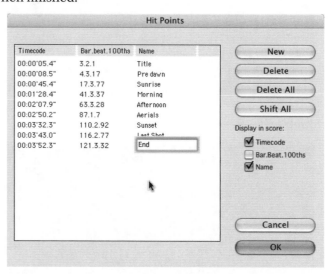

Setting a Start Time for the Score and Video

The first Hit Point should be at five seconds into the score. It is a waste of time to have to watch the countdown each time you press Play. Also, you would have to add blank measures to the beginning of the score to account for the time. I want the score to start on the title screen. Hit Point 1 is the where the title screen appears, so its current location is where the video should start to match the score. The first Hit Point is at 5.3".

1. Select **Play** > Video and Time > Timecode and Duration.

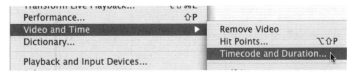

2. Under the Start Time heading, set "Timecode of first bar" to 5.3".
3. Set "Start video from" at 5.3".
4. Click OK.
5. Press P to check the new start point. You should see the title screen first, not the countdown screens.

You will notice that the Hit Points have now repositioned themselves earlier in the time line and the Timecode display has changed to reflect the new start time. Sibelius can be set to start a score at any time during the video. You cannot start a score before the video starts.

Back to the Beginning, or 5.3 Seconds to Be Exact

Now that you've added the points in time where the music and video must meet, it is time to use the musical tool of tempo to fit the music of "Heartland" to the video. The music begins with the Harp during the title screen to establish the mood. The pre-dawn section ends with a beat of silence just before the first picture where there is sun on the mountain peak, the location of Hit Point 3 (Sunrise). You will need to hear the computer playback again.

1. Be sure the playback volume is set correctly so you can hear MIDI playback.
2. Navigate back to page 1 of the score with the Timecode strip and Hit Points visible on the screen.

Entering Tempo Text

1. Double-click the Tempo text in bar 1 and then type 82.
2. Play the video and audio and see how the two match up. The Sunrise picture should appear on the screen at bar 15. Continue playback until the Morning Hit Point.

The tempo needs to be slower in the Sunrise section, bars 15 through 32, so the Morning Hit Point occurs at bar 33.

3. Navigate to bar 15, page 3 of the score, with the Timecode strip visible on the screen.

4. Select bar 15 and use the shortcut: Option-⌘-T (Mac); Alt-CTRL-T (Win) to create new Tempo text.

5. Press ⌘-4 (on the numeric keypad) (Mac) or CTRL-4 (on the numeric keypad) (Win) to enter a quarter note, press space, then the equals sign (=), press the space bar, and then type "75." Press Esc twice.

6. Press P to play back the audio and video again to check the timing. Let the play-back continue to the next Hit Point, Afternoon.

The tempo needs to be a bit faster in the Morning section.

7. Select bar 33 and use the shortcut: Option-⌘-T (Mac); Alt-CTRL-T (Win) to create new Tempo text.

8. Press ⌘-4 (on the numeric keypad) (Mac) or CTRL-4 (on the numeric keypad) (Win) to enter a quarter note, press space, then the equals sign (=), press the space bar, and then type "80." Press Esc twice.

9. Press P to play back the audio and video again to check the timing. Let the play-back continue to the next Hit Point, Afternoon.

The Morning section ends with two dramatic mountain pictures, which I have scored with a little flourish in the music. I want to lift the tempo just a little in these measures.

10. Select bar 45 and use the shortcut: Option-⌘-T (Mac); Alt-CTRL-T (Win) to create new Tempo text.

11. Press ⌘-4 (on the numeric keypad) (Mac) or CTRL-4 (on the numeric keypad) (Win) to enter a quarter note, press space, then the equals sign (=), press the space bar, and then type "82." Press Esc twice.

12. Select bar 49 and use the shortcut: Option-⌘-T (Mac); Alt-CTRL-T (Win) to create new Tempo text.

13. Press ⌘-4 (on the numeric keypad) (Mac) or CTRL-4 (on the numeric keypad) (Win) to enter a quarter note, press space, then the equals sign (=), press the space bar, and then type "85." Press Esc twice.

I've made a creative choice concerning the Afternoon Hit Point. I'm going to place the Hit Point on the resolution of the previous musical phrase (bar 51, page 5 of the score) and let it flow into the next section, which features water in each of the pictures. The musical Afternoon section begins in bar 53 and should be a faster tempo. Building into the modulation there should be a ritard at bar 68 and slow down a little more at bar 70. The Hit Point for the Aerial section should be on beat 3 of bar 71, where the Horns play the melody. The Aerial section should lock into tempo at 72.

14. Navigate to bar 53, page 5 of the score with the Timecode line visible on the screen.

15. Select bar 53 and use the shortcut: Option-⌘-T (Mac); Alt-CTRL-T (Win) to create new Tempo text.

16. Press ⌘-4 (on the numeric keypad) (Mac) or CTRL-4 (on the numeric keypad) (Win) to enter a quarter note, press space, then the equals sign (=), press the space bar, and then type "90." Press Esc twice.
17. Navigate so bars 68 through 72 are visible on the screen.
18. Select bar 68 and use the shortcut: Option-⌘-T (Mac); Alt-CTRL-T (Win) to create new Tempo text.
19. Press ⌘-4 (on the numeric keypad) (Mac) or CTRL-4 (on the numeric keypad) (Win) to enter a quarter note, press space, then the equals sign (=), press the space bar, and then type "84". Press Esc twice.
20. Select bar 70 and use the shortcut: Option-⌘-T (Mac); Alt-CTRL-T (Win) to create new Tempo text.
21. Press ⌘-4 (on the numeric keypad) (Mac) or CTRL-4 (on the numeric keypad) (Win) to enter a quarter note, press space, then the equals sign (=), press the space bar, and then type "78." Press Esc twice.
22. Select bar 72 and use the shortcut: Option-⌘-T (Mac); Alt-CTRL-T (Win) to create new Tempo text.
23. Press ⌘-4 (on the numeric keypad) (Mac) or CTRL-4 (on the numeric keypad) (Win) to enter a quarter note, press space, then the equals sign (=), press the space bar, and then type "75." Press Esc twice.
24. Save the file.
25. Play back the video and audio.

There should be a nice transition from a closeup picture to a distant picture at the beginning of measure 84 where the music begins to lighten orchestrally. The music comes down in volume to the end. The Last Shot Hit Point should be in measure 93 and the End Hit Point in measure 97 with the last chord ending with the fade out of the "The End" text.

How to Remove a Video

If you decide to download a higher, or lower, resolution file of the video, you will need to remove the one currently loaded before you can work with the new file. To remove a loaded video, select **Play** > Video and Time > Remove Video.

At this point, you are finished with syncing the score and video. When you saved the file, Sibelius remembers the location on your hard drive where the video vile currently resides. There is no need to reload it after closing and reopening the file, unless you move the video to another volume or hard drive on your system. If you do move it, Sibelius will prompt you to locate the file manually. If you click Yes, a dialog box will appear so you can locate and open the file from the new location. If you click No, Sibelius will not attempt to play any video but the score will still playback as before.

Where you take the project is up to you. One possibility is to use the Save As Audio feature to create and .aif (Mac) or .wav (Win) file an use a separate program to join the audio and video files and create a DVD. Just make sure you are using the Kontakt Player for playback. See section 7.10 in the Sibelius Reference for more information.

Playback with GPO Sibelius Edition

In Chapter 10 you may have used the Sibelius Rock & Pop Collection to play back the "Pop Quiz" score. In this chapter you will examine GPO Sibelius Edition and how to use it to play back the "Heartland" Score. GPO Sibelius Edition does not come with Sibelius and must be purchased separately. For more information and audio examples, go to *www.sibelius.com/products/gpo_sibelius/index.html*. If you don't own GPO Sibelius Edition, skip ahead to Parts on the next page.

1. Make the Mixer window active if it is not already on the desktop by pressing the letter M all by itself or clicking the Mixer button on the toolbar.
2. Select **Play** > Playback and Input Devices.
3. In the Device column, select Kontakt Player.
4. In the Sound Set column, click on Kontakt Gold and select "GPO 32 Slot Orchestra" from the pop-up list.

5. Click OK, and click Yes in the alert dialog box that follows.
6. In the Mixer window, click the Reset Sounds button.
7. Click Yes in the alert dialog box. Sibelius will begin loading the sounds into the Kontakt Player and assigning them to the staves of the score.

Loading the GPO sounds will take time, and Sibelius will have to do this every time the document is opened (or reloaded, if you are switching between documents). After the loading process is completed, you will need to make some changes in the instrument assignments made by Sibelius.

8. Click the Kontakt Player button in the toolbar to make the Player window active.

Since there is no dedicated Piccolo staff, Sibelius did not assign the piccolo to the bottom Flute staff. This also means that the transposition will not be correct, so for proper playback, the part must be transposed up one octave. Remember to transpose it back down an octave before printing.

9. Be sure to expand the Mixer window so it looks like the graphic below. Click on the arrow to expand or contract the window.
10. Click on Flute in the name strip under channel 2 in the Mixer window.
11. In the Sound pop-up menu, select the Woodwind submenu, and select Piccolo Solo KS.

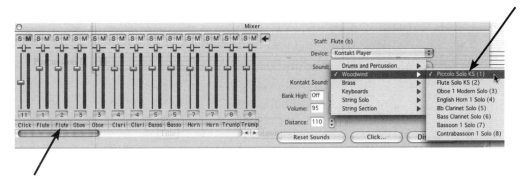

Parts

I won't step you through creating parts for the entire ensemble in this lesson, just cover the situations that have not been mentioned in the previous chapters. If you have gone through those chapters, you have the skills to format parts for a new page size and to transform parts all at once (Chapter 11) or by copying layout from part to part (Chapter 7).

1. From the Dynamic Parts menu in the toolbar, select the Flute part.
2. Convert the page size to letter, as you did in Chapter 11. Review the steps there if you need a refresher.

The Flute section was created using the "Extra staff" Below method when the Manuscript Paper was created at the beginning of this chapter, so all three of the Flute parts are gathered together in one combined part. This works for the score, but is usually not a good option to print for the performer since they will have to sift through extra information to follow their line through unisons and splits, at times switching between staves. It will take you some additional time to split the parts out to print the staves separately, but it will be worth it when rehearsal or recording time comes.

Extracting Parts into Separate Files

There are two ways to split parts, and both of them remove the convenience of having the parts and score in a single document. The first is to extract the staves needing separation into separate files where they can be processed independently from the score and other parts. In other words, they are not dynamically linked.

1. Activate the Parts window.
2. Click the Extract Parts button at the bottom of the Parts window.
3. Click Yes in the explanation dialog box.
4. In the Extract parts dialog box, under the Parts heading, Option-click (Mac) or Alt-click (Win) the Flute part so that it alone is selected.

Under Filenames, there are several choices for naming that use a percent sign and letter code that Sibelius will translate into the final file name. If you would like to choose something other than the default choices presented, select the field and enter the preferred choices. For "Heartland," replace the default setting with the title (%t) and the part name (%p). I prefer shorter file names with only the title of the piece and the name of the instrument.

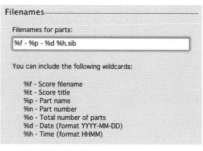

5. Highlight the "Filenames for parts:" field and type: "%t %p,sib."

There is an option to select a folder for the created files. If you wish to select a new folder, do it here. I will leave them in the Scores folder in the Sibelius main folder. There is also an option for opening the parts after extraction. If you plan on immediately working with these parts, leave it checked.

6. Click OK.

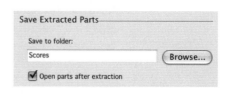

The extracted Flute part looks identical to the Flute part in the score, except the background color of the screen is score white instead of the parts' ivory. You will convert this into three parts. The Flute 3 will be easiest since it is already on a separate staff.

7. Use the shortcut: Shift-⌘-S (Mac); Shift-CTRL-S (Win) to save the file with a new name.

8. Name the file "Heartland-Flute 3.sib" and click Save.

9. Triple-click an empty part of the top staff to select it for the entire piece.

10. Press the Delete key to remove the Flute 1 and 2 staff.

11. Double-click the part name in the upper left of the page. You will see a dialog box suggesting you make the change in the Score Info dialog box. Click Yes.

12. In the Part Name field, enter Flute 3/ Piccolo and click OK.

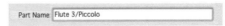

13. Format the part as required, then save and close the file.

14. Select **File** > Open Recent File > Heartland-Flute.

15. Triple-click the Flute 3 staff to select it for the entire piece.

16. Press the Delete key to remove the staff.

17. Use the shortcut: Shift-⌘-S (Mac); Shift –CTRL-S (Win) to save the file with a new name.

18. Name the file "Heartland-Flute 1.sib" and click Save.

19. Double-click the part name in the upper left of the page. You will see a dialog box suggesting you make the change in the Score Info Dialog box. Click Yes.

20. In the Part Name field, enter Flute 1 and click OK.

21. Triple-click the staff, or use the shortcut to select the whole document.

22. Select **Edit** > Filter > Player 2 (For Deletion). All of the lower notes will be highlighted blue, and the Voice 2 notes will be highlighted green.

23. Press the Delete key to remove the Flute 2 notes. The Voice 2 entries have been replaced by half rests; these will be removed in one more trip to the Filter.

24. Format the part as required, making sure there are no collisions between music, dynamics, and text; then save and close the file.

25. Select **File** > Open Recent File > Heartland—Flute.

26. Name the file "Heartland–Flute 2.sib" and click Save.

27. Double-click the part name in the upper left of the page. You will see a dialog box suggesting you make the change in the Score Info dialog box. Click Yes.

28. In the Part Name field, enter Flute 2 and click OK.

29. Select **Edit** > Filter > Player 1 (For Deletion). All of the lower notes will be highlighted blue, and the Voice 1 notes will also be highlighted blue.

30. Press the Delete key to remove the Flute 1 notes. The Voice 1 entries have been be replaced by half rests; these will be removed in one more trip to the Filter.

31. Press Esc.

32. Select bars 53 through 56.

33. Use the shortcut: Shift-Option-⌘-1 (Mac); Shift-Alt-CTRL-1 (Win) to select the Voice 1 rests.

34. Press the Delete key to remove the rests.

35. Select bars 53 through 56 once more.

36. Type Shift-V to swap Voice 1 and Voice 2. This will place the notes in Voice 1 and fix the position issue with the rests.

37. Format the part as required, then save and close the file.

This process will need to be repeated for the four Horns (if you wish to separate them into four parts), 2nd and 3rd Trumpets, all three Trombones, and Tuba. At the end of the process the original extracted file, Heartland-Flute can be deleted.

Creating a Parts-Only Score

The second method for printing parts is to save a copy of the score and create all the parts in one master part document. There you can add extra staves to the document so that each staff will have only one instrument. You can use the Arrange feature or the Player 1 and 2 Delete Filter to explode the multipart staves. Essentially, this process will use the current staves as little sketches that will be reorchestrated onto new staves. The advantage of this process is the parts will all remain in one document, so changes will have to be made in the main score document and the parts score document, not the score and many individual parts files.

1. Return to your original "Heartland" score document.
2. Use the shortcut: Shift-⌘-S (Mac); Shift-CTRL-S (Win) to save the file with a new name, "Heartland Parts."
3. Press the letter I all by itself to access the Instruments and Staves dialog box.
4. From the "Choose from" list, select "Orchestra Instruments."
5. From the Family list, select "Woodwind."
6. From the Instrument list, select "Flute" and click the Add to Score button twice to add two staves to the score.
7. Select "Piccolo" and add one staff to the score.
8. Scroll down to the bottom of the list to locate the new staves, and select all three staves (Flute, Flute, Piccolo).
9. Click the Up button to move the three staves up until they are underneath the two existing Flute staves.
10. Click OK.
11. Double-click the first new Flute staff name and add a 1 to the end of the name to create Flute 1.
12. Repeat step 11 and add a 2 to the second new Flute staff.

From this point you have a choice of methods to copy the original Flute staves onto the new staves that will be printed for the individual players.

Option 1:
- Copy the top Flute staff onto both new Flute staves.
- Use the Player 1 (for deletion) and Player 2 (for deletion) Filters as shown previously to create separate Flute 1 and 2 parts.
- Copy the bottom Flute staff to the new Piccolo staff.

Option 2:
- Select both original Flute staves and use the Arrange feature and select Explode from the Styles list to copy both staves into the three new Flute and Piccolo staves.

The best approach may be a combination of the two options.

 To decrease load times in extracted parts or parts-only scores, remove the video, and, if using any Kontakt Player sounds, return to the computer's internal sounds before extracting or saving.

Creating a New Part in a Score

The oboes and the rest of the woodwinds do not have the multipart staff problem, but the do have some issues to be addressed. Each single-part staff needs to be in a single-part document for printing.

1. Return to the original "Heartland" score document.
2. From the Dynamic Parts menu, select Oboe.
3. Activate the Parts window.
4. Select Oboe in the Parts window.
5. Click the Staves in Part button at the bottom of the Parts window.

6. In the Staves in Part list, select Oboe (b) and click the Remove from Part button.

7. Click OK. Now the Oboe part contains only the top staff.

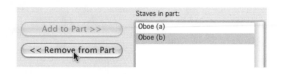

Now create a new a new part for the bottom staff.

8. Click the New Part button at the bottom of the Parts window.

9. In the New Part dialog box, select Oboe (b) in the "Staves available" list and click the Add to Part button. Both staves will be moved to the "Staves in part" list.

10. Select Oboe (a) in the "Staves in part" list and click the Remove from Part button.

11. Click OK.

In the Parts window, and the Dynamic Parts menu, there are two parts labeled Oboe. The next step is tricky. The staff name needs to be changed for each part, but you can't actually change the staff name or it will be altered in the score. You could change the name, print out the part, and then change the name back to the original, but that's certainly not the fastest way to go. There is an item in the Special Text submenu for instrument name at top left, but that will put the name on all parts, not just this one. What is needed is staff text that will appear only on this page.

1. Select **Create** > Text > Other Staff Text > Plain Text.
2. Type "Oboe 1."
3. Press Esc twice.

The existing staff name must be hidden and replaced with the name you just created.

4. Select the existing staff name.
5. Select **Edit** > Hide or Show > Show in Score.
6. Make the Properties window active.
7. Select the Oboe 1 text just created.
8. Click the Text tab in the Properties window.
9. Increase the text size to 14.0.
10. Position the text over the hidden staff name.
11. Repeat the process for the Oboe 2 part.

This process will have to be repeated for the woodwinds and the F horns. Much of the classical literature has two horn parts on the same staff. Since the parts for this orchestration are not that difficult, there is no problem with keeping both parts on the staff.

Multi-stave Parts

From multipart staves we go to the other end of the spectrum to cover multistave parts. These are most commonly found in string and percussion section parts. The system distribution will change and with that, some of the unison notes may no longer be necessary, or maybe additional music will need to be copied in the part. This presents the problem of altering the part that will affect the appearance of the score. Hiding the notes in the part or the score will not work because Sibelius will not hide a staff that has notation in a part. Once again the best choice is to extract the part and make the changes or create another document that is exclusively for parts.

1. Return to the "Heartland" parts document you created earlier.
2. Select Viola from the Dynamic Parts menu.

Create a system layout.

3. Select bars 1 through 14, the two gathered rests, and the 1/4 bar.
4. Select **Layout** > Format > Make into System or use the shortcut: Option-Shift-M (Mac); Alt-Shift-M (Win).
5. Select bars 15 through 26 and use the shortcut: Option-Shift-M (Mac); Alt-Shift-M (Win).
6. Select bars 27 through 32 and use the shortcut: Option -Shift-M (Mac); Alt-Shift-M (Win).
7. Select bars 33 through 41 and use the shortcut: Option -Shift-M (Mac); Alt-Shift-M (Win).
8. Select bars 42 through 47 and use the shortcut: Option -Shift-M (Mac); Alt-Shift-M (Win).

Bars 42 through 47 make up the first system with an incomplete bottom staff. Since the notes in the bottom staff are the same as the top staff, you can remove them and hide the bottom staff for this system.

9. Select bars 42 and 43 in the bottom staff.
11. Press the Delete key.
11. Select the entire bottom staff for that system.
12. Use the shortcut: Shift-Option-⌘-H (Mac); Shift-Alt-CTRL-H (Win) to hide the staff.

This finishes the first page. Resume grouping staves for the second page.

13. Group the following systems in any staff:
    a. bars 48 through 52
    b. bars 53 through 60
    c. bars 61 through 66
    d. bars 67 through 71
    e. bars 72 through 77
    f. bars 78 through 82
    g. bars 83 through 90 and 91 through to the end.

There are three multistave systems on page 2 to contend with. The first occurs at bars 53 through 60. The bottom staff is once again a unison passage and can be deleted.

14. Repeat steps 10 through 13 above to remove the music from the bottom system in bars 56 through 60, then hide the staff.

Bars 61 through 66 contain divisi notes, as do 67 through 69. The unison phrase in bar 70 is already copied to the bottom staff. To fit the score layout, finish the phrase by copying the notes in the top staff in bar 71.

15. Copy the contents of the top staff in bar 71 to the bottom staff. This includes the hairpin and courtesy clef, which will transfer using the normal copy and paste function.
16. To create a little more room between the staves in bars 76 through 71, select the bottom staff and use Shift-Option-down arrow (Mac) or Shift-Alt-down arrow (Win) to move the bottom staff down so the hairpin in the top staff of bar 71 does not touch the slur in the bottom staff.
17. Move the rit. in bar 68 to between the staves, so it is easier for players of the bottom staff to see.

Now the part is ready to print. Use what you have learned to format the Cello part.

20/20 Hindsight

Some of the problems you've just slogged through could have been averted by a more radical redesign of the Manuscript Paper, but some problems just don't hit you until you're up against them. Remember them for the next time you are choosing a Manuscript Paper option. The wind part situation could have been improved by replacing all of the staves with individual staves as opposed to the grouped staves. Some of this is just the constant state of affairs with large scores; the number of staves versus the readability of the score. In the end, all you can do is make the best choices possible given the situation and apply what you have learned to the next project.

Printing

Printing is usually the calm after the storm, unless your printer jams during printing or the computer and printer aren't speaking to one another thanks to some unknown error.

Page Sizes

This section is for anyone with a printer capable of printing on paper larger than letter and legal sizes. Large format printers offer greater readability by allowing larger staff sizes on the increased page size. There are a number of larger page formats that Sibelius is able to handle with the click of a mouse on a menu item.

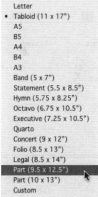

1. Use the shortcut: ⌘-D (Mac); CTRL-D (Win) to access the Document Setup dialog box.
2. Under Size, click on the pop-up list.

I would select Part (9.5″ × 12.5″) if this were headed for a recording session. A symphony orchestra might request Part (10″× 13″), but a publisher would request Concert (9″× 12″). Granted, these require a special nonstandard printer that can print on those sizes, but there are smaller sizes for marching band, choir, and, of course, letter and legal size.

 If you need to print a score at a size larger than your printer will accommodate, there are other options. Professional printers called "Service Bureaus," and businesses such as Kinkos that offer photocopying services also have computers and large format printers for such projects. Save the file in PDF format so Sibelius and the music fonts will not need to be on the computer from which you will be printing. Consult your local business for any size and file type restrictions first.

Scale Reduction

If you want to print the score for "Heartland" and do not have a printer that can print on $11'' \times 17''$ paper, here are the steps to make it work with the printer you own. The score is formatted for tabloid size paper, $11'' \times 17''$, in portrait format. If you were trying to make a photocopy of it, after asking permission from the copyright owner first of course, you would use the zoom reduction feature found on most copiers to reduce the copy to legal- or letter-size paper. This is possible with most printers.

The screenshots below may not be exactly the same as you see on your system. The reason is that every printer uses its own unique drivers or instructions.

1. Mac: Select **File** > Page Setup. Win: Select **File** > Print.

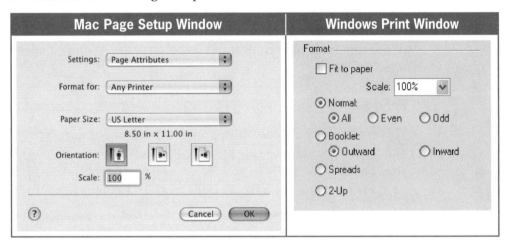

Look for the Scale setting. This number functions like the zoom reduction setting on a copier.

2. Enter 64 for the percent.
3. Use the shortcut ⌘-P (Mac) or CTRL-P (Win) to print the score on letter size paper.

Using this setting, you can print out any size Sibelius page on letter-size paper. When printing large scores, it's worth the investment in a pack of legal-size paper, as the proportional relation to $11 \times 17''$ paper is a bit better than normal paper.

 To create an $11'' \times 17''$ score with letter or legal-size paper, printed out on your printer, use a photocopier with a zoom enlargement feature, and enlarge it.

Back-to-Back Scores

If you want to print your score on both sides of each page (back-to-back), you need a printer with a duplexer, or if you don't own one, use this technique.

Mac:

1. Select **File** > Print.
2. Click on Copies & Pages and select Paper Handling from the pop-up menu.
3. Under the Print heading, click the "Odd numbered pages" button. The printer will print only pages 1, 3, 5, and so on.
4. Click Print.

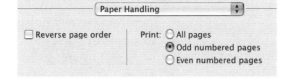

Windows:

2. Select **File** > Print
3. Under the Format heading, check Odd.
4. Click OK.

You want a stack of pages with page 1 on top, and face down, ready to load back in the printer. The direction the pages face will depend on how they come out of the printer and what side of the paper your printer prints on when loaded. Depending on the direction pages come out, you may want to check the "Reverse page order" box so the pages come out in the right order to go back through the printer.

5. Place the odd pages back in your printer tray so the printer will print the even pages on the back sides of the correct pages. For example, page 2 will print on the back of page 1, page 4 on page 3, and so on.
6. Select **File** > Print.
7. Mac:
   a. Click on Copies & Pages and select Paper Handling from the pop-up menu. Under the Print heading, click the "Even numbered pages" button.
   b. Click Print.
8. Win:
   a. Under the Format heading, click the Even button.
   b. Click OK.

 In future projects, you may encounter new situations that will require you to build on skills you have learned in this book. Sibelius is a tool, to be used to the best of your ability. The Sibelius company will continue to improve the program, and you should keep current on its features and how to best apply them to your music. This will help you to make the most of your investment in Sibelius and this book. See Chapters 13–15 for more suggestions on support and other areas.

Summary

In this chapter you took on the challenges of scoring to picture and adding many advanced scoring techniques. This is a list of the skills involved in this endeavor.

- create a Manuscript Paper
- customize that Manuscript Paper
- change the default position of text
- load a video clip into Sibelius
- play a video clip
- enter Hit Points
- name Hit Points
- move Hit Points
- use Focus on Staves
- enter multiple parts on the same staff
- use the Add Interval feature
- create divisi staff parts
- create boxed system text
- enter trills
- enter tremolos
- reposition individual staves
- hide staves
- sync the score to the video
- play back the score with PO Sibelius Edition
- extract parts from a multipart staff
- create a new part
- create a divisi staff part
- print documents larger than letter size on letter size paper
- print the score back to back

Review

1. Additional video clips are available on the Sibelius 4 CD or on the Sibelius Education Web site (*www.sibeliueducation.com*). Try composing a score for one of the clips. You can also download other royalty-free videos from:

   hubblesource.stsci.edu/sources/video/clips/
   memory.loc.gov/ammem/dihtml/divideos.html
   www.archive.org/details/movies

2. If you can transfer video or photos into your computer, try creating your own video or slide show to score.

3. After you create a score for a video, try creating another one where the music is completely the opposite mood of the first one you created.

SECTION IV

Getting the Most out of Sibelius

13

Importing and Exporting

This chapter deals with exporting or sending files from Sibelius to other programs and importing files into Sibelius scores. It is possible to exchange Sibelius files, send Sibelius files to other programs, and import MIDI and Music XML files into Sibelius. All of these options can be an enhancement to Sibelius users.

The areas to be addressed in this chapter include:

- sharing files between Mac and Windows
- exporting Sibelius 4 Files to earlier Sibelius versions
- exporting Sibelius files as MIDI files
- importing a MIDI file into Sibelius
- identifying sources of MIDI files to import into Sibelius
- importing files from other notation programs
- exporting and importing ASCII guitar tab
- copyright guidelines
- posting Scorch files on Web sites
- publishing music on *www.sibeliusmusic.com*
- importing and exporting graphic files

Sharing Files Between Mac and Windows

Since Sibelius was first introduced, Macintosh and Windows files have been and continue to be totally compatible. It is as simple as saving a file on one computer, moving it to the other, and opening it. It is helpful to include the Sibelius file suffix .sib at the end of the file name when saving a file on a Mac as Windows looks for a suffix at the end of the file name. Sibelius Windows version will save a file with the .sib suffix. Sometimes, it is helpful to open the file specifying that you want Sibelius to open it. To do this in Windows and Mac, use the contextual menus:

1. Open a folder that contains the Sibelius file to be opened.
2. To open the contextual menu, right-click (CTRL-click on a Mac with a one-button mouse) on the file icon, then select Open With and choose Sibelius 4 (or the most recent version of Sibelius that you own).

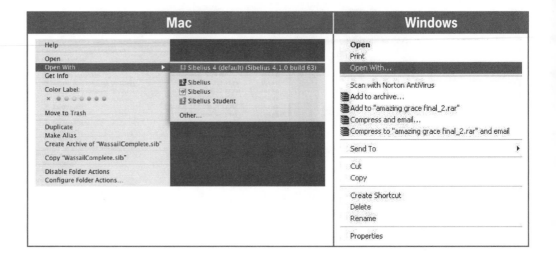

Exporting Sibelius 4 Files to Earlier Sibelius Versions

Sibelius 4 will open any file saved in an earlier version of the program, and can backwards save to earlier versions such as Sibelius 2, Sibelius 3, or Sibelius Student. This is helpful if you need to open a file in an earlier version of Sibelius. When you do this, the features unique to a later version are not supported. To save in an earlier Sibelius format:

1. Open the Sibelius file that you want to save in an earlier version.
2. Select **File** > Export > Sibelius 2, 3 or Student…
3. At the bottom of the Save As screen, choose either Sibelius 2 or Sibelius Student/ Sibelius 3.
4. Be sure to save it with a different file name than the original.

Some of the formatting may be lost when you backwards save, but this is an efficient way to share files with people who are using earlier versions of Sibelius.

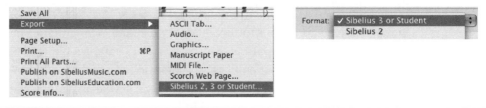

Exporting Sibelius Files in MIDI File Format

Chapter 1 mentioned that Sibelius has one major purpose: creating printed notation. There are times when it is helpful to send a Sibelius file to another program, such as a MIDI sequencer. For example, some users export a Sibelius file to a MIDI/digital audio sequencer and add digital audio tracks. All MIDI sequencers can read MIDI files in Standard MIDI File format. It is important to understand that when saving in MIDI format, only the notes, clefs, and ties are saved. One line of lyrics will also translate.

Things that do not translate include titles, articulations, lines, slurs, and other score markings.

To export Sibelius in MIDI format:

www.sibeliusbook.com

1. Open a Sibelius file. For this example, open the "Wassail Song" final version you created in Chapter 8. If you like, you can download the file from the *www.sibeliusbook.com* Web site in the Chapter 8 files folder.
2. Select **File** > Export > MIDI File. Sibelius will save the file in MIDI format so MIDI sequencers and other music notation programs can read it.
3. To open the MIDI file, open your MIDI sequencer program and consult the documentation on how to open/import it.

Importing a MIDI File Into Sibelius

It is possible to open MIDI files, created in other music software, in Sibelius. The main reason to do this is to save time entering the notation manually, depending on how the file was created. Also, some composers/arrangers prefer to work in a MIDI sequencer and then go to Sibelius to print out notation. Not all MIDI files will translate accurately into Sibelius, so don't get your hopes up too high!

 I have a basic philosophy about opening MIDI files: the more musical the file sounds, the worse the printout will be. And the opposite is usually true. The more mechanical the playback sounds, the more accurate the printout will be.

Follow these steps when opening a MIDI file in Sibelius:

1. In Sibelius, select **File** > Open or select **File** > Quick Start and click Open MIDI File.

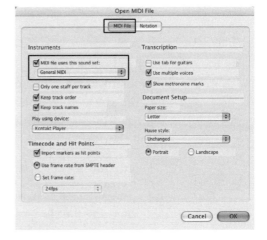

www.sibeliusbook.com

2. Choose the MIDI file to be opened. For this example, open the file Wassailcomplete.mid. This is a MIDI file version of the final Chapter 8 example, "Wassail Song." It can be downloaded from the *www.sibeliusbook. com* web site in the Chapter 13 files folder.

   When the MIDI file opens, a window, which will look familiar if you worked through the Flexi-time options in Chapter 6, appears. In the MIDI File options portion of the Open MIDI File window, there are many helpful options you can experiment with to improve the accuracy of the import.

3. Under Instruments, there is a pull-down menu that lists a host of MIDI synths. The most common choice is General MIDI, but if you use a specific synth make and model, you can select it at this point.

4. Next, click the Notation tab at the top of the Open MIDI Files dialog box.

5. In this dialog box, some important decisions must be made. First, take a guess at the smallest note value in the MIDI file. I usually guess based upon what the file sounded like when I played it. For example, with the "Wassail Song" arrangement, the smallest note value is an eighth note, so that should be selected under Note Values.

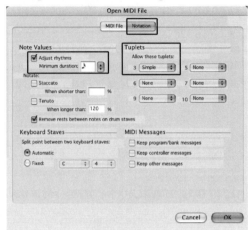

6. Next, determine if there are any triplets or tuplets in the score. I do this by listening to the file before I open it. If you think there are tuplets, select one or more of the tuplet options. I usually select Simple. See Chapter 6 (page 107) for more information on the various tuplet options or consult the *Sibelius Reference*.

7. When you complete the settings, click OK to close the Open MIDI File dialog box.

> Sibelius does its best to translate the MIDI file. When you open a MIDI file, give it a look. If it doesn't look like the printed music you expected, close the file without saving it and open it again, this time making some adjustments to the settings in the Open MIDI File dialog box to see if they improve it. For example, try a larger or smaller note value and add or subtract tuplet options. I usually will do this one or two more times before giving up on a particular MIDI file. Some MIDI files just will not print well, and you have to enter the notation from scratch.

When I opened the MIDI file version of the "Wassail Song" example, there were several problems that needed to be addressed. The staves were not in the correct order, some of the staves with rests were not displaying properly, and the voices were not recognized. The question at this point is, should I edit this file or just start from scratch? If you choose to edit the imported MIDI file, the following should be addressed:

Reorder the staves (instruments):

1. Press the letter I for Instruments or select **Layout** > Instruments and staves.

2. Reorder the staves so the percussion parts are below the vocal parts.

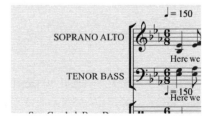

Even after reordering the staves, the Tambourine part is not visible in the first staff system. This is because Sibelius automatically turned on the

Hide Empty Staves feature to show only those staves that have notes in them. Staves with all rests in a system are hidden. This is sometimes referred to as optimizing staves and is done frequently in printed music of vocal and instrumental scores.

To reveal the Tambourine staff:

1. Select the entire score: **Edit** > Select > Select All or use the shortcut: ⌘-C (Mac); CTRL-C (Win).
2. Select **Layout** > Show Empty Staves.
3. Click OK.

There are some other problems with the MIDI translation. You will need to delete the 3/4 time signature in measure 2 and edit the notation. You will also need to use your changing voices skills, introduced in Chapter 9. You will also notice that only some of the lyrics came over in the translation. This is just to show you that often, when opening a MIDI file, you will need your Sibelius editing skills.

> Sibelius has a host of helpful plug-ins for converting a folder of files in many of the formats mentioned in this chapter. You can convert an entire folder of Finale, MIDI, Music XML, or other files. Once these files are in a folder, select **Plug-ins** > Batch Processing > [the option you require] (see below).

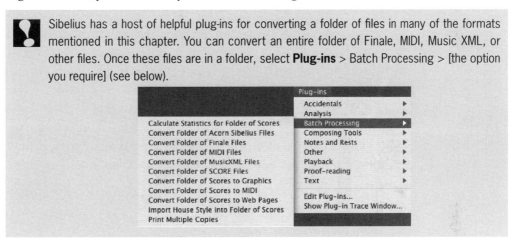

Sources of MIDI Files to Import Into Sibelius

There are various ways to locate and create MIDI files that can be read into Sibelius. MIDI files can be purchased from music publishers such as Hal Leonard, Warner Brothers, Silver Burdett, and others. You can also download MIDI files from the Internet.

Downloading MIDI Files from the Internet

There are thousands of MIDI files available via the Internet. To locate sources, use an Internet search engine such as *www.google.com* or *www.yahoo.com* and search for pages with MIDI files. An excellent source is the Classical MIDI Archives (*www.classicalarchives.com*). There are many other pages that offer MIDI files.

When you find a file you want to download from a Web page, listen to it by clicking on the name of the file or the link. After you listen and decide you want to copy it or download it to your hard drive:

1. Right-click on the link (CTRL-click on a Mac with a one-button mouse). From the contextual menu, choose "Save Link as" or "Download Link." Each Web browser has a slightly different way of handling downloads.
2. Rename the file if necessary and save it to your hard drive in a location that you will remember, such as the Documents folder. Be sure to rename the file to something that you will remember. Do leave the suffix .mid at the end of the file.
3. To open a MIDI file in Sibelius, select **File** > Open and choose the downloaded file.
4. After the file opens, save it in Sibelius. You will now have two versions of the file: one in MIDI format and the other in the translated Sibelius format. Name these files differently so you don't get them confused.

Note that you cannot open audio files, such as WAV, MP3, and AIFF, in Sibelius and turn them into music notation.

Importing Files from Other Notation Programs, Such as Finale, Overture, and Notion

There is a special file format, Music XML, that can be shared among different music notation programs. It is designed as an interchange format for notation and other software applications. It was developed by *www.recordare.com* and is currently supported by more than forty software applications. Sibelius 4 can read Music XML files and therefore can read files from other programs that also support Music XML. There is a distinct advantage to using Music XML over MIDI. In addition to reading the notes, clefs, key signatures, and ties, Music XML reads text, lyrics, articulations, and other markings. Only minor editing will be needed when exchanging files using Music XML.

1. In another notation program, such as Finale, first save the file in Music XML format.
2. In Sibelius, open the XML file. Sibelius will read Music XML files and translate them into notation.

Sending Sibelius Files to Other Notation Programs via XML

Sibelius 4 does not support saving in Music XML format, so Sibelius files cannot be opened in other notation programs that read Music XML. The only way to share Sibelius files with other applications via Music XML is to purchase a plug-in from Recordare (*www.recordare.com*). The cost is $125 for Mac and Windows. Of course, you could save Sibelius files in MIDI format and open them in other programs, such as Finale. However, as mentioned previously, many of the formatting, text, and other markings are not saved.

Exporting and Importing ASCII Guitar Tab

If you are a guitar player, you are probably aware of ASCII (pronounced *ask'-ee-too* or just *ask'-ee*) guitar tab. This is a popular format that is used to share thousands of guitar songs on the Internet. It is text-based, so it does not require the use of a notation program. Sibelius can open ASCII tab files and convert them into tab notation. Sibelius can also export Sibelius tab staves into ACSII format. Following is an example of ASCII guitar tab.

Exporting Tab Notation to ASCII

www.sibeliusbook.com

First, create or open a file in Sibelius that contains guitar tab. For this example, open the file from Chapter 10, "Pop Quiz." File name: *Chpt10Score.sib*. This file contains one guitar tab staff.

1. If you have a copy of the final version of the "Pop Quiz" score on your hard drive, open it. You can also download it from the *www.sibeliusbook.com* Web site in the Chapter 10 folder.
2. After opening the file, select **File** > Export > ASCII Tab.
3. Give the file a descriptive name and save it to a location that you will remember.

Sibelius will create a text file with a suffix of .txt that can be opened and pasted into a word processor or an HTML (HyperText Mark-up Language) editor or copied into a document for posting on the Internet.

Importing an ASCII Tab File

www.sibeliusbook.com

You can do an Internet search for ASCII guitar tab and find a plethora of hits. ASCII tab files usually have a .tab suffix or simply a .txt (text) suffix. There is a saved ASCII tab file on the *www.sibeliusbook.com* Web site. Download the Chapter 13 folder. To open the file, *Chpt10Scoreascii.tab*, or any other ASCII tab file, follow these steps:

1. In Sibelius, select **File** > Open.
2. Select the tab file you want and click Open.
3. In the Open ASCII Tab dialog box, leave the default selection as is, with "Only import rhythms when they are indicated" checked.
4. Click OK to open to file.

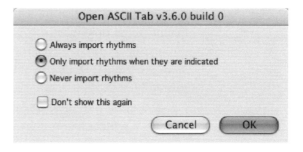

There is a special version of Sibelius for guitarists called Sibelius G7. It does not have all the features of Sibelius, but it can be an alternative for those who are primarily interested in writing guitar music. The Sibelius G7 Kontakt Edition has an integrated sample library containing realistic guitar, keyboard, drum, and orchestral voices. You can input chords and solos using an onscreen fretboard, view music as tab, and work with MIDI and ASCII tab files. For more information, check out *www.sibelius.com*.

Scanning Notation

With the proper software and hardware, it is also possible to scan printed music into Sibelius. See Chapter 7 for a detailed overview of this option.

Saving as Audio

Sibelius can save files in audio format, such as .wav and .aiff to burn to a CD. See Chapter 10, page 281, for an overview of this feature.

Saving as Manuscript Paper

You can customize the list of Manuscript Paper options that appears in the New Score setup window. This can be a helpful way to prepare templates of scores that you work with frequently. The steps for saving as Manuscript Paper were introduced in Chapter 6, page 104.

Sibelius Scorch

Scorch is free and lets you view, play, customize, and print Sibelius scores on the Internet. Scorch makes scores interactive via a Web browser, and the user does not need to own a copy of Sibelius. They simply download the Sibelius Web browser plug-in. This is a wonderful way to share scores with others, and Scorch is one of the industry's most popular music applications on the Web. Composers can post scores for others to view, teachers can post exercises for students, and much more. With Scorch, anyone with an Internet connection can view notation, turn pages, control the playback tempo, change the top instrument or key, save, and print. The composer can turn off some features of Scorch, like saving and printing. In addition, Scorch is used by music vendors and is used to purchase music online from publishers, including *www.jwpepper.com*, with their e-print technology.

Some examples of sites that use Scorch include:
www.mfiles.co.uk
www.music-scores.com
www.vtmidi.org

You will need to download the free Scorch plug-in in order to view the Scorch pages.

When you create a Scorch version of a Sibelius file, Sibelius creates two files: an HTML file and a Sibelius file. Both of these files must be in the same folder.

To create a Scorch file:

1. Open the Sibelius file you want convert into Scorch. Any of the book chapter examples can be used. Be sure there is some music in the score so you will be able to experiment with it.

2. Select **File** > Score Info and be sure there is text entered in the Title and Composer areas. If these fields are blank, enter text into them. This information will be displayed automatically at the top of the Scorch Web page.

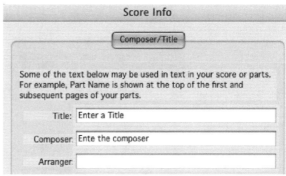

3. Select **File** > Export > Scorch Web Page, and enter a file name. Keep the names simple, with only letters and numbers. Sibelius will automatically remove spaces and shorten the name to a maximum of 27 characters so it will be able to load in most browsers.

4. Sibelius asks you to choose a template. The standard option is Classic. You can experiment with the others if you want, but Classic is what appears on most sites. You can also set the height and width of the page that will display.

5. If you want to allow Web site visitors to be able to save and print the music, be sure to check the "Allow printing and saving" option in the Export Scorch Web Page dialog box.

6. Click OK. Sibelius will create two files that must be together in the same folder when posted on your Web site.

To see the Scorch file you just saved:

1. Navigate to the folder where you saved the Scorch file. You should see two files, one with an .htm suffix and one with a .sib suffix. The files must be in the same location.
2. Double-click on the .htm file. It will launch your Web browser (Internet Explorer, Firefox, Safari, etc.). If you have trouble opening the file, open your browser first and from the File menu, select Open.

Below is the first page of "Wassail Song," saved in Scorch format and opened in a Web browser with saving and printing enabled:

For more detailed information on Scorch, review the Sibelius 4 Reference.

 Sibelius has a batch conversion plug-in that can convert a folder full of Sibelius files into Scorch files. This can be a fast way to convert many files at one time. It can be accessed via **Plug-ins** > Batch Processing > Convert folder of scores to web pages. For more information, consult the Sibelius Reference.

Publish Music on SibeliusMusic.com

SibeliusMusic.com offers composers the option to publicize and sell music worldwide. You can even include your biography, photograph, contact details, and list of scores on your own page on the site. Composers, arrangers, and teachers can publish any Sibelius file, such as coursework and complete scores, on the site. You can offer scores for free or for sale. Sibelius will pay you 50 percent of the sale price. What's more, you can publish your music for free. You can also set up a personal home page within *SibeliusMusic.com* with a memorable address to help people find your music quickly and easily. For more information, go to *www.sibliusmusic.com* and click on the question mark icon for detailed information.

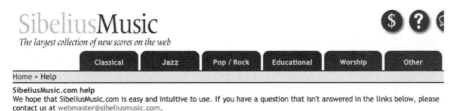

 If you are interested in selling music online on your Web site, then consider Sibelius Internet Edition. It is a complete solution for publishing sheet music on the Internet. Many major publishers use Sibelius Internet Edition to publish music securely online. For more information, go to *www.sibelius.com*. There's also the ability to create your own "store" at *SibeliusMusic. com*, which is for those planning to sell large amounts of sheet music. There's a monthly fee, but you make a higher percentage of each transaction.

Copyright Guidelines

Do be aware of the copyright restrictions with regard to importing music that is under copyright. Doing so without the permission of the copyright holder is a violation of the copyright law and it is forbidden by the Sibelius license agreement. The copyright owner of sheet music is usually listed at the bottom of the page. When in doubt, contact the copyright owner directly for permission. There are many compositions that are in the public domain and can be used without permission. Information on public domain can be obtained at *www.pdinfo.com*. Be aware that arrangements that have been written of public domain music may be under copyright, so check the sheet music before importing others' arrangements.

Importing Graphic Files into Sibelius

There are two ways to incorporate graphic files in Sibelius. One quick and easy way is to use the symbols built into Sibelius (not to be confused with cymbals—however, there are some graphic symbols of cymbals). Symbols were introduced in Chapters 5 and 10. These images can be used in any document. They cannot be resized or edited. To import a symbol into a Sibelius document:

1. Press the letter Z or select **Create** > Symbol.
2. From the Symbol dialog box, select the desired symbol.
3. At the bottom of the dialog box, select the desired size (normal, cue, etc.).
4. Click OK.
5. Click the mouse in the score where the symbol is to be used.

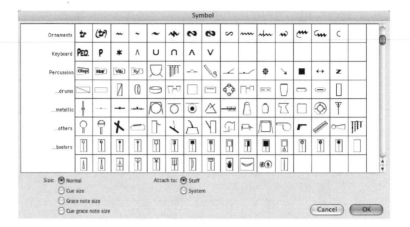

Importing TIFF Files

In Chapter 8, importing a graphic file was introduced. Sibelius can import TIFF graphic files. Perhaps you want to import a graphic logo into a Sibelius file, or maybe you just want to spice up your printouts with some added graphics, such as pictures of instruments or fingering charts.

TIFF stands for Tagged Image File Format, one of the most common graphic files formats. TIFF files usually have the suffix .tif. Sibelius 4 will only import TIFF files. It cannot import .jpeg, .gif, and other graphic formats. If you want to incorporate a non-TIFF graphic into a Sibelius file, you will have to convert it to TIFF format using a graphic editor, such as GraphicConverter (Mac) or Adobe Photoshop Elements (Mac/Win), or another graphic editor. The conversion to TIFF must be done outside of Sibelius. To import a TIFF file into a Sibelius document:

1. Press Esc.
2. Select **Create** > Graphic.
3. Select the TIFF file to be placed in the Sibelius document.
4. Click Open to select it.
5. Click the mouse in the desired location.
6. The file can be resized by dragging the handle (little box) in the lower left-hand or right-hand corner of the graphic.

Exporting Sibelius Pages and Selections to Other Programs

Sibelius can also go the other direction. Pages or portions of pages in Sibelius documents can be exported to other programs, including word processing applications such as Microsoft Word or WordPerfect and page layout software such as InDesign, PageMaker, Quark Xpress, and others.

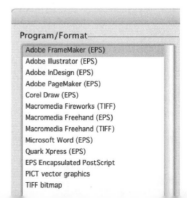

Exporting graphics is best when you are going to another program such as Microsoft Word or you want a page or a portion of a page for a newsletter or graphic design.

> When deciding whether to export a graphic to another program or do the layout inside of Sibelius: if the final version is mostly text, then export files from Sibelius to other programs. If there is mostly music and only some text, make the example in Sibelius and use the various text entry options to create the text.

Perhaps you would like to include a high-quality graphic of music notation in a word processing document, page layout file, or other applications. Sibelius can export in a variety of formats for use in other applications.

To export an entire Sibelius page:

1. Open the Sibelius file.
2. Select **File** > Export > Graphic.
3. Enter one or more pages to export.
4. Uncheck the Create Subfolder option.
5. Enter a file name in the appropriate box.
6. Click Browse to select the folder where the pages will save.
7. Select the appropriate format.
8. Click OK to save it.

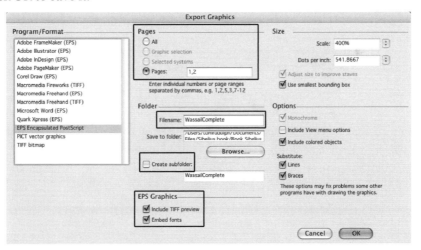

> For print documents such as books, EPS (Encapsulated PostScript) is the best option. You will notice that Sibelius offers a host of specific programs in EPS format. Be sure to select the closest match to the software you will be using. If the program is not listed, used the generic EPS format. TIFF files are best when exporting to non-print applications such as PowerPoint, Web pages, and the like.

To use the graphic file, open your word processor or page layout program. Choose Insert Picture, or consult the manual for the program you are using. Be sure that it is capable of reading the type of file format (EPS or TIFF) you exported from Sibelius.

To save a portion of a Sibelius page in graphic format:

1. Select **Edit** > Select > Select Graphic or use the shortcut: Option-G (Mac); Alt-G (Win).
2. Drag-select the area you want to capture. A box will appear around the selection. Edit the selection as needed. You can also pre-select the measures first and then follow steps 1 and 2 to capture the graphic.
3. Select **File** > Export > Graphic.
4. Under Pages, check Graphic Selection.
5. Uncheck the Create Subfolder option.
6. Enter a file name in the appropriate box.
7. Click Browse to select the folder where the pages will save.
8. Select the graphic file type.
9. Click OK to save it.

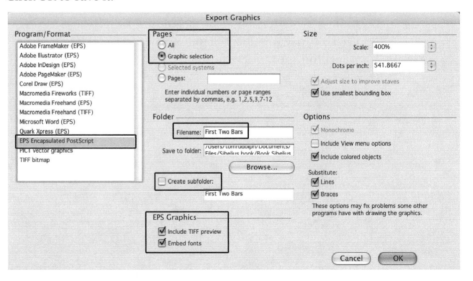

I usually create all of my graphic files and then import them into the appropriate application.

Basic Screen Capture of Sibelius Notation

It is also possible to get a quick screenshot of Sibelius notation and paste it into another program. This is referred to as a screen capture. The quality will not be as good as EPS or TIFF, but for a fast, usable graphic, it is an acceptable way to go.

With a Sibelius file open:

1. Select **Edit** > Select > Graphic or use the shortcut: Option-G (Mac); Alt-G (Win).

2. Select **Edit** > Copy or use the shortcut: ⌘-C (Mac); CTRL-C (Win).
3. Open your word processing, page layout, or other graphics program.
4. Paste it into the document (typically this is as simple as selecting **Edit** > Paste).

You can determine the dpi (dots per inch) that is going to be captured in the Sibelius Preferences. I usually leave it at 300 dpi. Fewer dots per inch will give you smaller file sizes and fuzzier output. To set these Preferences:

1. Mac: Select **Sibelius 4** > Preferences.
   Win: Select **File** > Preferences.
2. Select Other.
3. Under "Paste Graphics into Other Programs," leave it set to 300 (dpi), which is the default.

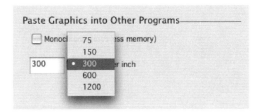

Summary

There are many options for importing and exporting a variety of files to and from Sibelius. This chapter explained how to do the following:

- share Sibelius files between Mac and Windows
- export Sibelius 4 files to earlier Sibelius versions
- export Sibelius files as MIDI files
- import a MIDI file into Sibelius
- find sources of MIDI files to import into Sibelius
- import files from other notation programs
- exporting and importing ASCII guitar tab
- follow copyright guidelines
- post Scorch files on Web sites
- publish music on *www.sibeliusmusic.com*
- import and export graphic files

Review

1. Search for MIDI files on the Internet. When you find some, download them, and import them into Sibelius. Try several different notation settings to see their effect on the piece.
2. Save a Sibelius file in MIDI format and open it in another music program, such as a sequencer.
3. Try exporting Sibelius graphics output to other programs, such as a word processor or page layout program.
4. Set up your own custom music Web page for free on *www.sibeliusmusic.com.*

14

Music Education Applications

The Sibelius Company has always had a penchant for music education. They are a huge supporter of music education and provide a host of materials for teachers and students. This chapter will review some of the music education applications for teachers and students using Sibelius music notation software.

 Be sure to check out the other software offerings that the Sibelius company offers. They are beyond the scope of this book. Go to *www.sibelius.com* and click on Products. You will see a list of Professional and Education products. There are excellent programs for all levels, kindergarten to university.

Notation software in general and Sibelius in particular can be applied in music education in two basic areas: for teacher use and as a composition/learning tool for students. Applications can be adapted for large group instruction as well as classroom and private lessons. The basic categories of applications can be organized as follows:

Teacher use:

- print out scores and parts
- prepare practice and assessment exercises and worksheets
- post files on educational Web sites

Student use:

- compose and print out original compositions and arrangements
- complete teacher-prepared worksheets
- practice, accompaniment, and assessment

Sibelius for Teachers

Sibelius can be an invaluable tool for a wide variety of teacher applications. The most obvious reasons for using a notation program are to save time and to produce readable pieces of music. Another advantage of Sibelius is the way it helps find mistakes. Simply play back the composition and proof-listen to the piece. It is often easier to find mistakes by listening than by solely inspecting the printed score. Some additional applications include:

Adding Note Names and Fingerings

There are many helpful plug-ins designed for use in education, such as those for automatic naming of notes, adding tonic sol-fa, brass fingerings, and string fingerings. The plug-ins are accessed by first selecting a note, passage, or entire score and then selecting the plug-in. Remember, plug-ins cannot be undone, so be sure to save your score before applying them. Consider using the following plug-ins in the **Plug-ins** > Text options:

- Add Brass Fingerings
- Add Note Names
- Add String Fingerings
- Add Tonic Sol-fa

Highlighting and Coloring Notes and Scores

There are several options for coloring notes and highlighting parts of scores for emphasis. For teachers who use Boomwhackers (*boomwhackers.com*) in the classroom, Sibelius includes a helpful plug-in that colors notes according to the color scheme used by Boomwhackers: **Plug-ins** > Boomwhacker Color Notes.

It is also possible to color specific notes. When using voices, colors can be turned on as described in Chapter 8. In addition, individual notes can be assigned specific colors. This can be helpful for analysis and for demonstration. You will need to have access to a color printer in order to print out the colors.

1. Select **Plug-ins** > Color Notes.
2. Choose specific colors for one or all pitches.

If you want to go back to a normal-looking score, select **View** > Note Colors > Notes out of range.

 A quick way to color notes is to select **View** > Note Colors > Pitch Spectrum. You can print these colors out on a color printer. The setting to control whether colored notes print or not is in the Print menu for Mac and Windows. Select **File** > Print and then under Annotations, check or uncheck the "Print colored objects" option.

The highlighting feature can also he helpful. Specific measures (bars) or passages can be highlighted for emphasis:

1. Select a note, bar, or bars.
2. Select **Create** > Highlight.

To clear highlights from a score: select **Plug-ins** > Other > Remove All Highlights.

Simplifying (Reorchestrating) Parts for Students

Octave Transposition

You might need a custom clarinet part for students not yet over the break, or perhaps the range of a particular piece goes above what's comfortable for your soprano section. Sibelius can be used to simplify a part. One way to do this is to enter the original part and then transpose it down an octave.

1. Enter a part into Sibelius.
2. Select any part or the entire composition.
3. Hold down ⌘ (Mac); CTRL (Win) and press the down arrow to move all selected notes down an octave. You can also press the up or down arrow to move a passage by step in either direction.

Re-input Pitches

One of the most helpful options when reorchestrating parts is the re-pitch option.

Enter the original part that you want to reorchestrate. This can be done by scanning or simply entering the original.

1. Select a single note or a chord.
2. Select **Notes** > Re-input Pitches. A dotted blue line will appear.
3. Play the new notes on a MIDI keyboard or type the note names on the computer keyboard. The pitches change but the rhythms stay the same.

Reorchestrating an Existing Arrangement (Transposing Parts)

In my middle school band, I have 18 alto saxes and 2 trombones. Yet the arrangements I purchase are usually written for 3 trombones and 2 alto saxes. I enter the second and third trombone parts and print them out for alto sax. Parts for all ensembles can be reorchestrated in this manner using Sibelius's built-in transposition capabilities. Parts can be entered in concert pitch and then automatically transposed and printed out for B♭ instruments, E♭ instruments, and so forth. Instrument transposition can be selected from the score setup. After the score has been created, new instruments can be created by pressing the letter "I" or choosing **Layout** > Instruments and Staves.

Transposing an Entire File

I frequently enter a part in concert pitch, print it, then go to the File menu and select Save As and give it a different file name. I then can change the key. The advantage of this method is that there is a separate file saved for each part. To change the key and pitches of an entire score:

1. Select **File** > Save As and rename a copy of the original score.

2. Select the entire piece: **Edit** > Select > Select All.

3. Select **Notes** > Transpose or use the shortcut Shift-T.

4. Select the transposition interval and note direction. Be sure to check "Transpose key signatures."

Using Staff (Instrument) Transposition

The other way to change key is by assigning specific instruments to staves. This is done in the New Score setup window or by pressing the letter I for instruments. When you select the name of a transposing instrument, Sibelius automatically creates the proper transposition. I frequently create parts for various instruments by the following steps:

1. Enter the original part; for example, trombone.
2. Press the letter I to add another instrument (staves).
3. Select the desired instrument.
4. Copy the original part (triple-click to select it) and Option-click (Mac); Alt-click (Win) the new staff to copy it. The part will automatically be transposed in the new part.

Creating Rhythm Parts

It is very easy to create rhythm examples and patterns using Sibelius. Any melody can be easily converted to rhythmic notation; for example, I often creating a set of rhythm patterns for students when they are learning a piece. It is also possible to create stemless notes and stems without noteheads. To create a rhythm version of a melody:

1. Create a melody in Sibelius (open one of the single-line scores in the first section of this book, such as "Greensleeves" or "Finlandia," to try these steps).
2. Add another staff to the score by pressing the letter I.
3. Copy the melody part to the new staff. Select the source staff and hold down Option (Mac); Alt (Win) and click in the first bar of the new staff to copy it.
4. Use the re-pitch option by selecting **Notes** > Re-input Pitches.
5. Select the first note of the melody or passage.
6. Hold down the letter B on the computer keyboard. This will change the melody to all Bs and since the typewriter keys repeat, will do it rather quickly.
7. To change the noteheads to slashes, for rhythmic notation, select the entire part or passage and open the Properties window by selecting **Windows** > Properties.
8. Open the Notes tab and select number 4 to change the noteheads to slashes.
9. Press the letter X to flip all stems up.

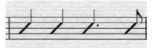

To create stemless notes and noteless stems:

Using the Properties Notes tab, you can also change one or more noteheads into stemless notes (8) or noteless stems (7). Select the passage and choose the appropriate number from the Properties > Notes tab. You can also access the various noteheads by selecting the notes or measures and then using the shortcut Shift-Option (Mac); Shift-Alt (Win) and pressing the appropriate number across the top of the computer keyboard: 0 = normal notation, 8 = stemless notes, and 7 = noteless stems.

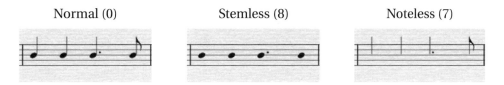

Normal (0)   Stemless (8)   Noteless (7)

Creating Ensemble Music, Such as Duets, Trios, and Quartets

As long as the music is your original composition or is in the public domain, you can create your own chamber music for any instrument combination. Imagine having duets that any instrument combination can play. I use Sibelius to create two-, three-, and four-part pieces for students to perform in chamber groups. As described above, once you have created a version of the duet or trio in concert pitch, you can transpose and shift the music for any combination of instruments. Consider importing MIDI files (see Chapter 13) to accomplish this task.

You can find a host of free arrangements and compositions as well as those for sale on *www.sibeliusmusic.com*. There is a special Educational section of the site.

In addition, there are many helpful features and postings on the Sibelius education Web site: *www.sibeliuseducation.com*.

Reduce a Piano Part So Students Can Accompany a Chorus or Other Ensemble

Many times with published arrangements, the piano accompaniment part is too difficult for students. Sibelius can help the teacher simplify the part. There is also an Arrange feature that will automatically create a piano reduction from a score or selected parts. To reduce a score:

1. Open the original score with multiple staves, such as "The Easy Winners" from Chapter 7.
2. Select all four parts (**Edit** > Select > Select All).

3. Create a piano part either in an entirely new score or in staves added at the bottom of "The Easy Winners."
4. Select the first bar of the new Piano part (both staves).
5. Select **Notes** > Arrange.
6. Choose Reduction from the Arrange window options.

 Educators should be aware of copyright law when simplifying compositions and arrangements that are copyrighted. The copyright notice is usually listed at the bottom of the music. Educators are permitted to make changes under the fair use clause of the copyright law. There is an excellent document at *www.menc.org/information/copyright/copyr.html*, which states: "Music teachers can edit or simplify purchased, printed copies, provided that the fundamental character of the work is not distorted or the lyrics, if any, are not altered or lyrics added if none exist."

Creating Worksheets and Readiness Exercises

Before I pass out a new arrangement to a performing group, I like to create a page or two of exercises that will help the students prepare for playing the piece. I include scales, rhythm patterns, and important melodies in unison for the entire group. Once the C part is completed, I simply copy and paste the music to create the other parts, often using the score template that can be accessed via Manuscript Paper in the New Score setup pages. I also use the Dynamic Part extraction techniques described in Chapter 7 to save time printing the individual parts.

Instant Scales and Arpeggios

There is a helpful plug-in designed to create scales and arpeggio exercises. They can be instantly created in a new or existing score.

1. Select **Plug-ins** > Other > Scales & Arpeggios.
2. Enter custom settings in the Scales & Arpeggios dialog box. Take your time to review the many options available.

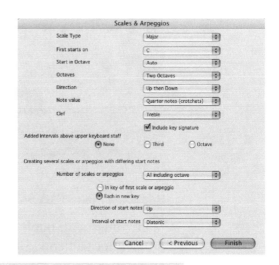

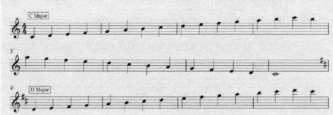

You can copy and paste the scales created via this plug-in into other staves. If you copy into a transposing score, the notes and keys will transpose. However, you will have to reenter the text above the staff indicating the various keys.

Hiding Key Signatures and Warning Key Signatures

If you prefer that your scales do not have key signatures, just select the key signatures and delete them. Sibelius will instantly add the appropriate accidentals.

You will notice that Sibelius entered a cautionary or warning key signature at the end of the line preceding each key change. This can be eliminated:

1. First, delete the key signature. Select it and press the Delete key.
2. Select the key signature that you just deleted by pressing the letter K for Key Signature.
3. Before you click it into the score, check the Hide box at the bottom of the Key Signature dialog box. This will hide the warning key signature.

Creating Warm-up and Practice Exercises

If you are an educator, you have probably developed some of your own favorite warm-up exercises. Sibelius can help you to print them out. For example, suppose you wanted to create a melody and instantly create it for an entire ensemble such as concert band, orchestra, jazz band, or other instrumental group. Use the Arrange feature to save time.

1. Create a single-staff document and enter a melody that you would like printed for an entire ensemble. For practice, open any of the single-line melodies from Chapters 2 through 6.
2. After entering the melody in a single-line staff, copy the entire melody to the clipboard by selecting **Edit** > Select > Select All.
3. Choose **Edit** > Copy.
4. Create a new blank score by selecting **File** > New.
5. In the Manuscript Paper list, select Concert Band (or any other instrumental ensemble). Click Finish.

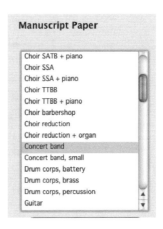

6. In the Concert Band blank score, select the first bar of all of the instruments.
7. Select **Notes** > Arrange.
8. In the Arrange Styles window, select Standard Arrangement and click OK.

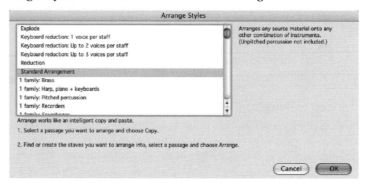

The arrange feature just assigned the single-line melody to every selected instrument and, in the majority of cases, to the correct octave. You can edit the parts before printing them separately. Use the Dynamic Parts options reviewed in Chapter 7 and you'll have a melody printed out for your ensemble in minutes.

Sibelius 4 Worksheets and Worksheet Creator

Sibelius 4 includes more than 1,700 worksheets designed for use in music education. I have often told music teachers that this alone is worth the price of Sibelius. Worksheets can be opened and new ones created and added. There is extensive information available in the Sibelius 4 Reference, section 5.21. Review this information to get a comprehensive overview of the worksheets that are included with Sibelius and how they can be edited and used. Additional information can be obtained online at:

www.sibelius.com/products/sibelius/4/worksheet.html

There are six main areas of worksheets. The categories include:

1. **Elements of Music**—Use these worksheets with students to assess and drill the fundamentals of music. Exercises can be completed on the computer or on paper.
2. **Writing and Creating Music**—A wide variety of worksheets that can be used with students to guide them through the process of composing music.
3. **Selected Repertoire**—Approximately 500 pieces of music and poetry, including melodies, rounds, and much more. These pieces are all in the public domain, so you and your students can use these as starting places for original arrangements.
4. **Reference**—A library of eighty scales, modes, and chord progressions. These could be incorporated in custom exercises.
5. **Posters, Flashcards, and Games**—Many materials that can be used in planning and decorating a classroom. I have used many of these for excellent substitute lesson plans when I am out of school on leave.
6. **UK KS3 & GCSE Projects**—Seven UK (United Kingdom) projects supporting the three main areas of study (performing, composing, and listening) designed for

stage 3 and GCSC (General Certificate of Secondary Education) classes, with comprehensive teacher's notes and ideas for extension.

 I suggest that music educators request an in-service day for the music staff to review the plethora of options included in the Sibelius Worksheets. There are so many options, it will take hours. Don't overlook this important aspect of Sibelius 4.

Write Your Own Compositions, Arrangements, or Even a Method Book

If you have been avoiding writing original compositions or arrangements because of the time needed to write and copy the parts, Sibelius can help. Also, once the composition is entered into Sibelius, it can be listened to, edited, and revised as often as you like.

 Write arrangements of songs in the public domain—there are many in the Worksheets section of Sibelius 4. Use these songs for arranging and/or print them out for classroom and rehearsal use.

Add Kontakt Gold to Gain Access to Marching Percussion Sounds

Kontakt Gold has been mentioned in Chapters 8 and 10. This is an add-on group of sounds for Sibelius. There are many advantages to using these sounds. For music educators, Kontakt Gold includes a host of marching percussion sounds and additional vocal and instrumental sounds that can be helpful for playback in educational arrangements. There are other sound libraries also available as add-ons for Sibelius 4. See more details at *www.sibelius.com/products*.

Burn Practice Audio CDs for Students

With either Kontakt Silver (free with Sibelius 4) or Kontakt Gold, or other software synths, teachers can convert Sibelius files to audio file format and burn them to a CD if the computer has a CD burner. Teachers can use this feature to create practice CDs for students.

1. With a Sibelius file open, select **File** > Export > Audio.
2. Enter a file name. Mac will save in .aiff format and Windows will save in .wav format.
3. Save the file to a folder that you will remember.
4. Open the CD burning software that came with your computer such as iTunes, EZ CD Creator, and the like.
5. Assemble the tracks and burn the CD.

Kidsib Music Font

Another add-on that can be helpful to music educators is the Kidsib font. With the font, Sibelius will automatically place the note names inside the noteheads. This is especially helpful for beginning band, strings, and keyboard exercises.

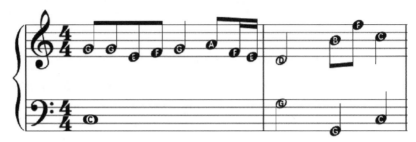

The Kidsib font must be purchased separately from *www.dvmpublications.com*. After purchasing and installing the font, the next step is to download the special plug-in for it from *www.sibelius.com/download/plugins/index.html?category=9* (or go to *www.sibelius.com*; click on Downloads; click on Extra Plug-ins; click on Notes and rests; scroll down to Apply Kidsib Font for Sibelius 4 [there is also a plug-in for Sibelius 3]).

Follow the printed instructions for downloading the plug-in and adding it to your version of Sibelius. Now, when you want to convert a passage to the Kidsib font, you can select the passage and go to **Plug-ins** > Notes and Rests and the Kidsib option will appear.

Scorch

Scorch was reviewed in Chapter 13. Teachers can use Scorch to post student compositions and files on school Web sites. Scorch can also be used to post notation and sound files on Web sites and with distance learning curricula. Since Scorch files do not require the purchase of any software, students can view and listen to pieces as well as change the tempo and key for practice.

Capturing Notation

Chapter 13 covered the process for capturing notation in Sibelius and exporting it to other programs such as word processors and page layout software. This combined with the Worksheets option gives teachers unlimited options for creating worksheets, tests, and the like.

Teacher Education

Many colleges and universities offer courses in music technology and music notation. The Technology Institute for Music Educators (*www.ti-me.org*) sponsors courses every summer throughout the country. Look for courses offering Sibelius (*www.ti-me.org/sites.html*). Also, check out the teaching suggestions on the Sibelius site:

www.sibelius.com/products/sibelius/features/teaching_with_sibelius.html

Sibelius also offers in-service training to teachers and schools. To inquire about scheduling a Sibelius training in your school, e-mail *trainingusa@sibelius.com*

Sibelius for Students

Sibelius is a fascinating tool in the hands of students. Sibelius will not teach them how to compose any more than a word processor will teach them how to write. However, just as a word processor can assist a student with editing, cutting, copying and pasting, spell checking, and so forth, Sibelius can assist in the music composition process. Sibelius gives students a fast and legible way to enter and print music, then hear what they have written.

 Sibelius offers an economical way to use Sibelius in school music technology and computer labs: a lite and less expensive version of Sibelius called Sibelius Student Edition. More information on this option can be obtained on the Sibelius Web site:

www.sibelius.com/products/sibelius_student/index.html

Sibelius Student Toolset

If you are using the full version of Sibelius with students, there is an option to turn on a reduced feature set so they have fewer features to worry about. In Sibelius, go to: **Preferences** > Menus and Shortcuts > School Features. When you turn on the school features, you will notice that many of the more advanced menus are grayed-out and not available.

Theory Exercises, Composing Tools, and Worksheets

Students can use Sibelius to create legible theory class assignments. Students in music theory classes at the high school and college levels should have access to computers to create legible exercises and assignments. Four-part writing can be greatly enhanced. The student gets the benefit of hearing the exercise as it is being entered and the teacher benefits by receiving a legible assignment. Theory assignments can be generated from the Worksheet creator or prepared from scratch. Students can take advantage of the plug-ins, including checking for parallel fifths and octaves (select a passage and choose **Plug-ins** > Proof-reading > Check for parallel 5th /8ves). Students can also use some composition tools when working with melodies. These include invert and retrograde (select the passage to be affected and choose **Plug-ins** > Composing Tools > Invert [or Retrograde]).

There are literally dozens of worksheets that can be culled from the 1,700 that come with Sibelius 4. Teachers can assign students specific exercises to complete using Sibelius.

Create Original Music

Students can learn to use Sibelius and begin to print out their own compositions. Every year I ask my middle school band members to compose a duet. I provide them with a melody and they write the harmony part. Notation software gives them the opportunity to hear their composition as it is being composed and produce a professional-looking printout. Also, consider assigning students to select a poem provided via the Worksheet creator or another source, then compose a melody to go with the poem.

Transcribe Melodies

Through the process of entering the notation, they will "discover" many aspects of music such as note values, number of beats per measure, direction of stems, etc.

Apply Concepts as They Are Learned

For example, if students are learning about theme and variations, ask them to compose their own variations using Sibelius. This can be applied to any musical concept.

Take Classes to the School Computer Lab

Since notes can be entered with the mouse or computer keyboard, students can compose using the computers in the computer lab. A site license or lab pack can be purchased at a lesser cost per computer in the lab.

Creativity Activities and Portfolio Assessment

Sibelius provides a tool for students to create and print out music. A printed piece of music is a tangible outcome that can be used for assessment.

Optional Colored Keyboard

Students (and teachers) should consider purchasing the Sibelius Colored Computer Keyboard. It is a fully functional computer keyboard with color-coded keys printed with shortcuts, note values, and other helpful keystrokes in Sibelius. More information is available on the *www.sibelius.com* Web site.

Summary

This chapter explored a variety of ways both teachers and students can use Sibelius to enhance teaching and learning.

Review

1. Make a list of all the ways you can use Sibelius to improve your teaching.
2. List the ways students can use Sibelius as a composition tool.
3. Select one piece you intend to teach this year. Make a list of the Sibelius techniques you can employ to create readiness exercises for the students
4. Consider joining the Technology Institute for Music Educators (*www.ti-me.org*). Member benefits include access to a database of teacher-created lesson plans as well as many other helpful features .

15

Support

If you have been going through all of the chapters in this book, you are probably quite impressed with the features that Sibelius offers. Not every Sibelius feature was included in this book. No doubt, there will still be times when you have questions about some aspect of Sibelius and need assistance. This chapter will highlight how you can get connected to help and find the answers. The options are organized into the following areas:

- Staying Current
- Getting Answers to Questions
- Additional Sibelius Training, Advice, and Third-Party Products

Register Sibelius

As soon as you purchase your Sibelius software, if you have not already, register it with Sibelius. You won't be able to save or print after a while if you don't, and you need to be registered in order to access some help options.

Use the Most Up-to-Date Version of Sibelius

Be sure to upgrade to the most recent version of Sibelius. Major upgrades come out every two to three years and are indicated by number: Sibelius 2, Sibelius 3, Sibelius 4. Check the Sibelius Web site (*www.sibelius.com*) to find out how to upgrade if you need to.

Download Maintenance Upgrades

If Sibelius tells you there is a maintenance upgrade available, download it. Maintenance upgrades are free and are usually posted between major upgrades. For example, Sibelius will fix certain bugs and then put out a maintenance upgrade. Sibelius 4 will automatically search the Sibelius.com Web site for upgrades so long as the option is checked in Sibelius Preferences. In the Preferences dialog box, click on Other to find the option that should be checked: "Check for updates every 90 days."

You can also check for maintenance upgrades manually by going to the Help menu and selecting the Check for Updates option. These are also listed on the *www.sibelius.com* Web site under Downloads.

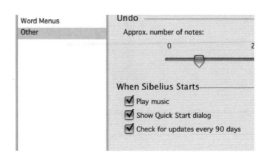

Download Additional Plug-ins from the Sibelius Web Site

Sibelius adds new and useful plug-ins that can be downloaded and installed into your version of Sibelius. Many of the plug-ins are free and new plug-ins are added frequently. Go to *www.sibelius.com* and click on Downloads and on the Extra Plug-ins link, or go directly to: *www.sibelius.com/download/plugins/index.html*

Getting Answers to Questions

Use This Book's Index

Since you have spent a good deal of time going through the chapters in this book, use the index in the back to look up steps for things you forget. If you don't find the answer there, move to the next option, below.

Use Sibelius Reference

The next place to go for answers is the Sibelius Reference, available in Sibelius from the help menu. Choose **Help** > Sibelius Help. You will have access to the index and you can search for specific terms. I also use the printed version of the Sibelius Reference quite a bit. It can be easier to read the book than to switch back and forth between Sibelius and the Web browser that displays the Reference Manual.

View the Sibelius Tutorial Videos

I have learned quite a bit from the videos that install with Sibelius 4. I don't use them to find the answers to specific problems; rather, I watch them to get new ideas on how to solve problems and to learn about new features. I try to jump back and forth from Sibelius and the video and try the steps suggested. The videos can be accessed from the Quick Start menu (**File** > Quick Start) and from the Help menu (**Help** > Tutorial Videos). This is the first place to go when tackling a new topic such as scanning, part extraction, etc.

Sibelius Help Center

If you can't get the answers from the above areas, the next level is the help center and tech support Sibelius offers. The first place to visit is the help center. Go to *www.sibelius.com* and click on the help center link at the top of the home page.

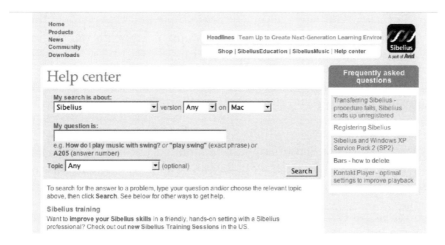

You can search the frequently asked questions and/or post a question. There are certified Sibelius technicians online and they will answer questions, usually within a twenty-four-hour period.

There is also a chat page where questions can be posted. It is not a live chat, more like a bulletin board or blog with questions and responses posted. It is possible to search the contents of the chat area.

Voice Telephone Tech Support

Another option is to call the Sibelius tech support phone number. The tech support line is free to new users for the first 90 days via the number: 888-280-9995. After the initial 90-day period, the tech support number (925-280-2101) is a toll call and can be accessed from the Help page on the *www.sibelius.com* Web site. When you call, have your Sibelius serial number handy. You will need it in order to get access to phone help. I also suggest you have your computer on and Sibelius running with the exact question or problem you are experiencing. Then you can try out the solutions as they are being offered by the tech support person.

Robin Hodson's *Sibelius QuickStart Guide*

Robin Hodson is the East Coast rep for Sibelius. He was one of the main reviewers of this book and has offered countless tips and advice to me over the years. He has a wonderful document that highlights many timesaving Sibelius tips. You can download the PDF file of the tips from *www.sibeliusmusic.com* or you can request a copy directly from Robin via his email address: *robin@sibelius.com*

Join a Sibelius User Group (E-mail List)

It is also a good idea to consider joining one or more Sibelius groups where users share ideas and solutions to common and not-so-common problems. An excellent reference list for all Sibelius user groups is located at *www.rpmseattle.com/sibelius/* under the Sibelius forums and mailing lists area. The current listings include the Sibelius Tech

Support and Chat page on the Sibelius site and independent Sibelius groups like the Southern California Sibelius Users Group, the Sibelius User's Group on Yahoo Groups, and the Sibelius Forum. All are free to join.

Additional Sibelius Training

Even with the above options, you might also consider taking some formal training on Sibelius. Sibelius has many certified trainers around the world and offers several training opportunities listed on their Web site. Go to *www.sibelius.com/courses/index.html* for a listing of courses and clinics in your area.

Third-Party Products

There is a growing list of third-party products for Sibelius, including companion products and fonts. The list of options can be viewed at *www.rpmseattle.com/sibelius*. Included are reference to third-party plug-ins, software synths, and a wide variety of customized fonts. Be sure to check if there are any products that would help you in your work with Sibelius.

Summary

This chapter included the following information on how to get support for Sibelius from various resources:

- register Sibelius
- use the most up-to-date version of Sibelius
- download maintenance upgrades (click Yes when prompted by Sibelius)
- use this book's index
- look it up in the Sibelius Reference (from the Help menu and print version)
- view the Sibelius Tutorial videos
- use the Sibelius online help center
- get tech support via voice (not toll-free): 925-280-2101
- join a Sibelius user group
- take a Sibelius training course
- investigate third-party Sibelius products

Review

1. Visit the Sibelius.com Web site and review the various support areas listed.
2. Join a Sibelius mailing list (user group). Read the messages and contribute to the list when possible.

Index